Contents – Text

Prague

Neil Wilson

LONELY PLANET PUBLICATIONS
Melbourne • Oakland • London • Paris

Prague
5th edition – January 2003
First published – June 1994

Published by
Lonely Planet Publications Pty Ltd ABN 36 005 607 983
90 Maribyrnong St, Footscray, Victoria 3011, Australia

Lonely Planet offices
Australia Locked Bag 1, Footscray, Victoria 3011
USA 150 Linden St, Oakland, CA 94607
UK 10a Spring Place, London NW5 3BH
France 1 rue du Dahomey, 75011 Paris

Photographs
Many of the images in this guide are available for licensing from Lonely Planet Images.
Web site: www.lonelyplanetimages.com

Front cover photograph
A tram in Malá Strana at dusk (Andrea Pistolesi, The Image Bank)

ISBN 1 74059 354 5

Printed through Colorcraft Ltd, Hong Kong
Printed in China

Contents – Maps

THINGS TO SEE & DO

WALKING TOURS

EXCURSIONS

COLOUR MAPS

MAP LEGEND

METRIC CONVERSION

The Author

Neil Wilson

After working as a petroleum geologist in Australia and the North Sea and doing geological research at Oxford University, Neil gave up the rock business for the more precarious life of a freelance writer and photographer. Since 1988 he has travelled in five continents and written around 35 travel and walking guidebooks for various publishers. He has worked on Lonely Planet's *Georgia, Armenia & Azerbaijan*, *Czech & Slovak Republics*, *Slovenia*, *Scotland* and *Edinburgh* guides. Although he was born in Glasgow, in the west of Scotland, Neil defected to the east at the age of 18 and has lived in Edinburgh ever since.

From Neil

Mockrat děkuji to the helpful staff at Prague Information Service, to Carol Downie for help with shops and restaurants, and to Richard Nebeský and Tomáš Harabíš for conversations over a cold *pivo* or six. Also, thanks to Tim Ryder and the editorial and cartographic staff at Lonely Planet.

This Book

John King and Richard Nebeský researched and wrote the first edition of *Prague*. Richard updated the second edition, John and Richard the third, and Neil Wilson and Richard the fourth. Neil went back to Prague to revise and update this edition.

From the Publisher

This fifth edition of *Prague* was produced in Lonely Planet's London office. The editing and proofing were coordinated by Sally Schafer and Emma Sangster, with assistance from Darren O'Connell and Tegan Murray. The mapping and design were coordinated by David Wenk. Ed Pickard drew the metro map, and Andrew Weatherill and Brendan Dempsey designed the cover. Thanks to Ed, Annika Roojun, Ryan Evans and Jain Lemos for invaluable last-minute help.

THANKS
Many thanks to the travellers who used the last edition and wrote to us with helpful hints, advice and interesting anecdotes. Your names appear at the back of the book.

Foreword

ABOUT LONELY PLANET GUIDEBOOKS

The story begins with a classic travel adventure: Tony and Maureen Wheeler's 1972 journey across Europe and Asia to Australia. There was no useful information about the overland trail then, so Tony and Maureen published the first Lonely Planet guidebook to meet a growing need.

From a kitchen table, Lonely Planet has grown to become the largest independent travel publisher in the world, with offices in Melbourne (Australia), London (UK), Oakland (USA) and Paris (France).

Today Lonely Planet guidebooks cover the globe. There is an ever-growing list of books and information in a variety of media. Some things haven't changed. The main aim is still to make it possible for adventurous travellers to get out there – to explore and better understand the world.

At Lonely Planet we believe travellers can make a positive contribution to the countries they visit – if they respect their host communities and spend their money wisely. Since 1986 a percentage of the income from each book has been donated to aid projects and human-rights campaigns, and, more recently, to wildlife conservation.

Although inclusion in a guidebook usually implies a recommendation, we can not list every good place. Exclusion does not necessarily imply criticism. In fact, there are a number of reasons why we might exclude a place – sometimes it is simply inappropriate to encourage an influx of travellers.

UPDATES & READER FEEDBACK

Things change – prices go up, schedules change, good places go bad and bad places go bankrupt. Nothing stays the same. So, if you find things better or worse, recently opened or long-since closed, please tell us and help make the next edition even more accurate and useful.

Lonely Planet thoroughly updates each guidebook as often as possible – usually every two years, although for some destinations the gap can be longer. Between editions, up-to-date information is available in our free, quarterly *Planet Talk* newsletter and monthly email bulletin *Comet*. The *Upgrades* section of our website (w www.lonelyplanet.com) is also regularly updated by Lonely Planet authors, and the site's *Scoop* section covers news and current affairs relevant to travellers. Lastly, the *Thorn Tree* bulletin board and *Postcards* section carry unverified, but fascinating, reports from travellers.

Tell us about it! We genuinely value your feedback. A well travelled team at Lonely Planet reads and acknowledges every email and letter we receive and ensures that every morsel of information finds its way to the relevant authors, editors and cartographers.

Everyone who writes to us will find their name listed in the next edition of the appropriate guidebook, and will receive the latest issue of *Comet* or *Planet Talk*. The very best contributions will be rewarded with a free guidebook.

We may edit, reproduce and incorporate your comments in Lonely Planet products such as guidebooks, websites and digital products, so let us know if you don't want your comments reproduced or your name acknowledged.

How to contact Lonely Planet:
Online: e talk2us@lonelyplanet.com.au, w www.lonelyplanet.com
Australia: Locked Bag 1, Footscray, Victoria 3011
UK: 10a Spring Place, London NW5 3BH
USA: 150 Linden St, Oakland, CA 94607

Introduction

The Czechs call it *matička Praha* – 'little mother Prague' – their national capital, the cradle of Czech culture, and one of the most beautiful and fascinating cities in Europe.

Kidnapped by communism for 40 years until it was freed by the Velvet Revolution of 1989, Prague has since become one of Europe's most popular tourist destinations. Largely undamaged by the ravages of WWII, the cityscape offers a smorgasbord of stunning architecture, from the soaring verticals of Gothic and the buxom exuberance of Baroque, to the sensuous elegance of Art Nouveau and the chiselled cheekbones of Cubist facades. Also on offer is an equally broad menu of musical delights, from the Prague Spring festival of classical music and opera, through countless jazz and rock venues, to some of Central Europe's top dance clubs.

In recent years Prague has seen its traditional pubs and eateries augmented by a wave of gourmet restaurants, cocktail bars and trendy cafés – though if you like, you can still feast on pork and dumplings, washed down with a beer, for less than 100Kč. And what beer! The Czechs have been brewing since at least the 9th century, and invented Pilsner – the world's first clear, golden beer – in 1842. Czech breweries still produce some of the world's finest beers.

Above all Prague is a place to be explored, whether venturing along the medieval lanes and hidden passages of the Staré Město (Old Town), strolling through the city's many wooded parks or taking a leisurely cruise along the Vltava River. Everywhere you go you will uncover some aspect of the city's multi-layered history – in its time Prague has been the capital of the Holy Roman Empire, the Habsburg Empire, the first Czechoslovak Republic (1918–38), the Nazi Protectorate of Bohemia and Moravia, the Communist Republic of Czechoslovakia, and the modern, democratic Czech Republic.

In August 2002 Prague suffered its worst flooding for nearly 200 years. But its 600-year-old Charles Bridge (Karlův most), one of the city's most famous landmarks, stood firm against the flood waters, a symbol of the city's steadfastness in the face of adversity. 'Little mother Prague' endures.

Facts about Prague

HISTORY

Prague's history has echoed not only through the Czech lands but across Europe. Among Prague flash points with major international consequences have been the rise and subsequent bloody splintering of the Hussite movement in the 15th century, the 17th-century anti-Habsburg uprising that set off the Thirty Years' War, and the communist putsch of 1948.

Prehistory

The oldest evidence of human habitation in the Prague valley dates from 600,000 BC, but more numerous clues were left by hunters during the last ice age, about 25,000 years ago. Permanent communities were established around 4000 BC in the northwestern parts of Prague, and the area was inhabited continuously by various Germanic and Celtic tribes before the arrival of the Slavs. It was from a Celtic tribe called Boii that Bohemia got its name, a name still used today for the western part of the Czech Republic.

The Coming of the Slavs

In the 6th century, two Slav tribes settled on opposite sides of a particularly appealing stretch of the Vltava River. The Czechs built a wooden fortress where Hradčany stands today, and the Zlíčani built theirs upstream at what is now Vyšehrad. They had barely dug in when nomadic Avars thundered in, to rule until the Frankish trader Samo united the Slav tribes and drove the Avars out. Samo held on for 35 years before the Slavs reverted to squabbling.

In the 9th century Prague was part of the short-lived Great Moravian Empire. Under its second ruler, Rastislav (r. 846–70), emissaries were invited to come from Constantinople, and Christianity took root in the region. The Moravians (the ancient lands of Moravia now form the eastern part of the Czech Republic) were ultimately undone by internal conflicts, especially with the Czechs, who finally broke away from the empire.

Přemysl Dynasty

Prague Castle (Pražský hrad) was built in the 870s by Prince Bořivoj as the main seat of the Přemysl dynasty. Vyšehrad sometimes served as an alternative in the 10th and 11th centuries (see Vyšehrad in the Things to See & Do chapter for more on the mythical founding of this dynasty).

Christianity became the state religion under the rule of Wenceslas (Václav), duke of Bohemia (r. c. 925–35), the 'Good King Wenceslas' of the old Christmas carol (in fact, he was never a king) and now the patron saint of the Czech Republic.

In 950 the German king, Otto I, conquered Bohemia and incorporated it into the Holy Roman Empire. By 993 Přemysl princes had forged a genuine Slav alliance, and ruled Bohemia on the Germans' behalf until 1212, when the pope granted Otakar I the right to rule as a king. Otakar bestowed royal privileges on the Staré Město (Old Town), and Malá Strana (Little Quarter) was established in 1257 by Otakar II.

Přemysl lands stretched at one point from modern-day Silesia (a region on the Czech-Polish border) to the Mediterranean Sea. However, their Austrian and Slovenian domains were lost when Otakar II died and his army was thrashed at the 1278 battle of Moravské Pole (fought near modern-day Dürnkrut in Austria) by the Austrian Habsburgs.

Prague's Golden Age

The murder of Wenceslas III in 1306 left no male heir to the Přemysl throne. Two Habsburg monarchs briefly ruled Bohemia until the Holy Roman Emperor, John of Luxembourg (Jan Lucemburský to the Czechs), also became king of Bohemia by marrying Wenceslas III's daughter Elyška in 1310. Under the rule of John's son Charles (Karel) IV (r. 1346–78), as king and Holy Roman Emperor, Prague grew into one of the continent's largest and most prosperous cities, acquiring its fine Gothic face, and landmarks including the Karolinum (Charles

University), Charles Bridge (Karlův most) and chrám sv Víta (St Vitus Cathedral).

The Hussite Revolution

The late 14th and early 15th centuries witnessed the Church-reform movement led by Jan Hus (see the boxed text). Hus' eventual conviction for heresy and his death at the stake in 1415 sparked a nationalist rebellion in Bohemia led by the Hussite preacher Jan Želivský. In 1419 several Catholic councillors were flung from the windows of Prague's Novoměstská radnice (New Town Hall) by Želivský's followers, thus introducing the word 'defenestration' (literally, the act of throwing someone out of a window) to the political lexicon.

After the death of Holy Roman Emperor and king of Bohemia Wenceslas IV in 1419, Prague was ruled by various Hussite committees. In 1420 combined Hussite forces led by the military commander Jan Žižka successfully defended Prague against the first anti-Hussite crusade, launched by Sigismund, the Holy Roman Emperor.

In the 1420s a split developed in the Hussite ranks between radical Taborites, who advocated total war on Catholics, and moderate Utraquists, who consisted mainly of nobles and were more concerned with transforming the Church.

In 1434 the Utraquists agreed to accept Sigismund's rule in return for religious tolerance; the Taborites kept fighting, only to be defeated in the same year at the battle of Lipany.

Following Sigismund's death, George of Poděbrady (Jiří z Poděbrad) ruled as Bohemia's one and only Hussite king, from 1452 to 1471, with the backing of Utraquist

Jan Hus

Jan Hus was the Czech lands' foremost, and one of Europe's earliest, Christian reformers, anticipating Martin Luther and the Lutheran Reformation by a century.

He was born into a poor family in southern Bohemia in 1372. At the age of 18 he enrolled at the Karolinum (Charles University), and two years after graduating he started work as a teacher there. Five years later he was made dean of the philosophy faculty, at a time when the university was caught up in a struggle against German influence.

Like many of his Czech colleagues, Hus was inspired by the English philosopher and radical reformist theologian John Wycliffe. The latter's ideas on reform of the Roman Catholic clergy meshed nicely with growing Czech resentment at the wealth and corruptness of the higher clergy, who together owned about half of all Bohemia, and their heavy taxation of the peasantry.

Prague reformers had in 1391 founded the Betlémská kaple (Bethlehem Chapel; see Southwestern Staré Město in the Things to See & Do chapter), where sermons were given in Czech rather than Latin. Hus preached here for about 10 years, while continuing his duties at the university.

Because German masters at the university enjoyed three votes to the Czech masters' one, anti-reform attitudes officially prevailed there. In 1403 the masters declared many of Wycliffe's writings to be heresy. During the Great Schism (1378–1417), when Roman Catholics had two popes, the masters opposed the 1409 Council of Pisa that was called to sort things out. This so infuriated Wenceslas IV that he abrogated the university constitution and gave the Czech masters three votes to the Germans' one, leading to a mass exodus of Germans from Prague.

In the chaos surrounding the Great Schism, one pope was persuaded to prohibit preaching in private chapels such as Betlémská kaple. Hus refused to obey, and was excommunicated, though he continued to preach at the chapel and teach at the university. A disagreement with Wenceslas IV over the sale of indulgences cost him the king's support. The Council of Constance, called to put a final end to the Schism, convicted Hus of heresy, and he was burned at the stake in 1415.

NICKY CASTLE

forces. He was centuries ahead of his time in suggesting a European council to solve international problems by diplomacy rather than war, but he couldn't convince the major European rulers or the pope. After George's death, two weak kings from the Polish Jagiellonian dynasty ruled Bohemia, though real power lay with the Utraquist nobles, the so-called Bohemian Estates.

Habsburg Rule

In 1526 the Austrian Catholic Habsburgs were again asked by the Czech nobility to rule Bohemia. In the second half of the century the city enjoyed great prosperity under Emperor Rudolf II, and was made the seat of the Habsburg Empire. Rudolf established great art collections, and renowned artists and scholars were invited to his court.

A huge fire in 1541 laid waste many sections of Malá Strana and Hradčany.

An ill-fated uprising of the Bohemian Estates in 1618, which began when two Habsburg councillors and their secretary were flung from an upper window in Prague Castle, dealt a blow to Czech fortunes for the next 300 years. This 'Second Defenestration of Prague' sparked off the Thirty Years' War, devastating much of Europe, and Bohemia in particular – a quarter of the Bohemian population perished.

The following year the Bohemian Estates elected Frederick of the Palatinate as their ruler. But because of ineffective leadership, low morale among their heavily mercenary army, and limited international support, the crucial battle of Bílá Hora (White Mountain) on 8 November 1620 was lost by the Protestants almost before the first shots were fired. The 'Winter King' (so-called because he ruled Bohemia for just one winter) fled and the 27 nobles who had instigated the revolt were executed in Old Town Square (Staroměstské náměstí).

The defeat slammed the door on Czech independence for almost three centuries. Czechs lost their privileges, rights and property, and almost their national identity due to forced Catholicisation and Germanisation (part of the wider Counter-Reformation movement). During the Thirty Years' War, Saxons occupied Prague from 1631 to 1632, and Swedes seized Hradčany and Malá Strana in 1648. Staré Město, though unconquered, suffered months of bombardment. Prague's population declined from 60,000 in 1620 to 24,600 in 1648. The Habsburgs moved their throne back to Vienna, reducing Prague to a provincial town, although it did get a major Baroque face-lift over the next century, particularly after a great fire in 1689.

In the 18th century the city was again on the move, economically and architecturally. The four towns of Prague – Staré Město, Nové Město (New Town), Malá Strana and Hradčany – were joined into a single, strong unit by imperial decree in 1784.

The Czech National Revival

In the 19th century, Prague became the centre of the so-called Czech National Revival (České národní obrození), which found its initial expression not in politics – political activity was forbidden by the Habsburgs – but in Czech-language journalism, literature and drama. Important figures included linguists Josef Jungmann and Josef Dobrovský, and František Palacký, author of *Dějiny národu českého* (History of the Czech Nation). A distinctive architecture also took form; Prague landmarks of this period include the Národní divadlo (National Theatre), Národní muzeum (National Museum) and Novoměstská radnice.

While many of the countries in post-Napoleonic Europe were swept up by similar nationalist sentiments, social and economic factors gave the Czech revival particular strength. Educational reforms by Empress Maria Theresa (r. 1740–80) had given even the poorest Czechs access to schooling, and a vocal middle class was emerging with the Industrial Revolution. Austrian economic reforms, plus changes in industrial production, were forcing Czech labourers into the bigger towns, cancelling out the influence of large German minorities there.

Prague also joined in the 1848 democratic revolutions that swept Europe, and the city was the first in the Austrian Empire to rise in favour of reform. Yet like most of the others, Prague's uprising was soon crushed.

In 1861 however, Czechs defeated Germans in Prague council elections and edged them out of power forever, though the shrinking German minority still wielded substantial influence well into the 1880s.

WWI & Independence

Czechs had no interest in fighting for their Austrian masters in WWI, and neighbouring Slovaks felt the same about their Hungarian rulers. Many defected to renegade legions fighting against the Germans and Austrians.

Meanwhile, Tomáš Garrigue Masaryk, Edvard Beneš and the Slovak Milan Štefánik began to argue the case – especially in the USA with President Wilson – for the Czechs' and Slovaks' long-cherished dream of independence. Wilson's interest was in keeping with his own goal of closer ties with Europe under the aegis of the League of Nations (the unsuccessful precursor to the United Nations). The most workable solution appeared to be a single federal state of two equal republics, and this was spelled out in agreements signed in Cleveland in 1915 and then in Pittsburgh in 1918.

As WWI drew to a close, Czechoslovakia declared its independence, with Allied support, on 28 October 1918. Prague became the capital, and the popular Masaryk, a writer and political philosopher, became the republic's first president.

On 1 January 1922 Greater Prague was established by the absorption of several surrounding towns and villages, growing to a city of 677,000. Like the rest of the country, Prague experienced an industrial boom until the Great Depression of the 1930s. By 1938 the population had grown to one million.

WWII

Unfortunately the new country was not left to live in peace. Most of Bohemia's and Moravia's three million German speakers wished to join Greater Germany, and in October 1938 the Nazis occupied the Sudetenland (the border regions with Germany and Austria), with the acquiescence of Britain and France in the infamous Munich Agreement. On 15 March 1939 Germany occupied all of Bohemia and Moravia, declaring the region a 'protectorate', while Slovakia proclaimed independence as a Nazi puppet state.

Prague suffered little physical damage during the war, although the Germans destroyed the Czech resistance – and hundreds of innocent Czech villagers – in retaliation for the assassination in Prague of SS General and Reichsprotektor Reinhard Heydrich (see the boxed text).

Prague's pre-WWII community of some 120,000 Jews was all but wiped out by the Nazis. Almost three-quarters of them – and some 90% of all the Jews in Bohemia and Moravia – died of starvation or were exterminated in camps from 1941 (see the boxed text 'The Jews of Prague' overleaf).

On 5 May 1945 the population of Prague rose against the German forces as the Red Army approached from the east. US troops

The Assassination of Heydrich

In 1941, in response to strikes and sabotage by the increasingly well organised Czech underground movement, the German government replaced its Reichsprotektor in Bohemia and Moravia with the SS General and antisubversion specialist Reinhard Heydrich, who cracked down on resistance activities with a vengeance.

In a clandestine operation, Britain trained a number of Czechoslovak paratroopers for an attempt to assassinate Heydrich. Astonishingly, it succeeded. Two paratroopers, Jan Kubiš and Jozef Gabčík, managed, on 27 May 1942, to bomb and shoot Heydrich as he rode in his official car in the city's Libeň district (see the boxed text 'Prague under the Nazis' in the Things to See & Do chapter for more on the area). He later died of his wounds. The assassins and five co-conspirators fled but were betrayed in their hiding place in the kostel sv Cyril a Metoděj (Church of SS Cyril & Methodius); in the ensuing siege all were killed or committed suicide.

The Nazis reacted with a frenzied wave of terror, including the annihilation a month later of two entire Czech villages, Lidice and Ležáky (see the Excursions chapter for more on the grim fate of Lidice), and the shattering of the underground movement.

had reached Plzeň, but held back in deference to their Soviet allies. The only help for Prague's lightly armed citizens came from Russian soldiers of the so-called Vlasov units, former POWs who had defected to the German side and now defected in turn to the Czech cause (they subsequently retreated to western Bohemia and surrendered to the Americans). Many people died before the Germans began pulling out on 8 May, having been granted free passage out of the city by the Czech resistance movement (in return for which the Germans left without destroying any more buildings or bridges).

Most of Prague was thus liberated by its own residents before Soviet forces arrived the following day. Liberation Day is now celebrated on 8 May; under communism it was 9 May.

Expulsion of Sudeten Germans

In 1945 Czechoslovakia was re-established as an independent state. One of the government's first acts was the expulsion of Sudeten Germans from the borderlands. By 1947 nearly 2.5 million Sudetenlanders had been stripped of their Czechoslovak citizenship and their land, and forcibly expelled to Germany (mainly Bavaria) and Austria. Thousands died during forced marches.

Despite a 1997 declaration of mutual apology for wartime misdeeds by the Czech Republic and Germany, the issue still brings emotions to the boil. Most Sudeten survivors feel their Czech citizenship and property were taken illegally. Many Czechs, on the other hand, remain convinced that Sudetenlanders forfeited their rights when they sought help from Nazi Germany, and that a formal apology by President Václav Havel in January 1990 was unwarranted.

Communism

In the 1946 elections the Communist Party of Czechoslovakia (KSČ) became the republic's dominant party with 36% of the popular vote, and formed a coalition government with other socialist parties.

The Jews of Prague

Prague's Jewish community was first moved into a walled ghetto in about the 13th century, in response to directives from Rome that Jews and Christians should live separately. Subsequent centuries of pogroms and official repression culminated in Ferdinand I's (r. 1526–64) threat, only grudgingly withdrawn, to throw all Jews out of Bohemia.

The reign of Rudolf II saw honour bestowed on Prague's Jews, a flowering of Jewish intellectual life, and prosperity in the ghetto. Mordechai Maisel (or Maisl), mayor of the ghetto, Rudolf's finance minister and Prague's wealthiest citizen, bankrolled some lavish redevelopment. Another major figure was Judah Löw ben Bezalel, or Rabbi Löw, prominent theologian, chief rabbi, student of the mystical teachings of the qabbala, and nowadays best known as the creator of the mythical golem – a kind of proto-robot made from the mud of the Vltava River.

When they helped to repel the Swedes on Charles Bridge (Karlův most) in 1648, Prague's Jews won the favour of Ferdinand III, to the extent that he had the ghetto enlarged. But a century later they were driven out of the city for over three years, to be welcomed back only because Praguers missed their business.

In the 1780s Emperor Joseph II outlawed many forms of discrimination, and in 1848 the ghetto walls were torn down, and the Jewish quarter – named Josefov in honour of Joseph II – was made a borough of Prague.

The demise of the quarter (which had slid into squalor as its population fell) came between 1893 and 1910 when it was cleared, ostensibly for public-health reasons, split down the middle by Pařížská třída and lined with Art Nouveau apartment buildings.

The community itself was all but eliminated by the Nazis and the communist regime slowly strangled what remained of Jewish cultural life. Thousands emigrated. Today only about 6000 Jews live in Prague.

Tension grew between democrats and communists, and in February 1948 the communists staged a coup d'état with the backing of the Soviet Union. A new constitution established the KSČ's dominance, and government was organised along Soviet lines. Thousands of noncommunists fled the country.

The 1950s were an era of harsh repression and decline, as communist economic policies nearly bankrupted the country. Many people were imprisoned. Hundreds were executed and thousands died in labour camps, often for little more than a belief in democracy. In a series of Stalin-style purges organised by the KSČ, many people, including top members of the party itself, were executed.

The 'Prague Spring' & Charter 77

In the late 1960s, Czechoslovakia enjoyed a gradual liberalisation under Alexander Dubček, the reformist general secretary of the KSČ. These reforms reflected a popular desire for full democracy and an end to censorship – 'socialism with a human face', as the party called it in its April 1968 'Action Programme'.

But Soviet leaders grew alarmed at the prospect of a democratic society within the Soviet bloc, and its certain domino effect in Poland and Hungary. The brief 'Prague Spring' was crushed by a Soviet-led Warsaw Pact invasion on the night of 20–21 August 1968. Prague was the major objective; Soviet special forces with help from the Czechoslovak secret service, the StB, secured Ruzyně airport for Soviet transport planes. At the end of the first day, 58 people had died. Passive resistance followed; street signs and numbers were removed from buildings throughout the country to disorient the invaders.

In 1969 Dubček was replaced by the orthodox Gustav Husák and exiled to the Slovak forestry department. Around 14,000 party functionaries and 280,000 members who refused to renounce their belief in 'socialism with a human face' were expelled from the party and lost their jobs. Many other educated professionals became street cleaners and manual labourers.

In January 1977 a group of 243 writers, artists and other intellectuals signed a public demand for basic human rights, Charta 77 (Charter 77), which became a focus for opponents of the regime. Prominent among them was the poet and playwright Václav Havel (see the boxed text overleaf).

The 'Velvet Revolution'

The communist regime remained in control until the breaching of the Berlin Wall in November 1989. On 17 November Prague's communist youth movement organised an officially sanctioned demonstration in memory of nine students executed by the Nazis in 1939. But the peaceful crowd of 50,000 was cornered in Národní street, where hundreds were beaten by police and about 100 were arrested.

Czechs were electrified by this wanton official violence, and the following days saw nonstop demonstrations by students, artists and finally most of the populace, peaking in a rally on Letná plain by some 750,000 people. Leading dissidents, with Havel at the forefront, formed an anticommunist coalition, which negotiated the government's resignation on 3 December. A 'Government of National Understanding' was formed, with the communists as a minority group. Havel was elected president of the republic by the federal assembly on 29 December.

The days following the 17 November demonstration have become known as the 'Velvet Revolution' (Sametová revoluce) because of its almost totally nonviolent character.

The 'Velvet Divorce'

Free elections to the federal assembly in 1990 were won by Civic Forum (OH) and its Slovak counterpart, People Against Violence (VPN). But Civic Forum soon split, over economic policy, into the right-of-centre Civic Democratic Party (ODS) led by Václav Klaus, and the left-of-centre Civic Forum led by Jiří Dienstbier. Klaus forced through tough economic policies, and their success gave the ODS a slim victory in the 1992 elections.

Václav Havel

Václav Havel was born in October 1936, the son of a wealthy Prague restaurateur. His family's property was confiscated after the communist coup of 1948, and as the child of bourgeois parents, he was denied easy access to education. He nevertheless finished high school and studied for a time at university before landing a job at the age of 23 as a stagehand at the divadlo na Zábradlí (Theatre on the Balustrade; see Drama under Theatre in the Entertainment chapter). Nine years later he was its resident playwright.

His enthusiasm over the liberal reforms of the 'Prague Spring', and his signature on the Charter 77 declaration, made him an enemy of the Husák government. His works – typically focusing on the absurdities and dehumanisation of totalitarian bureaucracy – were banned, his passport was seized and altogether he spent some four years in jail for his activities on behalf of human rights in Czechoslovakia.

The massive demonstrations of November 1989 thrust Havel into the limelight as a leading organiser of the noncommunist Civic Forum movement, which pressed for democratic reforms and ultimately negotiated a new government of national reconciliation. Havel himself was elected president of the country the following month, and the first president of the new Czech Republic in 1993.

NICKY CASTLE

In 1998 he was re-elected, with the slimmest of margins. Nevertheless, the dignified former playwright remains the Czechs' favourite elder statesman; many worry that there is no-one of similar status to succeed him when his term ends with the 2003 presidential election.

Meanwhile, separatists headed by Vladimír Mečiar won the 1992 elections in Slovakia, depriving the ODS of a parliamentary majority. The very different economic positions of Mečiar and Klaus made compromise almost impossible, with Mečiar favouring gradual transformation and independence for Slovakia. The two leaders decided that splitting the country was the best solution, and on 1 January 1993, Czechoslovakia ceased to exist for the second time this century.

Prague became the capital of the new Czech Republic, and Havel was elected as its first president.

After the Divorce

The first Czech-only elections, in 1996, ended inconclusively. Klaus' ODS won the biggest share of the vote but even with coalition partners, the Civic Democratic Alliance (ODA) and the Christian & Democratic Union (KDU-ČSL), it failed by one seat to score a parliamentary majority and was forced to negotiate with the second-strongest party, the Social Democrats (ČSSD). The ODS and its minority government were unable to govern effectively, and seemed to have lost the will for change. Allegations of corruption began to multiply, foreign investment slackened off and the Czech economy began to slump.

In December 1997 Klaus was forced to resign over a party-finance scandal, although this coincided with the fragile partnership with the KDU-ČSL nearing a collapse. President Havel succeeded in patching together an interim government, headed by former Central Bank boss Josef Tošovský. In January 1998 Havel just managed to get re-elected as president, by a margin of only one vote. His term in office will end with the next presidential election in 2003.

In the June 1998 parliamentary elections, the ČSSD won only 74 of 200 parliamentary seats, with the ODS a close second. In July, Havel asked the ČSSD leader, Miloš Zeman, to form a new government, though he only managed to do so with the help of the ODS, who in return insisted on several ministerial posts, the watering down of some of the ČSSD's left-of-centre positions, and the appointment of Václav Klaus as parliamentary speaker.

The ČSSD remained the largest party in the June 2002 elections with an increased share of the vote (30.2% but only 70 seats), headed by its new leader and the Czech Republic's prime minister, Vladimir Spidla. The ODS was second with 24.5% and 58 seats – their worst ever showing. The big surprise of 2002 was the Czech Communist Party (KSČM), which moved up to third place with 18.5% and 41 seats – up from 24 seats in 1998. The centrist Christian Democrat Coalition (Koalice; 14.3%, 31 seats) slipped to fourth. The turnout, however, was only 58%.

After several weeks of negotiations, Spidla formed a coalition government with Koalice and together the parties wield a wafer-thin majority of 101 seats in the 200-seat parliament.

Affordable housing remains in short supply in Prague, the health system is under strain, and pollution and crime rates are up. Nevertheless, Prague's booming tourism and a solid industrial base have left its citizens in better economic shape than the rest of the country. Unemployment here is minimal, shops are full, and many buildings have had or are getting face-lifts.

In the international arena, the Czech Republic has joined the big league: along with Poland and Hungary it became a member of NATO in 1999. The Lower House of the Czech parliament voted 154 to 38 in favour of NATO membership, though there was little public debate on the subject and no public referendum, as was held in Hungary (where 85% voted in favour).

Relations with Germany and Austria have in recent years been strained by the Czechs' refusal to decommission the ageing Temelin nuclear power station in southern Bohemia, and their continued upholding of the Beneš Decree, which saw the forced expulsion of Sudeten Germans from postwar Czechoslovakia.

The Czech Republic is expected to join the EU along with nine other countries in 2004.

CLIMATE

The Czech Republic has a transitional climate between maritime and continental, characterised by hot, showery summers; cold, snowy winters; and generally changeable conditions. A typical day in Prague from June to August sees the mercury range from about 12°C to 22°C. Temperatures from December to February push below freezing. Wide variations are common, sometimes surpassing 35°C in summer and –20°C in winter.

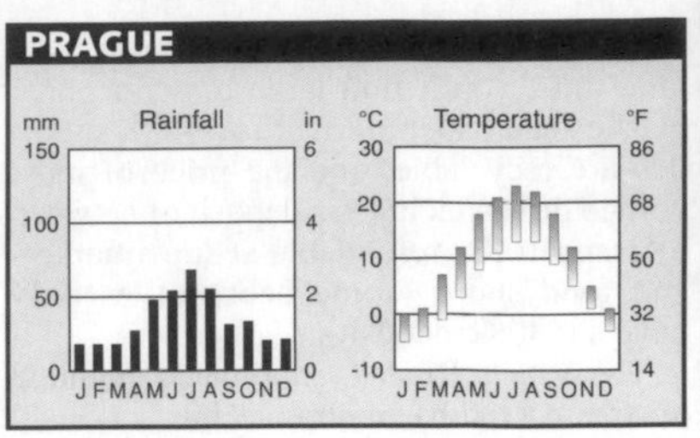

The closest thing to a 'dry season' is from January to March, when total precipitation (mostly as snow at that time) is less than a third of that during the wettest months, June to August. And yet January averages as many 'wet' days (about two out of five) as the summer months do. The summer's long, sunny, hot spells tend to be broken by sudden, heavy thunderstorms. May and September have the most pleasant weather.

ECOLOGY & ENVIRONMENT

During most of the year Prague's air is fairly breathable. But in mid-winter the air can get foul with vehicle emissions, particularly during inversions (a meteorological phenomenon in which air temperature increases with altitude, causing ultra-stable conditions). If you're just here for a few days, there's little to worry about, though Prague residents suffer from high rates of respiratory ailments.

Radio and TV stations provide bulletins about pollution levels, and the Prague Information Service (PIS; see Tourist Offices in the Facts for the Visitor chapter) should be able to tell you of any risk.

Central Prague's traffic becomes increasingly gridlocked as the number of new cars soars. Plans for a ring road around the city have so far been stalemated by opposition from every council through which it would pass.

Czechs have been recycling waste for a long time; you'll find large bins for glass, plastics and paper all over town. Most bottles are recyclable, and the price of most bottled drinks includes a deposit of between 3Kč and 10Kč, refundable at supermarkets and food shops (some beer bottles only have a 0.40Kč deposit).

The Vltava River is marginally polluted upstream (south) of Prague but seriously polluted downstream. In August 2002 the city suffered its worst floods for 200 years when the Vltava burst its banks and inundated most of Malá Strana and parts of Staré Město. Although sandbag defences saved Old Town Square, the clean-up is expected to cost more than US$2 billion and last until well into 2003.

GOVERNMENT & POLITICS

Prague is the capital of the Czech Republic and the seat of government, parliament and the president. The city itself is governed separately from other regions of the country by the Local Government of the Capital City of Prague, headed by a council and a mayor. The acting body of this government is the municipal office together with the council. Prague is divided into 10 districts and 57 suburbs, governed by district and local governments.

Since 1989 Prague citizens have voted heavily (typically about 60%) for right-of-centre parties. Václav Klaus (whose constituency included Prague) and his Civic Democratic Party (ODS) collected over 40% of the city's popular vote in the 1998 and 2002 elections, while the two other right-leaning parties together polled another 20%. Prague was in fact the only place in the country where the ODS polled at the top.

But country-wide, the ODS is in opposition to the left-of-centre Social Democrats (ČSSD), led by Vladimir Spidla, the current prime minister. Klaus, prime minister from 1992 to 1997 and the force behind many of the country's post-1989 reforms, was widely regarded as a Thatcherite, though others saw his policies as a practical mix of market reforms and socialism. Spidla, a historian and former labour and social affairs minister, is committed to expanding the welfare state, a policy at odds with the country's mounting budget deficit.

The Czech Communist Party (KSČM) is one of the few left in the world that still adheres to Marxist-Stalinist doctrine; it has a solid core of mostly elderly followers. In the 2002 elections it won 41 seats, up from 24 in 1998.

ECONOMY

Since the Industrial Revolution, Bohemia and Moravia have specialised in light industry, and in Central Europe their combined industrial output was once second only to Germany's. Under communist rule, industry and agriculture were nationalised, and heavy industry (mainly steel) was introduced along Soviet lines. Other important industries include vehicle and machinery manufacture, armaments, cement, plastics, cotton, ceramics and brewing.

Agricultural products include sugar beet, wheat, potatoes, corn, barley, rye, hops, lumber, cattle, pigs, poultry, horses and carp. The country lacks natural energy sources except large deposits of low-quality brown coal in North Bohemia and North Moravia. Its natural gas comes mainly from Russia and via a pipeline through Germany from Norway.

About 9% of Prague's population is employed in manufacturing (major industries are textiles, machinery and food), making it the largest industrial centre in the republic. Karlín and Smíchov are the two major industrial suburbs. Most of the population is employed in service industries, including tourism.

In 1998 the Czech economy, for years considered one of the healthiest in the former eastern bloc, suffered a slump and has had budget deficits ever since. Inflation rose from 8.8% in 1996 to 10.7% in 1998, but in 1999 was reined in and has remained steady at around 4% since 2000. Gross domestic product (GDP) growth of –2% in 1998 rose to +2.5% in 2001. An unemployment rate of 5.2% in 1997 climbed to over 9% by 1999 (though just 3% in Prague), and remained at that level in 2002.

The average monthly wage at the beginning of 2002 was about US$500 (15,700Kč), enough for a reasonably comfortable life – although for Prague residents living in the central tourist zones, costs have gone through the roof.

The devastating floods of August 2002 (see Ecology & Environment earlier in this chapter) are likely to have a lasting impact on the economy of both Prague and the Czech Republic as a whole.

Privatisation

In 1990 the government embarked on an ambitious privatisation programme. The 'small-privatisation' phase included restitution – the return of property to pre-1948 owners or their descendants – and the sale of smaller enterprises through auctions or straight to foreign buyers. All of Prague's hotels and restaurants are now privately owned, though the government still owns, and subsidises, most theatres and museums.

A 'large-privatisation' phase has concentrated on large enterprises, and small ones that had not yet found buyers. Sales were conducted mainly through a coupon system (in which every citizen had a chance to become a shareholder) or by auction. An important element was the April 1993 reopening of the Prague stock exchange.

A protracted third phase is focused on a handful of large, over-staffed and low-productivity companies, including most major banks and strategic industrial companies. It is taking longer than planned, in part because since 1996 the ODS lacked the majority needed to push privatisation and other reforms through parliament, and in part because many of the already-privatised companies had been bought by the banks themselves.

In 2001 the Komerční banka (Commercial Bank) became the last of the 'big four' banks to be privatised (the others are IPB, ČSOB and Česká spořitelna). Next up for privatisation are České drahy (ČD), the state railway operator, and the steel, petrochemical, gas, and energy sectors.

POPULATION & PEOPLE

Czechs are Western Slavs, as are Poles, Slovaks and Lusatians (Sorbs). Roughly one out of 13 Czech citizens lives in Prague, whose population in 2002 was around 1,213,000.

In addition to Slovak and Romany minorities, there are significant numbers of expatriates – especially Ukrainians, Americans and Germans – living and working in Prague. Based on work-permit statistics and educated guesses about the ratio of legal to illegal workers, it's thought there are between 20,000 and 60,000 of them.

ARTS

Music

Before Christianity, folk songs and dances were the main forms of music in the Czech lands. The Church tried to replace these with Christian songs, and introduced Gregorian plainsong. Hussite reformers promoted hymns in Czech and drew on popular folk melodies, providing fertile ground for the future development of Czech music. Remnants of old Czech tunes can still be found in Protestant German hymns.

The Counter-Reformation put a lid on Czech musical culture. Above the village level, it survived only among a handful of musicians composing and playing at the courts of other European rulers. The most notable of these expatriates was Jan Dismas Zelenka, who worked in Dresden during the 18th century.

The musical spirit returned in the mid-19th century with the rise of several great composers during the early stages of the National Revival. Bedřich Smetana (1824–84), the first great Czech composer, incorporated folk melodies into his classical compositions. His best-known works are *Prodaná nevěsta* (The Bartered Bride), *Dalibor a Libuše* (Dalibor & Libuše) and *Má Vlast* (My Country).

Antonín Dvořák (1841–1904) spent four years in the USA where he lectured on music and composed the symphony *From the New World*. Among his other well known works are the two *Slovanské tance* (Slavonic Dances; 1878 and 1881), the operas *Rusalka* and *Čert a Káča* (The Devil & Kate) and his religious masterpiece *Stabat Mater*. Another prominent composer of this generation was Zdeněk Fibich (1850–1900).

Moravian-born Leoš Janáček (1854–1928), who also incorporated folk elements into his heavier music, is a leading 20th-century Czech composer. Never as popular as Smetana or Dvořák in his native country, his better-known compositions include the opera *Jenůfa*, the *Glagolská mše* (Glagolitic Mass) and *Taras Bulba*, while one of his finest pieces is *Stories of Liška Bystrouška*.

Other well known composers are Josef Suk (1874–1935) and Bohuslav Martinů (1890–1959).

Jazz Jazz has a grip on Czech cultural life that is unmatched almost anywhere else in Europe. It was already being played in the mid-1930s, mostly for dancing. Czech musicians remained at the forefront of the European jazz scene until the communist takeover in 1948 when controls were imposed on the performance and publication of jazz music, which was considered to be a product of the capitalist system. In the late 1950s, Prague Radio had a permanent jazz orchestra led by Karel Krautgartner.

Restrictions were gradually lifted in the 1960s. One of the top bands in this period was the SH Quartet, which played for three years at Reduta, the first Czech professional jazz club, in Prague (see Jazz & Blues in the Entertainment chapter). Another leading band was the Junior Trio, with Jan Hamr and the brothers Miroslav and Allan Vitouš, who all left for the USA after 1968. Jan Hamr (keyboards) became prominent in 1970s American jazz-rock as Jan Hammer, while Miroslav Vitouš (bass) rose to fame in several American jazz-rock bands.

One of the most outstanding musicians in today's jazz scene is Jiřví Stivín who in the 1970s produced two excellent albums with the band System Tandem and since has been regarded as the most original European jazz musician. Another is Milan Viklický who also still performs in many of Prague's jazz clubs. Milan Svoboda, as well as being an accomplished pianist, is best known for his conducting abilities.

Rock & Pop Rock was often banned by communist authorities because of its 'corrupting influence', although certain local bands, and innocuous western groups such as Abba, were allowed. Karel Gott and Helena Vondráčková were the two most popular Czech pop stars before 1989.

The pioneers of Czech rock (*Big Beat* in Czech), Sputnici, were the best known of several 1960s bands recycling American hits. Malostranská beseda in Malá Strana was a popular venue (see Rock & Other Music in the Entertainment chapter). But serious rock remained an underground movement for small audiences in obscure pubs and country houses. Raids and arrests were common. Fans included political dissidents such as Václav Havel. Plastic People of the Universe achieved international fame by being imprisoned after a 1970s show trial intended to discourage underground music.

Since 1989, bands have proliferated. Though Prague's club scene is lively, many of the city's finest venues (especially those in city-owned properties) have shut down as a result of court actions over noise.

Popular bands on the home front include pop-oriented Buty; hard-rock bands Lucie and the less-refined Alice; and even a country-and-western rock band, Žlutý Pes (Yellow Dog). More alternative are several veteran outfits, including the grunge band Support Lesbiens, and Visací Zámek (Padlock). Lucie Bílá, diva of 1990s Czech pop, started out sounding like a toned-down Nina Hagen, but has lately turned to rock musicals and Czech versions of American and British hits. Newer talent includes Patti-Smith-like Načeva, and avant-garde violinist and vocalist Iva Bittová, who has made first-rate classical and modern recordings.

Literature

The earliest literary works were hymns and religious texts in Old Church Slavonic, replaced by Latin in the late 11th century. The 14th and 15th centuries saw the appearance of reformist theological texts, mostly in Czech, by Jan Hus and others.

With the imposition of the German language after the Thirty Years' War, Czech literature entered a dark age, re-emerging only in the early 19th century in the Czech-language works of the linguists Josef Dobrovský and Josef Jungmann. In the mid-19th century František Palacký published a five-volume history of Bohemia and Moravia.

Karel Hynek Mácha, possibly the greatest of all Czech poets, was the leading representative of Romanticism in the early 19th century; his most famous lyrical work is *Máj* (May). Mid-19th-century Romanticism produced outstanding pieces about life in the country, especially *Grandmother* by Božena Němcová (the first major female Czech writer), and Karel Erben's *Flowers*.

The radical political journalist Karel Havlíček Borovský criticised the Habsburg elite and wrote excellent satirical poems. Two poets of the time who took much inspiration from Czech history were Jan Neruda (who also wrote *Povídky malostranské*, or Prague Tales, a collection of stories about daily life in Malá Strana) and Svatopluk Čech.

At the end of the 19th century Alois Jirásek wrote *Staré pověsti české* (Old Czech Legends), a compendium of stories from the arrival of the Czechs in Bohemia to the Middle Ages, as well as nationalistic historical novels, his best being *Temno* (Darkness).

Kafka's Prague

Literary Prague at the onset of the 20th century was a unique melting pot of Czechs, Germans and Jews. Though he wrote in German, Franz Kafka is a son of the Czech capital. He lived in Prague all his life, haunting the city and being haunted by it, needing it and hating it. One could look at *The Trial* as a metaphysical geography of Staré Město (Old Town), whose Byzantine alleys and passages break down the usual boundaries between outer streets and inner courtyards, between public and private, new and old, real and imaginary.

Most of Kafka's life was lived around Josefov and Old Town Square (Staroměstské náměstí). He was born on 3 July 1883 in an apartment beside kostel sv Mikuláše (St Nicholas Church); only the stone portal remains of the original building. As a boy he lived at Celetná 2 (1888–89); dům U minuty, the Renaissance corner building that's now part of the Staroměstská radnice (Old Town Hall; 1889–96); and Celetná 3 (1896–1907), where his bedroom window looked into kostel panny Marie Před Týnem (Týn Church). He took classes between 1893 and 1901 at the Old Town State Gymnasium in palác Kinských (Kinský Palace) on the square, and for a time his father ran a clothing shop on the ground floor there.

On the southern side of the square, at No 17, Berta Fanta ran an intellectual salon in the early part of the 20th century to which she invited fashionable European thinkers of the time, including Kafka and fellow writers Max Brod (Kafka's friend and biographer), Franz Werfel and Egon Erwin Kisch.

After earning a law degree from the Karolinum in 1906, Kafka took his first job from 1907 to 1908, an unhappy one as an insurance clerk with the Italian firm Assicurazioni Generali, at Wenceslas Square (Václavské náměstí) 19 (on the corner of Jindřišská). At Na poříčí 7 in northern Nové Město (New Town) is the former headquarters of the Workers' Accident Insurance Co, where he toiled on the 5th floor from 1908 until his retirement in 1922.

The last place Kafka lived with his parents (1913–14) – and the setting for his horrific parable *Metamorphosis* – was a top-floor flat across Pařížská from kostel sv Mikuláše, facing Old Town Square. At the age of 33 he finally moved into a place of his own at Dlouhá 16 (at the narrow corner with Masná), where he lived from 1915 to 1917, during which time he also spent a productive winter (1916–17) at a cottage rented by his sister at Zlatá ulička (Golden Lane) 22, inside the Prague Castle (Pražský hrad) grounds. By this time, ill with tuberculosis, he took a flat for a few months in 1917 at the Schönborn Palace at Tržiště 15 (now the US embassy) in Malá Strana (Little Quarter).

Kafka died in Vienna on 3 June 1924 and is buried in the Jewish Cemetery at Žižkov.

NICKY CASTLE

A major political philosopher and writer of his time was Tomáš Garrigue Masaryk, later to become Czechoslovakia's first president.

One of the best-known Czech writers of all is Franz Kafka. Along with a circle of other German-speaking Jewish writers in Prague, he played a major role in the literary scene at the beginning of the 20th century (see the boxed text). His two complex and claustrophobic masterpieces are *The Trial* and *The Castle*. Others in the same circle were critic Max Brod and journalist Egon Erwin Kisch.

Among their Czech-speaking contemporaries was Jaroslav Hašek, now best known for *Dobrý voják Švejk* (The Good Soldier Švejk), which is full of good, low-brow WWI humour about the trials of Czechoslovakia's literary mascot, written in instalments from Prague's pubs.

The post-WWI Czech author Karel Čapek is famous for a science-fiction drama, *RUR* (Rossum's Universal Robots), from which the word 'robot' entered the English language. Well known poets of the interwar years are Jaroslav Seifert (awarded the Nobel Prize for Literature in 1984) and Vítěslav Nezval.

The early communist period produced little of literary value, though the 1960s saw a resurgence of writing as controls were relaxed. Writers such as Václav Havel, Josef Škvorecký, Milan Kundera and Ivo Klíma produced their first works in the years preceding the 1968 Soviet-led invasion. Klíma's best-known novel is *The Ship Named Hope*.

After the invasion some, including Havel, stayed and wrote for the underground *samizdat* press or had manuscripts smuggled to the West. Others left, producing their best work in exile. Kundera's best novel is probably *The Joke;* two other well known works are *The Unbearable Lightness of Being* and *The Book of Laughter and Forgetting*. Two good reads by Škvorecký are *Cowards* and *The Bride of Texas*. Other important figures of this time are philosopher Jan Patočka and poet Jiří Kolář.

Until his accidental death in 1997, the Czech Republic's leading contemporary novelist was Bohumil Hrabal. One of his most notable novels, *The Little Town That Stood Still*, portrays with good humour the interactions of a small, close-knit community. Another popular Hrabal work is *Closely Watched Trains*.

Painting

The luminously realistic, 14th-century paintings of Magister Theodoricus (Master Theodoric), whose work hangs in the kaple sv Kříže (Chapel of the Holy Cross) at Karlštejn Castle and in the kaple sv Václava (Chapel of St Wenceslas) in chrám sv Víta, influenced art throughout Central Europe.

Another gem of Czech Gothic art is a late-14th-century altar panel by an artist known only as the Master of the Třeboň Altar; what remains of it is in the klášter sv Jiří (Convent of St George) in Prague Castle.

The Baroque era saw a surge of Catholic religious art, dominated in Bohemia by Petr Brandl.

The Czech National Revival in the late 18th and early 19th centuries witnessed the appearance of a Czech style of realism, in particular by Mikuláš Aleš and the father and son Antonín and Josef Mánes. Alfons Mucha is well known for his late-19th-century Art Nouveau posters. Czech landscape art developed in the works of Anton Kosárek, followed by a wave of Impressionism and Symbolism at the hands of Antonín Slavíček, Max Švabinský and others. The earliest notable woman painter, Zdenka Braunerová, concentrated on painting and sketching Prague and the Czech countryside.

In the early 20th century, Prague developed as a centre of avant-garde art, concentrated in a group of artists called Osma (The Eight). Prague was also a focus for Cubist painters, including Josef Čapek. The functionalist movement flourished between WWI and WWII in a group called Devětsil, led by the adaptable Karel Teige. Surrealists followed, including Zdeněk Rykr and Josef Šíma.

Forty years of communism brought little art of interest, at least through official channels. Underground painters of the time included Mikuláš Medek (whose abstract, Surrealist art was exhibited in out-of-the-way galleries) and Jiří Kolář, an outstanding graphic artist and poet. Some of the never-exhibited artists of the postwar years have surfaced since 1989.

Sculpture

Medieval sculpture, like medieval painting, served religious ends. In the 12th and 13th centuries sculpture evolved from ornamentation into realism. The 14th century saw further realist tendencies, represented by the portraits of royal and noble figures in chrám sv Víta. Soon a more decorative style took over, best exemplified by the anonymous *Krumlov Virgin* in the klášter sv Jiří at Prague Castle.

Gothic realism in the late 15th century brought more lively forms, including the work of the so-called Žebrák Master of Sorrows, also in the klášter sv Jiří.

In the Baroque era, religious sculpture sprouted in public places, including 'Marian columns' erected in gratitude to the Virgin for protection against the plague. Two outstanding Baroque sculptors were Matthias Braun and Ferdinand Maximilian Brokoff. An important late-18th-century figure was Ignác František Platzer, whose decorative statues can be seen throughout Prague.

Bohemian sculpture declined until a mid-19th-century revival, in which Václav Levý was a principal figure. Josef Václav Myslbek dominated sculpture in the late 19th century with his romantic Slavonic style. His students, including Stanislav Sucharda, produced brilliant Symbolist pieces. Other sculptors were the Impressionists Ladislav Šaloun and Josef Mařatka.

One of the best-known Cubist sculptors was Otto Gutfreund. In the 1920s he switched to realism, influencing the next wave of sculptors such as Jan Lauda, Karel Pokorný and Karel Dvořák. Surrealism followed, one of its best-known figures being Ladislav Zívr.

Zdeněk Palcr (1927–96) was perhaps one of the best Czech sculptors of the 20th century with a unique style in which he tended to use geometrical lines rather than the true shapes of the human body to portray people in his sculptures.

Cinema

The pioneer of Czech cinema was the architect Jan Kříženecký who made three comedies in American slapstick style that were shown at the 1898 Exhibition of Architecture and Engineering.

The domestic film industry took off in the early years of this century and Czechs were leading innovators. The first film ever to show full frontal nudity was Gustaf Machatý's *Extase* (Ecstasy; 1932). It was a hit (and a scandal) at the 1934 Venice Film Festival. Revealing all was one Hedvige Kiesler, who went on to Hollywood as Hedy Lamarr. Hugo Haas directed a fine adaptation of Karel Čapek's anti-Nazi science-fiction novel *Bílá nemoc* (White Death) in 1937. Fear of persecution drove him to Hollywood, where he made and starred in many films.

The Nazis limited the movie industry to nationalistic comedies, while under communism the focus was on low-quality propaganda films. A 'new wave' of Czech cinema rose between 1963 and the Soviet-led invasion in 1968. Its young directors escaped censorship because they were among the first graduates of the communist-supervised Academy of Film. It was from this time that Czech films began to win international awards.

Among the earliest outstanding works was *Černý Petr* (Black Peter, known in the USA as *Peter & Paula*; 1963) by Miloš Forman, who fled after 1968 and became a successful Hollywood director with films such as *One Flew over the Cuckoo's Nest* (1975) and *Amadeus* (1984). Other prominent directors were Jiří Menzel, Věra Chytilová and Ivan Passer.

Some post-1968 films critical of the regime were banned or their production stopped. Probably the best film of the following two decades was Menzel's internationally screened 1985 comedy *Má vesnička středisková* (My Sweet Little Village), a subtle look at the workings and failings of socialism in a village cooperative.

Directors in the post-communist era are struggling to compete with Hollywood films, as well as the good Czech films of the 1960s. So far the only one who has succeeded is Jan

Svěrák, whose 1994 hit *Akumulátor* was the most expensive Czech film produced to date. In 1996 it was surpassed at the box office by the internationally acclaimed *Kolja* (Kolya), about a Russian boy raised by a Czech bachelor (played by the director's father). A year later *Kolja* won the best foreign film awards at the Cannes Film Festival and the US Academy Awards.

Věra Chytilová continues to produce good films and win prizes at film festivals. In 2000 another brilliant young director, David Ondříček, released *Samotáři*, the story of a group of seven people trying to find love and a partner in the 1990s.

More recently, Jan Hřejbek's superb black comedy *Musíme Si Pomáhat* (Divided We Fall; 2000), exploring the conflicting loyalties of small-town Czechs during WWII, won an Oscar nomination for best foreign film. In 2001 Jan Sverák, director of *Kolja,* produced another potential Oscar-winner with *Dark Blue World,* a story of two Czech fighter pilots who return home after WWII only to be sent to labour camps by the communist authorities.

The Czech film studios at Barrandov in southwestern Prague are known for their world-class animated and puppet films, many of which were made from the 1950s to the 1980s. The best of the puppet films, *A Midsummer Night's Dream* (1959), was produced by the talented Jiří Trnka.

Theatre

Czech-language theatre did not develop fully until the 16th century. Themes were mostly biblical and the intent was to moralise. At Prague's Karolinum, Latin drama was used for teaching. The best plays were written by Jan Ámos Komenský (John Comenius) in the years before the Thirty Years' War, after which plays in Czech were banned. German drama and Italian opera were popular during the 17th and 18th centuries, when many theatres were built.

In 1785 Czech drama reappeared at the Nostitz Theatre (now Stavovské divadlo, Estates Theatre; see Drama under Theatre in the Entertainment chapter), and Prague became the centre of Czech-language theatre. Major 19th-century playwrights were Josef Kajetán Tyl and Ján Kolár. Drama, historical plays and fairy tales flourished as part of the Czech National Revival. In 1862 the first independent Czech theatre, the Prozatimní divadlo (Temporary Theatre), opened in Prague.

Drama in the early years of Czechoslovakia was led by the brothers Karel and Josef Čapek, and also František Langer. Actor and playwright EF Burian later became known for his experimental dramas.

Under communism classical theatrical performances were of a high quality, but the modern scene was stifled. Exceptions included the pantomime of the Černé divadlo (Black Theatre) and the ultra-modern Laterna Magika (Magic Lantern), founded by Alfréd Radok.

Many fine plays, including those by Václav Havel, were not performed locally as a result of their anti-government tone, but appeared in the West. In the mid-1960s free expression was explored in Prague's divadlo na Zábradlí (Theatre on the Balustrade; see Drama under Theatre in the Entertainment chapter), with works by Havel, Ladislav Fialka and Milan Uhde, and performances by the comedy duo of Jiří Suchý and Jiří Šlitr.

Marionette & Puppet Theatre Marionette performances have been popular in Prague since the 16th century. A major figure of this art form was Matěj Kopecký (1775–1847).

Marionette theatres opened in Prague and Plzeň in the early 20th century. Josef Skupa's legendary Spejbl & Hurvínek (the Czech Punch & Judy) attracted large crowds, and still does.

Even during communism puppet and marionette theatre was officially approved and popular, and Czech performances were ranked among the best in the world, especially in the films of Jiří Trnka (see Cinema earlier in this chapter).

Architecture

See the Things to See & Do chapter for more information on the places mentioned in this section.

Romanesque (10th to 12th Centuries) The earliest Slavonic buildings in Bohemia were wooden and have not survived. The oldest nonperishable structures were stone-built Romanesque rotundas (circular churches), though most have since been incorporated into larger churches. The Romanesque style is typified by heavy walls and columns, barrel-vaulted ceilings and small doors and windows with semi-circular arches.

Prague's finest Romanesque structure is the bazilika sv Jiří (Basilica of St George; 920) in Prague Castle, although its exterior facade is a 17th-century Baroque addition. Other examples include the rotunda sv Martina (Rotunda of St Martin; late 11th century) at Vyšehrad, and the rotunda sv Longina (rotunda of St Longinus; late 11th century) and the kaple sv Kříže (rotunda of the Holy Cross; mid-12th century) in Nové Město.

Gothic (13th to 16th Centuries) The 13th century brought the Gothic style to churches, public buildings and entire town centres, with arcaded houses built around a central square. Gothic represented not just a new aesthetic but also a revolution in architectural design that allowed architects to build thinner walls and higher vaults. The style is characterised by tall, pointed arches, ribbed columns and vaults, external flying buttresses (to support the thinner walls) and tall, narrow windows with intricate tracery supporting great expanses of stained glass. As time went by, Gothic designs became ever taller, pointier and more elaborately decorated.

Czech Gothic architecture thrived during the rule of Charles IV, especially in the hands of German architect Peter Parler, best known for the eastern part of chrám sv Víta (late 14th century). A beautiful example of late-Gothic craftsmanship is the flowing, ribbed vault of Prague Castle's Vladislavský sál (Vladislav Hall; 1487–1500) by Benedikt Rejt.

Other fine Gothic structures are the klášter sv Anežky (Convent of St Agnes; 1233–1380), kostel panny Marie Před Týnem (Church of Our Lady Before Týn; 1365–1511), Charles Bridge and its towers (1357–early 15th century; also by Peter Parler) and the Prašná brána (Powder Gate; 1475).

Renaissance (15th to 17th Centuries) Renaissance architecture appeared in the early 16th century, with Italian designers invited to Prague by Habsburg rulers. It brought a new enthusiasm for classical forms and an obsession with grace and symmetry. The emphasis was more on chateaux and merchant houses than on churches.

The mixture of Italian and local styles gave rise to the unique 'Czech Renaissance' style, featuring heavy ornamental stucco decorations and paintings of historical or mythical scenes. The technique of sgraffito – creating patterns and pictures by scraping through an outer layer of pale plaster to reveal a darker surface beneath – was much used in exterior decoration.

Fine examples of Renaissance buildings include the Letohrádek (Summer, or Belvedere, Palace; 1538–63) and the Švarcenberský palác (Schwarzenberg Palace; 1546–67) at Hradčany; on a smaller scale is the dům U minuty (1564–1610), part of the Staroměstská radnice.

Baroque (17th and 18th Centuries) Re-Catholicisation and reconstruction after the Thirty Years' War introduced the Baroque style to Habsburg palaces, residences and new churches. This was the grandest period in Bohemian architecture, responsible for the Baroque 'face' of Prague today. The style's marble columns, florid sculpture, trompe l'oeil paintings, frescoed ceilings and rich, gilded ornamentation full of curves and ovals combined to create extravagant and awe-inspiring interiors.

In the early 18th century a distinctively Czech Baroque style emerged. Its best-known practitioners were the Bavarian father and son Kristof and Kilian Ignatz Dientzenhofer, the Italian Giovanni Santini and the Bohemian František Kaňka. The best examples in Prague – among dozens – include kostel sv Mikuláše (St Nicholas Church; 1704–55) in Malá Strana, the Loreta (1711–51) in Hradčany, kostel sv Mikuláše (1732–35) on Old Town Square, and Vila Amerika (1717–20) in Nové Město, all by the Dientzenhofers.

The final flourish of the late-Baroque period was the rococo style, a sort of 'super-Baroque' with even more (and even more elaborate) decoration. The palác Kinských (Kinský Palace; 1755–65) overlooking Old Town Square has a rococo facade.

Revivalist (late 18th and 19th Centuries) This period saw various revivals of older architectural styles – neoclassical, neogothic, neo-Renaissance – which in the middle of the century coincided with the Czech National Revival. Neoclassicism harked back to the classical architecture of ancient Greece and Rome, favouring huge, simple, symmetrical buildings with grand colonnades and pediments, as seen in the Stavovské divadlo (1781–83) in Staré Město. One of the finest works of this period is the neo-Renaissance Národní divadlo (1883) by Josef Zítek, on Národní. Other buildings in this style include the Národní muzeum (1885–90) on Wenceslas Square (Václavské náměstí) and the Rudolfinum (1876–84) on náměstí Jana Palacha.

Art Nouveau (c. 1899–1912) As in the rest of Europe, Czech architecture in the early 20th century was under the spell of Art Nouveau, with its sinuous, 'botanical' lines and colourful renderings of flowers and (mostly female) human figures. The term came from the French *l'art nouveau* (New Art) and was known as *secese* in Bohemia, *Sezessionstil* in Austria and *Jugendstil* in Germany.

The most visible Art Nouveau works in Prague are the Hotel Central on Hybernská in Nové Město, the Grand Hotel Europa (1903–05) on Wenceslas Square, the Praha hlavní nádraží (Prague's main train station; 1901–09), Obecní dům (Municipal House; 1903–12), and structures built for the Terrestrial Jubilee Exposition of 1891 in Bubeneč.

Modern (20th Century) Cubism had a strong influence on architecture before WWI, developing into a striking local style. Some of Prague's finest Cubist facades were designed by Josef Chochol between 1912 and 1914, and can be seen in the neighbourhood just below Vyšehrad; look at the houses at Libušina 49, Rašínovo nábřeží 6–10 and Neklanova 30. Other appealing examples are U černé Matky Boží (House of the Black Madonna; 1911–12) in Staré Město, twin houses on Tychonova in Dejvice (by Josef Gočár) and a 1921 apartment building at Elišky Krasnohorské 10–14 in Staré Mesto (by Otakar Novotný).

Prague has only a few examples of the interwar style called Art Deco, a latter-day term for an avant-garde 1920s and 30s style mixing traditional decoration with a modern look. They include the Bank of Czechoslovakian Legions (1921–23) at Na poříčí 24, and the dům Látek (Adria Palace; 1922–25), both in Nové Město. More avant-garde architecture can be found in the later work of Jan Kotěra, though Prague has few examples.

Constructivist-style buildings – typified by extreme geometric simplicity and functionalism – include the Veletržní palác (Trade Fair Palace; 1926–28) in Holešovice, and kostel sv Václava (St Wenceslas Church; 1927–30) in Vinohrady. The kostel Nejsvětějšího Srdce Páně (Church of the Most Sacred Heart of Our Lord; 1928–32) by Josip Plečnik in Vinohrady, is a modern classic inspired by the forms of Early Christian basilicas and Egyptian temples.

The architecture of the communist era was heavy-handed and Stalinist, producing many eyesores – including vast, prefabricated residential complexes – and little style or quality. Restoration concentrated on prime tourist sights while other buildings were neglected.

Post-1989 Architecture Prague's post-1989 architecture is a mixed bag, some quite out of keeping with its surroundings, some simply ugly, and some surprisingly attractive. One of Prague's most idiosyncratic and appealing examples of new architecture is the Tančící dům (Dancing Building; 1992-96), on Rašínovo nábřeží in Nové Město. For its strikingly fluid lines it was initially nicknamed the 'Fred & Ginger Building' after the legendary dancing duo, Astaire and Rogers. Prague law insists that any new structure in the historical centre must be in keeping with its neighbours, and this bumptious, weaving edifice, designed by the Czech Vlado Milunič and the American Frank O Gehry, somehow manages this perfectly.

By contrast, the bland, glass-and-metal facade of the Mýslbek Building, designed by the French firm Caisse des Dépots et Consignations, clashes unpleasantly with its *fin-de-siècle* neighbours on Na příkopě in Staré Město. On the other hand, the building's rear face, on Ovocný trh, fits in masterfully.

Other recent architecture has tended towards undistinguished commercial/office towers outside the city centre. One with a modicum of shape and personality is the Česká Spořitelna Building on Budějovické náměstí, in Prague 4.

Restoration work, both state-funded and private, has gone into high gear since 1990, though much remains to be done, and some structures are beyond help. Not all restoration has been in line with the city's poorly enforced laws on preserving the history of the city, and some unique and irreplaceable structures have been destroyed.

SOCIETY & CONDUCT

Czechs tend to be polite, mild-mannered people with a good sense of humour, not inclined to argue or fight. They can be quite conservative socially. If you're invited to someone's home, you'll find them very hospitable. Do at least bring flowers for your host, and remember to remove your shoes when you enter the house.

It's customary to say *dobrý den* (good day) when entering a shop, café or quiet bar, and to say *na shledanou* (goodbye) when you leave. On public transport, most younger people will give up their seat for the elderly, the sick, and pregnant women.

When attending a classical concert, opera, ballet or play in one of the traditional theatres, men typically wear a suit and tie, and women an evening dress. It's only foreigners who don't, drawing frowns from Czechs. Casual dress is fine at performances of modern music, plays and so on.

RELIGION

Many Czechs were converted to Christianity in the 9th century by the 'Apostles of the Slavs', the monks Cyril and Methodius of Thessaloniki. Christianity became the state religion under Wenceslas, duke of Bohemia (r. c. 925–35) and patron saint of the Czech Republic.

The Czech Church remained loyal to Rome until the end of the 14th century, when reformers including Jan Hus began to argue for the simpler, more accessible practices of early Christianity. Hussites preached in Czech, not Latin, and gave wine as well as bread in the Holy Communion, enraging their conservative colleagues. Hus was excommunicated in 1411 and burned at the stake in 1415, and Bohemia became a hotbed of anti-Catholic nationalism.

Although Hussitism eventually lost its military edge, Bohemia remained a Protestant and independent-minded part of the Holy Roman Empire for the following two centuries, until the Protestant Czechs were decisively defeated at the battle of Bíla Hóra (White Mountain) west of Prague in 1620. Bohemia was pulled into the Thirty Years' War and the Counter-Reformation, losing both its political and religious independence. The Habsburgs re-Catholicised the nation, though the Czechs never took to Catholicism as they had to Protestantism.

After 1948 communism brought state atheism and the systematic repression of all religion. Most religious institutions were closed and the clergy were imprisoned. Religion, however, was never stamped out; an underground religious network included many priests who secretly performed rites. Full religious freedom returned with the 'Velvet Revolution' of 1989.

The largest church in the country is the Roman Catholic Church, though only about 40% of Czechs call themselves Catholic. The reconstituted Hussite Church, with 400,000 members, is the second largest. Of half a dozen Protestant churches, the largest is the Evangelical Church of Czech Brethren with about 180,000 members.

Though church membership is not as strong as in many other European countries – a newspaper survey in 2000 found the Czech Republic to be 'the least religious country in Eastern Europe' with over 50% of the population calling themselves atheists – there has been a slight rise in church membership in recent years, and a significant rise in the number of children attending religious education.

Since WWII the Jewish community in the Czech Republic has shrunk from a prewar total of 120,000 to about only 6000.

LANGUAGE

Naturally enough for the capital of the Czech Republic, the dominant language in Prague is Czech, although you will find that many older Czechs speak some German. Under communism everybody learned Russian at school, but this has now been replaced by English. While you'll have little trouble finding English speakers in central Prague, they're scarce in the suburbs and beyond, as are translated menus.

For more information on Czech and a list of useful words and phrases, see the Language chapter at the back of this book.

Facts for the Visitor

WHEN TO GO

While attractions across much of the Czech Republic are closed or keep limited hours outside the summer season, Prague caters for visitors all year round. Periods when the tourist crush is especially oppressive include the Easter and Christmas/New Year holidays, as well as May and June. Many Czechs go on holiday in July and August, during which time the supply of bottom-end accommodation actually increases, as student hostels are opened to visitors.

If you can put up with the cold and the periodic smog alerts during weather inversions, hotel space is plentiful in winter (outside Christmas/New Year), and Prague is gorgeous under a mantle of snow.

ORIENTATION

Prague sits amid the gentle landscapes of the Bohemian plateau, straddling the Vltava (vl-**ta**-va; Moldau in German), the Czech Republic's longest river. At Mělník, 30km downstream (north), the Vltava joins the Labe, which drains northern Bohemia and then crosses Germany (as the Elbe) to the North Sea.

Central Prague consists of five historical towns. On a hill above the western bank of the Vltava is Hradčany, the castle district, dominated by Prague Castle (Pražský hrad) and chrám sv Víta (St Vitus Cathedral), which give the city its trademark skyline. Between the castle and the river is Malá Strana, the 13th-century 'Lesser (or Little) Quarter', marked by the green dome of kostel sv Mikuláše (St Nicholas Church). The finest panoramic views of the city are from Petřín Hill, south and west of Malá Strana.

On the Vltava's eastern bank, and linked to Malá Strana by the landmark Charles Bridge (Karlův most), is Staré Město, the 'Old Town'. This maze of Gothic and Baroque streets surrounds the huge expanse of Old Town Square (Staroměstské náměstí). Frozen in time in the northern part of Staré Město is Josefov, the former Jewish ghetto, now riven by the Art Nouveau–bravado of Pařížská. Nové Město, the 'New Town' – new in the 14th century, that is – wraps around Staré Město to the east and south, with the broad avenue of Wenceslas Square (Václavské náměstí) at its centre.

Within these historical districts lie most of the city's attractions. The whole compact maze is best appreciated on foot, aided by good public transport. Beyond the centre is 19th- and 20th-century Prague, where many districts began life as separate towns.

Flood Damage

In summer 2002 the Czech Republic, along with neighbouring countries, suffered its worst floods in over a century. The country was left with an estimated clean-up bill of €3 billion. Prague was severely affected – Charles Bridge (Karlův most) was at one stage under threat of collapse, and the Josefov, Karlín and Troja districts were badly damaged. At the time of writing it was estimated that the metro would be out of operation until the end of 2002. Tram and bus services were being used in their place.

Also affected was the fortress town of Terezín in North Bohemia. The 300-year-old stronghold, once exploited by the Nazis as a concentration camp, has had buildings damaged and much original furniture destroyed.

Visitors to Prague and other affected regions may find some attractions limited by repair work into 2003. For the latest updates on the situation contact the **Prague Information Service** *(PIS; ☎ 212 444; W www.prague-info.cz).*

Points of Arrival & Departure

See the Getting There & Away and Getting Around chapters for more details about gateways.

Air Ruzyně airport is 17km west of the centre. It's a 40-minute trip comprising a metro and bus ride.

Train Praha hlavní nádraží (Prague's main train station, also called Wilsonovo nádraží), is three blocks northeast of Wenceslas Square in eastern Nové Město. Other stations served by international trains are Praha-Holešovice, north of the centre, and Praha-Smíchov in the southwest. All three are beside metro stations of the same name.

The most likely stations for long-distance domestic trains are the main station, and Masarykovo nádraží two blocks to the north. Other stations where you might end up include Praha-Dejvice (two blocks from Hradčanská metro station); Praha-Smíchov; Praha-Vysočany, northeast of the centre (bus No 185, 209, 259 or 278 to Českomoravská metro station); and Praha-Vršovice (tram No 24 to Wenceslas Square).

Bus Most international coaches, all domestic long-distance buses and most of the regional services use Florenc bus station, beside Florenc metro station (Map 6), or streets nearby. Some regional buses depart from the stands near metro stations Anděl, Dejvická, Černý most, Hradčanská, Nádraží Holešovice, Radlická, Roztyly, Smíchovské nádraží, Zličín and Želivského.

Government Travel Advice

Most governments periodically update Consular Information Sheets or Travel Advisories, which contain useful information and advice for travellers, including entry requirements, medical facilities, crime information and warnings of areas considered to be dangerous.

Australia
Department of Foreign Affairs & Trade (☎ 02-6261 3305, toll-free ☎ 1300 555 135, faxback service 02-6261 1299, W www.dfat.gov.au/travel) RG Casey Bldg, John McEwen Crescent, Barton, ACT 0221

Canada
Department of Foreign Affairs & International Trade (☎ 613-944 6788, toll-free ☎ 800-267 6788, faxback service 613-944 2500, toll-free fax 800-575 2500, W www.dfait-maeci.gc.ca) 125 Sussex Dr, Ottawa K1A 0G2

UK
Foreign & Commonwealth Office (☎ 020-7008 0232/3, W www.fco.gov.uk) Travel Advice Unit, Consular Division, Foreign & Commonwealth Office, Old Admiralty Bldg, London SW1A 2PA. Regularly updated Foreign Office travel advice is also displayed on BBC2 Ceefax, from page 470.

USA
State Department Bureau of Consular Affairs (☎ 202-647 5225, faxback service 202-647 1488, W www.travel.state.gov) Overseas Citizens Services, Room 4800, Department of State, Washington, DC 20520-4818

MAPS

Lonely Planet's tough, plastic-coated *Prague* city map is good value, with sections covering central Prague, Prague Castle, greater Prague, the Prague metro, the area around Prague, as well as a walking tour. It also has an index of streets and sights.

Prague Information Service (PIS; see Tourist Offices later) stocks a free English-language pamphlet *Welcome to the Czech Republic,* which is produced by the Ministry of Interior. It features a map of the historical centre, transport routes in the centre, and information such as emergency and embassy addresses.

Maps are available at newsagents, bookshops and travel agencies for 80Kč or less. The most accurate and readable one of the city centre and inner suburbs is Kartografie Praha's *Praha – plán města* (1:10,000; 49Kč). It includes transport and parking information, an index, metro map, plans of the castle and Charles Bridge, and a brief description of the major historical sites.

If you are staying in Prague for a significant amount of time, Kartografie's pocket atlas *Praha – plán města – standard* (1:20,000; 129Kč), covering all of Prague, is invaluable.

A public transport map showing all day and night services (metro, tram and bus) is available from any of the six public information offices of Dopravní podnik (DP), the city transport department (see the Getting Around chapter), for a bargain 20Kč.

See Books & Maps in the Shopping chapter for good sources of maps.

Addresses

Confusingly, most buildings have two numbers. The one on a blue sign is its position on the street. These are ordered sequentially with odd numbers on one side and even on the other. The one on a red sign is its number in the district, which is part of the old house-numbering system and usually bears no relation to its neighbours.

In this book we use 'blue' numbers; if unavailable, the 'red' one is used. Sometimes both numbers are given and they are separated by a slash (/), with the red number given first in line with local practice.

Numbers of apartment buildings apply to the building only, and each apartment has a tag with the owner's name but rarely an apartment number.

From about the 14th century, houses were known by their emblems – such as the 'House of Two Suns' (dům U dvou slunců). Thus today most old houses in Malá Strana and Staré Město have three identification symbols: emblem, and red and blue numbers.

TOURIST OFFICES

There are only two state tourist organisations in Prague: Prague Information Service (PIS) and the Czech Tourist Authority (ČCCR). Several formerly state-run travel offices are now privatised commercial travel agencies; while staff are sometimes willing to answer questions, they're not there to provide free information to tourists. See the Getting There & Away chapter for a rundown of the most helpful agencies.

Prague Information Service (PIS)

The municipal **Prague Information Service** *(Pražská informační služba, PIS; ☎ 12444; W www.prague-info.cz; Betlémské náměstí 2, 116 98 Praha 1)* has the city well covered, with good maps and detailed brochures (including accommodation and historical monuments), all free. PIS also publishes the detailed what's-on guide (in Czech only), *Přehled,* and other general material.

There are four branches (the Betlémské náměstí address is for postal inquiries only):

Praha hlavní nádraží (Map 6) Wilsonova 2. Open 9am to 7pm Monday to Friday, 9am to 4pm Saturday and Sunday April to October; 9am to 6pm Monday to Friday, 9am to 3pm Saturday November to March.

Malá Strana Bridge Tower (Map 5) Mostecká 2, Malá Strana. Open 10am to 6pm daily April to October.

Na příkopě 20 (Map 7) Staré Město. Open 9am to 7pm Monday to Friday, 9am to 5pm Saturday and Sunday April to October; 9am to 6pm Monday to Friday, 9am to 3pm Saturday November to March.

Staroměstská radnice (Old Town Hall; Map 7) Staroměstské náměstí 1, Staré Město. Open 9am to 7pm Monday to Friday, 9am to 6pm Saturday and Sunday April to October; 9am to 6pm Monday to Friday, 9am to 5pm Saturday and Sunday November to March.

All four offices provide general information on Prague and the Czech Republic, concert/theatre tickets, and the services of the AVE agency for help in finding accommodation. AVE also has a pricey exchange office at the Staroměstská radnice branch, and sells one-, three- and seven-day public transport tickets.

PIS's affiliate **Pragotur** *(☎ 224 48 25 62, fax 224 48 23 80; open 9am-6pm Mon-Fri, 9am-4pm Sat & Sun)* offers foreign-language guide services from a desk at the Staroměstská radnice branch. The Staroměstská radnice and Na příkopě branches also offer city tours. See the Getting Around chapter for more on organised tours.

Other Tourist Publications *Přehled* is not the only guide to the action in Prague. There is also the monthly *Culture in Prague* and the free fortnightly pamphlet *Do města – Downtown* in English. Among the numerous advertiser-supported tourist handbooks sold at travel agencies and newsstands there are two other reasonable publications that also include practical information: the quarterly *Welcome to Prague* and the monthly *Prague This Month.*

Čedok

Čedok is the privatised former state tour operator and travel agency. The main office *(Map 7; ☎ 224 19 71 21; Na příkopě 18; open 9am-6pm Mon-Fri, 10am-3pm Sat)* is a good, if pricey, one-stop shop for excursions and

Info, Info Everywhere

The universal green *i* (information) symbol is used willy-nilly by anyone keen to attract the attention of Prague's sometimes disoriented visitors. Ironically, the one outfit that offers reliable, generally unbiased aid – PIS – doesn't use it. PIS has its own logo: a stylised crown spiked with three *i*'s.

concert/theatre tickets, as well as travel bookings. Services at the airport branch are limited to upper-end accommodation and car rental. See Travel Agencies in the Getting There & Away chapter for a complete list of Čedok branches.

Prague Tourist Center

This helpful and conveniently located private office *(Map 7; ☎/fax 224 21 22 09; ⓦ www.ptc.cz; Rytířská 12)* sells maps, guidebooks, souvenirs, concert/theatre tickets, tours and accommodation.

Czech Tourist Authority (ČCCR)

The Czech Tourist Authority *(Česká centrála cestovniho ruchu, ČCCR; Map 7; ☎ 224 82 69 84; ⓦ www.visitczechia.cz; Staroměstské náměstí 6; open 9am-6pm daily)* has information about sights, museums, festivals and other points of interest for the whole of the Czech Republic.

ČCCR Offices Abroad Representative offices include:

Austria (☎/fax 01-533 21 93, ⓔ tourinfo-wien@visitczechia.cz) Herrengasse 17, 1010 Vienna
Canada (☎ 416-363 9928, ⓔ ctacanada@iprimus.ca) Czech Airlines Office, 401 Bay St, Suite 1510, Toronto, Ontario M5H 2Y4
France (☎ 01 53 73 00 32, ⓔ crparis@attglobal.net) Rue Bonaparte 18, 75006 Paris
Germany (☎/fax 030-204 4770, ⓔ tourinfo@czech-tourist.de) Karl Liebknecht Strasse 34, 10178 Berlin
Netherlands (☎ 020-575 30 14, ⓔ ccamsterdam@czech.cz) Strawinskylaan 517, 1077 XX Amsterdam
UK (☎ 020-7631 0427, ⓔ schoppova@visitczechia.org.uk) Morley House, 320 Regent St, London W1B 3BG
USA (☎ 212-288 0830, ⓔ travelczech@pop.net) 1109-1111 Madison Ave, New York, NY 10028

VISAS & DOCUMENTS

Passport

When visiting the Czech Republic you'll need a passport that is valid until at least 90 days after your date of entry. Domestic passport offices and many embassies abroad can provide you with a new one, or insert new pages into your present one, fairly quickly.

Visitors with passports in poor condition have occasionally been refused entry into the Czech Republic.

Visas

Czech visa regulations change frequently, so check the latest situation with the **Czech Ministry of Foreign Affairs** *(ⓦ www.mzv.cz/washington/cons/visa.htm)*. If your country is *not* on the Visa Waiver list, then you *will* need a visa.

Citizens of EU countries, Switzerland, the USA, Japan and New Zealand can stay for up to 90 days without a visa; for UK citizens the limit is 180 days. At the time of writing, citizens of Australia, Canada and South Africa need a visa (even if you are only passing through the country by train or bus), which you should obtain in advance at a consulate in your own country. Visas are not available at border crossings or Prague's Ruzyně Airport – you must apply at a Czech embassy or consulate abroad, preferably in your own country. You'll be refused entry if you need a visa and arrive without one.

When applying, you will need one or two passport-sized photos, and cash or a money order for the fee, which varies according to your nationality. Most Czech embassies in Western capitals will accept applications by post if you include a self-addressed envelope with return postage for recorded (certified) delivery, and payment by postal money order; get the forms from the embassy (fax applications are best) or a travel agent. Processing of applications takes five working days.

All foreign visitors must register with the Czech immigration police within three days of arrival; this requirement is strictly enforced with a fine of 400Kč. Hotels, hostels and camp sites will automatically register you when you check in; otherwise – if you are staying with friends, for example – you will need to register at a foreigners' police office (see Visa Extensions for details of one office).

Arriving visitors are occasionally asked to show that they have the equivalent of at least 1100Kč (US$30) for every day of their intended stay, or a credit card. You may also be asked to produce evidence of travel health insurance.

Visa Extensions Extensions are granted once only for a maximum of 90 days. Apply at entrance B of the grim **Foreigners' Police & Passport Office** *(Úřadovna cizinecké policie a pasové služby; Map 8; Olšanská 2, Žižkov; tram No 9; open 7.30am-11.45am & 12.30pm-2.30pm Mon, Tues & Thur; 7.30am-11.30am & 12.30pm-5pm Wed; 7.30am-noon Fri)*, which is a 10-minute walk north from Flora metro station. An extension costs 1000Kč, and is payable with special stamps *(kolky)* sold there or at any post office. The paperwork takes about four working days. See Work later in this chapter if you intend to stay longer than the statutory tourist period.

Travel Insurance

A travel insurance policy to cover theft, loss and medical problems is a good idea. There is a wide variety of policies available, so check the small print. Some policies specifically exclude 'dangerous activities', which can include skiing, motorcycling, even trekking. A locally acquired motorcycle licence is not valid under some policies.

You may prefer a policy which pays doctors or hospitals directly rather than you having to pay on the spot and claim later. If you have to claim later make sure you keep all documentation. Some policies ask you to call back (reverse charges) to a centre in your home country where an immediate assessment of your problem is made.

Check that the policy covers ambulances or an emergency flight home.

Driving Licence & Permits

Officially, for stays of up to 60 days, the Czech Republic recognises any foreign driving licence bearing a photograph of its owner; if yours doesn't, you should get an international driving permit (IDP). That said, the author has presented a UK licence (without photo) to Czech traffic police on several occasions without problems. Drivers must also have vehicle registration papers and the 'green card' that shows they carry full liability insurance (for more on drivers' documents, see the Getting There & Away chapter).

If you plan to remain in the country for more than 60 days, you will need an IDP, which you can get from a national automobile association in your home country.

Useful Cards

Hostel Cards Many of the Czech Republic's hostels don't belong to the Hostelling International (HI) system, though some hostels do give discounts to HI members.

Student, Youth & Teacher Cards The international student identity card (ISIC) and teacher's card (ITIC) – valid from September to the end of the following year – are aimed at travel-related costs such as airline fares and museum admissions. Youth cards such as Euro 26 and IYTC – good for a year from the purchase date – provide more general discounts, for example in shops and cinemas, as well as on some accommodation and travel.

All of these cards are available from youth-oriented travel agencies around the world. Those in Prague include:

Charles University Information and Advisory Centre (IPC; Map 6; ☎ 224 49 18 96, ⓔ ipc@ruk.cuni.cz) Školská 13a, Nové Město. Open 1pm to 4pm Monday, Wednesday and Thursday; 10am to noon Tuesday.

CKM Travel Centre (Map 6; ☎ 222 72 15 95, ⓔ ckmprg@login.cz, Mánesova 77) Vinohrady. Open 10am to 6pm Monday to Thursday, 10am to 4pm Friday.

GTS International (Map 6; ☎ 222 21 12 04, ⓔ gts.smecky@gtsint.cz) Ve Smečkách 33. Open 8am to 6pm Monday to Friday, 11am to 3pm Saturday.

You'll need a passport-sized photo and solid proof of your age or student status. Prices at the time of research were about 200Kč. For further information, see the following websites: W www.istc.org (ISIC and ITIC); W www.euro26.org (Euro 26); and W www.counciltravel.com/idcards/ (ISIC, ITIC and IYTC).

Prague Card This is a three-day, tourist-oriented pass good for buses, trams, metro and the Petřín funicular railway, plus admission to city-run museums and state-run galleries. It costs 560Kč (students and children 460Kč) and is available from CKM Travel, Čedok, American Express (AmEx) and a few other travel agencies (see Travel Agencies in the Getting There & Away chapter).

Copies

All important documents (passport data page and visa page, credit cards, travellers cheque purchase receipts, travel insurance policy, air/bus/train tickets, driving licence etc) should be photocopied before you leave home. Leave one copy with someone at home and keep another with you, separate from the originals.

It's also a good idea to store details of your vital travel documents in Lonely Planet's free online Travel Vault in case you lose the photocopies or can't be bothered with them. Your password-protected Travel Vault is accessible online anywhere in the world – create it at W www.ekno.lonelyplanet.com.

EMBASSIES & CONSULATES

Czech Embassies & Consulates

Diplomatic representation abroad includes:

Australia
Embassy: (☎ 02-6290 1386) 38 Culgoa Circuit, O'Malley, Canberra, ACT 2606
Consulate: (☎ 02-9371 0860) 169 Military Rd, Dover Heights, Sydney, NSW 2031. Visas are issued only at the consulate.

Austria
Embassy: (☎ 01-894 21 25/6) Penzingerstrasse 11-13, 1140 Vienna

Canada
Embassy: (☎ 613-562 3875) 251 Cooper St, Ottawa, Ontario K2P 0G2

France
Embassy: (☎ 01 40 65 13 01) 15 Ave Charles Floquet, 75343 Paris Cedex 07

Germany
Embassy: (☎ 030-22 63 80) Wilhelmstrasse 44, 10117 Berlin
Branch Embassy: (☎ 0228-9 19 70) Ferdinandstrasse 27, 53127 Bonn

Ireland
Embassy: (☎ 031-668 1135) 57 Northumberland Rd, Ballsbridge, Dublin 4

Netherlands
Embassy: (☎ 070-346 97 12) Paleisstraat 4, 2514 JA The Hague

New Zealand
Honorary Consulate: (☎ 04-939 1610) 48 Hair St, PO Box 43035, Wainuiomata, Wellington. Visa applications for stays over 90 days, or for working or study visas, must be made to the Czech consulate in Sydney, Australia.

Poland
Embassy: (☎ 022-628 7221) Koszykowa 18, 00-555 Warsaw

Slovakia
Embassy: (☎ 02-59 20 33 03) Hviezdoslavovo náměstí, 81 000 Bratislava

UK
Embassy: (☎ 020-7243 1115) 26 Kensington Palace Gardens, London W8 4QY

USA
Embassy: (☎ 202-274 9100, W www.mfa.cz/washington) 3900 Spring of Freedom St NW, Washington, DC 20008
Consulate General: (☎ 310-473 0889) 10990 Wilshire Blvd, Suite 1100, Los Angeles, CA 90024
Consulate General: (☎ 212-717 5643) 1109-1111 Madison Ave, New York, NY 10028

Embassies & Consulates in Prague

It's important to realise what your own embassy – the embassy of the country of which you are a citizen – can and *cannot* do to help you if you get into trouble. Generally, it won't be much help if the trouble you're in is remotely your own fault. Remember that, while in Prague, you are bound by the laws of the Czech Republic. Your embassy will not be sympathetic if you end up in jail after committing a crime locally, even if such actions are legal in your own country.

In genuine emergencies you might get some assistance, but only if other channels have been exhausted. For example, if you

JONATHAN SMITH

Old Town Square: the bustling heart of the city

RICHARD NEBESKÝ

Renaissance elegance on Karlovo náměstí

JULIET COOMBE

A sumptuous knocker in Hradčany

RICHARD NEBESKÝ

Malá Strana in winter: icy quiet on Čertovka

RICHARD NEBESKÝ

Prague Castle in spring: soaring Gothic glimpsed through the cherry trees of Petřín Hill

VLADIMIR LIBA

Summer in the city: chilling out on Kampa

RICHARD NEBESKÝ

The rustling of autumn leaves on Slovanský ostrov (Slav Island)

need to get home urgently, a free ticket is highly unlikely – the embassy would expect you to have insurance. If you have all your money and documents stolen, it might assist with getting a new passport, but a loan for onward travel is almost always out of the question.

Most embassies are in or around Malá Strana and Hradčany, and are open for visa-related business until 11am or 1pm only.

Countries with embassies in Prague include:

Australia (Map 7; ☎ 251 01 83 51) Solitaire Office Bldg, Unit 6/3, Klimentska 10, Staré Město. This is an honorary consul for emergency assistance only (eg, a stolen passport); otherwise contact the Australian embassy in Vienna.
Austria (Map 9; ☎ 257 09 05 11) Viktora Huga 10, Smíchov
Canada (Map 3; ☎ 272 10 18 00) Mickiewiczova 6, Hradčany
France (Map 5; ☎ 251 17 17 11) Velkopřerovské náměstí 2, Malá Strana
Consular service: (☎ 251 17 17 31) Nosticova 10
Germany (Map 5; ☎ 257 11 31 11) Vlašská 19, Malá Strana
Ireland (Map 5; ☎ 257 53 00 61) Tržiště 13, Malá Strana
Netherlands (Map 3; ☎ 224 31 21 90) Gotthardská 6, Bubeneč
Poland (Map 5; ☎ 257 32 03 88) Valdštejnska 8, Malá Strana
Consular service: (Map 6; ☎ 224 22 87 22) Václavské náměstí 49, Nové Město
Slovakia (Map 3; ☎ 233 32 14 42) Pod hradbami 1, Dejvice
UK (Map 5; ☎ 257 40 21 11) Thunovská 14, Malá Strana
USA (Map 5; ☎ 257 53 06 63) Tržiště 15, Malá Strana

CUSTOMS

You can import a reasonable amount of personal effects and up to 6000Kč (around US$180) worth of gifts and other 'noncommercial' goods. If you're aged over 18, you can bring in 2L of wine, 1L of spirits and 200 cigarettes (or equivalent tobacco products).

Before you make a major purchase in Prague, find out how much it will cost to get it out of the country. Duty of 22% must be paid on consumer goods exceeding 30,000Kč (US$1000) in value.

You can't export genuine antiques, and customs officials are a suspicious lot. If you are unsure about what you're taking out, ask at the Národní muzeum (National Museum; Wenceslas Square) or Umělecko-průmyslové muzeum (Museum of Decorative Arts; 17.listopadu). Certification from them should satisfy airport or postal customs. For mailing any such items over 2kg, go to the **customs post office** *(Pobočka Celního Úřadu; Map 2; ☎ 257 21 37 36; Plzeňská 139; open 7am-3pm Mon-Tues & Thurs-Fri, 7am-6pm Wed)*. Take tram No 4, 7 or 9 to the Klamovka stop, three stops from Anděl metro station.

There is no limit to the amount of Czech or foreign currency that can be taken in or out of the country, but amounts exceeding 350,000Kč must be declared.

MONEY

Currency

The unit of Czech currency is the *koruna česká* (Czech crown), abbreviated Kč. The koruna is divided into 100 *haléřů* or heller (h). Notes come in 5000Kč, 2000Kč, 1000Kč, 500Kč, 200Kč, 100Kč, 50Kč and 20Kč denominations, and coins in 50Kč, 20Kč, 10Kč, 5Kč, 2Kč and 1Kč, and 50h, 20h and 10h.

Exchange Rates

country	unit	koruna
Australia	A$1	17.29
Canada	C$1	19.92
euro	€1	31.04
Japan	¥100	25.37
New Zealand	NZ$1	15.16
Singapore	S$1	17.53
UK	£1	49.08
USA	US$1	31.62

Exchanging Money

Debit Cards The easiest, cheapest way to carry money is in the form of a debit card from your bank, with which you can withdraw cash either over the counter or from an ATM. Charges are minimal at major Prague banks (typically from zero to about 2%) and some home banks charge nothing at all for the use of these cards. Provided you make withdrawals of at least several thousand koruna at a time, you'll pay less than the assorted commissions on travellers cheques. Make sure you know your personal identification number (PIN; four to six digits, numbers only), and check with your bank about transaction fees and withdrawal limits.

Cash The main banks – Komerční banka, Česká spořitelna, ČSOB and Živnostenská banka – are the best places to change cash. They charge 2% commission with a 50Kč minimum (but always check, as commissions can vary from branch to branch). They will also provide a cash advance on Visa or MasterCard without commission. Most banks are open at least from 8am to 4pm Monday to Friday and in smaller towns may close for lunch between noon and 1pm.

Hotels charge about 5% to 8% commission, while Čedok travel agencies and post offices charge 2% – similar rates to the banks.

Many private exchange offices in Prague charge exorbitant commissions *(výlohy)* of up to 10%. Some of these advertise higher rates and 0% commission but don't mention their sky-high 'handling fee', or charge no commission but have very poor exchange rates (see the boxed text 'Rates Rackets').

Travellers Cheques Banks charge 2% with a 50Kč minimum for changing travellers cheques. AmEx and Thomas Cook offices change their own-brand cheques without commission, but charge 2% or 3% for other brands, 3% or 4% for credit-card cash advances, and 5% for changing cash.

Lost travellers cheques can be reported to the telephone numbers listed under Credit Cards later.

ATMs There is a good network of ATMs, or *bankomaty,* throughout the city. Most accept Visa, Plus, Visa electron, MasterCard, Cirrus, Maestro, Euro and EC cards.

Credit Cards Many mid-range and top-end hotels and restaurants accept credit cards. You can use a card to get a cash advance in a bank or to withdraw money from

Rates Rackets

One of Prague's biggest cons is the poor rates of exchange given by private exchange bureaus *(směnárna)* in the popular tourist areas, and the tricks they use to conceal this. Remember that when you're changing foreign currency into Czech crowns the 'buy' rate applies (ie, they will be buying currency or travellers cheques from you). Most private exchange offices advertise the more attractive-looking 'sell' rate.

The following table shows how much Czech money you would have got by changing £100 in cash at various places in Prague on a particular day in June 2002, compared with using an ATM:

source	exchange rate	commission	koruna for £100
ATM	44.98	0%	4498Kč
Živnostenská banka	44.90	2%	4400Kč
American Express (AmEx)	44.90	5%	4265Kč
Acron (airport)	43.60	4%	4186Kč
TravelEx/Thomas Cook	43.47	5%	4130Kč
Chequepoint	37.05	0%	3705Kč

Note that on this day Chequepoint (a private agency) was prominently advertising a very attractive rate of 46.85Kč, but the small print showed that this was the *sell* rate – which only applies if you are selling Czech crowns! Chequepoint also advertised a reasonable buy rate of 43.95Kč, but this was only for transactions of more than 15,000Kč (around £340). The actual rate for the £100 transaction was dismal.

Banks & Exchange Offices

The city-centre offices of Prague's main foreign-exchange offices and banks are:

American Express (AmEx; Map 6; ☎ 222 80 02 37) Václavské náměstí 56
Česká spořitelna banka (Map 7; ☎ 222 00 41 11) Na příkopě 29
Československá obchodní banka (ČSOB; Map 7; ☎ 224 11 11 11) Na příkopě 14
Investiční a poštovní banka (IPB; Map 7; ☎ 222 04 11 11) Senovážné náměstí 32
Komerční banka (Map 7; ☎ 222 43 21 11) Na příkopě 33
Thomas Cook/TravelEx (Map 6; ☎ 221 10 53 71) Národní 28; (Map 6; ☎ 221 10 53 71) Karlova 3
Živnostenská banka (Map 7; ☎ 224 12 11 11) Na příkopě 20 (exchange bureau to the right of the main entrance). Even if you have no business, it's worth looking in at the main hall's lavish Art Nouveau interior.

ATMs, but charges will be higher than with a debit card. Your own bank may charge a fee of about US$3 and possibly a 1% commission for using an ATM, but this is still more favourable (if you take out large amounts) than the commissions and exchange rates charged on travellers cheques.

Report lost Visa cards on ☎ 224 12 53 53; MasterCard/Euro cards on ☎ 261 35 46 50; and AmEx cards on ☎ 222 80 01 11.

International Transfers If you're not an AmEx or Thomas Cook customer, the fastest way to get emergency money from home is through **Western Union** *(Map 6; ☎ 224 22 29 54; Václavské náměstí 15, Nové Město; open 8am-8pm Mon-Fri, 9am-5pm Sat, 10am-4pm Sun)*, which has agencies all over town, including branches at the main post office and Praha hlavní nádraží. You'll be paid in koruna.

Black Market The koruna became fully convertible in 1996. There is no longer a black market – anyone who approaches you on the street offering to change money is probably a thief, and there are plenty of them loitering around Na příkopě and the arcades on Jindřišská near the corner with Wenceslas Square.

Costs

Things are still relatively cheap in Prague for Western visitors (though not for locals in the historical centre). The big exception is accommodation, where tourist prices are in line with Western Europe.

By staying at cheap hostels or camp sites, sticking to self-catering and stand-up cafés, and going easy on the beer, you might get by on US$15 to US$20 per person per day in summer. If you stay in private accommodation or upmarket hostels away from the city centre, eat at cheap restaurants and use public transport, you can get by on US$25 to US$40. Sharing a double room with bathroom in a mid-range hotel or pension, and eating in good Czech or Western restaurants, will cost US$40 to US$80.

These costs don't include extras such as entertainment, souvenirs and tours. Eating and sleeping near the city centre will cost more, as will having a room to yourself. Rates may drop if you stay for more than one or two nights. Except for the Christmas/New Year and Easter periods, some places drop their prices outside the summer season. In nearby towns, such as those described in the Excursions chapter, prices are consistently lower.

Naturally, Bohemia's splendid beer will tempt you to increase your spending: half a litre can cost as little as 5Kč in local shops or 12Kč on draught in neighbourhood pubs, but ranges from 25Kč to 60Kč in tourist bars and costs 80Kč or more in posh restaurants.

A disappointing side of the Czech concept of a 'free market economy' is the official two-tier price system; foreigners can pay up to double the local price for some hotel rooms, airline and bus tickets, and museum and concert tickets. Most theatre tickets are snapped up by scalpers and travel agencies and resold to foreigners at several times the original price. Sometimes simply questioning the price difference results in an 'error correction'. With enough charm and enough Czech you can pay local prices by steering clear of 'tourist' rooms and by ordering from the Czech-language menu.

Discounts Many discounts – for transport, for tourist attractions, in hotels and in some restaurants – are available to full-time students and those aged under 26, and sometimes to their spouses and children. Many bargains are not advertised; the best way to find them is to wave an identity card at every opportunity. See Visas & Documents earlier in this chapter for details of available cards and how to get them.

Tipping & Bargaining

After fair service in a restaurant, round up the bill to the next 10Kč (or the next 20Kč if it's over about 100Kč). The same applies to tipping taxi drivers. If your driver is honest and turns on the meter then you should round up the fare at the end of your journey.

In restaurants, the usual protocol is for the waiter or waitress to show you the bill and for you, as you hand over the money, to tell them the total amount you want to pay with the tip included.

Change is usually counted out starting with the big notes, on down to the littlest coins. In more posh restaurants, if you say *děkuji* (thank you) during this process, your waiter may assume the rest is a tip.

There's little scope for bargaining Prague prices down, except possibly at the open-air markets (see the Shopping chapter).

Taxes & Refunds

Value-added tax (VAT, or DPH in Czech) is 5% on food, hotel rooms and restaurant meals, but 22% on luxury items (including alcohol). This tax is included in the marked price and not added at the cash register.

It is possible to claim VAT refunds for purchases worth more than 1000Kč made in shops displaying the 'Tax Free Shopping' sticker. They will give you a VAT Refund Form, which you must present to customs for validation when you leave the country. You can then claim your refund from a collecting agency within three months of the purchase date.

POST & COMMUNICATIONS

Post

The main **post office** *(Map 6; Jindřišská 14, Nové Město; open 7am-8pm daily)* is just off Wenceslas Square. There's an information desk just inside the main hall to the left.

Most of the city's other post offices open from 8am to 6pm or 7pm Monday to Friday, and until noon Saturdays. There's also a **'nonstop' post office** *(Map 6; Hybernská 15, Nové Město; open 12.30am-11.30pm daily)* near Masarykovo train station.

Postal Rates The Czech postal service is fairly efficient and not too expensive. However, anything you can't afford to lose should go by registered mail *(doporučený dopis)* or Express Mail Service (EMS).

Postcards and letters weighing up to 20g (automatically airmail) cost 9Kč to Europe and 14Kč to the USA and Canada.

A 2kg parcel (by airmail) costs 348Kč to Europe, and 691Kč to anywhere else. You can send parcels of books or printed matter up to 15kg at lower rates. For the fast and secure EMS, rates to Europe are 952Kč for up to 1kg and 1080Kč for up to 2kg.

Sending Mail You can buy stamps from street vendors and PNS newsagents as well as from post offices. Letters go in the orange boxes found outside post offices and around the city.

In Prague's main post office you must use the automatic queuing system. Take a ticket from one of the machines in the entrance corridors – press button No 1 for single-item stamps, letters and parcels, and No 4 for EMS. Then watch the display boards in the main hall – when your ticket number appears (flashing), go to the desk number shown.

Small-packet services and EMS close at noon on Saturday, and are closed Sunday. Always get a receipt *(potvrzení)* when sending anything larger than a letter by airmail, or using a more expensive service, to ensure it goes by the service you have paid for.

See Customs earlier in this chapter if you want to post out antiques (though it's best to carry anything of value out of the country yourself). In principle, anything else can be posted internationally from any major post office. In practice, many postal employees still suffer from communist-era anxieties about 'regulations', and may send you off to the customs post office if you want to send anything over 2kg, no matter what it is.

Parcels containing glass and crystal will not be accepted by the postal systems in the USA, Australia or New Zealand.

If you need a professional courier service, **DHL** *(Map 6; ☎ 800 10 30 00; Václavské náměstí 47, Nové Město; open 8am-6.30pm Mon-Fri, 9am-3pm Sat)* has a convenient office with English-speaking staff just off Wenceslas Square. It costs 1040Kč to send a 200g EasyPack of A4 documents to the USA.

Receiving Mail You can pick up poste-restante mail *(výdej listovních zásilek)* at desk Nos 1 and 2 (at far left) of the main post office from 7am to 8pm Monday to Friday and 7am to noon Saturday. Mail should be addressed to Poste Restante, Hlavní pošta, Jindřišská 14, 110 00 Praha 1, Czech Republic. You must present your passport to claim mail (check under your first name, too). Mail is held for one month.

Holders of AmEx cards or travellers cheques can have letters and faxes held for up to one month at the AmEx Prague office (see the boxed text 'Banks & Exchange Offices' earlier in this chapter for the location). The British and Canadian embassies will hold letters for their citizens for a few months. None of these offices will accept registered letters or parcels.

Telephone

Český Telecom has finally replaced its antiquated telephone network with a modern digital system. On 22 September 2002 all Czech phone numbers became nine-digit numbers, without an initial zero and without a separate area code – you have to dial all nine digits for any call, local or long-distance. For example, all Prague numbers (former area code 02) have changed from 02-xx xx xx xx to 2xx xx xx xx. You have to dial the '2' even if you are calling from within Prague. Czech mobile numbers have also dropped the initial zero.

Blue coin-phones only accept 2Kč, 5Kč, 10Kč and 20Kč coins, and can be used to make local, long-distance and international calls. A more common and convenient alternative is a *telekart* (telephone card), which is good for local, long-distance and international calls. Cards are sold at post offices, newsagents, PIS branches and the main telephone bureau, and come in 50-unit (175Kč) and 100-unit (320Kč) sizes.

Lonely Planet's ekno global communication service provides low-cost international calls – for local calls you're usually better off with a local phonecard. Ekno also offers free messaging services, email, travel information, and an online travel vault where you can securely store all your important documents. You can join online at **W** www.ekno.lonelyplanet.com, where you will find the local-access numbers for the 24-hour customer-service centre. Once you have joined, always check the ekno website for the latest access numbers for each country and updates on new features.

The simplest and cheapest (25% less than coin or cardphones) option is to pay a deposit at the main telephone bureau (to the left inside the main post office's right-hand entrance) and make your call in a soundproof booth, where a little meter ticks off your money.

Calls from hotel or restaurant telephones tend to cost at least twice as much as those

Telephone-Speak

The various signal-tones in Prague don't always sound like the ones back home. Here are the useful ones to know:

Ready to dial:	long tone, short tone
Ringing:	series of long tones
Engaged (busy):	series of short tones
Trying to connect:	very short pips
Number unobtainable:	series of three rising tones

from a public telephone. Calls to mobile telephones are more expensive than those to landlines.

Local Calls Using a pay phone for local calls will cost around 4Kč for two minutes at peak rate (7am to 7pm Monday to Friday).

For Prague directory information dial ☎ 1180.

Regional & Long-Distance Calls To call another city in the Czech Republic, just dial the full, nine-digit number. An intercity call costs around 6Kč per minute (40% of that during off-peak periods) at a pay phone.

The telephone bureau at the post office has directories for Prague and other major cities. For information about Czech numbers dial ☎ 1180. For the domestic operator dial ☎ 133 002.

International Calls To call out of the Czech Republic, dial 00 followed by the country code, the area code (you'll probably have to drop the first zero) and then the number.

You can make international telephone calls at the main post office's telephone bureau, or directly from pay phones. Three-minute international direct-dial (IDD) calls from a pay phone at peak rate cost around 35Kč to Germany; 42Kč to the UK, France, Australia, the USA and Canada; and 63Kč to New Zealand and Japan. Off-peak rates are about 10% less. Operator assistance adds about 50Kč.

For international directory inquiries and information on international rates and services, dial ☎ 1181. For operator assistance with international calls, call ☎ 133 004 (English), ☎ 133 003 (French), or ☎ 133 005 (German).

Reverse-Charge Calls You can place an international reverse-charge (collect) call from the telephone bureau without putting down any cash, or from a public telephone for the price of a local call. To make a reverse-charge call, dial ☎ 133 004 (English), ☎ 133 003 (French), or ☎ 133 005 (German).

It is also possible to use so-called 'country-direct' numbers for reverse-charge, account or credit-card calls; see the boxed text 'Country-Direct Numbers'.

Country-Direct Numbers

The Country-Direct service is available in the Czech Republic (you can get a full list of countries and numbers from any telephone office or directory). Use the following numbers, preceded by 00420, to make a charge-card or reverse-charge call to your home country:

Australia Direct	☎ 06101
Canada Direct	☎ 00151
Canada (AT&T)	☎ 00152
France Direct	☎ 03301
Deutschland Direct	☎ 04949
Netherlands	☎ 03101
UK Direct (BT)	☎ 04401
USA (AT&T)	☎ 00101
USA (MCI)	☎ 00112
USA (Sprint)	☎ 87187

Calls to Prague To call Prague from another country, dial that country's international access code, plus 420 (Czech Republic) and the full nine-digit number.

Mobile Phones The Czech Republic uses GSM 900, which is compatible with the rest of Europe, Australia and New Zealand but not with the North American GSM 1900 or the totally different system in Japan. However, some North Americans have GSM 1900/900 phones that do work here. If you have a GSM phone, check with your service provider about using it in Prague, and beware of calls being routed internationally (very expensive for a 'local' call). You can rent a mobile from **EuroTel Praha** *(☎ 267 01 67 01)* stores in Prague for around 1795Kč per week (plus a 5000Kč deposit). In this case, however, you can't use your existing mobile number.

Fax & Telegram

Faxes and telegrams can be sent and received 24 hours a day from the telephone bureau at the main post office. Fax rates are 10Kč to 12Kč per page plus transmission time (the same as telephone rates, with an A4-sized page taking about 1½ minutes). Incoming faxes cost 8Kč per page. Many hotels and agencies have fax services too, but rates are around twice the post office rate. AmEx members can receive (but not send) faxes at the Wenceslas Square office (for address details see the boxed text 'Banks & Exchange Offices' earlier in this chapter).

Telegrams cost 45Kč plus 3Kč per word, with a minimum charge of 10 words (75Kč). To dictate a telegram by phone dial ☎ 133 001.

Email & Internet Access

Prague has dozens of Internet cafés. The following is a selection of conveniently located ones:

Bohemia Bagel (Map 7; ☎ 224 81 25 60, ⓔ info@bohemiabagel.cz) Masná 2, Staré Město. Open 7am to midnight Monday to Friday, 8am to midnight Saturday and Sunday; 1Kč per minute, no minimum.

Cybeteria (Map 6; ☎ 222 23 07 07, ⓔ info@cream.cybeteria.cz) Štěpánská 18, Nové Město. Open 10am to 8pm Monday to Friday, noon to 8pm Saturday and Sunday; 1.70Kč per minute.

Internet Café Prague (Map 6; ☎ 221 08 52 84, ⓔ internetcafe@internetcafe.cz) Palác Metro arcade, Národní 25, Nové Město. Open 9am to 11pm Monday to Friday, 10am to 11pm Saturday and Sunday; 2Kč per minute. PCs and Macs are both available.

Internet Nescafé Live (Map 7; ☎ 221 63 71 68, ⓔ info@cybeteria.cz) Rathova Pasaž, Na příkopě 23, Staré Město. Open 9am to 10pm Monday to Friday, 10am to 8pm Saturday and Sunday; 1.70Kč per minute.

Internetová čajovna v Síti (Map 10; ☎ 732 96 35 67, ⓔ e-cajovna@post.cz) Jana Masaryka 46, Vinohrady. Open 10am to 10pm Monday to Friday, 2pm to 10pm Saturday and Sunday; 1.50Kč per minute, or 1Kč per minute if you buy tea (a selection of quality teas is available).

Pl@neta (Map 8; ☎ 267 31 11 82, ⓔ info@planeta.cz) Vinohradská 102, Žižkov. Open 8am to 10pm daily; 1.5Kč per minute.

Spika (Map 7; ☎ 224 21 15 21, ⓔ spika@spika.cz) Dlážděná 4, Nové Město. Open 8am to midnight daily; 20Kč per 15 minutes.

The Globe (Map 6; ☎ 224 91 62 64, ⓔ globe@globebookstore.cz) Pštrossova 6, Nové Město. Open 10am to midnight daily; 1Kč per minute, no minimum. The Globe has Ethernet sockets where you can connect your network-enabled laptop (also 1Kč per minute; cables provided, 50Kč deposit).

If you plan to take a laptop computer with you, remember that the power-supply voltage in the Czech Republic may be different from that at home, risking damage to your equipment. The best investment is a universal AC adaptor for your appliance, which will enable you to plug it in anywhere without frying its innards. You'll also need a European plug adaptor – often it's easiest to buy these before you leave home.

You should be able to log on from your hotel room for the cost of a local call by registering with an Internet roaming service such as **MaGlobe** (ⓦ *www.maglobe.com*), which has access numbers for Prague. Most newer, mid-range and top-end hotels have telephone jacks, usually US standard (RJ-11), which you can plug your modem cable into. Adaptors for the older, four-pin Czech phone jacks can be found in electronic supply shops.

Buy a line tester – a gadget that goes between your computer and the phone jack – so that you don't inadvertently fry your modem. Get on and off quickly; calls from hotels are expensive. An increasing number of Internet cafés in Prague now offer Ethernet sockets where you can connect a network-enabled laptop to the Internet. For more information on travelling with a laptop see ⓦ www.kropla.com.

Major Internet service providers such as **AOL** (ⓦ *www.aol.com*), **CompuServe** (ⓦ *www.compuserve.com*) and **AT&T** (ⓦ *www.attbusiness.net*) have dial-in nodes in Prague. If you have an account with one of these, you can download a list of local dial-in numbers before you leave home.

If you access your email account at home through a smaller ISP or your office or school network, your best option is to open a webmail account such as Yahoo or Hotmail before you leave, and either give your new webmail address to your friends and family, or use the account's 'Check Other Mail' option to download mail from your home account (this may not work for work-based email accounts).

A final option for checking email at cybercafés is to open a free ekno Web-based account online at W www.ekno.lonelyplanet.com. You can then access your mail from anywhere in the world from any net-connected machine running a standard Web browser.

DIGITAL RESOURCES

The Web is a rich resource for travellers. You can research your trip, hunt down bargain air fares, book hotels, check on weather conditions or chat with locals and other travellers about the best places to visit (or avoid!).

There's no better place to start your Web explorations than the Lonely Planet website (W www.lonelyplanet.com). Here you'll find succinct summaries on travelling to most places on earth, postcards from other travellers, and the Thorn Tree bulletin board where you can ask questions before you go, or dispense advice when you get back. You can also find travel news and updates to many of our most popular guidebooks, and the subWWWay section links you to the most useful travel resources elsewhere on the Web.

CzechSite (W www.czechsite.com) is a general site that covers travel planning for a trip to Prague, while Prague.TV (W www.prague.tv) is an invaluable source of off-beat news, reviews and events listings. AllPraha (W www.allpraha.com) is a comprehensive, searchable directory of all kinds of services and businesses in Prague.

News and current affairs in Prague and throughout the Czech Republic are covered on Radio Prague (W www.radio.cz) and Radio Free Europe/Radio Liberty (W www.rferl.org/bd/cz) sites. The *Prague Post* (W www.praguepost.cz) weekly newspaper's site has useful tourist information as well as news.

The Czech Ministry of Foreign Affairs (W www.czech.cz) has an English-language site with lots of official information. The weekly *Prague Castle* has a site (W www.hrad.cz) providing information for visitors as well as official news from the president's office.

BOOKS

For information on Prague bookshops, see the Shopping chapter.

Lonely Planet

If you're doing any further travelling in the region, pick up Lonely Planet's *Czech & Slovak Republics* or the wider-ranging *Central Europe* or *Eastern Europe* guidebooks. Lonely Planet's *Czech Phrasebook* or the Czech chapter in the *Central Europe* or *Eastern Europe* phrasebooks provide help with the Czech language.

History & Politics

The Coasts of Bohemia by Derek Sayer is a very readable exploration of the ironies of Czech history in the 19th and 20th centuries. *Prague in Black and Gold* by Peter Demetz is a fascinating history of the Czech capital by a Czech-born American professor who fled the country in 1949 and returned after the velvet revolution. Callum MacDonald's *The Killing of SS Obergruppenführer Reinhard Heydrich* is a gripping account of the assassination of Prague's WWII Nazi ruler.

The Oxford historian Timothy Garton Ash's *We the People: the Revolutions of 1989* features gripping 'I was there' accounts of the revolutions that swept away the region's old guard in 1989. William Shawcross' *Dubček & Czechoslovakia* is a biography of the late leader of the Prague Spring, with a hasty post-1989 update. Another good biography is Michael Simmons' *The Reluctant President: A Political Life of Václav Havel*.

General

The essays and memoirs of the dissident-turned-president Václav Havel offer a revealing 'inside' view. *Disturbing the Peace* is a collection of recent historical musings, *Letters to Olga* is a collection of letters to his wife from prison in the 1980s, while *Living in Truth* is a series of absorbing political essays.

Patrick Leigh Fermor's *A Time of Gifts* is the luminous first instalment of his trek through Europe, including Czechoslovakia, in the early 1930s.

Bruce Chatwin's *Utz* is a quiet, absorbing novella about a porcelain collector in Prague's old Jewish quarter.

The Widow Killer by Pavel Kohout – along with Václav Havel one of the signatories of Charta 77 – is a mystery thriller set in Prague in the final weeks of WWII.

Probably the best Czech novelist of the 20th century is Bohumil Hrabal (1914–97). One of his finest works is *The Little Town That Stood Still,* a novel set in a small town that shows, in a humorous way, how the close-knit community interacts.

For information on fiction by Czech authors, see Literature under Arts in the Facts about Prague chapter.

FILMS

Prague itself has become a major star in big-budget Hollywood films; Miloš Forman's Oscar-winning *Amadeus* (1984) was shot here (Miloš Forman thought the backstreets of Malá Strana looked more like old Vienna than any part of modern-day Vienna), as were Steven Soderbergh's *Kafka* (1991), Barbara Streisand's *Yentl* (1983) and *Mission Impossible* (1996). The sci-fi thriller *The League of Extraordinary Gentlemen* (in production in 2002), starring Sean Connery, was also shot in Prague.

NEWSPAPERS & MAGAZINES

Prague has no daily English-language newspaper, but the weekly *Prague Post* is good value for visitors at 50Kč. Along with local news and features, it has a 'Night & Day' arts and entertainment listings section, travel tips, and concert and restaurant reviews.

The *New Presence* (subtitled the Prague Journal of Central European Affairs; 80Kč) is a quarterly translation of the Czech *Nová Přítomnost,* with features and essays on current affairs, politics and business. For names of further business-oriented newspapers and magazines, see Doing Business later in this chapter. The alternative bilingual (Czech/English) free monthly magazine *Think* (W www.think.cz) has features on music, fashion and art.

Major European and American newspapers and magazines are on sale at kiosks in tourist zones and at Praha hlavní nádraží. Many of these are also stocked at the newspaper reading room of the City Library (see Libraries later in this chapter).

RADIO & TV

The **BBC World Service** *(W www.bbc.cz)* broadcasts both English-language and Czech news and cultural programmes locally on 101.1MHz FM, 24 hours a day. The programme is available on its website (in Czech).

The former Czechoslovakia was the second European nation after Britain to start its own radio station: Czech Radio (Český rozhlas) has been broadcasting since May 1923. **Radio Prague** *(W www.radio.cz)* has daily transcripts of its news bulletins and RealAudio/MP3 broadcasts on its website.

The FM band is full of local DJs playing Western pop and rock. Radio 1 (96MHz FM) plays mainly alternative music mixed with techno.

The former Czechoslovak National Assembly building adjacent to the Národní muzeum (National Museum) is now the world headquarters for Radio Free Europe, which broadcasts from a transmitter in the suburbs.

The only regular English-language programming on the two state-run TV channels is the 45-minute 'Euronews' bulletin on ČT 2 at noon Monday to Thursday and 7.15pm Friday to Sunday. There are two independent commercial channels: TV Nova and Prima TV. Nova shows lots of old American and European flicks and dubbed sitcoms. Anyone with a satellite dish can choose from an extensive menu of European stations.

PHOTOGRAPHY & VIDEO

Forty-five years of secret police lurking behind every shrub have made some people uneasy about being photographed, so ask first. 'May I take your photograph?' is '*Mohu si vás vyfotit?*'.

For more guidance on how to get the best out of your photos, see Lonely Planet's *Travel Photography: A Guide to Taking Better Pictures* by Richard I'Anson.

Film-Damaging Airport X-Rays

If you carry unprocessed film in your checked-in baggage, even in a lead-lined 'filmsafe' pouch, you're inviting trouble. Several international airports now use either the older 'smart' CTX 5000 or the new In-Vision L3 scanners for checked-in baggage. These scan first with a mild beam, then zero in ferociously on anything suspicious. A lead pouch would not only be ineffective but would invite further scans, and film inside is virtually certain to be ruined. Even tests by the manufacturer have confirmed this.

For obvious reasons there's no list of airports using the scanners, though they allegedly include some in the USA, the UK, France, the Netherlands, Belgium, Israel, South Africa and several Asian countries.

On the other hand, scanners for hand luggage at most major airports are relatively harmless, at least for slow- and medium-speed films. There are no plans yet to use the CTX 5000 or InVision L3 for hand luggage. The moral of the tale is obvious: always carry unprocessed film in your hand luggage, and if possible get officials to hand-inspect it. They may refuse, though having the film in clear plastic bags (and preferably clear canisters) can help to persuade them.

Film & Equipment

You can buy print film at one of the many small shops in Staré Město and Malá Strana offering one-hour or next-day processing services. Some Kodak franchises also stock Ektachrome (but not Kodachrome) slide film.

Typical prices are 200Kč for a pack of three 36-exposure colour print films (Fujicolor 100), and 130Kč for one 36-exposure slide film (Fujichrome Sensia 100), both excluding processing. Print processing typically costs 60Kč plus 9.90Kč per print – you get to look at a contact sheet, then choose which ones you want prints of. Slide (E6) processing costs about 80Kč per film.

The best places to buy slide and black-and-white film, both standard and professional, are **Milan Škoda Fototechnika** *(Map 6; ☎ 224 21 71 29; Vodičkova 36, Nové Me; open 8.30am-8pm Mon-Fri, 9am-6pm Sat)* and **ČTK Foto Shop** *(Czech News Agency; Map 6; ☎ 222 09 83 19; Opletalova 5/7, Nové Město; open 8am-7pm Mon-Fri, 9am-1pm Sat)*. Both of these places also offer good quality slide and monochrome processing services.

For passport or visa photos, try **Fotolab** *(Map 6; ☎ 222 21 11 34; Václavské náměstí 50, Nové Město; open 8.30am-7.30pm Mon-Fri, 9am-6pm Sat, 10am-6pm Sun)*. You can get Polaroid passport photos at ministudios in Praha hlavní nádraží and in the Můstek metro station lobby, below Wenceslas Square.

For camera repairs, try Milan Škoda Fototechnika (see earlier) or **Foto Jan Pazdera** *(Map 6; ☎ 224 23 54 04; Vodičkova 28, Nové Město; open 10am-6pm Mon-Fri)*.

Some shops stock 8mm video cassettes, but be careful: the Czech Republic uses the PAL system, which is incompatible with SECAM (France) and NTSC (North America and Japan) systems. Know what your home system uses.

TIME

The Czech Republic is on Central European Time, ie, GMT/UTC plus one hour. Clocks are set to daylight-saving time in summer, that is, forward one hour on the last weekend in March and back one hour on the last weekend in October.

Czechs use the 24-hour clock and there's no equivalent of am and pm, though they can commonly add *ráno* (morning), *dopoledne* (before noon), *odpoledne* (afternoon) or *večer* (evening).

ELECTRICITY

Electricity in Prague is 220V, 50Hz AC, and is quite reliable. Nearly all the outlets have the standard European socket with two small round holes; some also have a protruding earth (ground) pin. If you have a different plug or want to use the earth pin, bring an adaptor, as they are difficult to find in the Czech Republic. North American 110V appliances will also need a transformer if they don't have built-in voltage adjustment.

WEIGHTS & MEASURES

Czechs use the metric system. A comma is used instead of a decimal point, and full stops are used to indicate thousands, millions etc. A dash is used after prices rounded to the nearest koruna. Thus, for example, thirty thousand koruna would be written 30.000,- rather than 30,000.00. See the inside back cover for a conversion table.

LAUNDRY

Most of Prague's self-service laundries *(samoobslužná prádelna)* charge around 140Kč, and take 1½ hours to wash and dry a 6kg load of laundry.

The city's original laundrette is **Laundry Kings** *(Map 3; ☎ 233 34 37 43; Dejvická 16, Dejvice; metro Hradčanská; open 6am-10pm Mon-Fri, 8am-10pm Sat)*, which has a good bulletin board, snacks and newspapers, and a drop-off service.

Laundryland *(Map 10; ☎ 222 51 66 92, delivery service ☎ 603 41 10 05; Londýnská 71, Vinohrady; open 8am-10pm daily)* also has branches in the Pavilón shopping centre *(Map 10; Vinohradská 50, Vinohrady; open 9.30am-9pm Mon-Sat, noon-8pm Sun)* and in the Černá růže shopping centre *(Map 7; Na příkopě 1, Nové Město; open 9am-8pm Mon-Fri, 9am-7pm Sat, 11am-7pm Sun)*.

Two laundrettes that offer Internet access while you wash are **Astera** *(Map 6; ☎ 224 21 55 36; Jindřišská 5, Nové Město; open 7am-7pm Mon-Fri, 8am-noon Sat)* and **Prague Cyber Laundromat** *(Map 10; ☎ 222 51 01 80; Korunní 14, Vinohrady; open 8am-8pm daily)*; the latter – don't be put off by the graffitied exterior – also has a children's play area.

All of these laundrettes also offer dry-cleaning services.

Local laundries that will do a service wash for you are hard to find. Readers have recommended **Kussova prádelna** *(Map 7; ☎ 224 81 26 41; Rybná 27, Staré Město)*.

If you'd rather do yours in the hotel sink, bring along a universal sink plug and a bit of line.

TOILETS

Public toilets are free in state-run museums, galleries and concert halls. Most cafés and restaurants don't seem to mind nonguests using theirs – ask for *záchod*, *vé cé* (WC) or *toalet* – but many in tourist areas charge 2Kč or 5Kč.

Elsewhere, such as in train, bus and metro stations, toilets are staffed by mostly burly attendants who ask for 2Kč for use of the toilet (their only pay) and may sell a few sheets of toilet paper *(toaletní papír)* if you need it. Most places are fairly clean. Men's are marked *muži* or *páni*, and women's *ženy* or *dámy*.

HEALTH

No vaccinations are required for the Czech Republic. Public hygiene in Prague is good. For people with respiratory problems, Prague can be an unpleasant place to be in midwinter when vehicle emissions turn the air dangerously foul during periodic weather inversions.

Precautions

Prague's tap water is drinkable, though to delicate palates it's an unpleasant chlorinated brew. There have been isolated instances of contamination in outer districts in the past, though this is unlikely to affect most visitors. Cheap bottled water is available almost everywhere, as many Czechs prefer it to tap water.

Most restaurants and takeaway food outlets are as hygienic as anywhere in Europe, though you're safest with hot, freshly made items.

Bedbugs can be a problem in hostels not only in the Czech Republic but throughout Europe. Some hostels regularly fumigate their rooms but others don't. Many hostels that do fumigate don't allow their guests to use their own sleeping bags or sleeping sheets but provide sheets for guests. Bedbugs are most easily spread from hostel to hostel by people using their own bedding. The hostels recommended in the Places to Stay chapter were clean at the time of research.

Medical Services

Emergency treatment and nonhospital first aid are free for all visitors to the Czech Republic. Citizens of EU countries may get cheap or free treatment under reciprocal health-care treaties (check before you leave home). Others must pay for treatment, normally in koruna, and at least some must be paid upfront. Everyone must pay for prescribed medications.

A travel insurance policy that covers medical treatment abroad is a good idea; those offered by various youth-travel agencies are good value. All the places listed here accept credit cards.

Hospitals The best hospital in Prague is **Na Homolce** *(Map 2; ☎ 257 27 11 11, after hours ☎ 257 27 25 27; 5th floor, Foreign Pavilion, Roentgenova 2, Motol)*. It is equipped and staffed to Western standards, and staff speak English, French, German and Spanish, but there are no English speakers on the after-hours telephone number. Take bus No 167 from Anděl metro station and get off at the sixth stop.

District clinics have after-hours emergency services (open from 7pm to 7am, and all weekend). **Poliklinika na Národní** *(Polyclinic on Národní; Map 6; ☎ 222 07 51 20, 24-hr emergency number ☎ 7777 94 22 70; W www.poliklinika.narodni.cz; Národní 9, Staré Město; open 8.30am-5pm Mon-Fri)* is a central clinic with English-speaking staff. Expect to pay around 800Kč to 1200Kč for an initial consultation.

Prague has several pricey but professional private clinics with English-speaking doctors, some of them Western-trained, and a range of in- and out-patient services, where an initial consultation will cost from US$50 to US$200. They include the **Canadian Medical Centre** *(Map 2; ☎ 235 36 01 33, after hours ☎ 603 21 23 20; Veleslavínská 1, Veleslavín; tram Nos 20 & 26; open 8am-6pm Mon-Fri)* and the **American Medical Center** *(Map 4; 24hr ☎ 220 80 77 56; Janovského 48, Holešovice; tram Nos 5, 12 & 17; open 8am-6pm Mon-Fri)*. Both will open at any time for an emergency, but you need to call ahead.

Dental Services There are dental clinics at Na Homolce hospital, the Poliklinika na Národní (see Medical Services earlier) and at other clinics and hospitals. For after-hours emergencies in central Prague go to the **district clinic** *(Map 6; ☎ 224 94 69 81; Palackého 5, Nové Město)*.

Pharmacies There are plenty of pharmacies *(lekárna)*, and most city districts have one that stays open 24 hours a day. In Nové Město it's at the **district clinic** *(Map 6; ☎ 224 94 69 82; Palackého 5; open 7am-7pm Mon-Fri, 8am-noon Sat)*. Vinohrady's is **Lékárna U sv Ludmily** *(Map 10; ☎ 222 51 33 96; Belgická 37; open 7am-7pm Mon-Fri, 8am-noon Sat)*.

For emergency service after hours, ring the bell – you'll see a red button with a sign *zvonek lekárn*a (pharmacy bell) and/or *první pomoc* (first aid). Over-the-counter and prescription medicines are not always available, so it's wise to bring what you need.

Ticks

Ticks *(klíště)* are a common nuisance in forests, and even in suburban gardens, from May to September. About 5% of them carry tick-borne encephalitis (TBE), a cerebral inflammation that can cause death, and about 25% carry Lyme disease, a potentially serious bacterial infection that affects the nervous system, joints and skin.

The Křivoklátsko region, southwest of Prague (see the Excursions chapter), has one of the country's highest rates of TBE. In the Czech Republic and other European countries you can get a TBE vaccine as a series of two or three injections. The injections provide good protection against TBE and can be administered quickly: it takes about 10 days to get the three shots. The vaccination is not expensive and there are no side effects. TBE vaccinations are not available in Australia or the USA.

With Lyme disease, red blotches (sometimes several centimetres or more across, sometimes pale in the centre) may appear – though a tick bite can also cause blotches without Lyme disease. The disease is accompanied by tiredness, weakness and/or flu-like symptoms. If it's detected early it can be treated with antibiotics, so immediate medical attention is obviously in order. Lyme disease can also be transmitted by mosquitoes and gadflies.

Avoid ticks by wearing socks and long trousers when walking in woods and tall grass. If a tick buries itself in your skin, *don't* pick it off, but coax it out by covering it in vaseline or oil.

HIV & AIDS

Infection with HIV (Human Immunodeficiency Virus) may develop into AIDS (Acquired Immune Deficiency Syndrome) which is usually fatal. Any exposure to blood, blood products or bodily fluids may put an individual at risk. The major route of HIV transmission is via unprotected sex; apart from abstinence, the most effective preventative is always to practise safe sex using condoms. HIV can also be spread by dirty needles, so acupuncture, tattooing and body piercing are potentially as dangerous as intravenous drug use if the equipment is not clean.

In the Czech Republic, just over 500 people are officially registered as HIV positive, though the true number is estimated to be around 2500. Neither HIV testing nor any other medical checks are required for entry visas, or work or residency permits.

Organisations in Prague offering confidential HIV testing include the following:

The National AIDS Prevention Line (Národní linka prevence AIDS; Map 9; toll-free helpline ☎ 0800 144 444) KHS, Dittrichova 17, Nové Město. Open for blood samples from 8am to noon Monday to Friday, helpline open from 1pm to 6pm Monday to Friday.

Czech AIDS Help Society (Česká společnost AIDS pomoc, or ČSAP; Map 6; ☎ 224 81 42 84, help line ☎ 224 81 07 02) Malého 3, Karlín. Free and anonymous HIV testing takes place from 4pm to 7pm on Monday.

Drug Problems

The **Drop In Foundation** *(Map 6; ☎ 222 22 14 31; W www.dropin.cz; Karoliny Světlé 18, Staré Město; open 9am-6pm Mon-Fri)* is an easy-going and informal drug-counselling centre. Enter the centre from ulice Boršov.

WOMEN TRAVELLERS

To many Westerners the Czech Republic seems to be picking up, sexually speaking, where it left off in 1948. Some newsstands stock dozens of porno titles; even mainstream advertising has no qualms about using the occasional naked breast to sell products. The expatriate press in Prague bubbles with arguments about whether this is sexism or freedom of expression, while on the whole Czechs seem less fussed than foreigners about the matter.

The darker side is that sexual violence has been on the rise since 1989, at least in Prague. Most Czech women we talked to said they sometimes experienced whistling and catcalls. Attacks on local women have happened in all parts of Prague, but statistically speaking women are far safer here than in most large Western cities. The most dangerous area for women at night is the park in front of Praha hlavní nádraží.

Czech women have made a lot of progress towards the goal of equality in the workplace, and state financial support for maternity leave is good (six months on 90% of salary). At home, however, most are still expected to look after the kids and do all of the housework.

Women (especially solo travellers) may find the atmosphere in many nontouristy pubs a bit raw, as they tend to be exclusively male territory. *Kavárny* (coffee shops) often dispense beer and wine too, and are more congenial; *vinárny* (wine bars) are also good, relaxed places for drinks and a meal.

There are very few services for women such as helplines and refuge or rape crisis centres. The main organisation in Prague is the **White Circle of Safety** *(Bílý kruh bezpečí; ☎ 257 31 71 00; W www.bkb.cz; Duškova 20, Smíchov)*, which provides help and counselling to victims of criminal offences of all kinds.

GAY & LESBIAN TRAVELLERS

Homosexuality is legal in the Czech Republic (the age of consent is 15), but Czechs are not accustomed to seeing gays showing affection to each other in public; it's best to be discreet.

The bimonthly gay guide and contact magazine *Amigo* has a few pages in English, and a useful English website (W www.amigo.cz/indexe.htm). The Gay Guide Prague

(**W** www.gayguide.net/europe/czech/prague) is another useful source of information. See also Gay & Lesbian Venues in the Entertainment chapter.

Gay Iniciativa *(Gay Initiative; ☎/fax 224 22 38 11; **e** info@gay.iniciativa.cz; Senovážné náměstí 2, Nové Město)* is the national organisation for gays and lesbians; it can offer information on events, venues and resources.

DISABLED TRAVELLERS

Increasing, but still limited, attention is being paid to facilities for the disabled in Prague. Wheelchair ramps are becoming more common, especially at major street intersections and in top-end hotels (in the text we identify hotels with facilities for the disabled). For the blind or vision-impaired, most pedestrian-crossing lights in central Prague have a sound signal to indicate when it's safe to cross. McDonald's and KFC entrances and toilets are wheelchair-friendly.

The Stavovské Theatre is equipped for the hearing-impaired, and this and several other theatres are wheelchair-accessible. The monthly what's-on booklet *Přehled* (see Tourist Offices earlier in this chapter) indicates venues with wheelchair access.

Few buses and no trams have wheelchair access; special wheelchair-accessible buses operate Monday to Friday on line Nos 1 and 3, including between Florenc bus station and náměstí Republiky, and between Holešovice train station and náměstí Republiky (contact one of the DP information centres listed in the Getting Around chapter for more information, or visit the website at **W** www.dp-praha.cz).

Praha hlavní nádraží, Holešovice train station and a handful of metro stations (Hlavní nádraží, Hůrka, Luka, Lužiny, nádraží Holešovice, Stodůlky and Zličín) have self-operating lifts. Other metro stations (Chodov, Dejvická, Florenc C line, Háje, IP Pavlova, Opatov, Pankrác, Roztyly and Skalka) have modified lifts that can be used with the help of station staff. Czech Railways (ČD) claims that every large station in the country has wheelchair ramps and lifts, but in fact the service is poor.

When flying, disabled travellers should inform the airline of their needs when booking, and again when reconfirming, and again when checking in. Most international airports (including Prague's) have ramps, lifts, accessible toilets and telephones. Aircraft toilets, on the other hand, present problems for wheelchair travellers, who should discuss this early on with the airline and/or their doctor.

Information & Organisations

The **Prague Wheelchair Users Organisation** *(Pražská organizace vozíčkářů; Map 7; ☎ 224 82 72 10; **e** pov@gts.cz; **W** www.pov.cz; Benediktská 6, Josefov)* can organise a guide and transportation at about half the cost of a taxi, and has an online database of barrier-free places in Prague (currently in Czech only; an English translation is planned).

The vision-impaired are represented by the **Union of the Blind and Weak Sighted** *(Sjednocená organizace nevidomých a slabozrakých v ČR; Map 6; ☎ 221 46 21 46; **e** sons@braillnet.cz; Krakovská 21, Nove Město)*, which provides information but no services.

SENIOR TRAVELLERS

While senior residents of Prague get many concessions, such as on museum admission and public transport, there are no formal discounts for senior travellers here. But a senior card will get you sizable knockdowns on international travel, similar to those for under-26s, as noted in the Getting There & Away chapter.

A Prague travel agency advertising itself as a specialist in tours for senior travellers, including foreign visitors, is **Heart of Europe** *(CK Srdce Evropy; Map 6; ☎ 224 16 24 86, fax 224 16 24 82; **e** srdceevropy@vol.cz; V jámě 1, Nové Město)*.

Travellers aged over 50 can also check out tours and bargain fares offered by senior specialists **SAGA Holidays** *(toll-free ☎ 800-343 0273 in the USA, ☎ 0800 300 456 in the UK; **W** www.saga.co.uk)*.

PRAGUE FOR CHILDREN

Czechs are generally family-oriented and there are plenty of activities for children around the city. For details, prices and opening hours see the Things to See & Do chapter or the special section 'Prague Castle'.

Museums of possible interest to children include the **muzeum hraček** (Toy Museum), though it's frustratingly hands-off; the **Národní Technické muzeum** (National Technology Museum), especially the vast hall full of trains, cars and aeroplanes; the **Vojenské historické muzeum** (Museum of Military History); the **muzeum MHD** (Public Transport Museum); and the **muzeum letectví a kosmonautiky** (Museum of Aircraft & Space Exploration).

For outdoor activity, try the **zoo** or **Petřín Hill**, a large park where parents and kids alike can take a break from sightseeing. In the park itself you can enjoy the funicular railway, the mirror maze, Petřín Tower (with terrific views of Prague if the weather is clear), the Štefánik Planetarium and a playground. For the best views of all, go to the TV Tower.

In summer there are rowing and paddle boats for hire on the **river. Children's Island** was being redeveloped at the time of research, but there are other safe, fenced **playgrounds** nearby (all Map 5): by the entrance to Petřín park on náměstí Kinských; at the northern end of Kampa island; by the entrance to Kampa Park restaurant; and on Vlašská, just beyond the German embassy. Older children might enjoy **horse riding**, **tennis** or **bowling**. In winter there are plenty of **ice rinks**.

March is the time of the **spring fair**, when the fairgrounds in Bubeneč are full of rides, shooting galleries and candy floss. If there's a **circus** in town it will most likely be on Letná Plain, opposite the AC Sparta Praha Stadium in Bubeneč.

At weekends and on holidays between April and mid-November, **vintage tram cars** trundle along a special sightseeing route, No 91, around the historical centre; see the boxed text 'Vintage Trams' in the Getting Around chapter. And don't miss the **changing of the guard** at Prague Castle – but get in position before the crowds do, or the kids won't see a thing.

Several **theatres** cater for children, but nearly everything is in Czech. Two good ones are the **divadlo Minor** (see Theatre in the Entertainment chapter) and the **divadlo Spejbla a Hurvínka** *(Map 3; ☎ 224 31 67 84; Dejvická 38, Dejvice; box office open 10am-2pm & 3pm-6pm Tues-Fri, 1pm-5pm Sat & Sun)*. The latter is a marionette theatre named after Spejbl and Hurvínek, Josef Skupa's famous puppet duo of the early 20th century.

The Říše loutek, or Puppet Kingdom, of the **Narodni divadlo marionet** (National Marionette Theatre; see Theatre in the Entertainment chapter) is aimed at adults too, with its long-running production of Mozart's famous opera *Don Giovanni*. Programmes for these and many other theatres are provided in *Culture in Prague* or *Přehled* and in other cultural publications.

Czech restaurants do not specifically cater for children in the Western sense, with play areas and so on. Some restaurants have a children's menu *(dětský jídelníček)*, but even if they don't, they can usually provide smaller portions for a lower price.

Childcare

PIS usually has a list of babysitting *(hlídaní dětí)* agencies, and most top-end hotels provide a babysitting service; rates generally run from 80Kč to 120Kč per hour. Agencies that can provide English-speaking babysitters include:

Babysitting Praha (☎ 602 88 50 74, ⓔ blazinkk@centrum.cz)
Kid's Zone (☎ 608 17 48 37, 608 94 00 44, ⓦ www.kidszone.cz)
Markéta Tomlová (☎ 608 08 28 68, ⓔ tomkovam@seznam.cz) English- and French-speaking babysitters

LIBRARIES

The modern, barrier-free **City Library** *(Městská knihovna; Map 7; ☎ 222 11 33 71; Mariánské náměstí, Staré Město; main library open 9am-8pm Tues-Fri & 10am-5pm Sat, ground floor reading room open 9am-8pm Tues-Fri & 9am-5pm Sat)* has foreign-language material, including periodicals (to the left), fiction (to the right) and newspapers (on the ground floor). A library card costs 55/80Kč for six/12 months, plus a refundable 1000Kč deposit for nonresidents.

See Cultural Centres later in this chapter for information about other reading rooms.

UNIVERSITIES

The Czech Republic's oldest and most distinguished university is Charles University, founded in 1348 by Charles IV in the building called the **Karolinum** *(Map 7; Železná 9)*. Today it has 13 faculties and several research centres in about 160 buildings scattered all over the city (plus two faculties in Hradec Králové and one in Plzeň).

To find out about courses, student cards or student hang-outs, go to IPC, the university's **Information & Advisory Centre** *(Informačně poradenské centrum; Map 6; ☎ 224 49 18 96; e ipc@ruk.cuni.cz; Školská 13a; open 1pm-4pm Mon, Wed & Thur; 10am-noon Tues)*.

For details of Czech-language courses at the university, see Courses in the Things to See & Do chapter.

CULTURAL CENTRES

If you're looking for newspapers or information about other countries, try these centres:

France

Institut Français de Prague (Map 6; ☎ 221 40 10 11, W www.ifp.cz) Štěpánská 35, Nové Město. Open 9am to 6pm Monday to Friday; library open 10am to 7pm Tuesday, 11am to 7pm Wednesday and Thursday, 10am to 5pm Friday, 10am to 1pm Saturday. Has a café with French newspapers, a French-language multimedia library and a bookshop.

Germany

Goethe Institut (Map 6; ☎ 221 96 21 11, W www.goethe.de/ms/pra) Masarykovo nábřeží 32, Nové Město. Library open 1pm to 7pm Tuesday to Friday, 10am to 2pm Saturday. Has a German multimedia library.

Poland

Polish Cultural Centre (Map 6; ☎ 224 21 47 08, W www.polskyinstitut.cz) 1st floor, Václavské náměstí 49-51, Nové Město. Reading room open 10am to 5pm Monday to Thursday and 10am to 3pm Friday; library open 2pm to 5pm Tuesday and 1pm to 3.30pm Thursday.

Slovakia

Slovenský institut (Map 6; ☎ 224 94 81 35, W www.slovakemb.cz/#50) Purkyňova 4, Nové Město. Gallery open 10am to 6pm Tuesday to Friday, 1pm to 5pm Saturday and Sunday; library and reading room open 1pm to 4pm Monday to Wednesday, 10am to 1pm Thursday and Friday. Sells books and maps of Slovakia.

UK

British Council (Map 6; ☎ 221 91 11 11, W www.britishcouncil.cz) Národní 10, Nové Město. Open 9am to 5pm Monday to Friday. Has British papers and magazines, and satellite Sky TV news.

USA

American Embassy Information Resource Center (IRC; Map 7; ☎ 224 23 10 85) Hybernská 7a, Nové Město. Open 8am to 4.30pm Monday to Friday. Has American newspapers, magazines and reference books, plus a business reference service (available by appointment only).

DANGERS & ANNOYANCES

Tourists are charged two or three times more commission than Czechs at some independent exchange offices, for admission into some museums and for some theatre tickets. For information on taxi rip-offs, see the Getting Around chapter. Double pricing in hotels is noted in the Places to Stay chapter, overcharging in restaurants in the Places to Eat chapter.

Emergency telephone numbers are:

Emergency Services	☎ 112
Ambulance	☎ 155
Automobile Emergencies	☎ 1230 (ÚAMK)
	☎ 1240 (ABA)
Fire	☎ 150
Municipal Police	☎ 156
National Police	☎ 158

Theft

Tourism and heady commercialism have spawned an epidemic of petty (and not-so-petty) crime. Where tourists are concerned, this mainly means pickpockets. Naturally, the prime trouble spots are where tourists gather in crowds. These include Prague Castle (especially at the changing of the guard), Charles Bridge, Old Town Square (especially in the crowd watching the Astronomical Clock mark the hour), the entrance to Starý židovský hřbitov (the Old Jewish Cemetery), Wenceslas Square, Ruzyně airport, Praha hlavní nádraží, in the metro and on trams (especially getting on and off the crowded Nos 9 and 22). Be aware that people who lean over to look at your menu may be more interested in your wallet.

It's common sense to keep valuables well out of reach, such as inside your clothing. Be alert in crowds and on public transport. A classic scam involves someone asking directions and thrusting a map under your nose, or a woman with a baby hassling you for money – anything to attract your attention – while accomplices delve into your bags and pockets. If anything like this happens, immediately check your bags and look around you.

Over the last few years there have also been an increasing amount of reports from foreigners being robbed by bogus police. Men who claim that they are plain-clothes police investigating counterfeiting or illegal money-changing approach tourists and ask to see their money, which is returned after being examined. The unsuspecting tourist finds out later when they check their wallet that a substantial amount of money has been taken.

Another ploy involves a 'lost tourist' asking for directions (usually in halting English). Once you have been in conversation for a few minutes, two of the tourist's 'friends' interrupt, claiming to be plain-clothes policemen and accusing you of changing money illegally. They will demand to see your wallet and passport, but if you hand them over they are likely to run off with them. If in doubt, insist on accompanying them to a police station.

Lost or Stolen Belongings

Try your embassy first. The staff should give you a letter to take to the police, preferably in Czech, asking for a police report, without which you cannot collect on insurance. Try to get the embassy to provide its own report in your language too.

The British embassy has this down to an art and will also help you get in touch with a relative or the bank to get more money. For British and unrepresented Commonwealth citizens, it may even arrange an emergency passport to get you home.

For a police report, go to the Praha 1 **police station** *(Map 6; ☎ 261 45 17 60; Jungmannovo náměstí 9, Nové Město)*, as this is the only police station that can organise an interpreter. If the theft occurred in another district, the interpreter will take you to that district's police station to make a report. In Praha 1, there are two other main district **police stations** *(Bartolomějská 14 • Benedikstká 1)*. Unless you speak Czech, forget about telephoning the police, as they rarely speak English.

If your passport has been stolen and it contained a visa, apply for a replacement visa at the Foreigners' Police & Passport Office in Žižkov (see Visas & Documents earlier in this chapter). For advice on dealing with lost or stolen cards or travellers cheques, see Money earlier in this chapter.

For anything except travel documents, you might get lucky at the city's **lost & found office** *(ztráty a nálezy; Map 6; ☎ 224 23 50 85; Karoliny Světlé 5; open 8am-noon & 12.30pm-5.30pm Mon & Wed, 8am-noon & 12.30pm-4pm Tues & Thur, 8am-noon & 12.30pm-2pm Fri)*, east of the National Theatre. There's another **lost & found office** *(☎ 220 11 42 83; open 24 hrs)* at the airport.

Racism

You may be surprised at the level of casual prejudice directed against the Roma, whom people are quick to blame for the city's problems. Dark-skinned visitors may encounter low-level discrimination. Overt hostility towards visitors is rare, though there have been some assaults by skinheads on dark-skinned people.

LEGAL MATTERS

If you find yourself under arrest for any reason whatsoever, you are entitled to call your embassy. Note that it is technically illegal not to carry some form of identification (normally your passport). If you can't prove your identity, police have the right to detain you for up to 48 hours.

Penalties for possession of drugs are harsh and it's unlikely that your embassy can do much to help if you are caught. In the Czech Republic it was, until recently, legal to possess and use cannabis (though it was illegal to sell it). However, a new law came into force on 1 January 1999 (despite a veto by President Havel) which made it illegal to possess 'more than a small amount' of drugs. Unfortunately the law does not define 'a small amount' or specify which drugs, giving the police a free hand to nick anyone in possession of any amount of any drug. It's simply not worth the risk to import, export or possess any illegal substances.

Many of the older police officers retain a communist-era mistrust of foreigners. Younger officers are easier to deal with, but almost none speak fluent English. See Dangers & Annoyances earlier about where to go for a police report. The Foreigners' Police & Passport Office (see Visas & Documents earlier in this chapter) is the place for visa-related problems.

Drink-driving is strictly illegal; there is a zero blood-alcohol limit for drivers. Traffic fines are generally paid on the spot (ask for a receipt). For more information on road rules see the Getting There & Away chapter. The fine for littering is about 100Kč.

BUSINESS HOURS

Shops tend to open from 8.30am or 9am to 5pm or 6pm Monday to Friday, and to 11am or 1pm on Saturday. Department stores close at 8pm Monday to Friday, an hour or two earlier on Saturday, and at 6pm on Sunday. Touristy shops in central Prague are open later at night and on Saturdays and Sundays.

Restaurant hours vary, but most places operate from 11am to 11pm daily (some close on Monday). You will find hardly any places open during the Christmas holiday.

Major banks are open from at least 9am to 5pm Monday to Friday. Many exchange offices carry on until 11pm or later daily (see Money earlier in this chapter).

Government office hours are from 8.30am to 5pm Monday to Friday, though some tourist offices operate later and at weekends. The main post office at Jindřišská 14 (Map 6) opens from 7am to 8pm daily for some, but not all, services (see Post & Communications earlier in this chapter). Other post offices are open from about 8am to 6pm Monday to Friday and until noon on Saturday.

Most museums and galleries open from 9am or 10am to 5pm or 6pm year-round. Many close on Monday and sometimes the first working day after a holiday. Some of Prague's bigger churches are open similar hours.

Castles, chateaux and other historical monuments outside the city are open May to September, from 8am or 9am to 5pm or 6pm, except for a lunch break, daily except Monday and the first working day after a holiday. Most shut down from November to March, with some limited to weekends in October and April. But Karlštejn Castle is open from at least 9am to 4pm year-round (except the day after any public holiday, and Christmas Eve and New Year's Day). If you plan to take a guided tour, remember that ticket offices close an hour or so before the official closing time, depending on the length of the tour.

PUBLIC HOLIDAYS & SPECIAL EVENTS

Public Holidays

On the following public holidays banks, offices, department stores and some shops close. Restaurants, museums and tourist attractions tend to stay open.

New Year's Day (*Nový rok*) 1 January

Easter Monday (*Pondělí velikonoční*) March or April. The country collapses in a mirthful rite of spring: Czech men of all ages swat their favourite women on the legs with willow switches, and the women respond with gifts of hand-painted eggs, after which everybody parties. This is the culmination of several days of serious spring-cleaning, cooking and visiting.

Labour Day (*Svátek práce*) 1 May. Once the communist 'holy' day, it's now just a chance for a picnic or a day in the country. To celebrate the arrival of spring, many couples lay flowers at the statue of the 19th-century poet, Karel Hynek Mácha (Map 5), author of *Máj* (May), a poem about unrequited love. President Havel has been known to pay homage here (see also the boxed text 'Majáles' later in this chapter).

Liberation Day (*Den osvobození*) 8 May. Anniversary of the liberation of Prague by its citizens in 1945. Under communism this was celebrated on 9 May, the day the Red Army marched in.

Saints' Days

Practically every day of the year is the feast day of a particular saint, something Roman Catholics will be familiar with. To Czechs, a person's 'name day' (the day of the saint whose name that person bears) is very much like a birthday, and a small gift or gesture on that day never goes amiss.

SS Cyril & Methodius Day (*Den Cyrila a Metoděje*) 5 July. Recalls the Slavs' introduction to literacy and Christianity by the two missionary monks from Thessaloniki.

Jan Hus Day (*Den Jana Husa*) 6 July. Commemorates the 1415 burning at the stake of the great Bohemian religious reformer. The day is kicked off by low-key celebrations and bell-ringing at Prague's Bethlehem Chapel the evening before.

Czech Statehood Day 28 September

Independence Day (*Den vzniku Československa*) 28 October. The anniversary of the founding of the Czechoslovak Republic in 1918, now celebrated as the day of independence from the Austro-Hungarian Empire.

Struggle for Freedom and Democracy Day 17 November

'Generous Day', Christmas Eve (*Štědrý den*) 24 December. The big day for evening family meals and gift-giving.

Christmas Day (*Vánoce*) 25 December. The day for visiting friends and relatives, and a turkey and dumpling lunch.

St Stephen's Day (*Štěpána*) 26 December. Equivalent to Boxing Day.

Special Days

The following are not public holidays but special days *(významné dny)* for remembrance or celebration:

Three Kings' Day (*Tři králové*) 6 January. Formal end of the Christmas season, sometimes celebrated with carol singing, bell ringing and gifts to the poor.

Anniversary of Jan Palach's Death 19 January. In memory of the Charles University student who burned himself to death in 1969 in protest against the Soviet occupation.

Birthday of Tomáš Garrigue Masaryk 7 March. Commemorates Czechoslovakia's father-figure and first president.

Burning of the Witches (*Pálení čarodějnic*) 30 April. Czech version of a pre-Christian festival for warding off evil, featuring burning brooms at the Fairgrounds at Bubeneč, and all-night, end-of-winter bonfire parties on Kampa island and in suburban backyards.

Majáles 1 May (see the boxed text 'Majáles' later).

Czech Uprising (*České povstání*) 5 May. Anniversary of Prague's 1945 anti-Nazi uprising preceding liberation.

Start of the 'Velvet Revolution' 17 November. Anniversary of the 1989 beating of student demonstrators by security police, which triggered the fall of the communist regime.

Christmas/New Year 24 December–1 January. While many Czechs celebrate an extended holiday, stuffing themselves with carp (sold live from big tubs in the streets), Prague is engulfed by revellers from all over Europe and the tourist season is on again, briefly and furiously.

Festivals

The following festivals are among Prague's better annual events; for updates, check the PIS website (W www.prague-info.cz).

Febiofest January. This international festival of film, television and video features new works by international film-makers. Shown throughout the Czech Republic and Slovakia.

AghaRTA International Jazz Festival March–December. Held at AghaRTA Jazz Centrum and a few other venues.

Musica Ecumenica Early April. This international festival of spiritual music is held at major venues around the city.

Musica Sacra Praga Mid-April and October. This festival of sacred music is held in various concert halls and churches.

Festival of Chamber Music May. Music by Czech composers is performed at Bertramka.

Prague Spring (*Pražské jaro*) 12 May–4 June. This international music festival is Prague's most prestigious event, with classical music concerts in theatres, churches and historic buildings. It begins on the anniversary of Smetana's death with a procession from his grave at Vyšehrad to the Obecní dům (Municipal House) for a performance of his *Má vlast* (My Country). For more information, see the Entertainment chapter.

Tanec Praha June. An international festival of modern dance held at various theatres around Prague.

Open-Air Opera Festival July–August. Held at various venues, including Wallenstein Garden.

Prague Folk Festival July–September. Held at the theatre of the City Library.

Verdi Festival August–September. Features Verdi's works at the Statní opera (State Opera House).

Prague Autumn September. International music festival held mainly at the Rudolfinum.

Majáles

Until WWII, students regularly celebrated 1 May as Majáles, a spring festival dating back to at least the early 19th century. Banned by the Nazis and later under communism, it was revived during the 'Prague Spring' of the mid-1960s, only to disappear once more in 1969. Nobody got it together again until 1997.

Majáles 1998 coincided with a visit by Beat Generation writer Lawrence Ferlinghetti for the Prague Writers Festival, recalling the crowning of Allen Ginsburg as king of the 1965 Majáles. Ginsburg was allowed into the country on the strength of his anti-US government views, but he made his distaste for authoritarianism quite clear and was quickly thrown out. The secret service documents surrounding his expulsion were published in a booklet in 1998.

Today's Majáles kicks off with an early-afternoon parade – with bands, students in fancy dress, and a float with the Kral Majáles (King of Majáles) – from náměstí Jana Palacha, via Kaprova to the Old Town Square and the Karolinum. From there everybody moves on to Střelecký ostrov for an all-night bash, including live bands, student theatre and nonstop sausages and beer. For dates and details, check the website at w www.majales.cz.

Svatováclavské slavnosti September. St Wenceslas Festival of spiritual art (music, painting, sculpture).
Mozart v Praze October. Mozart Festival held at Bertramka and other major venues around town which runs for most of the month.
Lucerne International Jazz Festival October. Held at Lucerne Music Bar in Lucerne Passage, Staré Město.
Musica Iudaica October–November. Festival of Jewish Music, especially the composers of Terezín (see the Excursions chapter). Held at various venues.
Festival Bohuslava Martinů (*Bohuslav Martinů Music Festival*) December. Held at Rudolfinum and other venues.

DOING BUSINESS

A free-market economy has been evolving, haphazardly, in the Czech Republic since 1989. Laws and regulations have been written from scratch; some have worked, some have failed and all are full of loopholes. It's not unusual for locals to take advantage of innocent newcomers, or to renege on agreements. Money laundering is also a big problem. It's essential that a reliable Czech partner be found for any venture: someone to deal with complex procedures and steer clear of crooked deals. Lawsuits can take years, and many judges have not yet grasped the meaning of a free society. Entrenched bureaucratic habits remain in place, and corruption is still a problem. Another big obstacle is the only partially privatised banking sector, with its over-emphasis on cash as the basis of the economy.

The expatriate business community in Prague is well informed by a glossy monthly magazine, the *Prague Tribune* (w www.praguetribune.cz), and a weekly newspaper, the *Prague Business Journal* (w www.pbj.cz), with business-oriented regional news plus a few entertainment and restaurant listings. The *Prague Post* (w www.praguepost.cz) also has an extensive business section.

Useful Organisations

If you want to do business, talk to the commercial section of your embassy in Prague, or the **American Chamber of Commerce** *(AmCham; Map 7; ☎ 224 82 65 51/52, fax 224 82 60 82; e amcham@amcham.cz; w www.amcham.cz; Malá Štupartská 7, Staré Město)* about work permits and other matters. AmCham has lots of useful resources. Some that are on sale in bookshops and kiosks are free here. Two useful publications are:

City Invest Czech by CzechInvest (US$20), updated annually, covers everything you need to know to launch a business in the Czech Republic, along with an analysis of the current economic situation in the country.
Prague Business Journal Book of Lists (US$12 in the Czech Republic, US$29 if purchased abroad), an annual publication with graded business lists of accountants, lawyers, hotels, moving companies, printers, security firms, banks and so on.

Also check out **Trade Links** *(☎ 224 21 06 92, fax 224 21 86 92; PO Box 131, 110 01 Praha 1)*, which publishes a *Guide for Businessmen* with translations of Czech commercial, accounting and bankruptcy laws, as well as information about living in Prague.

The **Economic Chamber of the Czech Republic** *(Hospodářská komora ČR; Map 6; ☎ 224 09 61 11, fax 224 09 62 22; W www.hkcr.cz; Seifertova 22, Žižkov)* provides financial, legal and organisational advice to small and medium businesses. Two organisations with information for investors are the government agency **CzechInvest** *(Czech Agency for Foreign Investment; ☎ 296 34 25 00; W www.czechinvest.org; Štěpánská 15, Nové Město)*, and the **Confederation of Czech Industries** *(Svaz průmylsu a dopravy ČR; Map 6; ☎ 224 93 40 88; W www.spcr.cz; Mikulandská 7, Nové Město)*.

Of the many translating and interpreting firms in the city, **Artlingua** *(Map 6; ☎ 224 91 80 58; W www.artlingua.cz; Myslíkova 6, Nové Město)* is one of the most professional.

The leading Czech commercial banks are Československá obchodní banka (ČSOB), Komerční banka, Česká spořitelna and Živnostenská banka. Leading foreign banks are ABN Amro Bank, Banca Nacional del Lavoro, Bank Austria Creditanstalt and BNP Dresdner Bank.

WORK

Unemployment in Prague is low – less than 2% – and there are job opportunities for foreigners in English teaching, computing, finance, real estate and management firms.

You can find short- or long-term work teaching English (or other languages) at numerous language schools in Prague. If you can prove your qualifications to them, they'll take care of the paperwork for a work permit. Major, trustworthy schools include:

Angličtina Expres (☎ 224 25 14 82, W www.anglictinaexpres.cz) Korunni 2, Vinohrady
Berlitz (☎ 22 12 55 50, W www.berlitz.cz) Hybernská 24, Nové Město
London School of Modern Languages (☎ 224 25 34 37, W www.lsml.cz) Londýnská 8, Vinohrady
Státní jazyková škola (State Language School, ☎ 222 23 22 35, W www.sjs.cz) Školská 15, Nové Město

You might find employment in the expat-run restaurants, hostels and bars springing up like mushrooms around Prague. Possibilities also exist in many foreign-owned businesses. Investment, banking, real estate, IT and management firms need experienced staff and often employ non-Czech speakers, but the odds of getting such a job are better from home than in Prague. The *Prague Post* usually has a few advertisements for such positions.

Work-Related Documents

If you're planning to seek work in Prague, bring along your original birth certificate or a notarised copy of it, plus any credentials relevant to the work you want (such as TEFL certificate or diploma).

Permits

On 1 January 2000 the Czech government introduced a new residency law for foreigners. The laws governing the employment of foreigners in the Czech Republic are summarised on the website of the **Ministry of Foreign Affairs** *(W www.mzv.cz)* – on the English-language pages, follow the links to Travel & Living Abroad and Employment of Foreigners.

Its main effect is that you can no longer obtain a residency permit while you are in the country – you have to obtain a long-term visa at a Czech embassy or consulate outside the Czech Republic. (Note: you can do this through any Czech embassy or consulate around the world, not only in your home country.) If you wish to stay in the country longer than your tourist limit of 30, 90 or 180 days (see Visas & Documents earlier in this chapter) for the purposes of work or study, you must apply for a 'long-term visa', which allows you to stay in the country for up to one year.

If you want to set up your own business in Prague (see the preceding Doing Business section), the process is a lot more complex. It's easy to see why most people get help from their employers or from specialist agencies. One reliable Prague agency specialising in work and residency permits is **International Business Support** *(IBS; ☎ 226 44 13 34, fax 226 44 29 54; e ibs@terminal.cz; Žerotínova 31, Žižkov)*. It makes sense to arrange your job in advance so that much of the paperwork is done before you arrive.

Of course a great many expats work without permits. You can only extend a tourist visa once for a maximum period of 90 days. But be careful: police are cracking down on people who are working illegally, and employers who hire workers without permits can, if caught, be nailed with crippling fines.

When the Czech Republic becomes a member of the EU, EU citizens will no longer need to apply for a work permit, though they'll still need a residence permit.

Other Help

If you're settling in and looking for flatmates, Czech lessons, work, a haircut etc, there are good noticeboards at Laundry Kings and Prague Cyber Laundromat (see Laundry earlier in this chapter); The Globe and Big Ben bookshops (see the Shopping chapter); and FX Café (see Vegetarian in the Places to Eat chapter). You can also look for jobs on the Internet at ⓦ www.jobs.cz and in the classified-ad sections in the *Prague Post* and *Prague Business Journal*.

Volunteer Work

KMC *(Klub mladých cestovatelů, Young Travellers' Club; Map 6; ☎ 222 22 00 81; ⓔ kmc@kmc.cz; ⓦ www.kmc.cz, Karoliny Světlé 30)* organises international work camps from June to August. Projects include things such as work in a centre for children with disabilities, renovation work at the zoo and gardening at Průhonice park. Contracts are for a minimum of three weeks with no pay, but room and board are provided. The registration fee, if you book ahead through a volunteer or Hostelling International (HI) organisation in your home country, is US$50 to US$100 (some are free). There's a list of upcoming camps on the website.

Getting There & Away

Students and those aged under 26 or over 60 can get some big travel discounts. See Useful Cards under Visas & Documents in the Facts for the Visitor chapter for information about a range of discount cards.

AIR

Prague Ruzyně *(information ☎ 20 11 11 11; real-time arrivals and departures* Ⓦ *www.prague-airport.cz/en)*, on the western outskirts of the city, is the Czech Republic's only international airport. It is served by about 28 international carriers, including ČSA (České aerolinie), the state airline.

The high season for travel to Prague is roughly from May to September, plus the Easter and Christmas/New Year periods. Advance booking is essential at these times.

Departure Tax

The 700Kč international departure tax is invariably included in the ticket price.

Buying Tickets

With a bit of research – ringing around travel agents, checking Internet sites, perusing the travel ads in newspapers – you can often get yourself a good travel deal. Start early as some of the cheapest tickets need to be bought well in advance and popular flights can sell out.

Full-time students and those aged under 26 (under 30 in some countries) have access to better deals than other travellers. You have to show a document proving your date of birth or a valid International Student Identity Card (ISIC) when buying your ticket and boarding the plane.

Generally, there is nothing to be gained from buying a ticket direct from the airline. Discounted tickets are released to selected travel agents and specialist discount agencies, and these are usually the cheapest deals going.

One exception to this rule is the expanding number of 'no-frills' carriers, which mostly sell only direct to travellers. Unlike the 'full-service' airlines, no-frills carriers often make one-way tickets available at around half the return fare, meaning that it is easy to put together an open-jaw ticket when you fly to one place but leave from another.

The other exception is booking on the Internet. Many airlines (full-service and no-frills) offer some excellent fares to Web surfers. They may sell seats by auction or simply cut prices to reflect the reduced cost of electronic selling.

Many travel agencies around the world have websites, which can make the Internet a quick and easy way to compare prices. There are also an increasing number of online agents who operate only on the Internet.

Online ticket sales work well if you are doing a simple one-way or return trip on specified dates. However, online superfast fare generators are no substitute for a travel agent who knows all about special deals, has strategies for avoiding layovers and can offer advice on everything from which airline has the best vegetarian food to the best travel insurance to bundle with your ticket.

You may find the cheapest flights are advertised by obscure agencies. Most such firms are honest and solvent, but there are some rogue fly-by-night outfits around. Paying by credit card generally offers protection, as most card issuers provide refunds if you can prove you didn't get what you paid for. Similar protection can be obtained by buying a ticket from a bonded agent, such as one covered by the Air Travel Organiser's Licence (ATOL) scheme in the UK. Agents who accept only cash should hand over the tickets straight away and not tell you to 'come back tomorrow'. After you've made a booking or paid your deposit, call the airline and confirm that the booking has been made. It's generally not advisable to send money (even cheques) through the post unless the agent is very well established – some travellers have reported being ripped off by fly-by-night mail-order ticket agents.

If you purchase a ticket and later want to make changes to your route or get a refund, you need to contact the original travel agent. Airlines issue refunds only to the purchaser of a ticket – usually the travel agent who bought the ticket on your behalf. Many travellers change their routes halfway through their trips, so think carefully before you buy a ticket which is not easily refunded.

Travellers with Special Needs

If they're warned early enough, airlines can often make special arrangements for travellers, such as wheelchair assistance at airports or vegetarian meals on the flight. Children aged under two travel for 10% of the standard fare (or free on some airlines) as long as they don't occupy a seat. They don't get a baggage allowance. 'Skycots', baby food and nappies should be provided by the airline if requested in advance. Children aged between two and 12 can usually occupy a seat for around two-thirds of the full fare, and do get a baggage allowance.

The disability-friendly website W www.everybody.co.uk has an airline directory that provides information on the facilities offered by various airlines.

The UK & Ireland

Discount air travel is big business in London. Advertisements for many travel agencies appear in *Time Out,* the *Evening Standard,* the free magazine *TNT* and the travel pages of the weekend broadsheet newspapers.

British Airways *(BA; ☎ 0845 779 9977; W www.britishairways.com)* and **ČSA** *(☎ 020-7255 1898; W www.csa.cz/en)* have two or three direct flights a day between London Heathrow and Prague; these airlines and **KLM** *(☎ 0870 507 4074; W www.klm.com)* also offer connections to Prague from other UK cities. ČSA flies to Prague daily from London Stansted; six times a week from Manchester; four or five times a week from Birmingham; and once or twice a day from Dublin. KLM offers good deals from Edinburgh and Glasgow to Prague via Amsterdam.

The lowest ordinary discounted summer fare from London to Prague costs about £100 to £150 return, but flights as low as £55 return can be found (usually involving travel on a Sunday or Monday, and a stay of at least a week).

The budget airline **Go** *(☎ 0870 607 6543; W www.gofly.com)* operates direct flights to Prague from London Stansted, Bristol and East Midlands. Tickets can be booked online and can be as low as £35 one-way from Stansted, flying mid-week in the low season.

A good discount travel agent is **Trailfinders** *(☎ 020-7937 1234; W www.trailfinders.co.uk; 215 Kensington High St, London W8 6BD).* You could also try specialists such as **Regent Holidays** *(☎ 0117-921 1711; W www.regent-holidays.co.uk; 15 John St, Bristol BS1 2HR).*

A popular travel agency in the UK is **STA Travel** *(☎ 0870 160 0599; W www.statravel.co.uk; 86 Old Brompton Rd, London SW7 3LQ),* which has branches across the country. STA sells tickets to all travellers but caters especially to students and those aged under 26.

Elsewhere in Europe

From most Continental cities, routes to and from Prague are sewn up between the main airline from the home country and ČSA. Usually fares are agreed between the two airlines on a route, and revenue divided, so there is no real competition and fares are high.

ČSA has direct flights to Prague from many European cities, including Amsterdam, Brussels, Copenhagen, Frankfurt, Hamburg, Moscow, Munich, Oslo, Paris, Stockholm and Vienna. Typical return fares include €342 from Paris and €252 from Frankfurt. Return fares from Prague include 1990Kč to Bratislava, 9400Kč to Budapest and 10,700Kč to Sofia.

Recommended travel agents in Paris include **OTU Voyages** *(☎ 01 40 29 12 12; W www.otu.fr; 39 av Georges-Bernanos, 75005 Paris),* **Voyageurs du Monde** *(☎ 01 42 86 16 00; 55 rue Ste-Anne, 75002 Paris)* and **Nouvelles Frontières** *(nationwide ☎ 08 25 00 08 25, Paris ☎ 01 45 68 70 00; W www.nouvelles-frontieres.fr; 87 blvd de Grenelle, 75015 Paris).* All have branches across the country.

A good agency in Germany is **STA Travel** *(☎ 030-20 16 50 63; W www.statravel.de;*

Dorotheenstrasse 30, 10117 Berlin • ☎ 030-310 00 40; Hardenbergstrasse 9, 10623 Berlin), with branches in all major cities.

The USA & Canada

The only direct flights from North America to Prague are the daily services from New York JFK with **Delta** *(☎ 800-241 4141; W www.delta.com)* or **ČSA** *(☎ 800-223 2365; W www.csa.cz/en)*. Fares for these are likely to be high – around US$750 return for the cheapest and most restrictive ticket. A much wider range of departure points, and lower fares, are available on airlines that stop in a third country en route: **Air France** *(☎ 800-237 2747; W www.airfrance.com/us)* via Paris, **BA** *(☎ 800-403 0882; W wwwbritishairways.com)* via London and **Lufthansa Airlines** *(☎ 800-645 3380; W www.lufthansa.com)* via Frankfurt are the main ones. A return flight from New York to Prague with **Austrian Airlines** *(☎ 800-843 0002; W www.austrianair.com)* or **Scandinavian Airlines** *(SAS; ☎ 800-221 2350; W www.scandinavian.net)* starts at around US$500, plus about US$200 from the west coast.

STA Travel *(☎ 800-777 0112; W www.statravel.com)* has offices in Boston, Chicago, Miami, New York, Philadelphia, San Francisco and other major cities.

From Canada, ČSA has two to four flights a week from Toronto and Montreal to Prague. Canada's best bargain-ticket agency is **Travel Cuts** *(☎ 416-979 2406; W www.travelcuts.com; 187 College St, Toronto M5T 1P7)*, with some 50 offices in major cities. Its July fares are around C$950.

Australia

The best available high-season return fare from east-coast Australia to Prague is about A$2000 (about A$600 less in the low season).

Two well known agents for cheap fares are STA Travel and Flight Centre. **STA Travel** *(☎ 1300 733 035; W www.statravel.com.au)* has offices in all major cities and on many university campuses. **Flight Centre** *(Australia-wide ☎ 131 600; W www.flightcentre.com.au; 82 Elizabeth St, Sydney)* has dozens of offices throughout Australia.

Quite a few travel offices specialise in discounted air tickets. Some travel agents, particularly smaller ones, advertise cheap air fares in the travel sections of weekend newspapers.

Airline Offices

Airline offices in Prague include:

Aeroflot (☎ 224 81 26 82) Truhlářská 5, Staré Město
Air Canada (☎ 224 81 01 81) Kozí 3, Staré Město
Air France (☎ 224 22 71 64) Václavské náměstí 57, Nové Město
Air India (☎ 224 21 24 74) Václavské náměstí 15, Nové Město
Air Ukraine (☎ 224 24 88 28) Husova 5, Staré Město
Alitalia (☎ 224 19 41 50) Na můstků 9, Staré Město
Austrian Airlines (☎ 224 82 61 99) Revoluční 15, Nové Město
Balkan Bulgarian Airlines (☎ 220 56 05 94) Ruzyně airport
British Airways (BA; ☎ 222 11 44 44) Ovocný trh 8, Staré Město
České aerolinie (ČSA; ☎ 220 10 41 11) V celnici 5, Nové Město
Delta Air Lines (☎ 224 94 67 33) Národní 32, Nové Město
El Al Israel Airlines (☎ 224 22 66 24) Václavské náměstí 48, Nové Město
Finnair (☎ 224 21 19 86) Španělská 2, Nové Město
KLM-Royal Dutch Airlines (☎ 233 09 09 33) Na příkopě 21, Nové Město
Lufthansa Airlines (☎ 220 11 44 56) Ruzyně airport
MALÉV-Hungarian Airlines (☎ 224 22 44 71) Na příkopě 15, Nové Město
Sabena (☎ 220 56 23 65) Ruzyně airport
Scandinavian Airlines (SAS; ☎ 220 11 44 56) Ruzyně airport
Singapore Airlines (☎ 224 23 54 91) Národní 33, Nové Město
South African Airways (☎ 224 81 02 75) Kozí 1, Staré Město

BUS

Other Parts of the Czech Republic

Within the Czech Republic buses are often faster, cheaper and more convenient than the train, and by European standards both are cheap. Long-distance bus companies include the national carrier ČSAD and Čebus.

All domestic long-distance buses and most regional services (such as those for excursions around Prague) use **Florenc bus station** *(Map 6; information ☎ 12999; online time tables* **W** *www.jizdnirady.cz; Křižíkova 4, Karlín)*; on Czech timetables it's shown as 'ÚAN Florenc' (short for *Ústřední autobusové nádraží,* or 'central bus station'). Some regional buses depart from stands near metro stations Anděl, Dejvická, Černý Most, Hradčanská, Nádraží Holešovice, Radlická, Roztyly, Smíchovské Nádraží, Zličín and Želivského.

Agencies don't book seats on domestic buses, but they can tell you which stand is best for a particular trip – or indeed whether you're better off taking the train. You might get some help from the **ČSAD information line** *(☎ 1034; open 6am-8pm)*.

At Florenc bus station you can get information at **window No 8** *(open 6am-9pm daily)*, or use the touch-screen computer. If you get no joy there, try the friendly **Tourbus** *(☎ 224 21 02 21;* **W** *www.tourbuspraha.cz; open 8am-8pm Mon-Fri, 9am-8pm Sat-Sun)* travel agency at the far end of the hall.

There is a formidable maze of charts on the walls of the bus station, though they're not impossible to figure out. First, find the name of the town you want to travel to on the big A–Z list on the left-hand wall beyond the main hall; this will give you the number of the bus stand *(Odjedzové stání)* and the route number *(Čislo linky)*. You can then hunt through the timetables *(jízdní řády),* which are arranged in numerical order by stand number. The timetable lists the name of the bus company operating the route as well as departure and arrival times. The footnotes may drive you crazy – crossed hammers means the bus runs Monday to Friday only (*jede* means 'runs', *nejede* means 'doesn't run').

Short-haul tickets are sold on the bus. Long-distance domestic tickets are sold at the station from AMS window Nos 1 to 4 in the central hall. Tickets can be purchased from 10 days to 30 minutes prior to departure.

Čebus *(☎ 21 89 54 24;* **W** *www.cebus.cz)* operates several express buses a day between Prague and Brno; buy tickets at AMS window Nos 0 to 4 (140Kč one-way, two hours). The bus departs from stand No 10. Other popular destinations include Karlovy Vary (100Kč, two hours) and Český Krumlov (120Kč, three hours). You sometimes have to pay a small additional charge for checked luggage.

There are generally more departures in the morning. Buses, especially if full, sometimes leave a few minutes early, so be there about 10 minutes before departure time; if you have not taken your seat by five minutes before departure time, you may lose your reservation. Many services don't operate at weekends, so trains are a better bet then.

Florenc has a **left-luggage office** *(úschovna zavazadel; open 5am-11pm daily)* halfway up the stairs beyond the main hall.

Other Countries

Eurolines With the increase in availability of low air fares, buses no longer offer the cheapest public transport around Europe. But if you can't find a cheap flight or prefer to stay on the ground, buses are a good deal. The easiest way to book tickets is through Eurolines, a consortium of coach operators with offices all over Europe. Coaches are as fast as the trains and fairly comfortable, with on-board toilets, reclining seats and sometimes air-conditioning. They stop frequently for meals, though you'll save a bit by packing your own munchies. Book at least a few days ahead in summer.

The peak season for bus travel is from mid-June to the end of September, when there are daily Eurolines buses to Prague from London (£61/95 single/return, 23 hours), Paris (€68/122, 15 hours), Frankfurt (€44/69, nine hours), Vienna (€24/47, 4¾ hours) and Amsterdam (€73/130, 15 to 19 hours). Outside peak season daily services fall to two or three a week.

There are several buses daily from Prague to Bratislava (300Kč one-way, 4¾ hours), five a week to Budapest (1100Kč, seven hours) and three a week to Warsaw (550Kč, 10 hours) via Wroclaw (350Kč, five hours).

Discounts depend on the route, but children aged four to 12 typically get 30% to 40% off, and students, under-26s and seniors about 10%. For coach junkies, a Eurolines

Pass gives you unlimited travel to 36 major European cities for 15/30/60 days for a peak-season price of £155/229/267 (under-26s and seniors £130/186/205).

In Prague, the Eurolines coach operators are **Sodeli CZ** *(Map 7; ☎ 224 23 93 18; Ⓦ www.eurolines.cz; Senovážnénáměstí 6, Nové Město; open 8am-6pm Mon-Fri, 9am-1pm Sat)* and **Bohemia Euroexpress International** *(BEI; Map 6; ☎ 224 81 44 50; Ⓦ www.bei.cz; Florenc bus station, Křižíkova 4, Karlín; open 7am-12.30pm & 1pm-7pm Mon-Fri, 8am-12.30pm & 1pm-7pm Sat, 9am-12.30pm & 1pm-7pm Sun)*.

The 200 or so Eurolines offices throughout Europe include the following:

Deutsche Touring/Eurolines (☎ 069-79 03 50, Ⓦ www.eurolines.de) Am Romerhof 17, Frankfurt-am-Main
Eurolines France (☎ 08 36 69 52 52, Ⓦ www.eurolines.fr) Gare Routière Internationale de Paris, 28 Av de Général de Gaulle, Bagnolet, Paris
Eurolines Nederland (☎ 020-560 8788, Ⓦ www.eurolines.nl) Amstel Bus Station, Julianaplein 5, Amsterdam
Eurolines UK (☎ 0870 514 3219, Ⓦ www.eurolines.co.uk) 4 Cardiff Rd, Luton

Eurolines' agent in the USA is **British Travel International** *(toll-free ☎ 800-327 6097; Ⓦ www.britishtravel.com)*.

Busabout A UK-based budget alternative to Eurolines, **Busabout** *(☎ 020-7950 1661; Ⓦ www.busabout.co.uk; 258 Vauxhall Bridge Rd, London SW1V 1BS)* is aimed at younger travellers but has no upper age limit. It runs coaches along defined routes, covering major cities mostly in Western and Central Europe. Pick-up points are usually convenient for hostels and camp sites. In Prague, Busabout stops at the Arena Hostel in Holešovice (see Hostels in the Places to Stay chapter).

A Busabout Flexi Pass, which allows you to get off and on anywhere on the route, costs from £169 (£149 for youth and student cardholders) for six days travel in one month. You can buy Busabout tickets directly from the company or from agents such as STA Travel, London Flight Centre and Travel Cuts.

Other Coach Lines Independent operators serving the London–Prague route include:

Bohemian Express (Map 8; ☎ 224 81 00 13; Ⓦ www.jizdenky.cz) Sokolovská 93, Karlín
(☎ 020-7828 9008) London
Capital Express (Map 4; ☎ 220 87 03 68; Ⓦ www.capitalexpress.cz) U Výstaviště 3, Holešovice
(☎ 020-7243 0488) 57 Princedale Rd, Holland Park, London W11 4NP
Kingscourt Express (Map 7; ☎ 224 23 45 83; Ⓦ www.kce.cz) Havelská 8, Staré Město, Prague
(toll-free ☎ 0800 496 0001) 15 Balham High Rd, London SW12 9AJ

Their prices are lower than Eurolines – about £60 to £64 return. Bohemian Express also has services to Belgium, Luxembourg and Sweden.

Coach Stands Most international coaches, including Capital Express and Eurolines, use Florenc bus station (Map 6). Kingscourt Express buses use a stop on Ke Štvanici (opposite McDonald's), a block north of Florenc. Bohemian Express uses a stand at Nádraží Holešovice metro station (Map 4).

Although you can buy international tickets at Florenc, buying your bus ticket from a travel agency gives you the widest choice and usually the best price. Reliable ones include CKM Travel, GTS International, Bohemiatour, Čedok and the ČD agency at Praha hlavní nádraží (Prague's main train station; see Travel Agencies later in this chapter). Although Eurolines, BEI, Bohemian Express, Capital Express and Kingscourt Express have their own ticket offices, you can also buy their tickets through other agencies.

TRAIN

Other Parts of the Czech Republic

Czech Railways (ČD) provides cheap, efficient train services to most parts of the country. One-way 2nd-class fares cost around 64/120/224/424Kč for 50/100/200/400km; 1st-class fares are 50% more expensive.

Services include SuperCity (SC on timetables; only for 1st-class international trains), EuroCity (EC), Intercity (IC), Express (Ex),

Rapid (R), Fast (Sp) and Ordinary (Os). You can't make reservations on a Fast or Ordinary train; for the others, 'R' in the timetable indicates that reservations are recommended, and a boxed or circled 'R' means they're mandatory.

You can buy just a ticket *(jízdenka)*, or a ticket with a reservation *(místenka)* for a seat *(místo)*, couchette (*lehátkový vůz* – narrower than a sleeper and only a blanket is supplied) or sleeper (*lůžko* – like a bed with sheets included). You can't make a reservation without a ticket.

Tickets can be purchased up to 30 days ahead or 60 days if you make a reservation. Reservations cost 20Kč; supplements for faster trains include 60Kč for EC and 40Kč for IC trains. Only SC, IC, EC and express trains have a restaurant car *(restaurační vůz)*.

Some trains operate only on certain days, but the footnotes on the posted timetables are incomprehensible unless you speak Czech or have a timetable booklet *(Jízdní řád)* that explains them in English. The clerks at information counters seldom speak good English – see the boxed text 'You're Going Where?' opposite for advice on buying tickets. Alternatively, go to an Internet café and check train (and bus) timetables in English on **W** www.vlak-bus.cz. All train ticket offices in the Czech Republic are computerised and will give you a printout in English with information about your train.

There's no need to book domestic rail travel before arriving in the Czech Republic.

Headaches on the Rails

Overnight trains running the Berlin–Prague, Budapest–Prague and other major routes have experienced some bold thefts from sleeping passengers, so keep a grip on your bags.

Some Czech train conductors may claim there's something wrong with your ticket, usually in the hope of a bribe. Ensure that you have the right ticket for your train and don't pay any 'fine', 'supplement' or 'reservation fee' without a written receipt *(doklad)*. If the conductor won't provide this, you shouldn't pay.

Some conductors may take your ticket and promise to return it later, but don't. A conductor may only hold your ticket if you board a train on which you've reserved a couchette or sleeper, in which case the attendant keeps your ticket overnight so you don't have to be woken up for ticket controls. Don't forget to get it back.

Other Countries

Train travel is the easiest and the most comfortable way to get from Western Europe to the Czech Republic, but it's expensive compared to the bus, and expensive *and* slow compared to budget airlines. In summer you should book at least a few weeks ahead.

Sample returns to Prague include €180 from Paris via Frankfurt (15 hours); £209 from London via Brussels and Berlin (18 hours); €66 from Berlin (five hours); and €85 from Frankfurt (seven hours).

Special fares are available for under-26s through youth travel specialists such as STA Travel (see Air earlier in this chapter).

In the UK, information on train travel to Prague is available through the **Deutsche Bahn UK Booking Centre** *(☎ 0870 243 5363; **W** www.deutschebahn.sagenet.co.uk)*.

In France, book through **SNCF** *(in French ☎ 08 36 35 35 35, in English ☎ 08 36 35 35 39; **W** www.sncf.fr)*, in Germany through **Deutsche Bahn ReiseService** *(☎ 01805 99 66 33; **W** www.bahn.de)*.

Rail Passes

If you plan to travel widely in Europe, the following special tickets and rail passes may be better value for getting into and out of the Czech Republic, but not for travel within it. It is still cheaper to buy local tickets for travelling around the country than to travel with the following passes. Some of these may have different names in different countries.

InterRail Pass This pass gives travellers unlimited 2nd-class travel for up to one month on most of the state railways of Western and Central Europe (except in their own country). The 'Zone D' pass for travel in the Czech Republic, Slovakia, Hungary, Poland and Croatia costs £209 for 22 days (£139 for those aged under 26). If you want to go out of this zone into another then a two-zone pass, valid for a month, costs £265/189.

Czech Flexipass This pass costs from US$48 to US$78 for three to eight days travel in a 15-day period in the Czech Republic. It's available to those aged under 26, ISIC cardholders, teachers and their spouses and children. It can be difficult to buy and many conductors are not familiar with the ticket, so many do not know what to do with it when you present it.

EuroDomino Pass If you don't plan to be on the move all that much, this pass allows a few days per month of unrestricted train travel within a particular country. For example, in the Czech Republic any three/five/eight days in a designated month costs £30/43/63, travelling in 2nd class.

Eurail Pass Eurail passes are not valid for travel in the Czech Republic.

Arriving in Prague by Train

Most international trains arrive at Praha hlavní nádraží (Map 6). A few go to Praha-Holešovice (Map 4) or Praha-Smíchov (Map 9). All have their own metro stations. Masarykovo nádraží (Map 7; metro Náměstí Republiky), two blocks north of the main station, is the primary domestic station.

Praha hlavní nádraží You disembark at Level 3 of Prague's main train station into a swarm of currency-exchange desks, accommodation offices and people offering places to stay. Get your bearings and a map at the helpful **PIS booth** *(open 9am-7pm Mon-Fri, 9am-5pm Sat-Sun)* at the southern end of Level 2.

The original (and mostly abandoned) Art Nouveau station is on Level 4; Levels 3, 2 and 1 are the modern extension beneath Wilsonova třída. You'll find several metro station entrances on Level 2, with taxis outside the northern and southern ends. Public transport information is available from DP (Dopravní podnik; city transport department) beside the metro entrance at the northern end. Level 1 has a 24-hour left-luggage office (*úschovna zavazadel*; 15Kč or 30Kč per bag per day), luggage lockers (two 5Kč coins needed) and a baggage check-in counter.

Try not to arrive in the middle of the night without a hotel booking; the station closes from 12.40am to 3.40am, and the surrounding area is a magnet for pickpockets, crazies and urine-soaked drunks – at night it's a bad place to hang out. Most of the station's currency-exchange and accommodation offices close from about 11pm to 6am. The closest hostel with a night desk is Hostel Jednota, just north of the station, or there's the luxury Hotel Esplanade just a few minutes' walk away (see the Places to Stay chapter).

You're Going Where?

Although most staff at the international ticket counters in Praha hlavní nádraží (Prague's main train station) speak at least some English, those selling domestic tickets rarely do. In order to speed up the process of buying a ticket, and to avoid misunderstandings, it's often easier to write down what you want on a piece of paper and hand it to the clerk.

Write it down like this:

od: departure station, eg, PRAHA
do: destination station
čas: approximate departure time using 24-hour clock, and
datum: date, eg, for 2.30pm on 20 May, write '14.30h. 20/05'.
osoby: number of passengers
jednosměrný (one-way) or *zpáteční* (return)

If you're making a reservation on an EC or IC train, you may also want to specify *1. třídá* or *2. třídá* (1st or 2nd class), and whether you want an *okno* (window) or *chodba* (aisle) seat.

One-way domestic train tickets for distances of more than 50km are valid for 24 hours from time of purchase, but for distances under 50km only until 6am the next day. Note that domestic return *(zpáteční)* tickets (about 10% more expensive than singles) are only valid for 48 hours from time of purchase – if you plan to be away for more than two days, just buy two singles.

Leaving Prague by Train

You can buy international train tickets in advance from train stations or from ČD, GTS International or Čedok travel agencies (see Travel Agencies later). ČD and its agency branches also sell InterRail passes.

At the northern end of Level 3 of Praha hlavní nádraží, there is an English-speaking **Information Desk** *(open 3.15am-12.40am daily)* for international train services. You can buy domestic tickets *(vnitrostátní jízdenky)* at the odd-numbered ticket windows to the left of the platform entrance on Level 2, and international tickets and reservations *(mezínárodní jízdenky a rezervace)* at windows 12, 16, 18, 20, 22 and 24 to the right.

International tickets are valid for two months, with unlimited stopovers. See Other Parts of the Czech Republic earlier in this section for information on ČD services.

The big departures board on Level 2 shows *druh vlaku* (type of train – EC, IC etc), *čislo vlaku* (train number), *cilová stanice* (destination), *směer* (via), *odjezd* (departure time) and *nast* (platform number).

Train timetable information is also available on ☎ 224 22 42 00 and on the Web at W www.cdrail.cz.

CAR & MOTORCYCLE

See Car & Motorcycle in the Getting Around chapter for details about car rental, breakdown support and driving in Prague itself.

Documents

See Visas & Documents in the Facts for the Visitor chapter for information on driving licences. Drivers also need their passport, vehicle registration papers and the 'green card' that shows they carry full liability insurance (see your domestic insurer about this). If the car is not registered in your name, avoid potential headaches by carrying a letter from the owner saying you're allowed to drive it.

You will need to buy a motorway tax coupon *(nálepka),* costing 100/200/800Kč for 10 days/one month/one year for vehicles under 3.5 tonnes, in order to use Czech motorways; failure to display one risks a 5000Kč fine. They are on sale at border crossings, petrol stations and post offices.

Road Rules

As in the rest of Continental Europe, you drive on the right in the Czech Republic. The legal driving age is 18. Don't drink alcohol if you'll be driving – regulations permit no alcohol in the blood, and penalties are severe.

Speed limits vary in built-up areas from 40km/h to 50km/h. On major roads the maximum speed is 90km/h, and on motorways 130km/h (minimum speed limit 80km/h). Although the official speed limit at the country's many rail crossings is 30km/h, it's better to stop and look for oncoming trains, as many well used crossings have no barriers and some don't even have flashing lights.

If the car has seat belts, they must be worn by all passengers. Children aged under 12 are not allowed in the front seat. Each vehicle must be equipped with a first-aid kit and two red-and-white warning triangles (to be set up behind and in front of your car if you break down). You must also display a sticker on the rear indicating the country of registration.

The following laws were introduced in the Czech Republic in January 2001: pedestrians have the right of way at all pedestrian crossings; all vehicles must have their headlights turned on 24 hours a day between November and March; children under 150cm tall or up to 12 years old have to sit in special car seats; and mobile telephones can only be used with a hands-free set.

Riders of motorcycles must wear helmets and goggles, and their passengers must wear helmets. Headlights must be switched on day and night. The maximum speed for motorcycles is 90km/h, and police make a point of booking foreign motorcyclists who keep up with cars on the motorways.

You may not overtake a tram or bus if it is stationary and there is no passenger island. In Prague you may only overtake trams on the right; anywhere else, you can do so on the left if it is not possible on the right.

Driving Offences On-the-spot fines for driving offences can run as high as 2000Kč. Fines for foreigners are commonly inflated; if no docket/receipt *(paragon)* is given, it's possible you're being overcharged, so politely demand one.

Fuel
Petrol or gasoline *(benzín)* is widely available, but not all stations are open on Sunday (nor after 6pm Monday to Friday). Leaded petrol (*special* at 91 octane, *super* at 96 octane), unleaded petrol (*natural* at 95 and 98 octane) and diesel *(nafta)* are stocked by most petrol stations. LPG (liquefied petroleum gas, *autoplyn*) is available in every region, but at a limited number of outlets, and rarely at petrol stations.

See the Getting Around chapter for details about fuel in Prague.

HITCHING
Hitching is never entirely safe in any country in the world, and we don't recommend it. Travellers who decide to hitch should understand that they are taking a small but potentially serious risk. People who do choose to hitch will be safer if they travel in pairs and let someone know where they are planning to go. That said, many Czechs, women included, do hitch and do pick up hitchhikers, and it can be an easy way to get around.

TRAVEL AGENCIES
Following are the contact details of some of the better Prague travel and sales agencies dealing with international travel. For package tours, see Organised Tours at the end of this chapter.

Bohemiatour
Low-overhead Bohemiatour *(Map 6; ☎ 224 94 77 07; W www.bohemiatour.cz; Jungmannova 4, Nové Město; open 9am-6pm Mon-Fri, 9am-noon Sat)* sells international bus tickets, domestic accommodation and package tours.

ČD
The Czech Railways (ČD) travel agency *(☎ 224 21 48 86, international train information ☎ 224 21 79 48; W www.cdrail.cz; open 6am-7.30pm daily)*, outside the southern end of Level 3 at the Praha hlavní nádraží, offers domestic and international train bookings and tickets, and sells rail passes. It also sells bus tickets and youth-price air tickets, and accepts credit cards; there's also a glum, cash-only ČD office down in the main hall.

Čedok
Čedok *(Map 7; ☎ 224 19 71 11, fax 224 21 63 24; W www.cedok.cz; Na příkopě 18, Staré Město; open 9am-6pm Mon-Fri, 10am-3pm Sat)*, the former state tour operator and travel agency, is a good – if rather pricey and very busy – one-stop shop for excursions, and domestic and international travel bookings of all sorts (except the airport office, which is limited to upper-end accommodation and car rental). There are branches at Rytířská 16, Staré Město; Václavské náměstí 53, Nové Město; and at Ruzyně airport.

Representative offices abroad include:

France (☎ 01 44 94 87 50; e cedok@wanadoo.fr) 32 Av de l'Opéra, 75002 Paris
Germany (☎ 030-204 4644, e cedok.berlin@t-online.de) Seydelstrasse 27, 10117 Berlin
UK (☎ 020-7580 3778, e travel@cedok.co.uk) Suite 22-23, 5th floor, Morley House, 314-322 Regent St, London W1B 3BG

CKM Travel
The former state-run youth-travel office, CKM, is now a series of unrelated (but co-operating) private agencies across the country. **CKM Travel Centre** *(Map 6; ☎ 222 72 15 95; e ckmprg@login.cz; Mánesova 77, Vinohrady; open 10am-6pm Mon-Thur, 10am-4pm Fri)*, a short walk from the Náměstí Jiřího z Poděbrad metro station, is a good place for bus tickets, cheap air tickets and budget accommodation, and for youth, student and teacher cards.

Fischer
Fischer *(Map 6; toll-free ☎ 800 12 10 10; W www.fischer.cz; Národní 10, Nové Město)* is a very reliable Czech travel agency that specialises in reasonably priced air fares and tours out of the country. Fischer also has offices in many main towns around the Czech Republic.

GTS International
GTS International *(Map 6; ☎ 222 21 12 04; e gts.smecky@gtsint.cz; Ve Smečkách 33; open 8am-7pm Mon-Fri, 11am-3pm Sat • Map 7; ☎ 224 81 27 70; Lodecká 3; open 9am-6pm Mon-Fri, 10am-2pm Sat)* sells youth and

student cards, Eurolines and Busabout bus tickets, and train and air tickets.

Tourbus

Cheerful Tourbus *(Map 6; ☎ 224 21 02 21, fax 221 89 56 00; W www.tourbuspraha.cz; ÚAN Florenc, Křižíkova 4-6, Karlín; open 8am-8pm Mon-Fri, 9am-8pm Sat)*, upstairs at Florenc bus station, sells domestic and international bus tickets, city travel passes, tours, telephone cards and some accommodation assistance.

ORGANISED TOURS

From the Czech Republic

Čedok offers the widest range of short trips and package tours in the Czech Republic, though generally at the highest prices. Its offices abroad (see Travel Agencies earlier in this chapter) can make arrangements or identify local agencies who sell their packages. Čedok uses a local operator, **Prague Sightseeing Tours** *(☎ 222 31 46 61; W www.pstours.cz)*, for trips around Prague and Central Bohemia.

Prague Sightseeing Tours and **Best Tour** *(☎ 220 87 89 47; W www.besttour.cz)* run several long day trips by coach to the handsome spa town of Karlovy Vary (1390Kč); south to the home of the original Budvar (Budweiser) beer, České Budějovice (1660Kč); and to truly beautiful Český Krumlov (1660Kč), a Unesco World Heritage Site with a castle second only to Prague's. Čedok also offers golf, skiing, cycling, horse riding, fishing and spa holidays, and escorted driving tours around the Czech and Slovak Republics.

WARNING

The information in this chapter is particularly vulnerable to change: prices for international travel are volatile, routes are introduced and cancelled, schedules change, special deals come and go, and rules and visa requirements are amended. You should check directly with the airline or a travel agent to make sure you understand how a fare (and ticket you may buy) works and be aware of the security requirements for international travel.

The upshot of this is that you should get opinions, quotes and advice from as many airlines and travel agents as possible before you part with your hard-earned cash. The details given in this chapter should be regarded as pointers and are not a substitute for your own careful, up-to-date research.

From the UK

Travelsphere Holidays *(☎ 01858 410 818; W www.travelsphere.co.uk; Compass House, Rockingham Rd, Market Harborough, Leicestershire LE16 7QD)* offers seven days in Prague from £219, including return travel by coach, accommodation and breakfast.

A three-day/two-night Prague 'city break' with **Travelscene** *(☎ 0870 777 9987; W www.travelscene.co.uk; 11-15 St Ann's Rd, Harrow, Middlesex HA1 1LQ)*, costs from £260 to £480 depending on the season and quality of accommodation.

Martin Randall Travel *(☎ 020-8742 3355; W www.martinrandall.com; 10 Barley Mow Passage, Chiswick, London W4 4PH)* offers good but pricey cultural tours. Prague-related offerings include five- to six-day art and history tours guided by an art historian from £890, and lecturer-accompanied tours to the Prague Spring festival for around £1390.

From the USA

American-International Homestays *(☎ 303-258 3234; W www.aihtravel.com/homestays; PO Box 1754, Nederland, CO 80466)* organises multi-city homestays in which host families act as de facto guides to their city. The cost is US$100 per day for a single or US$175 per day for a double. The company doesn't do packages and prices each air itinerary separately.

From Australia

An Australian agency that runs tours to Prague is the **Eastern Europe Travel Bureau** *(☎ 02-9262 1144, fax 9262 4479; W www.eetbtravel.com; Level 5, 75 King St, Sydney NSW 2000)*. Packages start at A$300 per person, for three nights, including guided tours. Staff can also book homestays and apartments.

RICHARD NEBESKÝ

A medieval moment off Maltézské náměstí

RICHARD NEBESKÝ

Renaissance splendour: the Letohrádek

JONATHAN SMITH

The Gothic magnificence of Týn church

JONATHAN SMITH
The Loreta: an essay in baroque

MARTIN MOOS
A neo-Renaissance charge at the Národní divadlo

RICHARD NEBESKÝ
Before exploring the Obecní dům, admire *Homage to Prague*, the gorgeous mosaic outside.

NEIL WILSON
One of Czech Cubist Josef Chochol's creations in Vyšehrad

RICHARD NEBESKÝ
Let's dance: the Tančící dům

Getting Around

Prague's compact historic centre (Hradčany, Malá Strana, Staré Město and Nové Město) is best appreciated on foot, with the help of cheap, widespread public transport. Pollution, traffic congestion and traffic-vibration damage to old buildings have led to the creation of pedestrian-only zones, and restrictions on vehicle traffic.

THE AIRPORT

Ruzyně airport is 10km northwest of the city centre.

The arrivals hall and departure hall are next to each other, on the same level. The arrivals hall has exchange counters, ATMs, several accommodation and car-hire agencies, a public-transport information desk, taxi counters, and a 24-hour left-luggage office. The 'Information' windows mainly dispense flight information.

The departure hall has a fast-food place and a bar, an airport information office, airline offices, an exchange counter, and travel agencies including the reputable Fischer (see Travel Agencies in the Getting There & Away chapter).

There's a **post office** *(open 8am-6pm Mon-Fri, 8am-1pm Sat)* in the Administrative Centre across the car park from the arrivals hall.

TO/FROM THE AIRPORT

Public Transport

Buses into the city depart from outside door F in the arrivals hall (look for the 'BUS CENTRUM' sign). Bus No 119 runs about every 10 minutes (every 15 minutes at weekends) from 4.25am to 11.40pm between the airport and Evropská, outside metro station Dejvická at the northwestern end of line A. Bus No 100 runs at least every 30 minutes from 5.45am to 11.35pm to metro station Zličín at the western end of line B. It takes about 45 minutes, including the metro trip, on either route to/from the city centre.

Night bus No 510 runs hourly from 12.39am to 3.39am from the airport (the stop is across the car park from the No 100/119 stop) to Divoká Šárka, from where night tram No 51 continues hourly through the city centre to Želivského bus station.

Bus tickets (adult/child 12/6Kč, additional 6Kč for a rucksack or suitcase) can be bought from the public-transport desk *(open 7am-10pm)* in the arrivals hall, at the newsstand, from machines at the bus stop (coins only, change given), or from the bus driver for 15Kč (exact fare needed). Validate your ticket in the yellow machine on the bus (for validation times see the boxed text 'Ticket-Machine Mysteries' later in this chapter).

Minibus

Čedaz *(☎ 220 11 42 96)* minibuses depart on the hour and half-hour between 5.30am and 9.30pm from náměstí Republiky in the city centre, and on Evropská, near Dejvická metro station. From the airport they depart every 30 minutes between 6am and 9pm from immediately outside the arrivals hall. The fare is 90Kč per person; buy tickets from the driver.

Čedaz also runs minibuses to hotels and private addresses, taxi-style, at 360Kč for one to four people, 720Kč for five to eight.

Taxi

A private taxi company, **Airport Cars** *(Fix Car; ☎ 220 11 38 92)*, with a desk in the terminal, runs fixed-price, officially sanctioned taxis with polite drivers. The fare is 650Kč to Malá Strana (Little Quarter) or Staré Město (Old Town), or higher fixed fares to more distant points. They charge 20% less for the return trip to the airport.

A regular taxi fare to the airport should be around 450Kč from the vicinity of Old Town Square (Staroměstské náměstí) but some unscrupulous taxi drivers can charge much more. They cannot collect passengers at the airport arrivals hall.

PUBLIC TRANSPORT

Big-city transport is rarely a joy to travel on, but Prague's system is cheap, extensive and user-friendly, with detailed information at well marked stops, recorded next-stop information on many buses and trams, and good maps.

Information

The **Dopravní podnik** *(DP, city transport department; ☎ 222 62 37 77; W www.dp-praha.cz)* has information offices in five metro stations: Muzeum and Můstek *(open 7am-9pm)* and Karlovo náměstí, Nádraží Holešovice and Černý Most *(open 7am-6pm Mon-Fri)*, and at Ruzyně airport *(open 7am-10pm daily)*. Here you can get tickets, directions, a multilingual system map, a map of *Noční provoz* (night services), and a guide to the whole system.

PIS (see Tourist Offices in the Facts for the Visitor chapter) has an English-language Transport brochure with much the same information as DP's.

Tickets & Passes

Tickets Tickets are sold from machines at metro stations and major tram stops, at newsstands, Trafiky snack shops, PNS and other tobacco kiosks, hotels, all metro-station ticket offices, and DP information offices. A ticket can also be bought from drivers on bus route Nos 300 to 399 for 15Kč; the exact fare is required.

A *jízdenka* (transfer ticket) for metro, tram, bus or the Petřín funicular (see the Things to See & Do chapter) costs 12/6Kč per adult/child aged six to 15; large luggage and bicycles also need a 6Kč ticket. Kids under six ride for free.

There's also a short-hop 8Kč ticket, valid for 15 minutes on buses and trams, or for up to four metro stations. No transfers, except between metro lines, are allowed with these, and they're not valid on the Petřín funicular nor on night trams or night buses.

On metro trains and newer trams and buses, an electronic display shows the route number and the name of the next stop, and a recorded voice announces each station or stop. As the train, tram or bus pulls away, it says: *Příští stanice,* or *zastávka* – the next station, or stop, is – perhaps noting that it's a *přestupní stanice* (transfer station). At metro stations, signs point you towards the *výstup* (exit) or to a *přestup* (transfer to another line).

Passes Various DP travel passes are good for unlimited travel on the entire system – though you may find they aren't very good value unless you hate walking or are staying outside the centre. Passes are available for periods of 24 hours (70Kč), three (200Kč),

Ticket-Machine Mysteries

It is not uncommon to see tourists staring with incomprehension at the public-transport ticket machines in Prague's hlavní nádraží (main train station). Although there are instructions in English, and the procedure is pretty straightforward (once you know how!), the mass of buttons and Czech words seems to freeze people into helpless uncertainty.

Here's what to do: press the button for the ticket you need – probably the red 12Kč PLNOCENNÁ (full fare) at top left – once for one ticket, twice for two etc. You will then see the price clocking up in the fare window. Put your coins in the slot – as soon as the correct fare (or more) has been inserted, your tickets will be printed, and change given if necessary. If you make a mistake, press the STORNO (cancel) button and start again. That's all there is to it.

Validate (punch) your ticket by sticking it in the little yellow machine at the metro station entrance or on the bus or tram; this stamps the time and date on it. Once validated, 12Kč tickets remain valid for one hour from the time of stamping, if validated between 5am and 8pm Monday to Friday, and for one hour 30 minutes at all other times. Within this time period, unlimited transfers are allowed on all types of public transport.

Being caught without a validated ticket entails a 400Kč on-the-spot fine (but only 50Kč for not having a luggage ticket). Inspectors sometimes demand a higher fine from foreigners and pocket the difference, so insist on a *doklad* (receipt) if this happens to you.

Vintage Trams

At weekends and on holidays between late March and mid-November, vintage tram cars trundle around a special sightseeing route, line No 91. Starting from the muzeum MHD (Public Transport Museum) in Střešovice, they depart hourly from noon to 6pm and loop round via Malostranské náměstí, the Národní divadlo (National Theatre), Wenceslas Square (Václavské náměstí), náměstí Republiky and Štefánikův most to finish at Výstaviště (Exhibition Grounds). Tickets cost 25/10Kč per adult/child. Ordinary tickets and passes cannot be used on this line. Call ☎ 233 34 33 49 for more information.

seven (250Kč) and 15 (280Kč) days. These tickets can be bought at DP information desks, and at many other ticket offices in metro stations. You can also buy 24-hour tickets from vending machines. These must be validated on first use only.

Long-term visitors can get a *měsíční síťová jízdenka* (monthly season pass) valid for one/three/12 months for 420/1150/3800Kč. To get one, bring your passport and a passport-sized photo to **DP headquarters** *(Map 9; Na bojišti 5)*, near metro station IP Pavlova; any DP information office; or any of about half the city's metro stations (ideally up to the 8th or from the 25th of any month).

Prague Card This three-day pass, geared towards tourists, is valid for transport on the whole DP system, plus admission to most of the city's museums and state-run galleries. It costs 560/460Kč per adult/child at PIS offices, Čedok, American Express (AmEx), GTS International, KMC Travel Service and a few other travel agencies (details of these offices can be found in the Facts for the Visitor chapter).

Inspectors Plain-clothes inspectors pounce frequently and will fine you 400Kč on the spot if you don't have a signed pass or validated ticket. They'll flash a metal badge at you – information posters at metro stations and tram stops show what a genuine badge looks like. A dumb-foreigner act rarely cuts any ice with them. At such low prices, cheating is pretty unnecessary in any case.

Tram & Bus

Most trams and buses operate from 4.30am to 12.15am daily. Routes and schedules are posted at each stop. Tram-line numbers have one or two digits, buses have three (suburban bus numbers start with '3').

There is a limited night service (at 40-minute intervals) on certain lines from midnight to 5am: tram Nos 51 to 58 all pass the corner of Lazarská and Spálená (north of Karlovo náměstí; Map 6) so you can transfer from one tram to another, or to any of bus Nos 501 to 512, which connect with the trams here. At stops, night services are indicated by white numbers on a dark background. DP's map, *Noční provoz* (Night Service), is useful.

Metro

Like other Soviet-designed underground systems, Prague's 49-station, 50km network is reliable, efficient and clean. Trains run from 5am to midnight daily. User-friendly maps and diagrams make the system easy to understand for non-Czech-speakers. See the Prague Metro map at the back of the book.

Train

Prague's integrated public-transport system includes travel on 2nd-class trains within Prague for the regular price. There are four other zones around Prague, each with its own fare, and it is possible to get as far as Beroun.

CAR & MOTORCYCLE

Driving in Prague is no fun, especially in the narrow, winding streets of the city centre. Trying to find your way around – or to park legally – while coping with trams, buses, other drivers, cyclists and pedestrians, and police on the lookout for a little handout, can make you wish you'd left the car at home.

You can ease the trauma by avoiding weekday peak-traffic hours: in central

Prague from 4pm onwards (on Friday from as early as 2pm). Try not to arrive in or leave the city on a Friday or Sunday afternoon or evening, when half the population seems to head to/from their *chaty* (weekend houses).

Central Prague has many pedestrian-only streets, including parts of Wenceslas Square (Václavské náměstí), Na příkopě and 28 .října (all Map 6), most of Old Town Square (Map 7) and some streets leading into it. Most are marked with *Pěší zóna* (Pedestrian Zone) signs, and only service vehicles and taxis have special permits to drive in these areas.

PIS' *Transport* brochure has much useful information for drivers, including emergency breakdown services, where to find car-repair shops (according to make) and all-important parking tips. For general information about driving in the Czech Republic, including documents and road rules, see Car & Motorcycle in the Getting There & Away chapter.

Parking

Parking in most of Praha 1 is regulated with permit-only and parking-meter zones. Meter fees are 30Kč or 40Kč per hour, with time limits from two to six hours. Traffic inspectors willingly hand out fines, clamp wheels or tow away vehicles. Parking in one-way streets is normally only allowed on the right-hand side.

There are several car parks at the edges of Staré Město, and Park-and-Ride car parks around the outer city (most are marked on the 1:20,000 GeoClub SHOCart Praha and Žaket city maps), close to metro stations.

Convenient underground car parks include:

Praha hlavní nádraží (Prague's main train station; Map 6) Bolzanova, Wilsonova
Kotva department store (Map 7) náměstí Republiky
Hotel Inter-Continental (Map 7) Pařížská
Státní opera Praha (Prague State Opera; Map 6) Wilsonova
Konstruktiva (Map 7) under náměstí Jana Palacha
Tržnice Smíchov (Map 2) náměstí 14.října, Praha 5

Guarded parking lots include:

Masarykovo train station (Maps 6 and 7) Na Florenci
Náplavka (Map 6) corner of Na Františku and Revoluční
Národní divadlo (National Theatre; Map 6) Divadelní
Hotel Opera (Map 6) Těšnov
Malostranské náměstí (Map 5) Malá Strana

Car Theft

A western car with foreign plates is a prime target for thieves, especially in central Prague, though the chances of theft are no higher than in the West. Older Czech cars are also getting popular, for the domestic spare-parts market, as are smaller items such as windscreen wipers, antennae and car emblems. Of course, don't leave your possessions visible in the vehicle. Car alarms and steering-wheel locking devices are all the rage in Prague; if you're driving your own car in Prague, consider bringing a locking device.

Passing Trams

In Prague you may overtake a tram only on the right, and only if it's in motion. You must stop behind any tram taking on or letting off passengers where there's no passenger island. A tram has the right of way when making any signalled turn across your path. For more road rules, see the Getting There & Away chapter.

Fuel

Leaded and unleaded fuel are available from all Prague petrol stations, and diesel at most of them. There is at least one round-the-clock station on every major highway and road in and out of Prague. LPG (liquefied petroleum gas, *autoplyn*) is mostly not available from petrol stations but only from LPG stations; there is at least one in each suburb.

Emergencies

In case of an accident the police should be contacted immediately if repairs are likely to cost over 20,000Kč or if there is an injury. Even if damage is slight, if you're driving your own car it's a good idea to report the accident, as the police can issue an insurance report that will help you avoid headaches when you take the car out of the country.

For emergency breakdowns, the **ÚAMK** *(Ústřední auto-moto-klub, Czech Automobile and Motorcycle Club; Map 2; ☎ 261 10 43 33; Na strži 9, Nusle, Praha 4)* provides nationwide assistance. Its 24-hour numbers for the so-called 'Yellow Angels' (Žlatý andělé) service are ☎ 1230 and ☎ 261 10 41 11. **Autoturist** *(Map 9; ☎ 224 94 22 06; Na Rybníčku 16)* is a travel agency that promotes ÚAMK and its services.

ÚAMK has agreements with numerous national motoring organisations, the Alliance Internationale de Tourisme and the Fédération Internationale de l'Automobile. If you are a member of any of these, ÚAMK will help you on roughly the same terms as your own organisation would. If not, you must pay for all services.

Another outfit offering round-the-clock repair services nationwide is **Autoklub Bohemia Assistance** *(ABA or Autoklub české republiky; Map 6; ☎ 1240 or ☎ 222 24 12 57; Opletalova 29)*.

Repairs

Spare parts (other than for Škodas) can be hard to find, but most well known models can be repaired at a basic level by at least one garage in Prague. Repair shops for major foreign brands are listed in the PIS *Transport* booklet.

Car Hire

The main international car-hire chains all have airport pick-up points (where you may have to pay an extra 400Kč surcharge) as well as central offices, including:

A-Rent Car/Thrifty (Map 6; ☎ 224 21 15 87) Washingtonova 9
Avis (Map 7; ☎ 221 85 12 25) Klimentská 46
CS-Czechocar (Map 7; ☎ 21 63 74 23/24) Rathova pasáž, Na příkopě 23
Europcar (Map 7; ☎ 224 81 05 15) Pařížská 28
Hertz (Map 9; ☎ 222 23 10 10) Karlovo náměstí 28

A-Rent Car is the cheapest, charging 1684/9666Kč per day/week for a Škoda Felicia, including unlimited mileage, collision-damage waiver and tax. There's a 395Kč surcharge to pick up your vehicle from the airport, but delivery to hotels in central Prague is free. The other major companies are up to 100% more expensive. Most allow one-way rentals to their other locations in the Czech Republic at no additional charge.

Local car-hire companies offer better prices, though their staff may not speak fluent English; even so, it's easy enough to book by email. Typical rates for a Škoda Felicia at the time of writing were 680Kč to 1150Kč per day, or 4600Kč to 6300Kč per week, including VAT, unlimited kilometres, and collision-damage waiver. Some ask for a deposit of 5000Kč if they do not accept credit cards. Reputable local companies include:

Alimex ČR (Map 6; ☎ 800 150 170; e praha@alimexcr.cz) Václavské náměstí
Secco Car (Map 2; ☎ 283 87 10 31; e info@seccocar.cz) Přístavní 39
West Car Praha (Map 2; ☎ 235 36 53 07; e auto@westcarpraha.cz) Veleslavínská 17

TAXI

In 2002 Prague City Council finally cracked down on the city's notoriously dishonest taxi drivers by raising the maximum fine for overcharging to one million Kč. Teams of inspectors disguised as tourists found that around 60% of drivers were overcharging; serious offenders will now have their details posted on the council's Czech-only website *(w www.prague-city.cz)*, as well as being fined and/or having their licences revoked.

Until the reforms take effect, however, hailing a taxi on the street – at least in a tourist zone – still holds the risk of an inflated fare. The taxi stands around Wenceslas Square, Národní třída, Na příkopě, Praha hlavní nádraží, Old Town Square and Malostranské náměstí are the most notorious for rip-off spots; even Czechs are not safe.

You're much better off calling a radiotaxi than flagging one down, as they're better regulated and more responsible. From our experience the following companies, all with 24-hour service, have honest drivers, some of whom speak a little English:

AAA Radio Taxi (☎ 233 11 33 11)
Airport Cars (☎ 220 11 38 92)
Halo Taxi (☎ 244 11 44 11)
ProfiTaxi (☎ 261 31 41 51)

If you hail a taxi in the street, ask the approximate fare in advance and ask the driver to use the meter *(zapněte taximetr, prosím)*. If it's 'broken', find someone else or establish a price before setting off. If you get the rare driver who willingly turns on the meter, he deserves a tip just for that (Czechs usually leave the change).

At the time of writing, the official maximum rate for licensed cabs was 30Kč minimum plus 22Kč per kilometre, or 4Kč per minute while it's stalled in traffic or waits while you enjoy the view. On this basis, any trip within the city centre – say, from Wenceslas Square to Malá Strana – should cost around 100Kč to 150Kč. A trip to the suburbs should not exceed 250Kč, and to the airport 450Kč. Journeys outside Prague are not regulated.

Regulations say the meter must be at zero when you get in, and fares must be displayed. At the end of the journey the driver must give you a meter-printed receipt showing company name, taxi ID number, date and times of the journey, end points, rates, the total, the driver's name and his signature. Get one before you pay, and make sure it has all these things in case you want to make a claim.

There's no telephone number you can use for complaints. Instead, send the receipt, or the cab's licence number (displayed on the outside of the doors), to Prague City Hall, Marianské náměstí 2, 110 01 Praha 1. You won't get a refund, but hopefully the council will nail the driver.

BICYCLE

Prague is not a brilliant place to ride a bike. Traffic is heavy, exhaust fumes can be choking and there are no bicycle lanes. The cobblestones in older streets will loosen your teeth, and tram tracks are treacherous, especially when wet.

You'll need a good lock for wheels and frame: bikes are a popular target. Spare parts are available in the city's many bike shops and in larger and smaller towns.

According to a new law for cyclists, bikes have to be equipped with a bell, front and rear brakes as well as mudguards, a front white reflector, a rear red reflector, a proper front white light, a flashing rear light, and reflectors on pedals – if not, a cyclist can be fined up to 1000Kč. Cyclists up to the age of 15 have to wear helmets.

If you're aged at least 12 you can take your bicycle on the metro. You must keep it near the last door of the rear carriage, and only two bikes are allowed in. You can't do it at any time when the carriage is full, nor if there's already a pram in the carriage.

Bicycle Hire

The only regular place that rents out bicycles to the public is **City Bike** *(Map 7; mobile ☎ 776 180 284; Královdvorská 5; metro Náměstí Republiky; open 9am-7pm)*. This friendly, English-speaking bunch offer two-hour, guided group rides for 500Kč per person, or you can hire a bike and go exploring on your own for 500Kč per four hours.

Resources

The UK's **Cyclists' Touring Club** *(CTC; ☎ 0870-873 0060; W www.ctc.org.uk; Cotterell House, 69 Meadrow, Godalming GU7 3HS)* publishes a free information pack (for members only) on cycling in the Czech and Slovak Republics. CTC also offers tips on bikes, spares, insurance etc, and can put you in touch with others who have cycled there.

BOAT

From April to October, weather and water levels permitting, Pražská paroplavební společnost *(PPS, Prague Passenger Shipping; ☎ 224 93 00 17; W www.paroplavba.cz; Rašínovo nábřeží 2; metro Karlovo Náměstí)* runs cruise boats up and down the Vltava River. Boats depart from the central quay on Rašínovo nábrežié (Map 9).

Most photogenic is a two-hour jaunt north to Štvanice island and then south to Vyšehrad, departing at 3.30pm daily from April to October (250Kč). On Wednesday, Friday, Saturday and Sunday from May to August, this cruise is served by the historic steamer *Vltava* (350Kč).

A one-hour cruise between the Národní divadlo and Vyšehrad costs 150Kč and departs hourly from 10am to 8pm May to September, 10am to 6pm in April, and noon to 6pm in October.

At 9am on Fridays, Saturdays, Sundays and holidays from May to August, a boat goes 37km south (upstream) through a wild, green landscape to Třebrenice at the Slapy dam. This fine, all-day escape costs 250Kč, arriving back in the city at 6.30pm.

Boats heading downstream to the Troja landing (near the zoo and Trojský zámek, Troja chateau; 60Kč one way, one hour 15 minutes) depart at 8.30am (May and June only), 9.30am, 12.30pm and 3.30pm daily from May to August, and at weekends and holidays in September and October. Returning boats depart Troja at 11am, 2pm and 5pm.

Other more expensive trips go up and down the river while you lunch, snack, dine and dance to disco or country-and-western music.

There are also 50-minute cruises (200Kč) from the PPS landing in Kampa, next to Charles Bridge (Karlův most), with departures hourly from 11am to 8pm June to September; 11am to 6pm in May; and noon to 5pm in March, April and October to December.

Boat trips with **Evropská vodní doprava** *(EVD; Map 7; ☎ 224 81 00 30; Ⓦ www.evd.cz)*, which leave from the quay beside Čechův most (near the Hotel Inter-Continental), include a one-hour cruise departing hourly from 10am to 6pm (200Kč); a two-hour cruise including lunch and music, departing at noon (590Kč); and a three-hour evening cruise with dinner and music (690Kč). All run year-round.

Prague Venice *(Map 7; ☎ 603 819 947; Křížovnické náměestí 3 • Map 5; Čertovka, Kampa island, Malá Strana)* operates 30-minute cruises (270Kč per person including drink) in small boats, under the hidden arches of Charles Bridge, and along Čertovka (Devil's Stream) in Kampa. They run from 10.30am to 11pm daily July and August and from 10.30am to 8pm daily March to June, September and October.

Boat Hire

If you just want a quiet float on the river, rent a rowing boat (about 40Kč per hour) or pedal-boat (50Kč per hour) from one of three places on the northern end of Slovanský ostrov (Map 6); or from another just south of Mánesův most in Staré Město (Map 7). You can hire a paddle boat for 100Kč per hour at the back of the muzeum Bedřicha Smetany (Smetana Museum) on Novotného lávka (Map 7), just south of Charles Bridge.

ORGANISED TOURS

Pragotur (see the following Guides section) and various private companies operating from kiosks along Na příkopě (Map 7) offer three-hour city bus tours for 560Kč per person. These are fine if your time is very short, but the castle and other major sights get so crowded that you can't enjoy the tour, or even hear your guide.

Guides

Pragotur *(☎ 224 48 25 62, fax 224 48 23 80; ⓔ guides.pis@volny.cz; Staroměstské náměstí 1; open 9am-6pm Mon-Fri, by phone from 8am, 9am-4pm Sat-Sun)*, an affiliate of PIS, can arrange personal guides fluent in all major European languages. Rates for a three-hour tour are 1000Kč for one person, or 1200Kč for two people plus 300Kč for each additional person. Their desk is in the PIS office in the Staroměstská radnice (Old Town Hall).

Walking Tours

The corner of Old Town Square, outside the Staroměstská radnice is usually clogged with dozens of people touting for business as walking guides. Quality varies.

Among the better offerings are those from **City Walks** *(mobile ☎ 608 200 912; Ⓦ www.praguewalkingtours.com)* and **Prague Walks** *(☎ 261 21 46 03; Ⓦ www.praguewalks.com)*, both of whom offer guided walks lasting from one hour 30 minutes to four hours on themes ranging from 'Mysterious Prague' to Prague pubs to the Velvet Revolution. Most walks begin at the Astronomical Clock *(orloj)*; prices range from 300Kč to 450Kč per person.

Travellers have recommended **Praguemaster** *(☎ 607 820 158)*, who offer a five-hour 'Total Prague' walk for 750Kč (650Kč for students), including lunch and tram tickets (9.30am daily from Křížovnické náměstí, at the eastern end of Charles Bridge; Map 7); and a two-hour 'Iron Curtain' tour (300/250Kč) starting at 2pm on Tuesday, Thursday and Saturday from the fountain in front of the Národní muzeum (National Museum; Map 6).

Vintage-Car Tours

A couple of businesses offer tours around the city in genuine vintage Czech cars dating from the late 1920s and early 1930s. A one-hour tour with **Old Timer History Trip** *(mobile ☎ 602 236 488; W www.historytrip.cz)* costs 900Kč for one or two people, or 1300Kč for three or four people. A similar tour with **3 Old Timers** *(☎ 608 519 333; W www.3oldtimers.com)* costs 1150Kč for up to three passengers. Both have pick-up points on Staroměstské náměstí and Malé náměstí (both Map 7). There's no need to book ahead – just turn up at the starting point, and look for the cars; if there's none around, call to find out when the next tour is available.

Jewish-Interest Tours

Precious Legacy Tours *(Map 7; ☎/fax 222 32 03 98; W www.legacytours.cz; Maiselova 16)* offers guided tours of places of interest to Jewish visitors, including a three-hour walking tour of Prague's Josefov district (US$16 per person), and a six-hour excursion to Terezín (US$27 per person). All revenue goes towards supporting the activities of Prague's small Jewish community, including social work and the reconstruction of property returned after 1989.

Readers have also recommended **Wittmann Tours** *(Map 6; ☎ 222 25 24 72; W www.wittmann-tours.com; Mánesova 8)*, whose guided walks of Josefov (600/460Kč adult/child) depart from the square in front of the Hotel Inter-Continental on Pařížska at 10.30am and 2pm daily May to October, and at 10.30am Sunday to Friday mid-March to April, November and December.

Excursions

Pragotur and the kiosks along Na příkopě run half- and full-day coach excursions from Prague to Konopiště (790Kč), Karlštejn (750Kč) and Kutná Hora (820Kč).

Central European Adventures *(Map 7; ☎ 222 32 88 79; e cea@seznam.cz; Jáchymova 4)* offers one-day guided bicycle tours around Karlštejn and Koněprusy (680Kč; Tuesday to Sunday from April to September) and guided canoe tours on the Berounka River (810Kč; Saturday and Sunday May to September). Buy tickets at PIS offices or Ticketpro (see Buying Tickets in the Entertainment chapter) and meet by the Astronomical Clock on the Old Town Square at 8.30am.

Things to See & Do

Prague's prime attraction is its physical face. The city centre is a haphazard museum of some 900 years of architecture – stodgy Romanesque, sublime Gothic, handsome Renaissance, dazzling Baroque, 19th-century revivals of all of them, mouthwatering Art Nouveau, and linear Cubism – all amazingly undisturbed by the modern day and folded into a compact network of lanes, passages and cul-de-sacs.

Also on offer is a heady menu of entertainment: classical music, from world-class festivals to tourist concerts in every other church; opera and ballet; avant-garde drama; jazz and rock; a few excellent museums; and dozens of art galleries. There are some good restaurants, and plenty of ordinary ones full of good cheer and world-famous Czech beer. Within reach as day trips are a dozen medieval castles and Baroque chateaux.

Prague's greatest distraction is that it's now one of Europe's most popular tourist destinations, and consequently becomes choked with summer crowds.

HIGHLIGHTS

The historical core of the city – Hradčany (Castle District) and Malá Strana (Little Quarter) west of the river, Staré Město (Old Town) and Wenceslas Square (Václavské náměstí) to the east, with Charles Bridge (Karlův most) in between – covers only about 3 sq km and is pedestrian-friendly, so you can see a lot even on a short visit.

Concerts

The finest places to enjoy a classical concert are the Dvořák Hall in the Rudolfinum, and the Smetana Hall in the Obecni dům (Municipal House). In summer, chamber concerts are held in many halls and churches; equally impressive are organ recitals, for which kostel sv Jakub (St James Church) is said to have the best acoustics.

Museums & Galleries

If you like museums, don't miss the muzeum hlavního města Prahy (Prague City Museum) in northern Nové Město (New Town), and the Národní Technické muzeum (National Technology Museum) in Holešovice. The best of the National Gallery's permanent collections are of 19th- and 20th-century Czech art and early-20th-century European art at the Veletržní palác in Holešovice; of Gothic art at the klášter sv Anežky (Convent of St Agnes) in Staré Město; of Renaissance art at the klášter sv Jiří (Convent of St George) in Prague Castle (Pražský hrad); and of 20th-century art at the dům u zlatého prstenu (House at the Golden Ring) in Staré Město.

Architectural Highlights

The city's finest Romanesque structure is the bazilika sv Jiří (Basilica of St George). The choir of chrám sv Víta (St Vitus Cathedral), one of Europe's finest churches, is the clear winner in the Gothic category. The Letohrádek (Summer Palace) at Hradčany (see the special section 'Prague Castle') is certainly the finest Renaissance building.

Of Prague's many Baroque masterpieces, one of the most elegant is the almost rococo facade of the palác Kinských (Kinský Palace) on Old Town Square (Staroměstské náměstí), while kostel sv Mikuláše (St Nicholas Church) in Malá Strana draws fans of Baroque from all over Europe.

The city has a high concentration of superb Art Nouveau buildings; top of the list, inside and out, is the Obecní dům. And there are more Cubist buildings here than in any other city in the world. Some of the most striking Cubist facades are at dům U černé Matky Boží (House of the Black Madonna) in Staré Město; at Neklanova 30 near Vyšehrad; and at Tychonova 4–6 in Dejvice.

Rising above Prague's mostly humdrum modern architecture is the extraordinary (and controversial) Dancing Building in Nové Město.

SUGGESTED ITINERARIES

If you're on a weekend break, a walk along the Královská cesta (Royal Way) – the route of ancient coronation processions – takes in the best of the city's architectural treasures, ending at Prague Castle and chrám sv Víta. On a longer stay, devote a day to exploring the sights along each of the four walks described later in this chapter.

Hradčany (Map 5)

Hradčany is the residential area stretching west from Prague Castle to the Strahovský klašter (Strahov Monastery), made a town in its own right in 1320. It twice suffered heavy damage – in the Hussite wars and in the Great Fire of 1541 – before becoming a borough of Prague in 1598. After this, the Habsburg nobility built many palaces here in the hope of cementing their power at Prague Castle.

HRADČANSKÉ NÁMĚSTÍ

Hradčanské náměstí has kept its shape since the Middle Ages. At its centre is a plague column by Ferdinand Brokoff (1726). Several former canons' residences (Nos 6 to 12) have richly decorated facades.

The **Švarcenberský palác** (Schwarzenberg Palace) sports a sgraffito facade as startling as a Hawaiian shirt. The Schwarzenbergs acquired it in 1719. Inside is a **Vojenské historické muzeum** *(Museum of Military History; closed at time of writing for renovations)* and an adjacent room full of miscellaneous 'antiquities', including a big collection of tin soldiers.

Opposite is the rococo **Arcibiskupský palác** *(Archbishop's Palace; open only on the day before Good Friday)*, bought and remodelled by Archbishop Antonín Bruse of Mohelnice in 1562, and the seat of archbishops ever since. It has a wonderful interior, including a chapel with frescoes by Daniel Alexius (1600).

Behind the Arcibiskupský palác is the Baroque **Šternberský palác** *(Sternberg Palace; ☎ 220 51 45 99; adult/child 60/30Kč; open 10am-6pm Tues-Sun)*, home to the National Gallery's valuable collection of 14th- to 18th-century European art, including works by Goya and Rembrandt.

LORETÁNSKÉ NÁMĚSTÍ

From Hradčanské náměstí it's a short walk west to Loretánské náměstí, created early in the 18th century when the **Černínský palác** (Černín Palace; see the boxed text 'Prague under the Nazis') was built. At the northern end of the square is the **klášter kapucínů** (Capuchin Monastery; 1600–02), Bohemia's oldest working monastery.

Loreta

The square's main attraction is the Loreta *(adult/child 80/60Kč; open 9am-12.15pm & 1pm-4.30pm Tues-Sun)*, an extraordinary Baroque place of pilgrimage founded by Benigna Kateřina Lobkowicz in 1626, designed as a replica of the supposed house of the Santa Casa (Virgin Mary). Legend says that the original Santa Casa was carried by angels to the Italian town of Loreto as the Turks were advancing on Nazareth. The duplicate **Santa Casa**, with fragments of its original frescoes, is in the centre of the courtyard.

Behind the Santa Casa is the **kostel Narození Páně** (Church of the Nativity of Our Lord), built in 1737 to a design by Kristof Dientzenhofer. The claustrophobic interior includes two skeletons – of the Spanish saints Felicissima and Marcia – dressed in nobles' clothing with wax masks over their skulls.

At the corner of the courtyard there is the startling **kaple Panny Marie Bolestné** (Chapel of Our Lady of Sorrows), featuring a crucified bearded lady. She was St Starosta, pious daughter of a Portuguese king who promised her to the king of Sicily against her wishes. After a night of tearful prayers she awoke with a beard, the wedding was called off, and her father had her crucified. She was later made patron saint of the needy and godforsaken.

The most eye-popping attraction is the **treasury** on the first floor. It's been ransacked several times over the centuries, but some amazing items remain. Most over-the-top is a 90cm-tall monstrance called the **Pražské slunce** (Prague Sun), made of solid silver and gold and studded with 6222 diamonds.

Above the Loreta's entrance 27 bells, made in Amsterdam in the 17th century, play *We Greet Thee a Thousand Times* every hour.

Prague under the Nazis

From March 1939 to May 1945 Prague was capital of the Nazi Protectorate of Bohemia and Moravia. Many city landmarks that look innocuous to the visiting tourist still serve as unpleasant reminders of the Nazi occupation; most of them have a memorial of some sort.

Černínský palác *(Černin Palace; Map 5; Loretánské náměstí; closed to the public)* The Baroque 18th-century palace facing the Loreta served as the SS headquarters from 1939 to 1945. It now houses the Czech foreign ministry.

Pečkův palác *(Peček Palace; Map 6; Politických vězňů 20; closed to the public)* This gloomy neo-Renaissance palace served as the wartime headquarters of the Gestapo. A memorial on the corner of the building honours the many Czechs who were tortured and executed in the basement detention cells. Today it is home to the Ministry of Trade and Industry.

Věznice Pankrác *(Pankrác Prison; Map 2; Táborská 988; closed to the public)* During WWII, the Nazis used Prague's notorious Věznice Pankrác as a place of incarceration, interrogation, torture and execution. A guillotine installed in 1943 had claimed the lives of 1075 people by the end of the war. The prison, southeast of Vyšehrad, remains in use today as a state prison – grim and overcrowded.

Památník protifašistického odboje v Kobylisích *(Kobylisy Anti-Fascist Resistance Memorial; Žernosecká; admission free; open 24hr)* This grassy quadrangle of earthen embankments, ringed by trees and overlooked by modern apartment blocks, was once the Kobylisy Rifle Range. More than a hundred Czechs were executed here by firing squads during WWII. Today it is the site of a national memorial; a huge bronze plaque lists all the names of the dead, and – such was Nazi bureaucracy – the dates and times of their executions. Take tram No 10, 17 or 24 to the terminal at Ďáblická, then walk west for 10 minutes along Žernosecká.

V Holešovičkách The spot in the suburb of Libeň (Map 2) where Reichsprotektor SS Obergruppenführer Reinhard Heydrich was assassinated (see the boxed text 'The Assassination of Heydrich' in the Facts about Prague chapter) has changed considerably since 1942 – the tram tracks have gone and a modern road intersection has been built – but is still just about recognisable from old photos. It's where the slip road exits north from V Holešovičkách to Zenklova. The neighbouring streets, Gabčíkova and Kubišova, are named after the parachutists who carried out the attack. Take tram No 10 or 24 to the Zenklova stop and walk south for a few minutes.

Národní památník obětí heydrichiády *(National Memorial to the Victims of Post-Heydrich Terror; Map 9; cnr Resslova & Na Zderaze; adult/child 30/20Kč; open 10am-5pm Tues-Sun Apr-Oct, 10am-4pm Tues-Sun Nov-Mar)* In 1942 seven Czech paratroopers involved in the assassination of Heydrich holed up in the crypt of the Church of SS Cyril and Methodius in Nové Město (see later in this chapter for more on the church) for three weeks after the killing, until they were betrayed by the Czech traitor Karel Čurda. The Germans besieged the church, first attempting to smoke the paratroopers out and then flooding it with fire hoses. Three were killed in the ensuing fight; the other four took their own lives rather than surrender. The crypt now houses the moving national memorial to the men with an exhibit and video about Nazi persecution of the Czechs. In the crypt itself you can still see the bullet marks and shrapnel scars on the walls, and signs of the paratroopers' last desperate efforts to dig an escape tunnel to the sewer under the street. On the Resslova side of the church, the narrow gap in the wall of the crypt is still pitted with bullet marks.

Photography is not allowed, and the rule is enforced with a 1000Kč fine.

STRAHOVSKÝ KLÁŠTER

Strahovský klašter (Strahov Monastery) was founded in 1140 by Vladislav II for the Premonstratensian order. The present monastery buildings, completed in the 17th and 18th centuries, functioned until the communist government closed them down and imprisoned most of the monks, who have only recently returned.

Inside is the 1612 **kostel sv Rocha** (Church of St Roch), now an exhibition hall. The **kostel Nanebevzetí Panny Marie** (Church of the Assumption of Our Lady) was built in 1143, and heavily decorated in the 18th century in Baroque style. Mozart is said to have played the organ here.

The monastery's biggest attraction is the **Strahovská knihovna** *(Strahov Library; ☎ 220 51 66 71; Strahovské nádvoří 1; adult/child 50/30Kč; open 9am-noon & 1pm-5pm daily)*, the largest monastic library in the country. You can look through the door, but you cannot go into the two-storey Filozofický sál (Philosophy Hall), with its carved floor-to-ceiling shelves lined with beautiful old tomes. Covering the ceiling is the *Struggle of Mankind to Gain Real Wisdom,* a fresco by Franz Maulbertsch. Down the hall is the Theology Hall, with a ceiling fresco by Siard Nosecký. At the entrance is a tiny exhibit of miniature books that forms part of the national **Museum of Czech Literature** *(adult/child 30/15Kč; open 9am-5pm Tues-Sun)*.

In the second courtyard is the **Strahovská obrazárna** *(Strahov Picture Gallery; adult/ child 35/20Kč; open 9am-noon & 12.30pm-5pm Tues-Sun)*, with a valuable collection of Gothic, Baroque, rococo and Romantic monastery art on the first floor, and temporary exhibits on the ground floor.

Malá Strana (Map 5)

Malá Strana (Little Quarter) clusters around the foot of Prague Castle. Most tourists climb up to the castle along part of the Královská cesta (Royal Way), on Mostecká and Nerudova, but the narrow side streets of this Baroque district also have plenty of interest. Almost too picturesque for its own good, Malá Strana is now much in demand as a filming location.

Malá Strana began as a market settlement in the 8th or 9th century. In 1257 Přemysl Otakar II granted it town status. The district was almost destroyed on two occasions: during battles between Hussites and the Prague Castle garrison in 1419, and in the Great Fire of 1541. Renaissance buildings and palaces replaced the destroyed houses, followed in the 17th and 18th centuries by the Baroque churches and palaces that give Malá Strana its present charm.

NERUDOVA ULICE

Nerudova, part of the Královská cesta, is architecturally the quarter's most important street; most of its old Renaissance facades were later 'Baroquefied'.

Heading downhill from the castle via Ke Hradu, you first come to the **dům U dvou slunců** *(House of the Two Suns; Nerudova 47)*, an early Baroque building where the Czech poet Jan Neruda lived from 1845 to 1891. The **dům U zlaté podkovy** *(House of the Golden Horseshoe; Nerudova 34)* is named after the relief above the doorway of sv Václav (St Wenceslas), whose horse was said to be shod with gold.

The first pharmacy in Hradčany opened next door in 1749, and houses the **Expozice Historických lékáren** *(Museum of Historical Pharmacies; adult/child 20/5Kč; open noon-6pm Tues-Fri, 10am-6pm Sat-Sun)* with a small collection of pharmaceutical paraphernalia and original furnishings from the 19th century.

From 1765 Josef of Bretfeld made his **Bretfeld Palace** *(Nerudova 33)* a centre for social gatherings, with guests such as Mozart and Casanova. The Baroque **kostel Panny Marie ustavičné pomoci** *(Church of Our Lady of Unceasing Succour; Nerudova 24)* was a theatre (divadlo U Kajetánů) from 1834 to 1837, and staged Czech plays during the Czech National Revival.

Most houses bear emblems of some kind. Built in 1566, **St John of Nepomuk** *(Neru-*

dova 18) is named after the patron saint of the Czechs, whose image was added in about 1730. The **dům U tří housliček** *(House of the Three Fiddles; Nerudova 12)*, a Gothic building rebuilt in Renaissance style in the 17th century, once belonged to a family of violin makers.

MALOSTRANSKÉ NÁMĚSTÍ

Kostel sv Mikuláše (St Nicholas Church), Malá Strana's primary landmark, divides Malostranské náměstí into an upper and lower square. The square has been the hub of Malá Strana since the 10th century, though it lost some of its character when Karmelitská was widened early in the 20th century. Today it's a mixture of official buildings and touristy restaurants, with a tram line through the middle of the lower square.

The Malostranská beseda nightclub and restaurant at No 21 was once the old town hall. Here in 1575 non-Catholic nobles wrote the so-called *České konfese* (Czech Confession), a pioneering demand for religious tolerance addressed to the Habsburg emperor and eventually passed into Czech law by Rudolf II in 1609. On 22 May 1618 Czech nobles gathered at the **Smiřický Palace** *(Nerudova 18)*; the next day they flung two Habsburg councillors out of a window in Prague Castle, setting off the Thirty Years' War.

Kostel sv Mikuláše

Malá Strana is dominated by the huge green cupola of kostel sv Mikuláše *(St Nicholas Church; adult/child 45/20Kč; church open 9am-4pm daily; bell tower 10am-6pm daily Apr-Oct, 10am-5pm Sat-Sun Nov-Mar)*, one of Central Europe's finest Baroque buildings. (Don't confuse it with the other kostel sv Mikuláše on Old Town Square.) It was begun by Kristof Dientzenhofer; his son Kilian continued the work and Anselmo Lurago finished the job in 1755.

On the ceiling, Johann Kracker's 1770 *Life of St Nicholas* is Europe's largest fresco. In the first chapel on the left is a mural by Karel Škréta, which includes the church official who kept track of the artist as he worked; he is looking out through a window in the upper corner.

NORTHERN MALÁ STRANA

From the northern side of Malostranské náměstí, Thunovská and the **Zámecké schody** (Castle Steps) lead up to the castle. At the eastern end of Thunovská, on Sněmovní, is the **Sněmovna** (Czech Parliament House), seat of the lower house of today's parliament, and formerly of the national assembly that deposed the Habsburgs from the Czech throne on 14 November 1918.

Around Valdštejnské Náměstí

This small square to the northeast of Malostranské náměstí is dominated by the **Valdštejnský palác** *(Wallenstein Palace; closed to the public)*, a monumental palace built in 1630 by Albrecht of Wallenstein, generalissimo of the Habsburg armies. It displaced 23 houses, a brickworks and three gardens, and was financed by the confiscation of properties from the Protestant nobles defeated at the Battle of Bílá Hora (White Mountain) in 1620.

The Renaissance and Baroque palace now houses the Senate of the Czech Republic, but you can wander through the courtyard into the enormous **Valdštejnská zahrada** *(Wallenstein Garden; admission free; open 10am-6pm daily Apr-Oct)*. Its finest feature is the huge **loggia** decorated with scenes from the Trojan Wars. The bronze statues of Greek gods that line the avenue opposite the loggia are copies – the originals were carted away by marauding Swedes in 1648 and now stand outside the royal palace of Drottningholm near Stockholm. At the eastern end of the garden is the **Valdštejnská jízdárna** (Wallenstein Riding School), home to changing exhibitions of modern art. There is another entrance to the garden on Letenská.

The **Pedagogické muzeum JA Komenského** *(Pedagogical Museum of JA Comenius; Valdštejnská 20; admission 10Kč; open 10am-12.30pm & 1pm-4.30pm Tues-Sun)* would be tedious if it wasn't for the caretaker's interesting guided tour in English explaining the life and teaching methods of this great 17th-century educator.

East along Valdštejnská is the main entrance to the **Palácové zahrady pod Pražským hradem** *(Palace Gardens Beneath Prague*

Castle; admission 95/40Kč; open 10am-6pm daily). These terraced gardens on the steep southern slope of the castle hill date from the 17th and 18th centuries, when they were created for the owners of the adjoining palaces. They were restored in the 1990s, and contain a Renaissance loggia with frescoes of Pompeii and a Baroque portal with sundial that cleverly catches the sunlight reflected from the water in the triton fountain in front of it.

The quiet **Vojanovy sady** *(Vojan Gardens; open 8am-7pm daily Apr-Oct, 8am-5pm daily Nov-Mar)*, entered from U lužického semináře, is all that remains of Prague's oldest park, established in 1248.

SOUTHERN MALÁ STRANA

The **Vrtbovská zahrada** *(Vrtbov Garden; Tržiště 25; open 10am-6pm daily Apr-Oct)* contains Baroque statues and urns by Matthias Braun and a terrace with good views of Prague Castle and Malá Strana.

The **kostel Panny Marie Vítězné** *(Church of Our Lady Victorious; Karmelitská)*, built in 1613, has on its central altar a waxwork figure of the baby Jesus brought from Spain in 1628. Known as the **Pražské jezulátko** (Infant Jesus of Prague), it is said to have protected Prague from the plague and from the destruction of the Thirty Years' War, and is visited by a steady stream of pilgrims, especially from Italy, Spain and Latin America. An 18th-century German prior, ES Stephano, wrote about the miracles, kicking off what eventually became a worldwide cult. The Infant's wardrobe consists of 60 costumes donated from all over the world, changed in accordance with a religious calendar.

At the back of the church is the **muzeum Pražského Jezulátka** *(Museum of the Infant Jesus of Prague; admission by donation; open 9.30am-9pm Mon-Sat & 1pm-6pm Sun June-Sept, 9.30am-5.30pm Mon-Sat & 1pm-5pm Sun Oct-May)*, displaying a selection from the Infant's wardrobe. A visit here makes you think about the Second Commandment ('Thou shalt not make unto thee any graven image…') and the Reformation. Jan Hus must be spinning in his grave.

Around Maltézské Náměstí

This quiet square takes its name from the knights of Malta, who in 1169 established a monastery beside the austere, early-Gothic towers of the **kostel Panny Marie pod řetězem** (Church of Our Lady Below the Chain).

South of the church is Velkopřevorské náměstí and the French embassy, opposite which is the **John Lennon Wall**. Before 1989, when most Western pop music was banned by the communists – some Czech musicians were jailed for playing it – the wall was a political focus for Prague youth. After his murder on 8 December 1980, John Lennon became a pacifist hero for many young Czechs. An image of Lennon was painted on the wall, along with political grafitti and Beatles lyrics; the secret police never managed to keep it clean for long. Post-1989 weathering and lightweight graffiti ate away at the political messages and images, until little remained of Lennon but his eyes. The wall was whitewashed in 1998 but was soon covered in more inconsequential graffiti, including various inferior likenesses of Lennon.

Kampa

An 'island' separated from the mainland by the Čertovka (Devil's Stream), Kampa is the most peaceful and picturesque part of Malá Strana. In the 13th century the town's first mill, the Sovovský mlýn, was built on Čertovka, and other mills followed. Kampa was once used as farmland, but the island was settled in the 16th century after being raised above flood level. In 1939 the river was so low that it was again joined to the mainland, and many coins and items of jewellery were found in the dry channel.

The area along the stream and under Charles Bridge is sometimes called 'Prague's Venice' (see Boat in the Getting Around chapter). Cafés beckon from Na Kampě square, south of the bridge, though the summer sun is ferocious here. The southern part of Kampa is a wooded park with views across to Staré Město.

Around Újezd

Near the southern end of Kampa lies one of Malá Strana's oldest Gothic buildings, the

kostel sv Jana Na prádle (Church of St John at the Laundry), built in 1142 as a local parish church. Inside are the remains of 14th-century frescoes.

Around the corner is the **Pop Museum** *(Besední 3; admission 30Kč; open 2pm-6pm Fri-Sun)*, with plenty of photos, old record covers, TV screens playing Czech 60s and 70s hits and a good collection of electric guitars. Unfortunately, all labels are in Czech but on the stage there are some guitars, keyboards and drums available for anyone to test their playing ability.

Střelecký Ostrov

Střelecký Ostrov (Marksmen's Island), to the south of Kampa, is crossed by the Legií most (Legion Bridge). Its name originates in its use in the 16th century as a cannon and rifle target for the Prague garrison. Prague students celebrate their annual Majáles festival here in early May (for details see the boxed text 'Majáles' in the Facts for the Visitor chapter), and during summer it has an open-air cinema and concert venue.

PETŘÍN

This 318m hill, called simply Petřín by Czechs, is one of Prague's largest single green spaces. It's great for cool, quiet walks and fine views over the 'city of 100 spires'. There were once vineyards here, and a quarry that provided the stone for most of Prague's Romanesque and Gothic buildings.

Petřín is easily accessible from Hradčany and Strahov, or you can ride the **lanová dráha** (funicular railway) from Újezd up to the top. The funicular uses ordinary city transit tickets and passes – remember to validate your ticket at the bottom station. It runs every 10 to 20 minutes from 9.15am to 8.45pm. You can also get off two-thirds of the way up at Restaurant Nebozízek.

Just south of the top station is **Štefánikova hvězdárna** *(Štefánik Observatory; ☎ 257 32 05 40; adult/child 30/20Kč; open 2pm-7pm & 9pm-11pm Tues-Fri; 10am-noon, 2pm-7pm & 9pm-11pm Sat-Sun Apr-Aug; 7pm-9pm Mon-Fri, 10am-noon, 2pm-6pm & 7pm-9pm Sat-Sun Mar, Sept & Oct; 6pm-8pm Mon-Fri, 10am-noon & 2pm-8pm Sat-Sun Nov-Feb)*, a 'people's observatory' where you can view the stars on clear nights, or look at photos and old instruments.

To the north is **Petřínská rozhledna** *(Petřín Tower; adult/child 40/30Kč; open 10am-7pm daily Apr-Oct)*, a 62m Eiffel Tower lookalike built in 1891 for the Prague Exposition. You can climb its 299 steps for some of the best views of Prague; on clear days you can see the forests of Central Bohemia.

On the way to the tower you cross the **Hladová zeď** (Hunger Wall), running from Újezd to Strahov. These fortifications were built in 1362 under Charles IV, and are so named because they were built by the poor of the city in return for food – an early job creation scheme.

Below the tower is the **Bludiště** *(Maze; adult/child 40/30Kč; open 10am-10pm daily Apr-Aug, 10am-6pm daily Sept-Oct, 10am-5pm Sat-Sun Nov-Mar)*, also built for the 1891 Prague Exposition. Inside is a mirror maze that's good for a laugh, as well as a diorama of the 1648 battle between Praguers and Swedes on Charles Bridge. Opposite is the **kostel sv Vavřince** (Church of St Lawrence), which contains a ceiling fresco depicting the founding of the church in 991 at a pagan site with a sacred flame.

In the peaceful **Kinského zahrada** (Kinský Garden), on the southern side of Petřín, is the 18th-century wooden **kostel sv Michala** (Church of St Michael), transferred here, log by log, from the village of Medveďov in Ukraine. Such structures are rare in Bohemia, though still common in Ukraine and north-eastern Slovakia.

Staré Město

By the 10th century a settlement and marketplace existed on Vltava River's eastern bank. In the 12th century this was linked to the castle district by the forerunner of the Charles Bridge, and in 1231 Wenceslas I honoured it with a town charter and the start of a fortification. This 'Old Town' – Staré Město – has since been Prague's working heart. The town walls are long gone, but their route is traced by Národní, Na příkopě and Revoluční.

Staré Město shared in the boom when Charles IV gave Prague a Gothic face befitting its new status as capital of the Holy Roman Empire. Charles founded the Karolinum in Staré Město in 1348, and began Charles Bridge in 1357. When Emperor Joseph II united Prague's towns into a single city in 1784, Staroměstská radnice (Old Town Hall) became its seat of government.

Many of Staré Město's buildings have Gothic interiors and Romanesque basements. To ease the devastation of frequent flooding by the Vltava River, the level of the town was gradually raised, beginning in the 13th century, with new construction simply rising on top of older foundations. You can see an example of this at Můstek metro station (corner of Na můstku and Na příkopě). Go down the stairs, and as you enter the station – on the left just before the escalators – there are some of the arches of the stone bridge that once spanned the moat. A huge fire in 1689 contributed to an orgy of rebuilding during the Catholic Counter-Reformation of the 17th and 18th centuries, giving the formerly Gothic district a heavily Baroque face.

The only intrusions into Staré Město's medieval layout have been the appropriation of a huge block in the west for the Jesuits' massive college, the Klementinum, in the 16th and 17th centuries, and the 'slum clearance' of Josefov, the Jewish quarter, at the end of the 19th century.

At the centre of everything is Old Town Square. If the maze of alleys around it can be said to have an 'artery', it's the so-called Královská cesta (Royal Way), the ancient coronation route to Prague Castle. In this part of the city, it runs from the Prašná brána (Powder Gate), along Celetná to Old Town Square and Malé náměstí, then along Karlova and over Charles Bridge.

OLD TOWN SQUARE (STAROMĚSTSKÉ NÁMĚSTÍ; MAP 7)

Old Town Square (Staroměstské náměstí or Staromák) is one of Europe's biggest and most beautiful public spaces. It has been Prague's heart since the 10th century, and was its main marketplace until the beginning of the 20th century.

Despite the over-the-top commercialism and crowds of tourists that swarm around the square, it's impossible not to enjoy the place – the cafés spilling onto the pavement, the omnipresent buskers and performing dogs, and the horse-drawn beer wagons. There's also alfresco concerts, political meetings, and even fashion shows. Its pastel gingerbread Baroque and neo-Renaissance facades reveal nothing of the crumbling interiors, and there's hardly a hint of the harrowing history that the square has witnessed (see the boxed text 'Czech History in Old Town Square').

Jan Hus Statue

Ladislav Šaloun's brooding Art Nouveau sculpture of Jan Hus dominates the square in the same way that Hus' mythic memory dominates Czech history (see the boxed text 'Jan Hus' under History in the Facts about Prague chapter). It was unveiled on 6 July 1915, the 500th anniversary of Hus' death at the stake, to patriotic noises but less than unanimous artistic approval. The steps at its base – once the only place in the square where you could sit down without having to pay for something – have now been protected by a ring of flower beds, but the police seem to have given up on ordering people to keep off, and there's now a beaten path through the flowers.

The brass strip on the ground nearby is the so-called **Prague Meridian**. Until 1915 the square's main ornament was a 17th-century column (see the boxed text 'Missing Monuments' later in this chapter), whose shadow used to cross the meridian at high noon.

Staroměstská Radnice

The Staroměstská radnice *(Old Town Hall; adult/child 30/20Kč, free 1st Tues of month; open 11am-6pm Mon & 9am-6pm Tues-Sun Apr-Oct, 9am-5pm Tues-Sat & 11am-5pm Sun Nov-Mar)*, founded in 1338, looks like a row of private buildings with a tower at the end – the result of its having been gradually assembled from existing buildings by a medieval town council short of funds.

The arcaded building at the corner, **dům U minuty**, is covered with Renaissance sgraffito. Franz Kafka lived in it as a child just before it was bought for the town hall.

Czech History in Old Town Square

Old Town Square has been the scene of some momentous events in Czech history:

1338 John of Luxembourg grants Staré Město the right to a town hall, and a private house is purchased for this purpose

1422 Execution of Jan Želivský, the Hussite preacher who led Prague's first defenestration, touching off the Hussite Wars

1437 Execution of 57 more Hussites

1458 Election of the Hussite George of Poděbrady as king of Bohemia, in the town hall

1621 Twenty-seven Protestants beheaded on 21 June after the Battle of Bílá Hora

1784 The town hall becomes the governmental seat of a newly unified Prague city

1915 Statue of Jan Hus unveiled on 6 July, the 500th anniversary of his martyrdom

1918 On 2 November, five days after the declaration of Czecholslovak independence, the 270-year-old Marian Column is toppled

1945 On 8 May Nazi SS units attempt to demolish the Staroměstská radnice (Old Town Hall) as German troops begin pulling out after three days of fighting against Prague residents; the following day, the Red Army marches in

1948 On 21 February Klement Gottwald proclaims a communist government from the balcony of palác Kinských (Kinský Palace)

1968 On 21 August Warsaw Pact tanks roll across the square as the 'Prague Spring' comes to an end; the Jan Hus statue is draped in black

A Gothic chapel and a neogothic northern wing were destroyed by Nazi shells in 1945, on the day before the Soviet army marched into Prague. The chapel has been laboriously reconstructed.

A plaque on the tower's eastern face contains a roll call of the 27 Czech Protestant nobles beheaded in 1621 after the Battle of Bílá Hora; crosses on the ground mark where the deed was done. Another plaque commemorates a critical WWII victory by Red Army and Czechoslovak units at Dukla Pass in Slovakia.

It's *de rigueur* to wait for the hourly show by the hall's splendid **Astronomical Clock**, or *orloj* (see the boxed text 'The Astronomical Clock' later). You can also see selected rooms of the town hall, the Gothic chapel and the Apostles from behind the scenes (30Kč).

Apart from the clock, the hall's best feature is the view from the 60m **tower** *(adult/child 30/20Kč)*, which is certainly worth the additional fee. There's a lift that allows access for wheelchair users.

Kostel sv Mikuláše

The Baroque wedding cake in the northwestern corner of the square is kostel sv Mikuláše (St Nicholas Church), built in the 1730s by Kilian Dientzenhofer (not to be confused with at least two other St Nicholas churches in Prague, including the Dientzenhofers' masterwork in Malá Strana). Considerable grandeur has been worked into a very tight space; originally the church was wedged behind Staroměstská radnice's northern wing (destroyed in 1945). Chamber concerts are often held beneath its stucco decorations, a visually splendid (though acoustically mediocre) setting.

Franz Kafka was born next door, at what is now a privately run **Expozice Franze Kafky** *(Franz Kafka Exhibition; U radnice 5; admission 20Kč; open 10am-6pm Tues-Fri, 10am-5pm Sat)*, a so-so photo exhibit.

Palác Kinských

Fronting the late-Baroque palác Kinských Kinský *(Goltz-Kinský Palace; Staroměstské náměstí 12)* is probably the city's finest rococo facade, completed in 1765 by the redoubtable Kilian Dientzenhofer.

Alfred Nobel, the Swedish inventor of dynamite, once stayed here; his crush on pacifist Bertha Kinský may have influenced him to establish the Nobel Peace Prize. Many living

Charles Bridge (Karlův Most)

Charles Bridge (Maps 5 & 7) was begun by Charles IV to replace an earlier bridge that had been washed away by floods. Designed by Peter Parler, it was completed in about 1400, though it only got Charles' name in the 19th century. Despite occasional flood damage, it withstood wheeled traffic for 600 years – thanks, legend says, to eggs mixed into the mortar – until it was made pedestrian-only after WWII.

Strolling on Charles Bridge is everybody's favourite Prague activity. By 9am it's a 500m-long fairground, with an army of tourists squeezing through a gauntlet of hawkers and buskers, beneath ranks of imposing Baroque statuary.

In the crush, don't forget to look at the bridge itself and the grand views up and down the river. In the summer you can climb the towers at either end, built originally for its defence. Admission to each costs 30/15Kč per adult/child. They're normally open from 10am to 6pm; the Malostranská mostecká věž (Malá Strana Bridge Tower; with a PIS branch office inside) is closed from November to March. Each tower has a small exhibit.

Gangs of pickpockets work the bridge day and night, so keep track of your purse or wallet.

Towers & Statues

The bridge's first monument was the crucifix near the eastern end, erected in 1657. The first, and most popular statue – the Jesuits' 1683 monument to St John of Nepomuk – inspired other Catholic orders, and over the next 30 years a score more went up, like ecclesiastical billboards. New ones were added in the mid-19th century, and one (plus replacements for some lost to floods) in the 20th century.

As most statues were of soft sandstone, several weathered originals have been replaced with copies. Some of the originals are in an exhibit in the *kasematy* (casemates) under the walls at Vyšehrad, while others are in the Lapidárium at Výstaviště (Exhibition Grounds) in Holešovice.

There are actually two bridge towers at the Malá Strana end. The lower one was originally part of the long-gone 12th-century Judith Bridge. The taller tower was built in the mid-15th century in imitation of the one at the Staré Město end. You can see the only surviving arch of the Judith Bridge by taking a boat trip with Prague Venice (see Boat in the Getting Around chapter), from the square at the Staré Město end.

From the western (Malá Strana) end, the statues that line the bridge are:

1 SS Cosmas & Damian, charitable 3rd-century physician brothers (1709)
2 St Wenceslas (sv Václav; 1858)
3 St Vitus (sv Víta; 1714)
4 SS John of Matha & Félix de Valois, 12th-century French founders of the Trinitarian order, for the ransom of enslaved Christians (represented by a Tatar standing guard over a group of them), with St Ivo (1714)
5 St Philip Benizi (sv Benicius; 1714)
6 St Adalbert (sv Vojtěch), Prague's first Czech bishop, canonised in the 10th century (1709, replica)
7 St Cajetan, Italian founder of the Theatine order in the 15th century (1709)
8 The Vision of St Luitgard, agreed by most to be the finest piece on the bridge, in which Christ appears to the blind saint and allows her to kiss his wounds (1710)
9 St Augustine (1708; replica)
10 St Nicholas of Tolentino (1706; replica)
11 St Jude Thaddaeus, Apostle and patron saint of hopeless causes (1708); further along on the right, beyond the railing, is a column with a statue of the eponymous hero of the 11th-century epic poem, Song of Roland (Bruncvík)
12 St Vincent Ferrer, a 14th-century Spanish priest, and St Procopius, Hussite warrior-priest (1712)
13 St Anthony of Padua, 13th-century Portuguese disciple of St Francis of Assisi (1707)
14 St Francis Seraphicus (1855)
15 St John of Nepomuk, patron saint of Czechs: according to the legend illustrated on the base of the statue, Wenceslas IV had him trussed up in a suit of armour and thrown off the bridge in 1393 for refusing to divulge confessions by the queen, though the real reason had to do with

Charles Bridge (Karlův Most)

the bitter conflict between church and state; the stars in his halo allegedly followed his corpse down the river. Legend has it that if you rub the bronze plaque, you will one day return to Prague (1683; bronze)

16 St Wenceslas as a boy, with his grandmother and guardian St Ludmilla, patroness of Bohemia (c. 1730)

17 St Wenceslas with St Sigismund (son of Charles IV and Holy Roman Emperor) and St Norbert, 12th-century German founder of the Premonstratensian order (1853)

18 St Francis Borgia, 16th-century Spanish priest (1710)

19 St John the Baptist (1857); further ahead on the right, a bronze cross on the railing marks the place where St John of Nepomuk was thrown off (see No 15 earlier)

20 St Christopher, patron saint of travellers (1857)

21 SS Cyril and Methodius, who brought Christianity and a written language to the Slavs in the 9th century (1938; the newest statue)

22 St Francis Xavier, 16th-century Spanish missionary celebrated for his work in the Orient (1711; replica)

23 St Anne with Madonna and Child (1707)

24 St Joseph (1854)

25 Crucifix (1657; gilded bronze), with an invocation in Hebrew saying 'holy, holy, holy Lord', funded by the fine of a Jew who had mocked it (in 1696); the stone figures date from 1861

26 Pietá (1859)

27 Madonna with St Dominic, Spanish founder of the Dominicans in the 12th century, and St Thomas Aquinas (1709; replica)

28 St Barbara, 2nd-century patron saint of miners; St Margaret, 3rd- or 4th-century patron saint of expectant mothers; and St Elizabeth, a 13th-century Slovak princess who renounced the good life to serve the poor (1707)

29 Madonna with St Bernard, founder of the Cistercian order in the 12th century (1709; replica)

30 St Ivo, 11th-century bishop of Chartres (1711; replica)

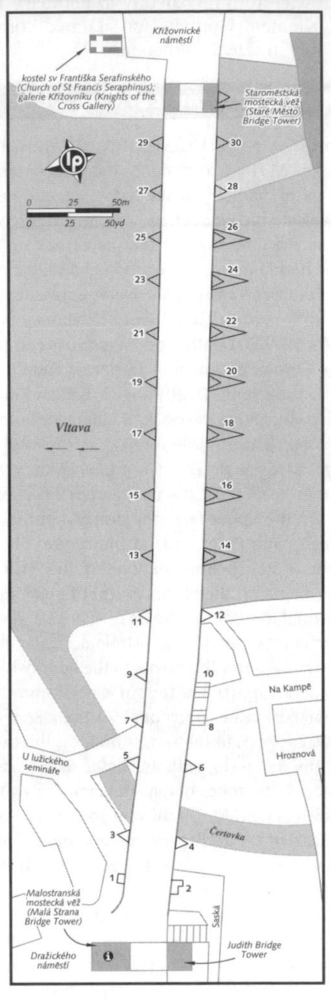

The elegant late-14th-century Staroměstská mostecká věž (Staré Město Bridge Tower) was, like the bridge, designed by Peter Parler. Here, at the end of the Thirty Years' War, a Swedish army was finally turned back by a band of students and Jewish ghetto residents. Looking out from the eastern face of the tower are SS Adalbert & Procopius, and below them Charles IV, St Vitus and Wenceslas IV. The tower also features a bit of 'Gothic porno': below these worthies on the left side of the arch is a stone relief of a man with his hand up the skirt of what appears to be a nun.

Praguers have a darker memory of the place, for it was from its balcony in February 1948 that Klement Gottwald proclaimed communist rule in Czechoslovakia.

The Astronomical Clock

The Staroměstská radnice (Old Town Hall) tower was given a clock in 1410 by the master clockmaker Mikuláš of Kadaně; this was improved in 1490 by one Master Hanuš, producing the mechanical marvel you see today. Legend has it that Hanuš was afterwards blinded so he could not duplicate the work elsewhere, and in revenge crawled up into the clock and disabled it. (Documents from the time suggest that he carried on as clock master for years, unblinded, although the clock apparently didn't work properly until it was repaired in about 1570.)

Four figures beside the clock represent the deepest civic anxieties of 15th-century Praguers: Vanity (with a mirror), Greed (with his money bag; originally a Jewish moneylender, cosmetically altered after WWII), Death, and Pagan Invasion (represented by a Turk). The four figures below these are the Chronicler, Angel, Astronomer and Philosopher.

On the hour, Death rings a bell and inverts his hourglass, and the 12 Apostles parade past the windows above the clock, nodding to the crowd. On the left side are Paul (with a sword and a book), Thomas (lance), Jude (book), Simon (saw), Bartholomew (book) and Barnabas (parchment); on the right side are Peter (with a key), Matthew (axe), John (snake), Andrew (cross), Philip (cross) and James (mallet). At the end, a cock crows and the hour is rung.

On the upper face, the disk (**A**) in the middle of the fixed part depicts the world known at the time – with Prague (**B**) at the centre, of course. The gold sun (**C**) traces a circle through the blue zone of day, the brown zone of dusk (**CREPUSCULUM** in Latin) in the west (**OCCASUS**, **D** on the diagram), the black disc (**E**) of night, and dawn (**AURORA**) in the east (**ORTUS**, **F** on the diagram). From this the hours of sunrise and sunset can be read. The curved lines (**G**) with black Arabic numerals are part of an astrological 'star clock'.

The sun-arm (**H**) points to the hour (without any daylight-saving time adjustment) on the Roman-numeral ring (**I**); the top XII is noon and the bottom XII is midnight. The outer ring (**J**), with Gothic numerals, reads traditional 24-hour Bohemian time, counted from sunset; the number 24 (**K**) is always opposite the sunset hour on the fixed (inner) face.

The moon (**L**), with its phases shown, also traces a path through the zones of day and night, riding on the offset moving ring (**M**). On the ring you can also read which houses of the zodiac the sun and moon are in. The hand with a little star at the end of it (**N**) indicates sidereal (stellar) time.

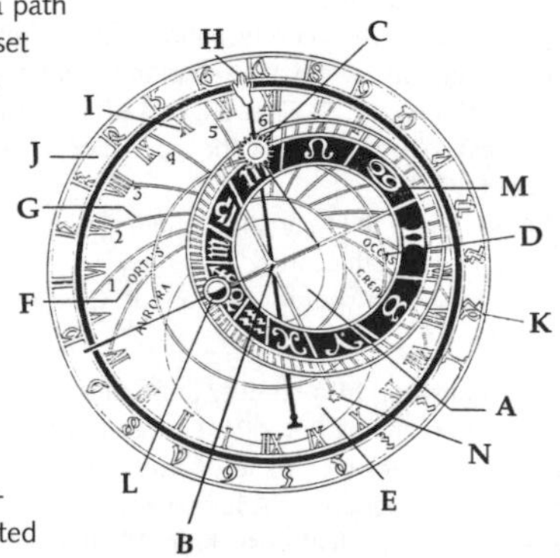

The calendar-wheel beneath all this astronomical wizardry, with 12 seasonal scenes celebrating rural Bohemian life, is a duplicate of one painted in 1866 by the Czech Revivalist Josef Mánes. You can have a close look at the beautiful original in the muzeum hlavního města Prahy (Prague City Museum; see Nové Město later in this chapter). Most of the dates around the calendar-wheel are marked with the names of their associated saints; 6 July honours Jan Hus.

Dům U Kamenného Zvonu

Next door is the dům U Kamenného Zvonu *(House of the Stone Bell; Staroměstské náměstí 13; adult/child 60/30Kč, free on 1st Tues of month; open 10am-6pm Tues-Sun)*, its 14th-century Gothic dignity rescued in the 1960s from a second-rate Baroque renovation. Inside, two restored Gothic chapels now serve as a branch of the Prague City Gallery, with changing exhibits of modern art, and as a chamber-concert venue.

Kostel Panny Marie Před Týnem

The spiky-topped kostel Panny Marie Před Týnem (Church of Our Lady Before Týn, or Týn Church) is early Gothic, though it takes some imagination to visualise the original in its entirety because it's strangely hidden behind the four-storey Týn School (not a Habsburg plot to obscure this 15th-century Hussite stronghold, but almost contemporaneous with it). Inside the church is smothered in heavy Baroque.

The entrance is up a passage to the right of Café Italia. Two of the church's most striking features are a huge rococo altar on the northern wall, and the beautiful north-eastern entrance. On the lower southern wall are two tiny windows that once looked in from the house at Celetná 3 – one from the bedroom of the teenage Franz Kafka (from 1896 to 1907).

The Danish astronomer Tycho Brahe, one of Rudolf II's most illustrious 'consultants' (who died in 1601 of a burst bladder during a royal piss-up), is buried near the chancel. The Týn Church is an occasional concert venue and has a very grand-sounding pipe organ.

Týnský Dvůr

The Týn Church's name comes from a medieval courtyard for foreign merchants, the Týnský dvůr or just Týn, behind the church on Štupartská. The renovated courtyard now houses shops, restaurants and the Hotel Ungelt.

In the restored Renaissance **dům U zlatého prstenu** *(House at the Golden Ring; adult/child 60/30Kč; open 10am-6pm Tues-Sun)*, on the corner of Týnská, just outside the western entrance to Týnský dvůr, is a branch of the Prague City Gallery, with a fine collection of 20th-century Czech art. Note the original painted ceiling beams in some rooms.

Kostel sv Jakuba

The large Gothic kostel sv Jakuba *(St James Church; Malá Štupartská)*, at the far side of Týnský dvůr, began in the 14th century as a Minorite monastery church, but was given a beautiful Baroque face-lift in the early 18th century. Pride of place goes to the over-the-top tomb of Count Jan Vratislav of Mitrovice, an 18th-century lord chancellor of Bohemia, in the northern aisle.

In the midst of the gilt and whitewash is a grisly memento. Hanging to the left of the main door is a shrivelled human arm. In about 1400 a thief apparently tried to steal the jewels from the statue of the Virgin. Legend says the Virgin grabbed his wrist in such an iron grip that his arm had to be lopped off. (The truth may not be far behind: the church was a favourite of the guild of butchers, who may have administered their own justice.)

It's well worth a visit to enjoy St James' splendid pipe organ and famous acoustics. Recitals – free ones at 10.30am or 11am after Sunday Mass – and occasional other concerts are not always advertised by ticket agencies, so check the notice board outside.

JOSEFOV (MAP 7)

The slice of Staré Město bounded by Kaprova, Dlouhá and Kozí contains the remains of the once-thriving quarter of Josefov, Prague's former Jewish ghetto, with half a dozen old synagogues, the town hall, a ceremonial hall and the powerfully melancholy Starý židovský hřbitov (Old Jewish Cemetery). In an act of grotesque irony, the Nazis spared these to be a 'museum of an extinct race'. Instead they have survived as a memorial to seven centuries of oppression.

Staronová synagóga (Old-New Synagogue) is still used for religious services; the others have been converted into exhibition halls holding what is probably the world's biggest collection of sacred Jewish artefacts, many of them saved from demolished Bohemian synagogues.

The floods that hit Prague in the summer of 2002 affected Josefov particularly badly. It's possible that access to some attractions may still be limited by repair work when you read this.

Mendelssohn Is on the Roof

The roof of the Rudolfinum – a complex of concert halls and offices built in the late 19th century – is decorated with statues of famous composers. It housed the German administration during WWII, when the Nazi authorities ordered that the statue of Felix Mendelssohn – who was Jewish – be removed.

In *Mendelssohn Is on the Roof,* a darkly comic novel about life in wartime Prague, the Jewish writer Jiří Weil weaves a wryly amusing story around this true-life event. The two labourers given the task of removing the statue can't tell which of the two dozen or so figures is Mendelssohn – they all look the same, as far as they can tell. Their boss, remembering his lectures in 'racial science', tells them that Jews have big noses. 'Whichever one has the biggest nose, that's the Jew.'

So the workmen single out the statue with the biggest conk – 'Look! That one over there with the beret. None of the others has a nose like him.' – sling a noose around its neck, and start to haul it away. As their boss walks across to join them, he gapes in horror as they start to topple the figure of the only composer that he *does* recognise – Richard Wagner.

Židovské Muzeum Praha

Josefov retains a fascinating variety of Jewish monuments, all of which are now part of the Židovské muzeum Praha *(Prague Jewish Museum; ☎ 222 31 71 91; Ⓦ www.jewishmuseum.cz; adult/child 500/340Kč; open 9am-6pm Sun-Fri Apr-Oct, 9am-4.30pm Sun-Fri Nov-Mar, closed on Jewish holidays)*. The various sights are well worth visiting, but the tickets – which are sold at the Obřadní Síň (Ceremonial Hall), Pinkasova synagóga (Pinkas Synagogue), Španělská synagóga (Spanish Synagogue) and Matana travel agency – are a bit of a rip-off. You also have the option of buying a ticket for the Staronová synagóga only (adult/child 200/140Kč) or for all the sights except the Staronová (adult/child 300/200Kč).

Staronová Synagóga Completed about 1270, the Staronová synagóga *(Old-New Synagogue; Červená 1)* is Europe's oldest working synagogue and one of Prague's earliest Gothic buildings. You step down into it because it predates the raising of Staré Město's street level to guard against floods.

Men must cover their heads (a hat, bandanna or the paper yarmulkes sold at the entrance for 5Kč). Around the central chamber are an entry hall, a winter prayer hall and the room from which women watch the men-only services. The interior, with a pulpit surrounded by a 15th-century wrought-iron grill, looks much as it would have 500 years ago. The 17th-century scriptures on the walls were recovered from under a later 'restoration'. On the eastern wall is the Holy Ark that holds the Torah scrolls. In a glass case at the rear, little light bulbs beside the names of the prominent deceased are lit on their death days.

With its steep roof and Gothic gables, this looks like a place with secrets, and at least one version of the golem legend (see the boxed text 'The Jews of Prague' in the Facts about Prague chapter) ends here. Apparently, left alone on the Sabbath, the creature runs amok; Rabbi Löw rushes out in the middle of a service, removes its magic talisman and carries the lifeless body into the synagogue's attic, where some insist it still lies.

Vysoká Synagóga Opposite the Staronová synagóga is the elegant 16th-century Vysoká synagóga (High Synagogue), so called because its prayer hall *(closed to the public)* is upstairs. On the ground floor is a Jewish Museum shop.

Židovská Radnice Built by Maisel in 1586 and given its rococo facade in the 18th century, the only part of the Židovská radnice *(Jewish Town Hall; closed to the public)* that can be visited is the Kosher Eatery on the ground floor. It has a clock tower with one Hebrew face whose hands, like the Hebrew script, run 'backwards'.

Klauzová Synagóga The Baroque Klauzová synagóga *(Klaus Synagogue; U Starého hřbitova 1)* by the cemetery entrance houses a good exhibit on Jewish ceremonies of birth and death, worship and special holy days.

Obřadní Síň The nearby Obřadní Síň *(Ceremonial Hall; U Starého hřbitova 3)* was built around 1906. Inside is an exhibit on Jewish traditions, similar to that in the Klauzová synagóga.

Pinkasova Synagóga The handsome Pinkasova synagóga *(Pinkas Synagogue; Široká 3; not likely to reopen until winter 2003 due to flood damage)* was built in 1535 and used for worship until 1941. After WWII it was converted into a powerful memorial, with the names, birth dates, and dates of disappearance of the 77,297 Bohemian and Moravian victims of the Nazis inscribed across wall after wall. It also has a collection of paintings and drawings by children held in the Terezín concentration camp during WWII (see the Excursions chapter).

Maiselova Synagóga The neogothic Maiselova synagóga *(Maisel Synagogue; Maiselova 10)* replaced a Renaissance original built by Maisel and destroyed by fire. It houses another exhibit of synagogue silver, textiles, prints and books.

Španělská Synagóga Named after its striking Moorish interior, the Španělská synagóga *(Spanish Synagogue; Vězeňská 1)*, dating from 1868, has an exhibit on Jews in the Czech Republic from emancipation to the present day.

Starý Židovský Hřbitov Founded in the early 15th century, the Starý židovský hřbitov (Old Jewish Cemetery) is Europe's oldest surviving Jewish cemetery, truly a monument to dignity in the face of great suffering. It has a palpable atmosphere of mourning even after two centuries of disuse (it was closed in 1787). Some 12,000 crumbling stones (some brought from other, long-gone cemeteries) are heaped together, but beneath them are perhaps 100,000 graves, piled in layers because of space limitations. Most contain the name of the deceased and his or her father, the date of death (and sometimes of burial), and poetic texts. Elaborate markers from the 17th and 18th centuries have bas-relief and sculpture, some of it indicating the deceased's occupation and lineage. The oldest standing stone (now replaced by a replica), dating from 1439, is that of Avigdor Karo, a chief rabbi and court poet to Wenceslas IV.

The most prominent graves, marked by pairs of marble tablets with a 'roof' between them, are near the main gate. They include those of Mordechai Maisel and Rabbi Löw.

You enter the cemetery through the Pinkasova synagóga on Široká and exit through a gate between Klauzová synagóga and the Obřadní Síň on U starého hřbitova. This is one of Prague's most popular sights, and the chattering tour groups tend to break its spell.

Since the cemetery was closed, burials have taken place at Olšanské hřbitovy (Olšany Cemetery) in Žižkov. There are remnants of another old Jewish burial ground at the foot of the TV tower in Žižkov (see later in this chapter).

Pařížská Třída

Despite their association with the demise of the Jewish quarter, Pařížská třída (Paris Avenue) and the adjacent streets are themselves a kind of museum. The ghetto was cleared at a time of general infatuation with the French Art Nouveau style, and its old lanes were lined with courtly four- and five-storey residential buildings – their stained glass and sculptural flourishes are now slipping into disrepair. Pařížská třída's many trees give it a Parisian flavour.

Umělecko-Průmyslové Muzeum

The neo-Renaissance Umělecko-průmyslové muzeum *(Museum of Decorative Arts; ☎ 251 09 31 11; 17.listopadu 2; adult/child 80/40Kč; open 10am-6pm Tues-Sun)*, built in 1890, arose as part of a European movement to encourage a return to the aesthetic values sacrificed to the Industrial Revolution. Its four halls are a feast for the eyes, full of 16th- to 19th-century artefacts, including furniture, tapestries, porcelain and a fabulous trove of glasswork. Don't miss the rococo grandfather of all grandfather clocks in room No 3.

Labels are in Czech but detailed English and French texts are available in each room. What you see is only a fraction of the collection; other bits appear now and then in single-theme exhibitions.

Náměstí Jana Palacha

Náměstí Jana Palacha (Jan Palach Square) is named after the young Charles University student who in January 1969 set himself alight in Wenceslas Square in protest against the Soviet invasion (see the boxed text 'Student Sacrifices' later in this chapter). On the eastern side of the square, beside the entrance to the philosophy faculty building where Palach was a student, is a plaque with a spooky death mask.

Presiding over the square is the **Rudolfinum**, home of the Czech Philharmonic. This and the Národní divadlo (National Theatre), both designed by architects Josef Schulz and Josef Zítek, are considered Prague's finest neo-Renaissance buildings. Completed in 1884, the Rudolfinum served between the wars as the seat of the Czechoslovak parliament.

KLÁŠTER SV ANEŽKY

In the northeastern corner of Staré Město is the former Klášter sv Anežky *(Convent of St Agnes; ☎ 224 81 06 28; U milosrdných 17; adult/child 100/50Kč; open 10am-6pm Tues-Sun)*, Prague's oldest surviving Gothic building, now restored and used by the National Gallery.

In 1234 the Franciscan Order of the Poor Clares was founded by the Přemysl king Wenceslas I, who made his sister Anežka (Agnes) its first abbess. Agnes was beatified in the 19th century, and with timing that could hardly be accidental, Pope John Paul II canonised her as St Agnes of Bohemia just weeks before the revolutionary events of November 1989.

In the 16th century the buildings were handed over to the Dominicans, and after Joseph II dissolved the monasteries, they became a squatter's paradise. They've only been restored in the last few decades.

The complex consists mainly of the cloister, a sanctuary and a church in French Gothic style. The graves of St Agnes and of Wenceslas I's Queen Cunegund are in the kaple Panny Marie (Chapel of the Virgin Mary) in the **svatyně sv Salvatora** (Sanctuary of the Holy Saviour). Alongside this is the smaller **kostel sv Františka** (Church of St Francis), where Wenceslas I is buried. Part of its ruined nave and other rooms have been rebuilt as a chilly concert and lecture hall.

The first-floor rooms now hold the National Gallery's permanent collection of medieval art (1200–1550) from Bohemia and Central Europe.

ALONG KRALOVSKÉ CESTA

The Kralovské Cesta (Royal Way) was the processional route followed by Czech kings on their way to chrám sv Víta for coronation. The route leads from the Prašná brána (Powder Gate) along Celetná, through Old Town Square and Malé náměstí, along Karlova and across Charles Bridge and Malostranské náměstí, before climbing up Nerudova to the castle.

Prašná Brána

The 65m-tall Prašná brána *(Powder Gate; Map 7; adult/child 30/20Kč; open 10am-6pm daily Apr-Oct)* was begun in 1475 on the site of one of Staré Město's original 13 gates. Built during the reign of King Vladislav II Jagiello as a ceremonial entrance to the city, it was left unfinished after the king moved from the neighbouring Royal Court to Prague Castle in 1483. The name comes from its use as a gunpowder magazine in the 18th century. Josef Mocker rebuilt, decorated and steepled it between 1875 and 1886, giving it its neo-gothic icing. There are great views from the top, and a tiny exhibit about the tower.

Obecní Dům

Don't miss Obecní dům *(Municipal House; Map 7; ☎ 222 00 21 00; náměstí Republiky 5; guided tours 150Kč; open 7.30am-11pm daily, guided tours 10am-6pm daily)*, Prague's most sensually beautiful building, with an unrivalled Art Nouveau interior and a facade that looks like a Victorian Easter egg.

It stands on the site of the Royal Court, seat of Bohemia's kings from 1383 to 1483 (when Vladislav II moved to Prague Castle) and only demolished at the end of the 19th century. Between 1906 and 1912 the Obecní dům was built in its place – a lavish joint effort by some 30 of the leading artists of the

continued on page 97

PRAGUE CASTLE (PRAŽSKÝ HRAD)

Prague Castle (Pražský hrad, or just *hrad* to Czechs) is the most popular sight in Prague. According to *Guinness World Records*, it's the largest ancient castle in the world – 570m long, an average of 128m wide and covering a total area bigger than seven football fields.

Its history starts in the 9th century when Prince Bořivoj founded a fortified settlement here. It grew as rulers made their own additions, which explains its mixture of styles. The castle has always been the seat of Czech rulers as well as the official residence, although the current president, Václav Havel, has chosen to live in his own house on the outskirts of the city.

Prague Castle has had four major reconstructions, from that of Prince Soběslav in the 12th century to a classical face-lift under Empress Maria Theresa. In the 1920s President Masaryk hired a Slovene architect, Jože Plečník, to renovate the castle.

Information

The castle's own **information centre** *(☎ 224 37 33 68 or ☎ 224 37 24 34; open 9am-5pm daily Apr-Oct, 9am-4pm daily Nov-Mar)* is in the Third Courtyard, opposite the main entrance to chrám sv Víta (St Vitus Cathedral). Here you can get a free castle map, buy admission tickets, rent an audio-guide and organise a guided tour.

You can buy tickets for concerts and other events at the **box office** *(☎ 1080; open 9am-5pm)* in the kaple sv Kříže (Chapel of the Holy Cross) in the Second Courtyard.

There's a **post office** *(open 8am-7pm Mon-Fri, 10am-7pm Sat)* and **currency exchange** *(open 8.10am-6.10pm daily)* next to the information centre, and an **ATM** in the information centre.

Tickets Entrance to the castle courtyards and gardens, and to the nave of chrám sv Víta, is free. There are three different tickets, which allow entry to various combinations of sights:

Ticket A (adult/concession 220/110Kč): chrám sv Víta, Starý Královský palác (Old Royal Palace), Bazilika sv Jiří (Basilica of St George), Prašná věž (Powder Tower), Zlatá ulička (Golden Lane) and Dalibor Tower.
Ticket B (180/90Kč): chrám sv Víta, Starý Královský palác, Zlatá ulička and Dalibor Tower.
Ticket C (40Kč, no concessions): Zlatá ulička and Dalibor Tower only.

Concession prices are for those aged seven to 16, students and disabled visitors; children aged six or under get in free. There is also a family ticket (300Kč for A, 270Kč for B), valid for two adults and their children.

Castle Highlights

You need at least half a day to fully appreciate the castle, but if you only have an hour or so to spare, buy Ticket B and make sure you see chrám sv Víta (St Vitus Cathedral) – including kaple sv Václava (St Wenceslas Chapel), the Tomb of St John of Nepomuk and the Mucha stained-glass window – and the Starý Královský palác (Old Royal Palace), including Vladislavský sál (Vladislav Hall) and the view from the terrace.

Two hours? Buy Ticket A and add on the bazilika sv Jiří (Basilica of St George) and a visit to the klášter sv Jiří (Convent of St George) gallery.

You can buy tickets at the information centre in the Third Courtyard, or at the entrance to the main sights, but *not* in the 'Ticket Office' in the kaple sv Kříže in the Second Courtyard.

These tickets do not include admission to the other art galleries and museums within the castle grounds mentioned later in this section. Tickets are valid for one day only.

Places to Eat

Food prices here are as high as the castle itself. If you're on a budget, eat before you get here or bring a picnic!

Café Poet *(Na baště; mains 145-200Kč, 3-course lunches 200Kč; open 10am-6pm)*, to the left of the castle's main gate, is the place to try for cakes, good coffee, salads, pizzas and grills. An alternative is Bistro Rudolf II at the western end of Zlatauli.

Cafe U Kanovníků *(náměstí U sv Jiří)* serves overpriced supermarket sandwiches, apple pie and drinks to tourists at outdoor tables. You can also get drinks and snacks at Bistro Zlatá ulička, and Café Gallery. All three are open from 10am to 6pm daily.

Guided Tours From Tuesday to Sunday, one-hour guided tours are available in Czech (150Kč for up to five people, plus 30Kč per extra person), and in English, French, German, Italian, Russian and Spanish (400Kč, plus 80Kč per extra person).

Alternatively you can rent an audio-guide (cassette player and headphones) for 145/180Kč for two/three hours.

Opening Hours From April to October, the castle grounds are open from 5am to midnight, and the gardens from 10am to 6pm, daily. The cathedral and other historic buildings accessible by ticket are open from 9am to 5pm daily.

From November to March, the grounds open from 6am to 11pm daily, and the historic buildings from 9am to 4pm daily. The gardens are closed.

First Courtyard

The castle's **main gate**, on Hradčanské náměstí, is flanked by huge, Baroque statues of battling Titans (1767–70), which dwarf the castle guards who stand beneath them. President Havel hired the costume designer from the film *Amadeus* (1984) to replace their communist-era khaki uniforms with the present pale blue kit, which harks back to the first Czechoslovak Republic.

The **changing of the guard** takes place every hour on the hour, but the longest and most impressive display is at noon, when banners are exchanged while a brass band plays a fanfare from the windows of the **Plečníkova síň** (Plečník Hall).

This impressive hall, which opens off the left side of the Baroque **Matyášova brána** (Matthias Gate; 1614), was created by Slovenian architect Jože Plečník as part of the 1920s restoration of the castle; the pointy flagpoles in the First Courtyard are also Plečník's.

Second Courtyard

You pass through the Matyášova brána into the Second Courtyard, centred on a Baroque fountain and a 17th-century well with Renaissance lattice work. The **kaple sv Kříže** (Chapel of the Holy Cross; 1763) on the right was once the treasury of chrám sv Víta; today it houses the castle's box office and shop.

At the northern end of the courtyard is the **Obrazárna Pražvského hradu** *(Prague Castle Gallery; ☎ 224 37 33 68; Pražský hrad, II. nádvoří; adult/concession 100/50Kč; open 10am-6pm daily)*, whose collection of 16th- to 18th-century European and Czech art includes works by Rubens, Tintoretto and Titian.

The magnificent **Španělský sál** (Spanish Hall) and **Rudolfova galerie** (Rudolph Gallery) in the northern wing of the courtyard are reserved for state receptions and special concerts (open to the public just one or two days a year, on special occasions).

Královská Zahrada The gate to the right of Obrazárna Pražvského hradu leads to the **Prašný most** (Powder Bridge; 1540), spanning the **Jelení příkop** (Stag Moat). A gate on the outer wall of the castle, overlooking the moat, leads to a bomb shelter started by the communists in the 1950s but never completed. Its tunnels run under most of the castle.

The **Královská zahrada** (Royal Garden), on the far side of the Jelení příkop, started life as a Renaissance garden built by Ferdinand I in 1534. The most beautiful of the garden's buildings is the **Míčovna** (Ball-Game

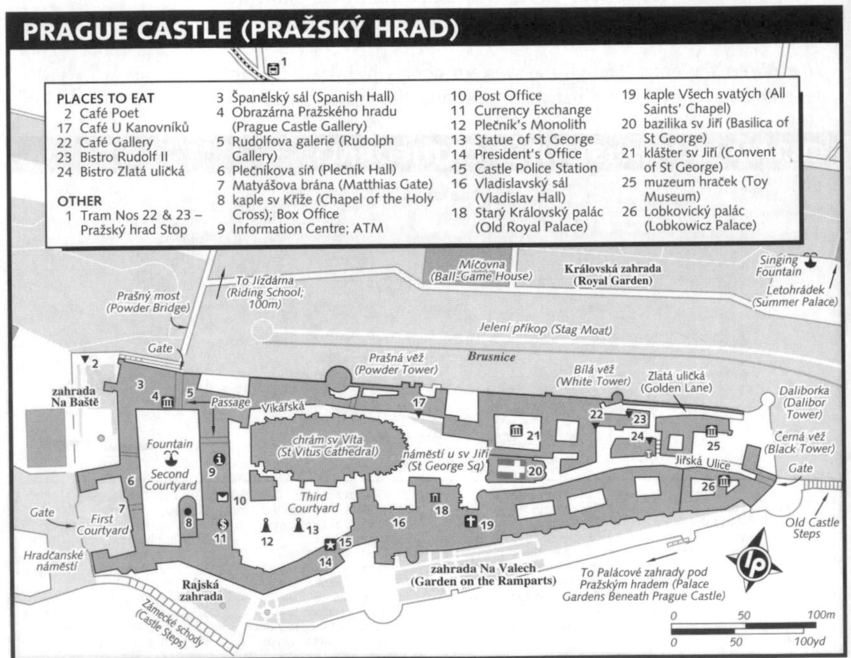

House; 1569), a masterpiece of Renaissance sgraffito where the Habsburgs once played a primitive version of badminton. To the east is the **Letohrádek** (Summer, or Belvedere, Palace; 1564), the most authentic Italian Renaissance building outside Italy, and to the west the former **Jízdárna** (Riding School; 1695). All three are used as venues for temporary modern-art exhibitions.

Chrám sv Víta As you exit the passage on the eastern side of the Second Courtyard, the huge western facade of chrám sv Víta (St Vitus Cathedral) soars directly above you. At first glance it may appear impressively Gothic, but in fact the triple doorway dates only from 1948 to 1953, one of the last parts of the church to be completed.

The cathedral's foundation stone was laid in 1344 by Emperor Charles IV, on the site of a 10th-century Romanesque rotunda built by Duke Wenceslas. Charles' original architect, Matthias of Arras, began work on the choir in the French Gothic style, but died eight years later.

His German successor, Peter Parler – a veteran of Cologne's cathedral – completed most of the eastern part of the cathedral in a freer, late-Gothic style before he too died in 1399. Renaissance and Baroque details were added over the following centuries, but it was only in 1861, during the Czech National Revival, that a concerted effort was made to finish the cathedral; it was finally consecrated in 1929.

The Nave You enter through the western door, which leads into the neogothic nave; everything between here and the crossing was built

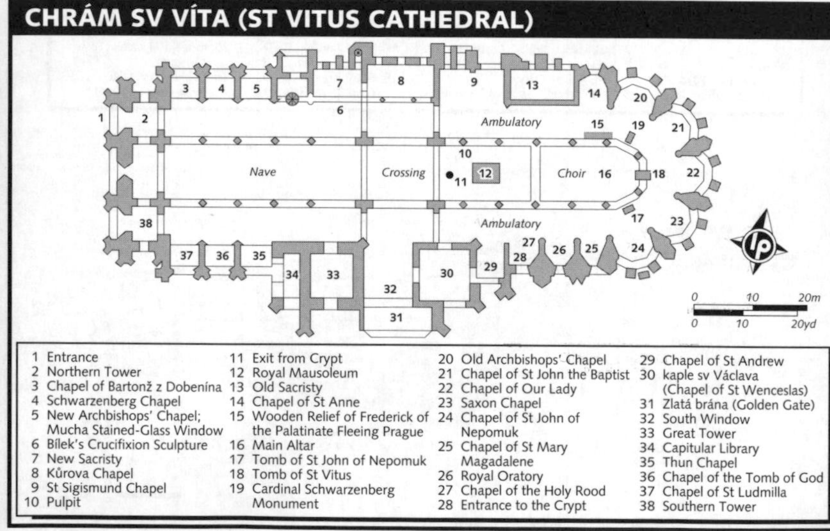

during the late 19th and early 20th centuries. The nave is enhanced by beautiful **stained-glass windows** dating from the early 20th century – note the one by Art Nouveau artist Alfons Mucha (third chapel on the northern side), depicting the lives of SS Cyril & Methodius (1909). Nearby is a wooden sculpture of the Crucifixion (1899) by František Bílek.

Walk up to the crossing, where the nave and transept meet, and look at the huge **south window** (1938) by Max Švabinský, depicting the Last Judgement – note the fires of Hell burning brightly in the lower right-hand corner.

Just to the right of the southern transept is the entrance to the 96m-tall **Great Tower** *(open 9am-5pm daily, last admission 4.15pm, Apr-Oct)*. You can climb the 297 slightly claustrophobic steps to the top for excellent views, and you also get a close look at the clockworks (1597). The tower's Sigismund Bell, made by Tomáš Jaroš in 1549, is Bohemia's largest. (NB: The tower is closed during bad weather.)

The Choir & Ambulatory You'll need your ticket to enter the eastern end of the cathedral, whose graceful late-Gothic vaulting dates from the 14th century. In the centre lies the ornate **Royal Mausoleum** (1571–89) with its cold marble effigies of Ferdinand I, his wife Anna Jagellonská and son Maximilián II.

On the ambulatory's northern side, just beyond the old sacristy and the confessional booths, a **wooden relief** (1630) by Caspar Bechterle shows Protestant Frederick of the Palatinate (in his horse-drawn coach) legging it out of Prague after the Catholic victory at the battle of Bílá Hora.

As you round the far end of the ambulatory you pass the **tomb of sv Víta** – the brass crosiers set in the floor mark the tombs of bishops – and reach the spectacular, Baroque silver **tomb of St John of Nepomuk**, its draped canopy supported by chubby, silver angels (the tomb contains two tonnes of silver in all).

The nearby **Chapel of St Mary Magdalene** contains the grave slabs of Matyáš z Arrasu (Matthias of Arras) and Petr Parléř (Peter Parler), the cathedral's architects. Beyond is the ornate, late-Gothic **Royal Oratory**, a fancy balcony with ribbed vaulting carved to look like tree branches.

The Crypt Stairs in the corner of the Chapel of the Holy Rood lead down to the crypt, where you can see the remains of earlier churches that stood on the site of the cathedral, including an 11th-century Romanesque basilica. Beyond, you can crowd around the entrance to the **Royal Crypt** to see the marble sarcophagi (dating only from the 1930s) which contain the remains of Czech rulers including Charles IV, Wenceslas IV, George of Poděbrady and Rudolf II.

Kaple sv Václava The biggest and most beautiful of the cathedral's numerous side chapels is Parler's **kaple sv Václava** (Chapel of St Wenceslas). Its walls are adorned with gilded panels containing polished slabs of semiprecious stones. Early-16th-century wall paintings depict scenes from the life of the Czechs' patron saint, while even older frescoes show scenes from the life of Christ.

On the southern side of the chapel, a small door – locked with seven locks – hides a staircase leading to the Coronation Chamber above the Zlatá brána (Golden Gate), where the Czech **crown jewels** are kept. Rarely exhibited to the public (you can see replicas at the museum in the Lobkovický palác; see the section on Jiřská ulice later), they include the gold crown of St Wenceslas, which was made for Charles IV in 1346 from the gold of the original Přemysl crown.

Third Courtyard

Turn left as you leave the cathedral to reach the Third Courtyard, which contains a granite **monolith** (1928) dedicated to the victims of WWI, designed by Jože Plečník, and a copy of a 14th-century bronze **statue of St George** slaying the dragon (the original is in the klášter sv Jiří, Convent of St George).

The southern doorway of sv Víta is known as the **Zlatá brána** (Golden Gate), an elegant, triple-arched Gothic porch designed by Peter Parler. Above it is a **mosaic** (1370–71) of the Last Judgment – on the left, the godly rise from their tombs and are raised into Heaven by angels; on the right, sinners are cast down into Hell by demons. In the centre, Christ reigns in glory, and beneath, on either side of the central arch, Charles IV and his wife kneel in prayer.

To the left of the gate is the **Great Tower**, which was left unfinished by Parler's sons in the 15th century; its soaring Gothic lines are capped by a Renaissance gallery and bulging spire that were added in the late 16th century.

Starý Královský palác The Starý Královský palác (Old Royal Palace), at the courtyard's eastern end, is one of the oldest parts of the castle, dating from 1135. It was originally used only by Czech princesses, but from the 13th to the 16th century it was the king's own palace.

At its heart is the **Vladislavský sál** (Vladislav Hall), famous for its beautiful, late-Gothic vaulted roof (1493–1502) designed by Benedikt Ried. Though around 500 years old, the flowing, interpenetrating lines of the vaults have an almost Art Nouveau feel, in contrast to the rectilinear form of the Renaissance windows. The vast hall was used for banquets, councils and coronations, and also for indoor jousting tournaments – hence the **Jezdecké schody** (Riders' Staircase) on the northern side, designed to admit a mounted knight. All the presidents of the republic have been sworn in here.

A door in the hall's southwestern corner leads to the former offices of the **České kanceláře** (Bohemian Chancellery). On 23 May 1618, in the second room, Protestant nobles rebelling against Emperor Matthias threw two of his councillors and their secretary out of the window. They survived, their fall broken by the dung-filled moat, but this so-called Second Defenestration of Prague sparked off the Thirty Years' War.

At the eastern end of Vladislavský sál is a balcony that overlooks **kaple Všech svatých** (All Saints' Chapel); a door to the right leads to a terrace with great views across the city. To the right of the Jezdecké schody, an unusual Renaissance doorway framed by twisted columns leads to the **Sněmovna** (Diet, or Assembly Hall), with another beautifully vaulted ceiling. To the left, a spiral staircase leads up to the **Říšská dvorská kancelář** (New Land Rolls Room), the old repository for land titles, where the walls are covered with the clerks' coats of arms.

The plain, 14th-century Gothic chambers beneath the hall, reached via the stairs at the foot of the Jezdecké schody, are of no great interest.

Náměstí U sv Jiří Náměstí U sv Jiří (St George Square), the plaza to the east of chrám sv Víta, lies at the heart of the castle complex.

Bazilika sv Jiří The striking, brick-red, early-Baroque facade that dominates the square conceals the Czech Republic's best-preserved Romanesque church, bazilika sv Jiří (Basilica of St George), established in the 10th century by Vratislav I (the father of St Wenceslas). What you see today is mostly the result of restorations made between 1887 and 1908.

The austerity of the Romanesque nave is relieved by a Baroque double staircase leading to the apse, where fragments of 12th-century frescoes survive. In front of the stairs lie the tombs of Prince Boleslav II (d. 997; on the left) and Prince Vratislav I (d. 921), the church's founder. The arch beneath the stairs allows a glimpse of the 12th-century crypt; Přemysl kings are buried here and in the nave.

The tiny Baroque chapel beside the entrance is dedicated to St John of Nepomuk.

Klášter sv Jiří The very ordinary-looking building to the left of the basilica was Bohemia's first convent, klášter sv Jiří (Convent of St George), established in 973 by Boleslav II. Closed and converted to an army barracks in 1782, it now a houses a branch of the **National Gallery** (*☎ 257 32 05 36; Jiřské náměstí 33; adult/concession 50/20Kč; open 10am-6pm Tues-Sun*), with an excellent collection of Renaissance and Baroque art.

Prašná věž A passage to the north of chrám sv Víta leads to Prašná věž (Powder Tower; also called the Mihulka), built at the end of the 15th century as part of the castle's defences. Later it became the workshop of the cannon- and bell-maker Tomáš Jaroš, who cast the bells for chrám sv Víta. Alchemists employed by Rudolf II also worked here. Today it houses a missable museum of alchemy, metal-working, and Renaissance life in Prague Castle (labels in Czech only).

Zlatá ulička Zlatá ulička (Golden Lane) is a picturesque, cobbled alley running along the northern wall of the castle. Its tiny, colourful cottages were built in the 16th century for the sharpshooters of the castle guard, but were later used by goldsmiths. In the 18th and 19th centuries they were occupied by squatters, and then by artists including the writer Franz Kafka (who stayed at his sister's house at No 22 from 1916 to 1917) and the Nobel-laureate poet Jaroslav Seifert. Today, the lane is an over-crowded tourist trap lined with craft and souvenir shops.

At the western end of the lane is the **Bílá věž** (White Tower), where the Irish alchemist Edward Kelley was imprisoned by Rudolf II. At its eastern end is the **Daliborka**, a round tower named after the knight Dalibor of Kozojedy, imprisoned here in 1498 for supporting a peasant rebellion, and later executed. According to an old tale, he played a violin during his imprisonment, which could be heard throughout the castle. Smetana based his 1868 opera *Dalibor* on the tale.

Jiřská Ulice (George St) Just inside the castle's eastern gate is the **Lobkovický palác** *(Lobkowicz Palace; ☎ 257 53 59 79; adult/concession 40/20Kč; open 9am-5pm Tues-Sun)*. Built in the 1570s, it now houses a branch of the **National Museum**, with a good collection on Czech history from prehistoric times until 1848. Exhibits include replicas of the Czech crown jewels, the sword of executioner Jan Mydlář (who lopped off the heads of 27 rebellious Protestant nobles in Old Town Square in 1621) and some of the oldest marionettes in the Czech Republic.

In the tower of the Nejvyšší Purkrabství (Burgrave's Palace) across the street is the **Muzeum hraček** *(Toy Museum; ☎ 224 37 22 94; Jiřská 4; adult/concession 40/20Kč; open 9.30am-5.30pm daily)*. Said to be the second largest of its kind in the world, the museum has exhibits going back to Greek antiquity. It's an amazing collection, but sure to be frustrating for kids as most displays are hands-off.

Zahrada Na Valech At the castle's eastern gate, you can either descend the Old Castle Steps to Malostranská metro station, or turn sharp right and wander back to Hradčanské náměstí through the Zahrada Na Valech (Garden on the Ramparts). The terrace garden enjoys superb views across the rooftops of Malá Strana, and permits a peek into the back garden of the British Embassy.

Alternatively, you can descend to Malá Strana through the **Palácové zahrady pod Pražským hradem** (Palace Gardens Beneath Prague Castle; admission 95/40Kč) – see Northern Malá Strana in the Things to See & Do chapter.

Getting There & Around

From Malostranská metro station, the shortest route to the castle is on foot via the Old Castle Steps – on leaving the metro, turn left along Klárov and take the second street on the left.

Lazybones can take tram No 22 or 23 from the stop across the street from the metro station to the second (Pražský hrad) stop, and stroll south along U prašného mostu to the Second Courtyard. If you want to wander through Hradčany before visiting the castle, stay on tram No 22 or 23 for two more stops and get off at Pohořelec.

Other approaches include walking along Nerudova or Thunovská from Malostranské náměstí, or climbing up through the Palácové zahrady pod Pražským hradem (see the Zahrada Na Valech section).

There is wheelchair access to chrám sv Víta, Starý Královský palác, bazilika sv Jiří, Obrazárna Pražvského hradu, the castle gardens, and to public toilets in the castle grounds.

RICHARD NEBESKÝ

Take me higher: the soaring facade of chrám sv Víta (St Vitus Cathedral)

RICHARD NEBESKÝ

A Titan at the castle gates

JULIET COOMBE

A castle guard's badge

RICHARD NEBESKÝ

Explore the castle by lamplight.

JULIET COOMBE

Holy light pours through the exquisite stained glass of chrám sv Víta.

JONATHAN SMITH

While hurrying to Mass, a priest passes in front of Renaissance sgraffiti on Hradčanské náměstí.

RICHARD NEBESKÝ

Statuary a go-go near the Stavovské divadlo (Estates Theatre) on Ovocný trh

continued from page 88

day, creating a cultural centre that was to be the architectural climax of the Czech National Revival.

The mosaic above the entrance, *Homage to Prague,* is set between sculptures representing the oppression and rebirth of the Czech people. You pass beneath a wrought-iron and stained-glass canopy into an interior that is Art Nouveau down to the doorknobs.

The restaurant and the *kavárna* (café) flanking the entrance are like walk-in museums of design, and even the basement club and restaurant are handsome. Upstairs are half a dozen over-the-top salons – including the Lord Mayor's Hall, decorated entirely by Alfons Mucha, whose paintings and posters have made him an international symbol of Art Nouveau. Also here is the Smetana Hall, Prague's biggest concert hall (see the Entertainment chapter).

On 28 October 1918 an independent Czechoslovak Republic was proclaimed in the Obecní dům, and in November 1989 meetings took place here between Civic Forum and the Jakeš regime. The Prague Spring (Pražské jaro) music festival always opens on 12 May, the anniversary of Smetana's death, with a procession from Vyšehrad (High Castle) to the Obecní dům, and a gala performance of his symphonic cycle *Má Vlast* (My Country) in the Smetana Hall (for more on Smetana see Arts in the Facts about Prague chapter).

Celetná Ulice

This pedestrianised street between Powder Gate and Old Town Square is an open-air museum of well groomed, pastel-painted Baroque facades over Gothic frames (and Romanesque foundations, deliberately buried to raise Staré Město above the Vltava River's floods).

But the most interesting building dates only from 1912: Josef Gočár's delightful Cubist facade (Prague's first) on the **dům U černé Matky Boží** (House of the Black Madonna) at the corner with Ovocný trh (Fruit Market). The building now houses a bookshop and a branch of the **České muzeum výtvarných umění** *(Czech Museum of Fine Arts; Celetná 34; adult/child 40/20Kč; open 10am-9pm Tues-Sun)*, with an interesting permanent exhibition on Czech Cubism.

Malé Náměstí (Map 7)

Malé náměstí (Little Square), the southwestern extension of Old Town Square, has a Renaissance fountain and 16th-century wrought-iron grill. Here several fine Baroque and neo-Renaissance exteriors adorn some of Staré Město's oldest structures. The most colourful is the **VJ Rott Building** (1890), decorated with wall paintings by Mikulaš Aleš, and now housing four floors of crystal, garnet and jewellery shops.

Klementinum (Map 7)

To boost the power of the Roman Catholic Church in Bohemia, the Habsburg emperor Ferdinand I invited the Jesuits to Prague in 1556. They selected one of the city's choicest pieces of real estate and in 1587 set to work on kostel Nejsvě-tějšího Spasitele (Church of the Holy Saviour), Prague's flagship of the Counter-Reformation. After gradually buying up most of the adjacent neighbourhood, the Jesuits started building their college, the Klementinum, in 1653. By its completion a century later, it was the largest building in the city after Prague Castle. When the Jesuits fell out with the pope in 1773, it became part of Charles University.

The Klementinum is a vast complex of beautiful Baroque and rococo halls, now occupied by the Czech National Library. Most of it is closed to the public, but you can visit the **Baroque Library Hall and Astronomical Tower** *(mobile ☎ 603 23 12 41; open 10am-7pm daily July, 2pm-7pm Mon-Fri & 10am-7pm Sat-Sun Aug-Oct)* on a guided tour (adult/child 150/50Kč). Gates on Křižovnická, Karlova and Seminářská allow free access to the Klementinum's courtyards, which offer a less crowded alternative to Karlova if you're walking to or from Charles Bridge.

Three churches line the southern wall of the Klementinum along Karlova ulice. The **kostel sv Klimenta** (St Clement Church), lavishly rehabilitated in Baroque style from

northern end of Jindřišská, a busy street running northeast from Wenceslas Square.

Around the corner is the colourful Moorish facade of the **Jubilejní synagóga** *(Jubilee Synagogue; Map 7; Jeruzalémská 7; admission 30Kč; open 1pm-5pm Sun-Fri, closed on Jewish holidays)*, also called the Velká (Great) synagóga, dating from 1906. Note the names of the donors on the stained-glass windows, and the grand organ above the entrance.

The **Muchovo muzeum** *(Mucha Museum; Map 6; ☎ 221 45 13 33; Panská 7; adult/child 120/60Kč; open 10am-6pm daily)* features the sensuous Art Nouveau posters, paintings and decorative panels of Alfons Mucha (1860–1939), as well as many sketches, photographs and other memorabilia. There's also a 30-minute documentary on his life (available in English).

Praha Hlavní Nádraží

Take a look at the grimy, soot-blackened splendour of the original Art Nouveau section of Praha hlavní nádraží *(Prague's main train station; Map 6)*, designed by Josef Fanta and built between 1901 and 1909. The domed interior is adorned with two nubile ladies framing a mosaic with the words *Praga: mater urbium* (Prague, Mother of Cities) and the date '28.říjen r:1918' (28 October 1918 – Czechoslovakia's Independence Day).

A statue at the northern end of the park in front of the station was meant to celebrate the Soviet liberation of Prague at the end of WWII but has always been vaguely insulting, with its submissive Czech soldier embracing his bigger Soviet comrade. Now stripped of its plaque, it looks more like a celebration of gay love in the military.

NÁRODNÍ MUZEUM

Looming above Wenceslas Square is the neo-Renaissance bulk of the Národní muzeum *(National Museum; Map 6; ☎ 224 49 71 11; adult/child 80/40Kč, free 1st Mon of month; open 10am-6pm daily except 1st Tues of month)*, designed in the 1880s by Josef Schulz as an architectural symbol of the Czech National Revival.

The museum was founded in 1818 as a natural history collection by a group of Czech aristocrats. However, it was Caspar Sternberg who originally conceived the idea of a national museum and who is credited with most of the work of establishing it. Its first home was at the Šternberský palác in Hradčany, but in 1846 it was moved to a building on Na příkopě where the Živnostenská bank now stands. Today's Národní muzeum building was built from 1885 to 1891 on the site of the former Horse Gate.

The main displays of rocks, fossils and stuffed animals have a rather old-fashioned feel – serried ranks of glass display cabinets arranged on creaking parquet floors – but even if trilobites and taxidermy are not your thing it's still worth a visit just to enjoy the marbled splendour of the interior and the views down Wenceslas Square. The opulent **main staircase** is an extravaganza of polished limestone and serpentine, lined with paintings of Bohemian castles and medallions of kings and emperors. The domed **pantheon**, with four huge lunette paintings of (strangely womanless) Czech legend and history by František Ženíšek and Václav Brožík, houses bronze busts and statues of the great and the good of Czech art and science.

Light-coloured areas on the facade of the museum are patched-up bullet holes. In 1968 Warsaw Pact troops apparently mistook the museum for the former National Assembly or the radio station, and raked it with gunfire.

Across the road to the northeast is the former Federal Assembly building, built in 1973 on the site of the former Stock Exchange (1936–38; parts of its walls can be seen inside). It's now the headquarters of **Radio Free Europe** *(Map 6)*; since 11 September 2001 it has been guarded by the military because of the threat of terrorist attack.

Beside it is the 19th-century **Statní opera** *(State Opera House; Map 6)*.

WENCESLAS SQUARE (VÁCLAVSKÉ NÁMĚSTÍ)

A horse market in medieval times, Wenceslas Square (Václavské náměstí, also called Václavák) got its present name during the nationalist revival of the mid-19th century; since then it has witnessed a great deal of Czech history. A giant Mass was held in the

Student Sacrifices

Throughout Czech history – from the time of Jan Hus to the Velvet Revolution – Prague's university students have not been afraid to stand up for what they believe in; many of them sacrificed their lives for their beliefs. Two student names that have gone down in 20th-century history are Jan Opletal and Jan Palach.

On 28 October 1939 – the 21st anniversary of the declaration of Czechoslovak independence – Jan Opletal, a medical student, was shot and fatally injured by police attempting to break up an anti-Nazi demonstration. After his funeral on 15 November, Prague students took to the streets, defacing German street signs, chanting anti-German slogans and taunting the police. The Nazi retaliation was swift and savage.

In the early hours of 17 November – a day now known in Czech as the 'day of the students' – the Nazi authorities raided Prague's student dormitories and arrested around 1200 students before carting them off to various concentration camps. Some were executed, and many others died in the camps. Prague's universities were closed down for the duration of WWII.

The street in northwestern Staré Město called 17.listopadu (17 November) was named in honour of the students who suffered death and deportation on 17 November 1939. Exactly 50 years later, students marching along Národní třída in memory of that day were attacked and clubbed by police. The national outrage triggered by this event pushed the communist government towards its final collapse a few days later. There's a memorial plaque with a hand making the peace sign and the date 17.11.89 inside the arcade at Národní 16.

On 16 January 1969, university student Jan Palach set himself on fire on the steps of Národní muzeum (National Museum) in protest at the Warsaw Pact invasion of Prague. He staggered down the steps in flames and collapsed on the pavement at the foot of the stairs. The following day around 200,000 people gathered in the square in his honour.

Jan took four agonising days to die, and his body was buried in Olšanské hřbitovy in Žižkov (see later in this chapter). But his grave later became a focus for demonstrations and in 1974 his remains were moved to his home village. By popular demand he was re-interred in Olšany in 1990. A cross-shaped monument set into the pavement to the left of the fountain in front of the Národní muzeum marks the spot where he fell.

square during the revolutionary upheavals of 1848, and in 1918 the creation of the new Czechoslovak Republic was celebrated here.

Following the 17 November 1989 beating of students on Národní třída (see the boxed text 'Student Sacrifices' earlier in this chapter), thousands gathered here in anger, night after night. A week later, in a stunning mirror-image of Klement Gottwald's 1948 proclamation of communist rule in Staroměstské náměstí, Alexander Dubček and Václav Havel stepped onto the balcony of the Melantrich Building to a thunderous and tearful ovation, and proclaimed the end of communism in Czechoslovakia.

At the top of the square is Josef Myslbek's muscular equestrian **statue of St Wenceslas** (sv Václav), the 10th-century pacifist duke of Bohemia and the 'Good King Wenceslas' of the Christmas carol – never a king but decidedly good. Flanked by other patron saints of Bohemia – Prokop, Adalbert, Agnes, and Wenceslas' grandmother Ludmilla – he has been plastered with posters and bunting at every one of the square's historical moments. Near the statue, a small **memorial** to the victims of communism bears photographs and handwritten epitaphs to Jan Palach and other anticommunist rebels.

In contrast to the solemnity of this shrine, the square beyond it has become a monument to capitalism, a gaudy gallery of cafés, fast-food outlets, expensive shops, greedy cabbies and pricey hotels. Noteworthy buildings (from the top of the square, even numbers on the western side) include:

No 25
Grand Hotel Evropa (Map 6; 1906) The most beautiful building on the square, Art Nouveau inside and out; have a peep at the French restaurant at the rear of the ground floor, and at the second floor atrium

No 36
Melantrich Building (Map 6; 1914) Where Havel and Dubček appeared on the balcony in November 1989

No 34
Wiehl House (Map 6; 1896) With a facade decorated with neo-Renaissance murals by Mikuláš Aleš and others, named after its designer, Antonín Wiehl

No 12
Peterkův dům (Peterka House; Map 6; 1901) Art Nouveau building by Jan Kotěra

No 6
Baťa shoe store (Map 6; 1929) Designed by Ludvík Kysela for Tomáš Baťa, art patron, progressive industrialist and founder of the worldwide shoe empire

No 4
Lindt Building (Map 6; 1927) Also designed by Ludvík Kysela, and one of the republic's first constructivist buildings

No 1
Koruna Palace (Map 7; 1914) An Art Nouveau design by Antonín Pfeiffer, with a tower topped with a crown of pearls; note its charming tiny facade around the corner on Na příkopě

At its foot, Wenceslas Square intersects the upmarket shopping street of Na příkopě (see Staré Město earlier in this chapter) at the so-called 'Golden Cross'.

WEST OF WENCESLAS SQUARE (MAP 6)

The most elegant of Nové Město's many passages runs beneath the Art Nouveau **Lucerna Palace** (1920), between Štěpánská 61 and Vodičkova 36. This shopping arcade was designed by Václav Havel, the president's grandfather, and is still partially owned by the president's sister-in-law. The Lucerna complex includes theatres, a cinema, shops, a rock club-cum-restaurant, and cafés. In the marbled atrium hangs a satirical counterpart to the equestrian statue of St Wenceslas (sv Václav) in Wenceslas Square.

The neighbouring **Novák Arcade**, connected to the Lucerna and riddled by a maze of passages, has one of Prague's finest Art Nouveau facades (overlooking Vodičkova), complete with mosaics of country life.

The most sublime attraction in the neighbourhood is the Gothic **kostel Panny Marie Sněžné** (Church of Our Lady of the Snows) at the bottom of Wenceslas Square. It was begun in the 14th century by Charles IV but only the chancel was ever completed, which accounts for its proportions: seemingly taller than it is long. Charles had intended it to be the grandest church in Prague; the nave is higher than that of chrám sv Víta, and the altar is the city's tallest. It was a Hussite stronghold, ringing to the sermons of Jan Želivský, who led the 1419 defenestration that touched off the Hussite Wars.

The church is approached through an arch in the Austrian Cultural Institute at Jungmannovo náměstí 18. Beside the church is the **kaple Panny Marie Pasovské** (Chapel of the Pasov Virgin), now a venue for temporary art exhibitions.

Rest your feet in the **Františkánská zahrada**, former monastery gardens built beside the church by the Franciscans, and now a peaceful park in the middle of the block.

ALONG NÁRODNÍ TŘÍDA (MAP 6)

Národní třída (National Avenue) is central Prague's 'high street', a stately row of mid-range shops and grand government buildings, notably the Národní divadlo at the Vltava River end.

Fronting Jungmannovo náměstí, at the eastern end, is an age-blackened, imitation Venetian palace known as the dům Látek (Cloth House) or **Adria Palace** *(Národní 40)*. Beneath it is the Adria Theatre, birthplace of Laterna Magika (see the Entertainment chapter) and meeting place of Civic Forum in the heady days of the Velvet Revolution. From here, Dubček and Havel walked to the Lucerna Passage and their 24 November 1989 appearance on the balcony of the Melantrich Building.

The **bronze plaque** on the wall inside the arcade near No 16, with a hand making the peace sign and the date '17.11.89', is in memory of the students clubbed in the street on that date (see the boxed text 'Student Sacrifices' earlier in this chapter).

West of Voršilská, the lemon-yellow walls of the **klášter sv Voršila** (Convent of St Ursula) frame a pink church, which has a lush Baroque interior that includes a battalion of Apostle statues. Out the front is St John of Nepomuk, and on the building's lower right niche is a statue of St Agatha holding her severed breasts.

Across the road at No 7 is the fine Art Nouveau facade (by Osvald Polívka) of the **Viola Building**, former home of the Prague Insurance Co, with the huge letters 'PRAHA' around five circular windows, and mosaics spelling out *život, kapitál, důchod, věno* and *pojišťuje* (life, capital, income, dowry and insurance). The building next door, a former publishing house, is also a Polívka design.

On the southern side at No 4, looking like it has been bubble-wrapped by Christo, is Nová Scéna (1983), the 'New National Theatre' building, home of Laterna Magika.

Finally, facing the Vltava River near Smetanovo nábřeží, is the **Národní divadlo** (National Theatre), the neo-Renaissance flagship of the Czech National Revival, funded entirely by private donations and decorated inside and out by a roll call of prominent Czech artists. Architect Josef Zítek's masterpiece burned down within weeks of its 1881 opening but, incredibly, was funded again and restored under Josef Schulz in less than two years. It's now mainly used for ballet and opera performances.

Across from the theatre is the **Kavárna Slavia** (see the Places to Eat chapter), known for its river views and Art Deco interior, once *the* place to be seen or to grab an after-theatre meal. Now renovated, it's once again the place to be seen – though mainly by other tourists.

MASARYKOVO NÁBŘEŽÍ (MAP 6)

About 200m south of the Národní divadlo, along Masarykovo nábřeží (Masaryk Embankment), is a grand Art Nouveau building at No 32, once the East German embassy, now occupied by the **Goethe Institut** (the German Cultural Institute).

Opposite is **Slovanský ostrov** *(Slav Island; Map 6)*, a sleepy, dog-eared sandbank with river views and gardens. Its banks were reinforced with stone in 1784, and a spa and a dye works were built in the early part of the following century. Bohemia's first train had a demonstration run here in 1841, roaring down the island at 11km/h. In 1925 the island was named after Slav conventions held here since 1848. In the middle of the island is a 19th-century meeting hall and a restaurant. At the southern end is **Šitovská věž**, a 15th-century water tower (once part of a mill) with an 18th-century onion-dome roof.

Beneath the tower is the Mánes Building, which houses the **Mánes Gallery** *(admission 25Kč; open 10am-6pm Tues-Sun)*. The gallery was founded in the 1920s by a group of artists headed by painter Josef Mánes, as an alternative to the Czech Academy of Arts. It still has one of Prague's better displays of contemporary art, with changing exhibits.

KARLOVO NÁMĚSTÍ & AROUND

At over seven hectares, Karlovo náměstí (Charles Square) is Prague's biggest square; it's more of a park, really. Presiding over it is **kostel sv Ignáce** *(St Ignatius Church; Map 9)*, a 1660s Baroque *tour de force* designed by Carlo Lurago for the Jesuits. It's worth a look for its huge stone portal and lavish interior.

The square's historical focus is the **Novoměstská radnice** *(New Town Hall; Map 6)* at the northern end, built when the 'New Town' was still new. From its windows two of Wenceslas IV's Catholic councillors were flung to their deaths in 1419 by followers of the Hussite preacher Jan Želivský, giving defenestration (throwing out of the window) – a tactic that would be repeated at Prague Castle in 1618 – a new political meaning, and sparking off the Hussite Wars.

The 23m **tower** *(admission 20Kč; open 10am-6pm Tues-Sun Apr-Sept)* was added 35 years later. You can climb the 221 steps to the top, and visit the Gothic Hall of Justice, site of the defenestration.

The Baroque palace at the southern end of the square belongs to Charles University. It's known as **Faustův dům** *(Faust House; Map 9)* because, according to a popular story, Mephisto took Dr Faust to hell through a hole in the ceiling here; and because of associations with Rudolf II's Irish court alchemist, Edward Kelley, who toiled here in the 16th century trying to convert lead to gold.

Resslova Ulice (Map 9)

Resslova ulice runs west from Karlovo náměstí to the river. Halfway along is the Baroque **kostel sv Cyril a Metoděj** (Church of SS Cyril & Methodius), a 1730s work by Kilian Dientzenhofer and Paul Bayer. The assassination of Reinhard Heydrich took place here (see the boxed text 'The Assassination of Heydrich' in the Facts about Prague chapter).

The crypt now houses the moving **Národní památník obětí heydrichiády** (National Memorial to the Victims of Post-Heydrich Terror; see the boxed text 'Prague under the Nazis' earlier in this chapter).

On the other side of Resslova is the 14th-century Gothic **kostel sv Václava na Zderaze** (Church of St Wenceslas in Zderaz), the former parish church of Zderaz, a village that predates Nové Město. On its western side are parts of a wall and windows from its 12th-century Romanesque predecessor.

Rašínovo Nábřeží (Map 9)

The junction where Resslova meets the river at Rašínovo nábřeží is dominated by the famous **Tančící dům** (Dancing Building), built in 1996 by architects Vlado Milunič and the American Frank O Gehry. The curved lines of the narrow-waisted glass tower clutched against its more upright and formal partner led to it being christened the 'Fred & Ginger Building', after the legendary dancing duo of Astaire and Rogers. It's surprising how well it fits in with its ageing neighbours.

A top-floor flat in the apartment building round the corner at **Rašínovo nábřeží 78** was where Václav Havel first chose to live (in preference to Prague Castle) after being elected as president in December 1989 – surely the world's least pompous presidential residence. He later moved to a house in the outskirts of Prague 6.

Here the Vltava River is lined with elegant *fin-de-siècle* apartment buildings. Two blocks south, on Palackého náměstí, is Stanislav Sucharda's extraordinary **František Palacký Memorial** – an Art Nouveau swarm of haunted bronze figures around a stodgy statue of the 19th-century historian and giant of the Czech National Revival.

Klášter Emauzy & Around (Map 9)

A block inland from Palackého náměstí is klášter Emauzy *(Emmaus Monastery; Vyšehradská 49)*, originally called Na Slovanech Monastery. It was completed in 1372 for a Slavonic Benedictine order at the request of Charles IV, who persuaded the pope to allow the Old Church Slavonic liturgy here, possibly in the hope of undermining the Orthodox Church in neighbouring Slavonic states. These un-Roman Catholic beginnings probably saved it from later Hussite plundering. Spanish Benedictines renamed it Emmaus.

The monastery's Gothic **kostel Panny Marie** (St Mary Church) was damaged by Allied bombs in February 1945. A few ceiling frescoes are still visible. The asymmetrical spires, added in the 1960s, look vaguely out of place. The attached cloisters have some fine, faded original frescoes, salted with bits of pagan symbolism.

Across Vyšehradská is the Baroque **kostel sv Jana Nepomuckého na Skalce** (Church of St John of Nepomuk on the Rock), built in 1739, one of the city's most beautiful Dientzenhofer churches.

Just south on Na slupi is Charles University's **botanická zahrada** *(botanical garden; Na slupi; admission free; open 9am-6pm daily)*. Founded in 1775, and moved from Smíchov to its present site in 1898, it's the country's oldest botanical garden.

EAST OF KARLOVO NÁMĚSTÍ

The area to the east of Karlovo náměstí is occupied by Charles University's medical faculty, and is full of hospitals and clinics.

Halfway between Žitná and Ječná is the 14th-century **kostel sv Štěpána** (St Stephen

Church), with a 15th-century tower, 17th- and 18th-century chapels, and an 1870s neo-gothic face-lift by Josef Mocker. Behind it on Na Rybníčku II is one of Prague's three surviving Romanesque rotundas, the **rotunda sv Longina** *(Rotunda of St Longinus; closed to the public)*, built in the early 12th century.

The most striking building in the drab neighbourhood south of Ječná is the **Vila Amerika** *(☎ 224 91 80 13; Ke Karlovu 20; adult/child 40/20Kč; open 10am-5pm Tues-Sun)*. This 1720s, French-style summerhouse, designed by (you guessed it) Kilian Dientzenhofer, is one of the city's finest Baroque houses, and now houses a museum dedicated to the composer Antonín Dvořák. Special concerts of Dvořák's music are staged here (see the Entertainment chapter).

Around the corner is the pub called **U kalicha** *(At the Chalice; Na bojišti 12)*. This is where the hapless Švejk was arrested at the beginning of Jaroslav Hašek's comic novel of WWI, *The Good Soldier Švejk* (which Hašek cranked out in instalments from his own local pub). U kalicha is milking the connection, as you'll see from all the tour buses outside.

At the southern end of Ke Karlovu is a little church with a big name: **kostel Nanebevzetí Panny Marie a Karla Velikého** (Church of the Assumption of the Virgin Mary & Charlemagne), founded by Charles IV in 1350 and modelled on Charlemagne's burial chapel in Aachen. In the 16th century it acquired its fabulous ribbed vault, whose revolutionary unsupported span was attributed by some to witchcraft.

From the terrace beyond the church you can see some of Nové Město's original fortifications, and look out at the Nuselský most (Nusle Bridge), which vaults the valley of the Botič creek to Vyšehrad, with six lanes of traffic on top and the metro inside.

Vyšehrad (Map 9)

Archaeologists know that various early Slavonic tribes set up camp near Hradčany and at Vyšehrad (High Castle), a crag above the Vltava River south of the Nusle valley. But Vyšehrad alone is regarded as Prague's *mythical* birthplace. According to legend, the wise chieftain Krok built a castle here in the 7th century. Libuše, the cleverest of his three daughters, prophesied that a great city would rise here. Taking as her king a ploughman named Přemysl, she founded Praha and the Přemyslid dynasty.

Vyšehrad may in fact have been settled as early as the 9th century, and Boleslav II (r. 972–99) may have lived here for a time. There was a fortified town by the mid-11th century. Vratislav II (r. 1061–92) moved here from Hradčany, beefing up the walls, and adding a castle, the bazilika sv Vavřince (St Lawrence Basilica), kostel sv Petra a Pavla (Church of SS Peter & Paul) and the Rotunda sv Martina (Rotunda of St Martin). His successors stayed until 1140, when Vladislav II returned to Hradčany.

Vyšehrad then faded until Charles IV, aware of its symbolic importance, repaired the walls and joined them to those of his new town, Nové Město. He built a small palace, and decreed that the coronations of Bohemian kings should begin with a procession from here to Hradčany.

Nearly everything was wiped out during the Hussite Wars. The hill remained a ruin – except for a township of artisans and traders – until after the Thirty Years' War, when Leopold I refortified it.

The Czech National Revival generated new interest in Vyšehrad as a symbol of Czech history. Painters painted it, poets sang about the old days, Smetana set his opera *Libuše* there. Many fortifications were dismantled in 1866 and the parish graveyard was converted into a national memorial cemetery.

Vyšehrad retains a place in Czech hearts, and is a popular destination for weekend family outings. Since the 1920s the old fortress has been a quiet park, with splendid panoramas of the Vltava valley. Take along a picnic and find a quiet spot among the trees, or with a view over the river.

VYŠEHRAD FORTRESS

From Vyšehrad metro station, head west past the Kongresové centrum (Congress Centre) to the Táborská brána (Tábor Gate). Inside are the remains of another gate (Špička brána), an **information office** *(open 9.30am-6.30pm daily)*, a café, and the Leopoldova brána, the most elegant of the fort's gates. Táborská brána and Leopoldova brána were erected, and the Gothic Špička gate pulled down, in the course of refortification after the Thirty Years' War.

You can also walk uphill from the No 7, 18 or 24 tram stop on Ostrčilovo náměstí, through the 1842 Cihelná brána (Brick Gate, also called Pražská or Vyšehradská brána). Check out the fine views of the Nusle valley from the northeastern bastion.

A more strenuous approach is from the tram No 3, 16, 17 or 21 stop on the riverside Rašínovo nábřeží. Continue under the railway bridge and across the busy traffic junction, then go left on the lane just past Libušina and up the long stairs to the western end of the fortress.

A good booklet about Vyšehrad's buildings is available from the kasematy (casemates), bazilika sv Vavřince and the galérie Vyšehrad (Vyšehrad Gallery).

Rotunda sv Martina

Vratislav II's little chapel, the rotunda sv Martina (Rotunda of St Martin), built in the 11th century, is Prague's oldest surviving building. In the 18th century it was used as a powder magazine. The door and frescoes date from a renovation in about 1880.

Nearby are a 1714 plague column and the Baroque **kaple Panny Marie v hradbách** (St Mary Chapel in the Ramparts), dating from about 1750, and behind them the remains of the 14th-century **kostelík Stětí sv Jana Křtitele** (Church of the Beheading of St John the Baptist).

Kostel sv Petra a Pavla

Vratislav II's kostel sv Petra a Pavla *(Church of SS Peter & Paul; admission 20Kč; open 9am-noon & 1pm-5pm Mon, Wed, Thur & Sat; 9am-noon Fri; 11am-5pm Sun)* has been built and rebuilt over the centuries, culminating in a neogothic work-over by Josef Mocker in the 1880s. The twin steeples, a distinctive feature of the Vyšehrad skyline, were added in 1903. The interior is a swirling acid-trip of colourful Art Nouveau frescoes, painted in the 1920s by various Czech artists.

Vyšehradský Hřbitov

For Czechs, the Vyšehradský hřbitov *(Vyšehrad Cemetery; admission free; open 8am-7pm daily May-Sept; 8am-6pm daily Mar, Apr & Oct; 9am-4pm daily Nov-Feb)* is the hill's main attraction. In the late 19th century, the parish graveyard was made into a memorial cemetery for famous figures of Czech culture, with a graceful, neo-Renaissance arcade running along the northern and western sides. For the real heroes, an elaborate pantheon called the **Slavín** (loosely, Hall of Fame), designed by Antonín Wiehl, was added at the eastern end in 1894; its 50-odd occupants include painter Alfons Mucha, sculptor Josef Myslbek and architect Josef Gočár. The motto reads 'ACZEMERJESMLUVÍ' – 'Though dead, they still speak'.

The 600 or so graves in the rest of the cemetery include those of composers Smetana and Dvořák, and writers Karel Čapek, Jan Neruda and Božena Němcová; there's a directory of famous names at the entrance. Some of the most beautiful headstones bear names few foreigners will recognise.

The Prague Spring (Pražské jaro) music festival kicks off every 12 May, the anniversary of Smetana's death, with a procession from his grave at Vyšehrad to the Obecní dům.

Vyšehradské Sady

South of the church are the Vyšehradské sady (Vyšehrad Gardens), with four statues by Josef Myslbek based on Czech legends. Libuše and Přemysl are in the northwestern corner; in the southeast are Šárka and Ctirad (see the boxed text 'Love Hurts' later in this chapter). On Sunday from May to August, open-air concerts are held here at 2.30pm, with anything from jazz to oompah to chamber music.

Other Sights

At the Cihelná brána is the entrance to the vaulted **kasematy** *(casemates; admission 20Kč; open 9.30am-5.30pm daily May-Oct,*

9.30am-4.30pm daily Nov-Apr) beneath the ramparts. The guided tour leads through several of these chambers, now used as a historical exhibit and for storing four of the original Baroque statues from Charles Bridge (other originals are at the Lapidárium in Holešovice; see Inner Suburbs later in this chapter).

You can also examine the foundations of the 11th-century Romanesque **bazilika sv Vavřince** *(St Lawrence Basilica; admission 10Kč; open 11am-6pm daily)*. Ask for the key in the snack bar next door.

In front of the southwestern bastion are the foundations of a small **royal palace** built by Charles IV, and then dismantled in 1655. Perched on the bastion is the **galérie Vyšehrad** *(Vyšehrad Gallery; admission 10Kč; open 9.30am-5.30pm Tues-Sun)*, with temporary exhibitions. Below the bastion are some ruined guard towers poetically named Libuše's Bath.

In the northwestern corner is the former **Nové proboštství** (New Provost's House), built in 1874. In the adjacent park is an open-air **Letní scéna** (Summer Theatre) where you can catch a concert or cultural show from 6pm on most Thursdays or the odd children's performance on Tuesday afternoon (usually around 2pm).

CUBIST ARCHITECTURE

If you've taken the trouble to come out to Vyšehrad, don't miss the chance to see some of Prague's finest Cubist buildings. Cubist architecture, with its eye-catching use of elementary geometric forms, is more or less unique to the Czech Republic, and particularly to Prague.

Best of the lot is the simple, striking facade of the apartment block at **Neklanova 30** by the dean of Czech Cubist architects, Josef Chochol. Other buildings by Chochol are the **Villa Libušina** at the corner of Vnislavova and Rašínovo nábřeží, and a **terrace** of three houses at Rašínovo nábřeží 6–10, just before it tunnels beneath Vyšehrad rock. All date from around 1912 to 1913. Other Cubist works by lesser lights are scattered around the neighbourhood.

Inner Suburbs

BUBENEČ & HOLEŠOVICE

This patch of Prague inside Vltava River's 'big bend' grew from two old settlements, Holešovice and the fishing village of Bubny. Both remained small until industry arrived in the mid-19th century and the Hlávkův most (1868) linked it to Nové Město. Close behind came a horse-drawn tram line, a river port and the exhibition grounds. The area was made part of Prague in 1884.

Strictly speaking, the boundary between Bubeneč (to the west) and Holešovice (to the east) lies along Čechova ulice, between the Stromovka and Letná parks.

Výstaviště

This vast exhibition area *(Maps 3 & 4; ☎ 220 10 31 11; U Výstaviště)* grew up around several buildings erected for the 1891 Terrestrial Jubilee Exposition. These include the Pavilón hlavního města Prahy (Prague Pavilion), which houses the Lapidárium, and the Průmuslový palác (Palace of Industry).

This was once the venue for the big spring and autumn trade fairs, but these are moving to a new exhibition centre at Letňany in the northeastern suburbs, now partially open and due for final completion in 2006. Výstaviště still hosts the popular annual funfair **Matějská pouť** (St Matthew's Fair) in March, when it's full of roller-coasters, candyfloss, and half of Prague having fun.

The **Lapidárium** *(Map 4; ☎ 233 37 56 36; admission 20/10Kč; open noon-6pm Tues-Fri, 10am-12.30pm & 1pm-6pm Sat-Sun)* is a repository for some 400 sculptures from the 11th to the 19th centuries. They include the Lions of Kouřim – Bohemia's oldest surviving stone sculpture – parts of the Renaissance Krocín Fountain that once stood in Old Town Square, 10 of Charles Bridge's original statues, and many other superb sculptures. This is an often overlooked gem of a museum.

You can watch the musical **Křižíkova Fontána** *(Křižík Fountain; Map 3; ☎ 220 10 32 80; Ⓦ www.krizikovafontana.cz)* do its thing in the evenings: a computer-controlled dance to

The Missing Monuments

Prague witnessed several profound changes of political regime during the 20th century: from Habsburg Empire to independent Czechoslovak Republic in 1918; to Nazi Protectorate from 1938 to 1945; to communist state in 1948; and back to democratic republic in 1989.

Each change was accompanied by widespread renaming of city streets and squares to reflect the heroes of the new regime. The square in front of the Rudolfinum in Staré Město, for example, was known variously as Smetanovo náměstí (Smetana Square; 1918–39); Mozartplatz (Mozart Square; 1939–45); náměstí Krasnoarmějců (Red Army Square; 1948–89); and náměstí Jana Palacha (Jan Palach Square; 1989–present).

This renaming was often followed by the removal of monuments erected by the previous regime. Here are five of Prague's most prominent 'missing monuments':

The Missing Virgin

If you look at the ground in Old Town Square (Staroměstské náměstí; Map 7) about 50m south of the Jan Hus monument, you'll see a circular stone slab set among the cobblestones. This was the site of a Marian Column (a pillar bearing a statue of the Virgin Mary), erected in 1650 in celebration of the Habsburg victory over the Swedes in 1648. It was surrounded by figures of angels crushing and beating down demons – symbolic of a resurgent Catholic Church defeating the Protestant Reformation.

The column was toppled by a mob – who saw it as a symbol of Habsburg repression – on 3 November 1918, five days after the declaration of Czechoslovak independence. Its remains can be seen in the Lapidárium at Výstaviště (see earlier in this chapter).

The Missing Emperor

Before 1918, Smetanovo nábřeží (Smetana Embankment; Map 6), between Charles Bridge and the Národní divadlo (National Theatre), was known as Emperor Francis I Embankment, after the Habsburg ruler. A block north of the theatre is a little garden with an elaborately pinnacled neogothic monument; take a second look, however, and you'll see that the pedestal at the top of the monument is empty. The equestrian statue of Francis I that once stood here was moved to the Lapidárium in 1918; plans for a statue of Smetana never materialised, and the plinth has been empty ever since.

The Missing General

Another victim of the change of regime in 1918 was the statue of Field Marshal Vacláv Radecký (1766–1858) – or Count Josef Radetzky, to give him his Austrian name – that once stood in the upper

recorded music. Performances range from classical music such as Dvořák's 'From the New World' to modern works by Jean Michel Jarre and Vangelis, rock music by Queen, and music from popular films. Prices for shows hover around 200Kč. Starting times are generally 8pm, 9pm, 10pm and 11pm daily. Call or check out the website for details of what's on (in Czech only – click the 'program' link and select 'na týden dopředu' for the following week's programme. It's best after sunset, lit with coloured lights.

Behind the fountain pavilion is the **divadlo Spirála** *(Spiral Theatre; Map 3)*, a venue for Czech-language musicals (see the Entertainment chapter). **Dětský svět** *(Children's World; Map 3)* is a children's theatre with regular weekend performances. The **Maroldovo Panorama** *(Map 3; open 2pm-5pm Tues-Fri, 10am-5pm Sat-Sun)* is an impressive 360° diorama of the 1434 battle of Lipany (in which the Hussite Taborites lost to the Hussite Utraquists and Emperor Zikmund's forces).

To get there, take tram No 12 westbound from outside metro Nádraží Holešovice, or tram No 5 northbound from náměstí Republiky.

The Missing Monuments

part of Malostranské náměstí (Map 5); it too is now in the Lápidarium. Although Radecký was a Czech, his fame derived from leading the Habsburg armies to victory against Napoleon, and crushing the Italians at the battles of Custoza and Novara. (Composer Johann Strauss the Elder wrote the *Radetzky March* in his honour.) A Baroque religious sculpture now occupies the site of Radecký's former pedestal.

The Missing Dictator

If you stand on Old Town Square (Map 7) and look north along the avenue of Pařížská you will see, on a huge terrace at the far side of Čechův most (Bohemia Bridge), a giant metronome. If the monumental setting seems out of scale with the monument, that's because the terrace was designed to accommodate the world's biggest statue of Stalin. Unveiled in 1955 – two years after Stalin's death – the 30m-high, 14,000-tonne monument showed Uncle Joe at the head of two lines of communist heroes, Czech on one side, Soviet on the other. Cynical Praguers quickly nicknamed it '*fronta na maso*' ('the meat queue').

The monument was dynamited in 1962, in deference to Krushcev's attempt to airbrush Stalin out of history. The demolition crew were instructed: 'It must go quickly, there musn't be much of a bang, and it should be seen by as few people as possible'. The Museum of Communism (see the boxed text 'Communist Prague' later in this chapter) has a superb photo of the monument – and of its destruction.

The Missing Tank

Náměstí Kinských (Map 5), at the southern edge of Malá Strana, was until 1989 known as náměstí Sovětských tankistů (Soviet Tank Crews Square), named in memory of the Soviet soldiers who 'liberated' Prague on 9 May 1945. For many years a Soviet T-34 tank – allegedly the first to enter the city – squatted menacingly atop a pedestal here (in fact it was a later Soviet 'gift').

In 1991, artist David Černý decided that the tank was an inappropriate monument to the Soviet soldiers and painted it bright pink. The authorities had it painted green again, and charged Černý with a crime against the state. This infuriated many parliamentarians, 12 of whom re-painted the tank pink. Their parliamentary immunity saved them from arrest and secured Černý's release.

After complaints from the Soviet Union, the tank was removed. Only a grassy patch between two rusting flagpoles remains, where every 9 May a few die-hard communists celebrate their own version of Liberation Day. The tank still exists, and is still pink – it's at the Military Museum in Lešany, near Týnec nad Sázavou, 30km south of Prague.

Stromovka

Stromovka, west of Výstaviště, is Prague's largest park. In the Middle Ages it was a royal hunting preserve, which is why it's sometimes called the Královská obora (Royal Deer Park). Rudolf II had rare trees planted and several lakes created (fed from the Vltava River via a still-functioning canal).

Stromovka has a **Planetárium** *(Map 3; ☎ 233 37 64 52; Královská obora 233; exhibition adult/child 10/5Kč, shows 30-120Kč; open 11am-8pm Sat-Thur)* just outside Výstaviště. There are various slide and video shows in addition to the astronomical shows, or you can just wander through the exhibition in the main hall.

Ekotechnické Muzeum

Near the banks of the Vltava River is the Ekotechnické muzeum *(Ecotechnical Museum; Map 3; ☎ 233 32 55 00; Papírenská 6, Bubeneč; admission 30Kč; open 10am-5pm Sat-Sun Apr-Oct)*, the former Waste Water Treatment Plant built between 1895 and 1906, following a design by the English architect WH Lindley. Surprisingly, it was in service until 1967 as the plant was designed to service a city of 500,000 people but by the time the plant closed, Prague had a population of over a million. There are several steam-powered engines in operation and more are being repaired. During the first weekend in September all the machinery is demonstrated in full working order. Take bus No 131 from Pod kaštany, near Hradčanská metro station, two stops to Praha-Bubeneč (nádraží) train station.

Veletržní Palác

In 1996 the huge, grimly functionalist Veletržní palác (Trade Fair Palace; 1928) became the new home of the National Gallery's **Centre for Modern & Contemporary Art** *(Map 4; ☎ 224 30 11 11; Dukelských hrdinů 47; adult/child 100/50Kč per floor or 200/100Kč for all 4 floors, free 1st Wed of month; open 10am-6pm Tues, Wed & Fri-Sun; 10am-9pm Thur)*. The superb collection of 19th- and 20th-century Czech and European art is spread over three floors of the vast, ocean-liner-like building.

You could easily spend a whole day here, but if you only have an hour to spare, head for the third floor (Czech Art 1900–30, and 19th- & 20th-century French Art) to see the *Sunbeam Motorcyclist* sculpture by Otokar Svec; the paintings of František Kupka, pioneer of abstract art; and the art, furniture and ceramics of the Czech Cubists. The French section includes some sculpture by Rodin, a few unexceptional Impressionist works, Gaugin's *Flight* and Van Gogh's *Green Wheat*.

Highlights of the fourth floor (19th-century Czech Art) include the Art Nouveau sculpture of Josef Myslbek, Stanislav Sucharda and Bohumil Kafka; the glowing portraits by Josef Mánes; and the forest landscapes by Július Mařák.

The first floor (20th-century Foreign Art) includes works by Picasso, Warhol and Lichtenstein, while the second floor (Czech Art 1930 to present day) has early examples of kinetic art, some Socialist Realist stuff from the communist era, and various amusing works by contemporary artists – check out the grotesque *Dog Family* by Karel Pauzer.

Take tram No 12 west from Nádraží Holešovice metro station to the Veletržní stop, or No 5 north from náměstí Republiky.

Národní Technické Muzeum

The fun Národní Technické muzeum *(National Technology Museum; Map 3; ☎ 220 39 91 11; Kostelní 42; adult/child 70/30Kč, with audioguide 120/80Kč; open 9am-5pm Tues-Sun)* has a huge main hall full of old trains, planes and automobiles, including 1920s and 30s Škoda and Tatra cars and a fine collection of Bugattis. The motorcycle exhibit has a 1926 BSA 350-L in perfect nick, and among the vintage bicycles you'll find a 1921 predecessor of the 1970s Raleigh Chopper. Upstairs you can fool around with the cameras in a working TV studio, or head for the basement for a tour down a simulated mineshaft.

From Vltavská metro station, take tram No 1 or 25 west, three stops to Letenské náměstí, and walk down Nad štolou and Muzejní streets.

Letná (Map 3)

Letná is a vast open area between Hradčany and Holešovice, with a parade ground to the north and a peaceful park, the **Letenské sady** (Letná Gardens), descending to the Vltava River with postcard views of the city and its bridges. In 1261 Přemysl Otakar II held his coronation celebrations here, and during communist times Letná was the site of Moscow-style May Day military parades. In 1989 750,000 people gathered here in support of the Velvet Revolution, and in 1990, Pope John Paul II gave an open-air Mass here to more than a million people. See the boxed texts 'Missing Monuments' and 'Communist Prague' in this chapter for more information.

In the southwestern corner is the charming Art Nouveau **Hanavský Pavilón**, built by Otto Prieser for the 1891 Jubilee Exposition.

ŽIŽKOV

Named after the one-eyed Hussite hero, Jan Žižka, who whipped Holy Roman Emperor Sigismund here in 1420, Žižkov has always been a rough-and-ready, working-class neighbourhood, full of revolutionary fizz well before 1948. Streets near the centre are slowly getting a face-lift but much of the district is still grimy and run down. It's famous for its numerous bars and nightclubs, and the views from Vítkov and the futuristic TV Tower.

Žižkov Hill (Vítkov)

The famous battle of Vítkov – it was not renamed Žižkov Hill until much later – took place in July 1420 on this long ridge separating Žižkov and Karlín districts. A colossal **statue of Jan Žižka** *(Map 8)*, the Hussite general, was erected here in 1950, commanding superb views across Staré Město to Prague Castle. It's said to be the biggest equestrian statue in the world.

Behind it is the **Národní památník** *(National Memorial; Map 8)*. See the boxed text 'Communist Prague' later in this chapter for more information. The massive memorial building – which has all the elegance of the reactor house at a nuclear power station – is closed to the public.

From Florenc or Praha hlavní nádraží (Prague's main train station), walk along Husitská; after the first railway bridge, turn left up U památníku. On the way up, battle freaks can stop at the grim-looking **Armádní muzeum** *(Army Museum; Map 6; ☎ 220 20 49 24; U památníku 2; adult/child 40/20Kč; open 10am-6pm Tues-Sun May-Oct, 9am-5pm Mon-Fri Nov-Apr)*, with a courtyard full of rusting tanks, and exhibits on the history of the Czechoslovak army and resistance movement from 1918 to 1945.

Televizní Vysílač

Prague's tallest, ugliest landmark is the 216m Televizní Vysílač *(TV Tower; Map 8; ☎ 267 00 57 78; Mahlerovy sady 1; adult/child 120/60Kč; open 10am-11pm daily)*, erected between 1985 and 1992. The viewing platforms, reached by high-speed lifts, have good information boards in English and French explaining what you can see. There is also a restaurant (at 63m). Ten giant crawling babies with slots for faces appear to be exploring the outside of the tower – an installation called *Miminka* (Mummy) by artist David Černý.

The tower is built on the site of a **Jewish cemetery** *(admission 20Kč; open 9am-1pm Tues & Thur)* that was opened after Josefov's was closed, and remained in use until 1890. What's left of the cemetery is just north of the tower.

Olšanské Hřbitovy

Olšanské hřbitovy *(Olšany Cemetery; Map 8; Vinohradská 153; admission free; open 8am-7pm daily May-Sept; 8am-6pm Mar, Apr & Oct; 9am-4pm Nov-Feb)*, Prague's main burial place, was founded in 1680 during a plague epidemic. Its oldest stones are in the northwestern corner, near the 17th-century **kaple sv Rocha** (St Roch Chapel).

There are several entrances to the cemetery along Vinohradská, east of Flora metro station. Jan Palach, the student who set himself on fire in January 1969 in protest at the Soviet invasion, is buried here (see the boxed text 'Student Sacrifices' earlier in this chapter). To find his grave, enter the main gate (flanked by flower shops) and turn right – it's about 50m along on the left of the path.

Židovské Hřbitovy

Franz Kafka is buried in the Židovské hřbitovy *(Jewish Cemetery; Map 2; admission free; open 9am-5pm Sun-Thur & 9am-2pm Fri Apr-Oct, 9am-4pm Sun-Thur & 9am-2pm Fri Nov-Mar, closed on Jewish holidays)*, which opened around 1890 when the previous Jewish cemetery – now at the foot of the Televizní Vysílač – was closed. To find Kafka's grave, follow the main avenue east (signposted), turn right at row 21, then left at the wall; it's at the end of the 'block'. Fans make a pilgrimage on June 3, the anniversary of his death.

The entrance is beside Želivského metro station; men should cover their heads (yarmulkes are available at the gate). Last admission is half an hour before closing.

VINOHRADY

Vinohrady lies southeast of the Národní muzeum and Praha hlavní nádraží. The name refers to vineyards that grew here centuries ago; even as recently as 200 years ago there was little urbanisation. Today it is an upmarket residential district of elegant, early-20th-century apartment blocks and wooded parks.

Vinohrady's physical and commercial heart is **náměstí Míru** (Peace Square), dominated by the neogothic **kostel sv Ludmily** *(St*

Ludmilla Church; Map 10). Right behind it is the neo-Renaissance **Národní dům** *(National House; Map 10)*, with exhibition and concert halls. On the northern side of the square is the **divadlo na Vinohradech** *(Vinohrady Theatre; Map 10)*, which was built in 1909 and is a popular drama venue.

At the eastern end of Vinohrady is the striking **kostel Nejsvětějšího Srdce Páně** *(Church of the Most Sacred Heart of Our Lord; Map 8; náměstí Jiřího z Poděbrad)*. It was built in 1932 and is probably Prague's most original church. It's the work of Jože Plečník, the Slovenian architect who also raised a few eyebrows with his additions to Prague Castle. Inspired by Egyptian temples and early Christian basilicas, the glazed brick building sports a massive, tombstone-like bell tower pierced by a circular glass clock-window.

Another architectural surprise from the same period is Josef Gočár's constructivist **kostel sv Václava** *(St Wenceslas Church; Map*

Communist Prague

It would be difficult to think of a more ironic site for Prague's new **Museum of Communism** *(Map 7; ☎ 224 21 29 66; Na příkopě 10; adult/child 180/140Kč; open 9am-9pm daily)* – it occupies part of an 18th-century aristocrat's palace, stuck between a casino on one side and a McDonald's burger restaurant on the other. Put together by an American expat and his Czech partner, the museum tells the story of Czechoslovakia's years behind the Iron Curtain in photos, words and a fascinating and varied collection of… well, stuff.

Here are a few more prominent reminders of Prague's 41 years as a communist capital:

Letná terása *(Letná Terrace; Map 3)* The monumental, stepped terrace overlooking the river on the southern edge of Letenské sady (park) dates from the early 1950s, when a huge statue of Stalin, the world's biggest, was erected here by the Communist Party of Czechoslovakia, only to be blown up in 1962 by the same sycophants when Stalin was no longer flavour of the decade (see the boxed text 'Missing Monuments' earlier in this chapter). A peculiar giant metronome – a symbolic reminder of the passing of time – has stood in its place since 1991. The latest plans for the area include the building of a giant oceanarium (opening late 2004).

Hotel Crowne Plaza Prague *(Map 3; see the Places to Stay chapter)* The silhouette of this huge Stalinist building in northern Dejvice will be familiar to anyone who has visited the Russian capital. Originally called the Hotel International, it was built in the 1950s to a design inspired by the tower of Moscow University, right down to the Soviet-style star on top of the spire (though this one is green, not red).

Nip into the gleamingly restored, marble-clad lobby bar (to the right), and take a look at the large tapestry hanging on the wall in the far left-hand corner. Entitled *Praga Regina Musicae* (Prague, Queen of Music), and created by Cyril Bouda around 1956, it shows an exaggerated aerial view of central Prague. Bang in the centre is the former Stalin Monument on Letná terása, and at the bottom edge you can spot the now-departed Soviet Tank memorial (see the boxed text 'Missing Monuments' earlier in this chapter).

Národní památník *(National Monument; Map 8)* Although not, strictly speaking, a legacy of the communist era – it was completed in the 1930s – the huge monument atop Žižkov Hill is, in the minds of most Praguers over a certain age, inextricably linked with the Communist Party of Czechoslovakia, and in particular with Klement Gottwald, the country's first 'worker-president'.

Designed in the 1920s as a memorial to the 15th-century Hussite commander Jan Žižka, and to the soldiers who had fought for Czechoslovak independence, it was still under construction in the

2; náměstí Svatopluka Čecha). Built in 1930 it has a fragile-looking tower and climbs the steep hillside. Take tram No 4 or 22 from Karlovo náměstí.

SMÍCHOV (MAP 9)

The suburb of Smíchov became part of Prague in 1838 and grew into an industrial quarter full of chimney stacks, railway yards and the sprawling Staropramen brewery.

Mozart stayed at the elegant 17th-century villa called **Bertramka** (☎ *257 31 74 65; Mozartova 169; adult/child 90/50Kč; open 9.30am-6pm daily Apr-Oct, 9.30am-5pm daily Nov-Mar)* during his visits to Prague in 1787 and 1791, as guest of composer František Dušek. Here he finished his opera *Don Giovanni*. Today the house is a modest Mozart museum. Regular concerts (adult/child 350/230Kč) are held in the salon, and in the garden (April to October). Take tram No 4, 7 or 9 from Anděl metro station.

Communist Prague

late 1930s. The occupation of Czechoslovakia by Nazi Germany in 1939 made the 'Monument to National Liberation', as it was called, seem like a sick joke.

After 1948 the Communist Party appropriated Jan Žižka and the Hussites for the purposes of propaganda, extolling them as shining examples of Czech peasant power. The communists completed the Národní památník with the installation of the Tomb of the Unknown Soldier, and Bohumil Kafka's gargantuan bronze statue of Žižka. But they didn't stop there.

In 1953 the monument's mausoleum – originally intended for the remains of Czechoslovakia's founding father, Tomáš Masaryk – received the embalmed body of Klement Gottwald, displayed to the public in a refrigerated glass chamber, just like his more illustrious comrade Lenin in Moscow's Red Square. It soon became a compulsory outing for school groups and bus-loads of visiting Soviet-bloc tourists.

However, Gottwald's morticians were apparently not as adept as the Russians – by 1962 the body had decayed so badly that it had to be cremated. Since 1989 the monument has been closed to the public except on a few special occasions, although you can wander freely around the exterior. This is a pity, as the interior is a spectacular extravaganza of polished marble and gilt, and its memorials – Soviet as well as Czech – allow a glimpse of a period of Czech history that many would prefer to forget. At the time of writing there were plans under consideration for the re-opening of the site, but it remains to be seen what comes of them.

Paneláky Prague's outer suburbs consist mainly of huge 1970s and 80s housing estates characterised by serried ranks of high-rise apartment blocks, known in Czech as *paneláky* (singular *panelák*) because they were built using prefabricated, reinforced concrete panels. Each block contains hundreds of identical flats, and each estate contains dozens of identical blocks.

Western visitors often assume that these concrete suburbs must be sink estates, filled with the city's poor and riddled with crime and drugs. Nothing could be further from the truth. The *panelák* suburbs are home to a broad spectrum of Czech society, from students to surgeons and from lawyers to street sweepers. Local services and public transport are good, there is plenty of open parkland, and there is a surprisingly strong sense of community.

Although perhaps lacking in aesthetic appeal, Prague's *paneláky* were neither particularly cheap nor quick to build, in contrast to the often shoddy residential blocks of similar vintage that blight many Russian cities. The prime motive for their construction was, rather, ideological. Their very uniformity was the antithesis of bourgeois individuality, and spoke of a new order where all were to be equal.

The biggest conglomeration of *paneláky* is in Jižní Město (South Town; Map 2) on the southeastern edge of the city, comprising the suburbs of Háje, Opatov and Chodov. Take metro line C to the end of the line at Háje for a quick stroll among the concrete canyons.

DEJVICE

Near the northeastern edge of Hradčany is the striking, red-brick **Bílkova vila** *(Bílek Villa; Map 3; Mickiewiczova 1; admission 50Kč, free 1st Tues of month; open 9am-6pm daily mid-May–mid-Oct, 9am-5pm daily mid-Oct–mid-May)*, designed by the sculptor František Bílek in 1911 as his own home, and now a museum of his unconventional stone and wood reliefs, furniture and graphics. A sign in front also calls it František Bílek Sochařský Atelier (Sculpture Studio). Take tram No 18 one stop north from Malostranská metro station.

Nearby are a marvellous matching pair of **Cubist houses** *(Map 3; Tychonova 4-6)* designed by the architect Josef Gočár as his residence.

North of Dejvice, the unusual villa suburb of **Baba** *(Map 2)* was a Functionalist project (1933–40) by a team of artists and designers, to build cheap, attractive, single-family houses. The **Hanspaulka** *(Map 1)* suburb to the south was a similar project, built between 1925 and 1930.

Outer Suburbs

Prague's outer suburbs are described clockwise, starting from the north.

TROJA

Facing the Vltava River north of the 'big bend' is **Trojský zámek** *(Troja Chateau; Map 2; ☎ 283 85 16 14; U Trojského zámku 1; adult/child 120/60Kč, free 1st Tues of month; open 10am-6pm Tues-Sun Apr-Oct, 10am-5pm Sat-Sun Nov-Mar)*, a 17th-century Baroque palace with a gang of stone giants on the balustrade above its French gardens. On the walls and ceiling of the main hall is a vast, obsequious mural depicting the Habsburgs in full transcendental glory. The chateau, which houses part of the Prague City Gallery's collection of 19th-century Czech paintings, can be visited by guided tour only, but you're free to wander in the beautiful gardens.

Across the road is the city **zoo** *(adult/child 60/30Kč; open 10am-7pm daily)*, set in 60 hectares of wooded grounds. Pride of place, at the top of the hill, goes to a herd of Przewalski's horses, little steppe-dwellers that still survive in the wilds of Mongolia and are successfully bred here.

To get to the chateau from Nádraží Holešovice metro station (Map 4) take bus No 112 to the end of the line. Tram No 5 from náměstí Republiky (Map 7) goes to within 15 minutes' walk of the zoo; head west from the tram stop along Trojská. Or take a boat trip from the city centre (see Boat in the Getting Around chapter). Or walk through Stromovka from Výstaviště (20 minutes).

KBELY

The Kbely airfield in northeastern Prague is home to the **muzeum letectví a kosmonautiky** *(Air & Space Museum; Map 2; ☎ 220 20 75 04; Mladoboleslavská; adult/child 40/20Kč; open 10am-6pm Tues-Thur & Sat-Sun May-Oct)*, where you can have a close look at Russian MiG fighter planes and a host of exhibits on aeronautics and space flight. The impressive collection amounts to no less than 275 aircraft.

Take bus No 185 or 259 six stops east from Českomoravská metro station.

ZBRASLAV

This town, 10km south of the city centre (see the Excursions map), was only incorporated into Greater Prague recently. As early as 1268 Přemysl Otakar II built a hunting lodge and a chapel here, later rebuilt as a Cistercian monastery. In 1784 it was converted into a Baroque chateau, the **Zámek Zbraslav** *(☎ 257 92 16 38; Bartoňova 2; adult/child 80/40Kč; open 10am-6pm Tues-Sun)*. It houses the National Gallery's permanent collection of Oriental and Asian art, with copies of well known Czech sculptures in the gardens.

Take bus No 129, 241 or 243 from Smíchovské Nádraží metro station (Map 9).

BARRANDOV (MAP 2)

The southern suburb of Barrandov, on the western bank of the Vltava River, was developed in the 1930s by Václav Havel, the father of President Havel. It is famous for the **Barrandov Studios**, the film studios founded by Miloš Havel (the president's uncle) in 1931, and increasingly popular today with Hollywood producers – *Mission Impossible* (1996), *Blade 2* (2001) and *The League of Extraordinary Gentlemen* (2002) were shot here.

The suburb was named after the 19th-century French geologist, Joachim Barrande, who studied the fossils in the contorted limestone of the **Barrandovské skály** (Barrandov Cliffs) – hundreds of them are on display in the Národní muzeum.

STŘEŠOVICE

The **muzeum MHD** *(Map 5; Public Transport Museum; ☎ 233 32 24 32; Patočkova 4; admission 20Kč; open 9am-5pm Sat-Sun & holidays Apr-Oct)*, at the Střešovice tram depot, has a large collection of trams and buses, from an 1886 horse-drawn tram to present-day vehicles. It's great for kids as they can climb into some of the vehicles. Take tram No 1 or 8 from Hradčanská metro station (Map 3) two stops to the Vozovna Střešovice stop.

Fans of modern architecture will appreciate the Functionalist **Müllerova vila** *(Map 2; Müller Villa; ☎ 224 31 20 12; Nad hradním vodojemem 14; admission 300Kč, open 9am-5pm Tues, Thur & Sat-Sun)*. The villa was designed by the Viennese architect Adolf Loos, whose ultramodernist exterior contrasts with the classically decorated interior. The overpriced (an extra 100Kč) English- or German-language 90-minute tour has to be booked in advance. To get there take tram No 1 or 18 from Hradčanská metro station (Map 3) four stops to Ořechovka.

BŘEVNOV (MAP 2)

Břevnovský klášter *(Břevnov Monastery; Map 2; ☎ 220 40 61 11; open 9am-5pm Sat-Sun mid-Apr–mid-Oct, 10am-3pm Sat-Sun mid-Oct–mid-Apr)* is the Czech Republic's oldest Benedictine monastery, founded in 993 by Boleslav II and Bishop St Vojtěch Slavníkovec. The men, from opposing and powerful families intent on dominating Bohemia, met at Vojtěška spring, each having had a dream that this was the place to found a monastery. The name comes from *břevno* (beam), after the beam laid across the spring where they met.

The present Baroque monastery building and the nearby **bazilika sv Markéty** (Church of St Margaret) were completed in 1720 by Kristof Dientzenhofer. In 1993 (the 1000th anniversary of the monastery's founding) the restored first floor, with its fine ceiling frescoes, and the Romanesque crypt, with the original foundations and a few skeletons, were opened to the public for the first time.

The monastery was used as a secret-police archive until 1990. Jan Patočka (1907–77), a leading figure of the Charta 77 movement who died after interrogation by the secret police, is buried in the cemetery behind the monastery.

The church, crypt and parts of the monastery can be seen by guided tour (50Kč) only. You can also visit the **monastery gardens** *(admission free; open 10am-6pm Sun)*.

Take tram No 8 from Hradčanská metro station (Map 3), or tram No 22 from náměstí Míru (Map 10), Karlovo náměstí (Map 9) or Malostranská metro stations (Map 5), to the Břevnovský klášter stop.

Bílá Hora (Off Map 2)

The 381m Bílá Hora (White Mountain) – more of a hillock really – on the western outskirts of Prague was the site of the 1620 Protestant military collapse that ended Czech independence for almost 300 years. The only reminder of the battle is a small cairn on a mound in the middle of a field.

Take the same trams as for Břevnovský klášter, but continue to the end of the line. Continue west past the **kostel Panny Maria Vítězná** (Church of Our Lady of Victory), an early-18th-century celebration of the Habsburg victory at Bílá Hora, and turn right; the field is visible up ahead.

LIBOC

Poking above the trees to the northeast of Bílá Hora is the pointed roof of the **Leto hrádek Hvězda** *(Star Summer Palace; ☎ 235 35 26 00; adult/child 30/15Kč; open 9am-5pm Tues-Sun May-Sept, 10am-6pm Tues-Sun Apr & Oct)*, a Renaissance summer palace in the shape of a six-pointed star built for Archduke Ferdinand of Tyrol in 1556. It sits at the end of a long avenue through the lovely wooded park of Obora Hvězda, a hunting reserve established by Ferdinand I in 1530.

The palace houses a small museum about its history, and a so-so exhibit on the battle of Bílá Hora.

Take tram No 8 or 22 to the Vypich stop, and bear right across open parkland to the white archway in the wall; the avenue on the far side leads to the palace (a 15-minute walk from the tram).

DIVOKÁ ŠÁRKA

The valley of the Šárecký potok *(Šárka Creek; Map 2)* is one of Prague's best-known and most popular nature parks. It's named after the warrior Šárka, who threw herself off a cliff here.

From metro station Dejvická (Map 3), catch tram No 20 or 26 west to the terminus at Divoká Šárka. The most attractive area is nearby, among the rugged cliffs near the Džbán Reservoir. You can swim in the reservoir.

From there it's a 7km walk northeast down the valley on a red-marked trail to the suburb of Podbaba, where the creek empties into the Vltava River. There's a bus stop by the Vltava at Podbaba, for the trip back to the centre, or you can walk south about 1.5km on Podbabská to the northern terminus of tram Nos 20 and 25, opposite the Hotel Crowne Plaza Prague in Dejvice (Map 3). Bus No 116 to Dejvice runs along the lower half of the Šárka Valley, should you want to cut your walk short.

Love Hurts

Šárka was one of a renegade army of women who fled across the Vltava River after the death of Libuše, mother of the Přemysl line. She was chosen as a decoy to trap Ctirad, captain of the men's army. Unfortunately she fell in love with him, and after her cohorts did him in, she threw herself into the Šárka Valley in remorse. The women were slaughtered by the men of Hradčany in a final battle.

There's a monumental statue of Šárka and Ctirad in the Vyšehradské sady (Vyšehrad Gardens; see Vyšehrad earlier in this chapter).

What's Free

You can wander through the grounds of Prague Castle, and even explore the nave of chrám sv Víta, without having to pay for a ticket. Visits to most churches, except kostel sv Mikuláše (Malá Strana) and kostel sv Cyril a Metoděj, are free. So is the muzeum Pražského Jezulátka in the kostel Panny Marie Vítězné (Malá Strana). The beautiful Valdštejnská zahrada in Malá Strana is also free.

In the evening you can stroll along Charles Bridge, where buskers play for the crowds, or Wenceslas Square, where fast-food stands, cinemas and bars stay open until late. However, Můstek at the lower end of Wenceslas Square, Skořepka, and Perlová are thick with prostitutes after dark and black-market moneychangers during the day are found along Můstek, lower Wenceslas Square and Jindřišská. The floodlit Staroměstské náměstí and the Charles Bridge are magical nocturnal attractions.

Admission to the Národní muzeum is free on the first Monday of each month. All the Prague City Galleries – dům U Kamenného Zvonu, Staroměstská radnice, City Library, Trojský zámek and the Bílkova vila – are free on the first Tuesday of each month. The National Gallery's Centre for Modern and Contemporary Art, in the Veletržní palác in Holešovice, is free on the first Wednesday of each month, and muzeum hlavního města Prahy (Prague City Museum) is free on the first Thursday of each month.

Activities

For a full list of Prague's sports halls and complexes, contact PIS or consult the *Welcome to Prague, Prague This Month* or *Přehled* booklets (see Tourist Offices in the Facts for the Visitor chapter).

Note that theft – even from lockers – is a problem in many swimming pools and gyms; it's best to leave valuables at the reception desk, or use your own padlock on the locker (if possible). Alternatively, buy a waterproof pouch and keep your valuables with you.

SWIMMING

There's a 25m pool at the **Sportcentrum YMCA** *(Map 7; ☎ 224 87 58 11; Na poříčí 12; open 6.30am-1pm & 4pm-10pm Mon-Fri, 10am-9pm Sat-Sun)* where admission costs 66/30Kč per hour for adults/kids under 140cm tall. **Esquo Relax Club** (see the following Tennis & Squash section), by Strahov Stadium, also has a swimming pool.

The pool and sauna at the **Sportcentrum Hotel Čechie** *(Map 2; ☎ 266 19 41 00; U Sluncové 618; open 4pm-11pm Mon, 1pm-11pm Tues-Fri, 10am-11pm Sat-Sun)* costs 200/100Kč for adults/under-15s for up to three hours. The **Olšanka Hotel** in Žižkov *(Map 8; see the Places to Stay chapter)* also has a fitness centre with a pool.

There are Olympic-sized indoor and outdoor pools at the **Plavecký stadión** *(Swimming Stadium; Map 2; ☎ 261 21 43 43; Podolská 74; open 6am-9.45pm Mon-Fri, 8am-7.45pm Sat-Sun)* in Podolí, which cost 80Kč for up to three hours. To get there, take tram No 3 or 16 to the Dvorce stop, from where it's a five-minute walk. Bring footwear for the grotty showers.

You can go swimming for free at the reservoir at Divoká Šárka (see Outer Suburbs earlier in this chapter).

TENNIS & SQUASH

Among the many places in town to play tennis is the prestigious **TJ Slavoj Praha** *(Štvanice Tennis Club; Map 4; ☎ 232 63 23; Ostrov Štvanice)* on Chase Island; take tram No 3 north from Wenceslas Square.

The **Hradčany Tennis Courts** *(Map 5; ☎ 220 51 40 15; Diskařská 1; open 8am-midnight daily)* are in the shadow of the Hradčany fortifications, west of Strahovský klašter. Summer rates for outdoor courts range from 100Kč per hour in the morning to 200Kč per hour in the evening.

You can rent outdoor clay courts for 200Kč per hour, and indoor courts for 400Kč to 650Kč per hour, at the **Sportcentrum Hotel Čechie** *(see Swimming earlier; open 7am-11pm Mon-Fri, 8am-11pm Sat-Sun)*. It also has squash courts for 260Kč to 350Kč per hour.

The **Esquo Squashcentrum** *(Map 5; ☎ 220 51 36 09; Vaníčkova 2b; open 7am-11pm Mon-Fri, 8am-11pm Sat-Sun)* in Strahov offers squash courts for 170Kč to 370Kč per hour, depending on the time of day; 9am to 4pm weekdays and early or late at weekends are the cheapest times.

FITNESS CENTRES

You can use the *posilovna* (weight room) at the **Sportcentrum YMCA** (see Swimming earlier) for 66Kč per hour. **Esquo Squashcentrum** (see Tennis & Squash earlier) has a fitness centre, which costs 50Kč per hour. The weights room at the **Sportcentrum Hotel Čechie** (see Swimming earlier) charges 100Kč to 120Kč for unlimited time.

Centrum krásy *(Beauty Centre; Map 6; ☎ 224 23 56 09; pasáž Jalta, Václavské náměstí 43)* has a fitness centre, sauna, massage and cosmetic centre.

The luxurious **Cybex Health Club & Spa** *(Map 6; ☎ 224 84 23 75; Pobřežní 1; open 6am-10pm Mon-Fri, 7am-10pm Sat-Sun)* in the Hotel Hilton Prague charges 900Kč for a day pass, which gives access to the gym, pool, sauna, Jacuzzi and steam room.

CYCLING

See Cycling in the Getting Around chapter for details on where to hire bicycles.

ICE-SKATING

There are many places to skate in winter. When it's below zero, sections of parks are sprayed with water and turned into ice rinks. Indoor rinks at *zimní stadiony* (winter-sports complexes) are open to the public during certain hours from September to March or April, including the **Zimní stadión Štvanice** *(Map 4; Ostrov Štvanice)* for 40Kč, and the cheaper **Hvězda HC zimní stadion** *(Map 2; Na rozdílu 1)* for 20Kč.

GOLF

Prague has one nine-hole golf course, the **Golf Club Praha** *(Map 2; ☎ 257 21 65 84; Plzeňská 401/2)*, behind the Hotel Golf in

Motol, Praha 5. Green fees are 900Kč on weekdays, 1000Kč at weekends and on holidays. You can hire a set of clubs for 800Kč.

The **Golf and Country Club Hodkovičký** *(Off Map 2; ☎ 244 46 04 35; Vltavanů 982; open 7am-9pm daily May-Oct, 10am-4pm daily Nov-Apr)*, in the south of the city, has a driving range and chipping and putting greens. Admission costs 50Kč plus 50Kč per 50 balls.

The closest 18-hole course is the prestigious **Karlštejn Golf Course** *(☎ 311 68 47 16, mobile ☎ 724 084 600; Běleč 280, Líteň)* overlooking Karlštejn Castle southwest of Prague (see the Excursions map). It's several kilometres from Karlštejn village, on the southern bank of the Berounka River. Green fees are 1200Kč on weekdays, and 2400Kč at weekends and on holidays.

BILLIARDS & BOWLING

Pool and billiards are popular, and the city has many clubs. A popular place is the **Louvre Billiard Club** *(Map 6; Národní 22)* with tables for 100Kč per hour.

For American-style ten-pin bowling, try the **Hotel Corinthia Towers** *(Map 10; ☎ 261 19 13 26; Kongresová 1; open 2pm-midnight daily)*, where one of four lanes costs 290Kč per hour (half-price before 6pm). The **Sportcentrum Hotel Čechie** *(see Swimming earlier; open 4pm-1am Mon-Fri, 2pm-1am Sat-Sun)* has a single lane costing 300Kč per hour.

HORSE RIDING

Year-round horse riding is offered at **Jezdecké středisko Zmrzlík** *(Zmrzlík Riding Centre; off Map 2; ☎ 257 96 02 45; Zmrzlík 3, Řeporyje)* for around 250Kč per person per hour. Take bus No 256 from Nové Butovice metro station to the Zmrzlík stop. Booking ahead is essential.

Riding is also available at **Jízdárna Koloděje** *(Koloděje Riding School; off Map 2; ☎ 281 97 00 55; Podzámecká 213)*, on the eastern fringes of the city, for 250Kč per hour. A course of riding lessons totalling 12 hours costs 2760Kč. Take bus No 229 from Skalka metro station to the end of the line.

PRAGUE INTERNATIONAL MARATHON

If you'd like to participate in Prague's own International Marathon, see Spectator Sports in the Entertainment chapter for details of how to register.

Courses

The **Information-Advisory Centre of Charles University** *(IPC; Map 6; ☎ 224 49 18 96 or ☎ 222 23 24 52, fax 222 23 22 52; ⓔ ipc@ruk.cuni.cz; Školská 13a)* is the place to go for general information on university courses.

Charles University's **Institute of Linguistics & Professional Training** *(Ústav jazykové a odborné přípravý, or UJOP; Map 9; ☎ 224 99 04 17/12, fax 224 99 04 40; ⓔ ujop@ruk.cuni.cz; Vratislavova 10)* runs four-week Czech language courses for foreigners in July and August. The application deadline is mid-June. No prior knowledge of the Czech language is required, and the course fee is US$590, not including accommodation. You can also opt for individual lessons (45 minutes) at US$16 each. Further details and an application form are on the university's website at ⓦ www.cuni.cz/cuni/ujop/czech.htm.

Charles University also offers intensive courses lasting from six weeks to 10 months for those interested in further study at Czech universities or specialisation in Slavonic studies at a foreign university. Note that students wishing to have credits transferred to their home university must obtain written approval from the head of their department before enrolling.

From June to November **Angličtina Expres** *(Map 10; ☎ 222 51 30 40, fax 224 51 30 40; ⓦ www.anexpres.cz; Korunní 2; office open 8am-8pm Mon-Fri)*, offers four- and eight-week courses in Czech for native speakers of English and German. Courses cost 4500Kč to 4800Kč, not including teaching materials.

The **Prague Center for Further Education** *(Map 5; ☎ 257 53 40 13; ⓦ www.prague-center.cz; Karmelitska 18)* offers English-language courses on a whole range of subjects from photography and computer skills to music, dance and crafts.

WALKING TOURS

The following walking tours are not so much a way to get your bearings, but a suggestion for how to arrange your entire visit. Take your time: Prague is a pleasure on foot.

Walk 1: Královská Cesta (Royal Way)

The Královská cesta is the ancient coronation route from the Prašná brána (Powder Gate) to Prague Castle (Pražský hrad), leading through some of the most picturesque parts of Staré Město (Old Town) and Malá Strana (Little Quarter). Start outside Náměstí Republiky metro station.

Facing náměstí Republiky is the Art Nouveau facade of Prague's most sumptuous building, the **Obecní dům** (Municipal House; 1). Next door is the 15th-century **Prašná brána** (2).

Go under the tower and west along Celetná. On the corner with Ovocný trh, the former fruit market, is one of the earliest Cubist facades in a city famous for them, on the **dům U černé Matky Boží** (House of the Black Madonna; 3); inside is a museum on Czech Cubism. Continuing west towards Old Town Square (Staroměstské náměstí), Celetná is an open-air museum of pastel Baroque facades.

Backtrack a bit and turn off the Královská cesta, north onto Králodvorská. This area, the Králův dvůr (Royal Court), was once the royal stables. On U Obecního domu is the Art Nouveau **Hotel Paříž** (4), built in 1907 and recently restored. Just before reaching the Kotva department store, turn left onto Jakubská. At the western end of Jakubská is **kostel sv Jakuba** (St James Church; 5), famous for its pipe organ and acoustics.

The block across from the church was once a medieval merchants' inn, the **Týnský dvůr** (6), now lined with shops and cafés. Go through the courtyard (enter at No 5) and exit at the far end beneath the **kostel Panny Marie Před Týnem** (Church of Our Lady Before Týn; 7). Admire the beautiful northern door around to the right, then return around the western end of the church to Celetná and the Královská cesta. Pass No 3, Franz Kafka's boyhood home from 1896 to 1907, and No 2, where his family lived from 1888 to 1889, and you're in Old Town Square.

Beyond the Staroměstská radnice (Old Town Hall) tower, the corner building covered in Renaissance sgraffito is **dům U minuty** (8), another Kafka home. Beyond this is Malé náměstí (Little Square), with a Renaissance fountain and fine Baroque and neo-Renaissance facades.

Bear left, then right onto Karlova. All along the right side of Karlova is the **Klementinum** (9), once a Jesuit college and now part of the Czech National Library. Along its high wall are three churches: the Greek Catholic **kostel sv Klimenta** (St Clement Church; 10), the little Vlašská **kaple Nanebevzetí Panny Marie** (Assumption Chapel; 11) and the grand **kostel Nejsvětějšího Spasitele** (Church of the Holy Saviour; 12).

You're now looking at the Staré Město tower of **Charles Bridge** (Karlův most). Cross the bridge, through the crowds and the rows of Baroque statues, drinking in the views of Prague Castle.

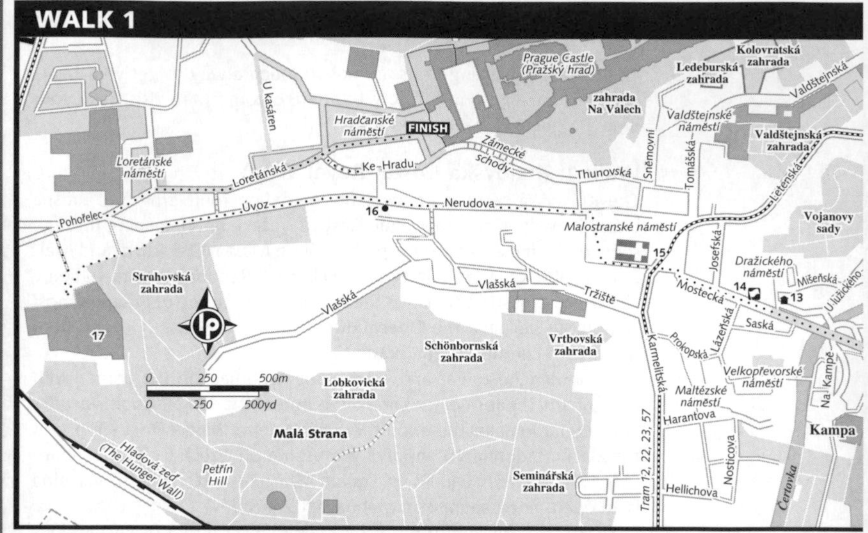

The western end of Charles Bridge crosses Kampa, separated from Malá Strana by the Čertovka channel. Just before the Malá Strana bridge towers, look right to the **Hotel U tří pštrosů** (13), one of Prague's posher establishments; the 16th-century house still has traces of its painted facade.

Walk beneath the towers and you're on Mostecká. The upper facades of some of the houses are worth noting, especially the rococo **Kounický palác** (Kounický Palace; 14) at No 277, now the Yugoslav embassy.

At the top of Mostecká is Malostranské náměstí, bisected by tram lines and centred on one of Prague's finest Baroque structures, **kostel sv Mikuláše** (St Nicholas Church; 15). Cross the square to picturesque Nerudova, named after the poet Jan Neruda, who lived at No 47 in the **dům U dvou slunců** (House of Two Suns; 16). On many of the street's mostly Baroque facades are colourful emblems that have given these buildings their popular names.

Go along Úvoz to the **Strahovský klášter** (Strahov Monastery; 17), and head back east, via Loretánská, to Hradčanské náměstí (or go back down Nerudova and climb the stairs at Ke Hradu). At the eastern end of the square is the entrance to the castle. Before going in, check out the royal view of the city from the corner of the square. On your right is Petřín Hill, below you the rooftops of Malá Strana. Looking across the Vltava River to Staré Město, it's easy to see why Prague is called the 'city of 100 spires'.

Walk 2: Around Wenceslas Square

Start at the steps in front of the neo-Renaissance **Národní muzeum** (National Museum; 1), which dominates the upper end of Wenceslas Square

WALK 1

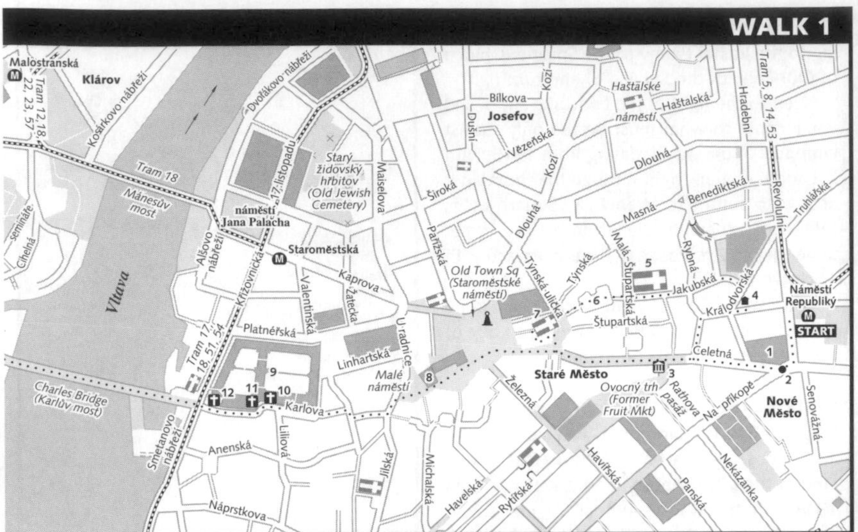

(Václavské náměstí; metro Muzeum). From the steps you have a grand view down the square, a focal point of Czech history since the 19th century. At the foot of the stairs is a pavement memorial to student Jan Palach.

Cross the busy traffic artery of Mezibranská to Prague's media-famous landmark, the equestrian **statue of sv Václav** (St Wenceslas; 2), the Christmas carol's 10th-century 'Good King Wenceslas'. Below is a modest **memorial** (3) to those who died for their resistance to communism.

Wander down the middle of the square, admiring the grand buildings on either side. The finest is the 1906 Art Nouveau **Grand Hotel Evropa** (4) at No 25, about halfway down on the right. Across the street at No 36 is the **Melantrich Building** (5), from whose balcony the obituary of Czech communism was pronounced by Alexander Dubček and Václav Havel on 24 November 1989.

Turn left into Hvězda Pasáz, a shopping arcade directly across the street from the Grand Hotel Evropa. It leads to the central atrium of the **Lucerna Palace**, graced by David Černý's ironic twist on the Wenceslas statue in the square outside (it helps to know that the first prime minister of the Czech Republic was also a Václav).

Turn right beneath the dead horse (you'll see when you get there), and follow the passage to Vodičkova. Bear right across the street and enter the Světozor arcade. Up ahead you'll see a stained-glass window dating from the late 1940s that's actually an advertisement (for Tesla Radio).

At the arcade's far end, turn left into the **Františkánská zahrada** (Franciscan Gardens), a hidden oasis of peace and greenery. Make your way diagonally to the far corner of the gardens, where you'll find an exit to

Jungmannovo náměstí. Go past the arch leading to the **kostel Panny Marie Sněžné** (Church of Our Lady of the Snows; 6) and turn right.

Keep to the right of the Lancôme shop, and you'll come to what must be the only **Cubist lamppost** in the world, dating from 1915. Turn left and then duck right through the short Lindt arcade to return to Wenceslas Square at its foot. Look up and to the left to see the corner tower of the Art Nouveau **Koruna Palace** with its crown of pearls.

You can now head right along Na příkopě to the beginning of Walk 1, or retire to one of the many nearby bars and cafés.

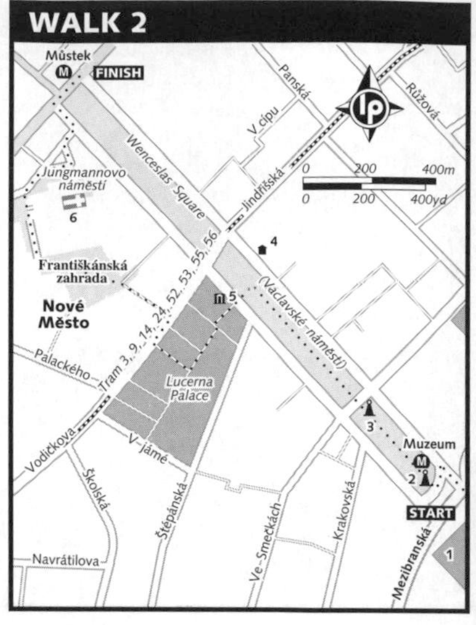

Walk 3: Josefov

Prague's Jewish community was confined to a walled ghetto in Staré Město (Old Town) around the 13th century, and it was not until 1848 that the walls eventually came down. A drastic clearance at the end of the 19th century resulted in the end of the ghetto as a community. Begin this walk at the northwestern corner of Old Town Square (Staroměstské náměstí).

From here Maiselova runs into the heart of Josefov. At the beginning of the street is the **birthplace of Franz Kafka** (1), though the building is not the same one. In the second block is the neo-Gothic **Maiselova synagóga** (Maisel Synagogue; 2). Beyond the **Židovská radnice** (Jewish Town Hall; 3) in the third block is the **Staronová synagóga** (Old-New Synagogue; 4), Europe's oldest active synagogue, completed about 1270. Beside it is the 16th-century **Vysoká synagóga** (High Synagogue; 5).

Left down U starého hřbitova are the walls of the melancholy **Starý židovský hřbitov** (Old Jewish Cemetery), Europe's oldest surviving Jewish burial ground – spared, ironically, because of a Nazi plan for a memorial to an 'extinguished race'. Continuing along the cemetery wall, a left turn onto Břehová brings you to 17.listopadu, with Charles University's Law Faculty across the road.

Turn left to the **Umělecko-průmyslové muzeum** (Museum of Decorative Arts; 6), with a treasure trove of eye-popping 16th- to 19th-century furnishings. Across the road is the **Rudolfinum** (7), interwar seat of the Czechoslovak Parliament and now home to the Czech Philharmonic. From náměstí Jana Palacha (Jan Palach Square), beside the Rudolfinum, you catch your first views of Prague Castle (Pražský hrad).

Turn left (east) onto Široká, past the 16th-century **Pinkasova synagóga** (Pinkas Synagogue; 8), now a memorial to Bohemian and Moravian victims of the Nazis. The eponymous 'hero' of Bruce Chatwin's novella *Utz* had his fictional home in this street, overlooking the cemetery.

Two blocks on, in a sudden change of atmosphere, you come to Pařížská, testament to Prague's late-19th-century infatuation with Art Nouveau architecture. Look left, across the river to the **Letná terása** (Letná Terrace), where a gigantic metronome tick-tocks on the spot once occupied by a 14,000-tonne statue of Stalin.

If your feet are sore, head back to Old Town Square. If you're game for more, go a block north along Pařížská and turn right onto Bílkova. At the end, turn left onto Kozí and right onto U milosrdných, to Prague's oldest Gothic structure, the former **klášter sv Anežky** (Convent of St Agnes; 9), home to the National Gallery's fine collection of medieval art.

Return to Old Town Square via Haštalské náměstí, Kozí and Dlouhá.

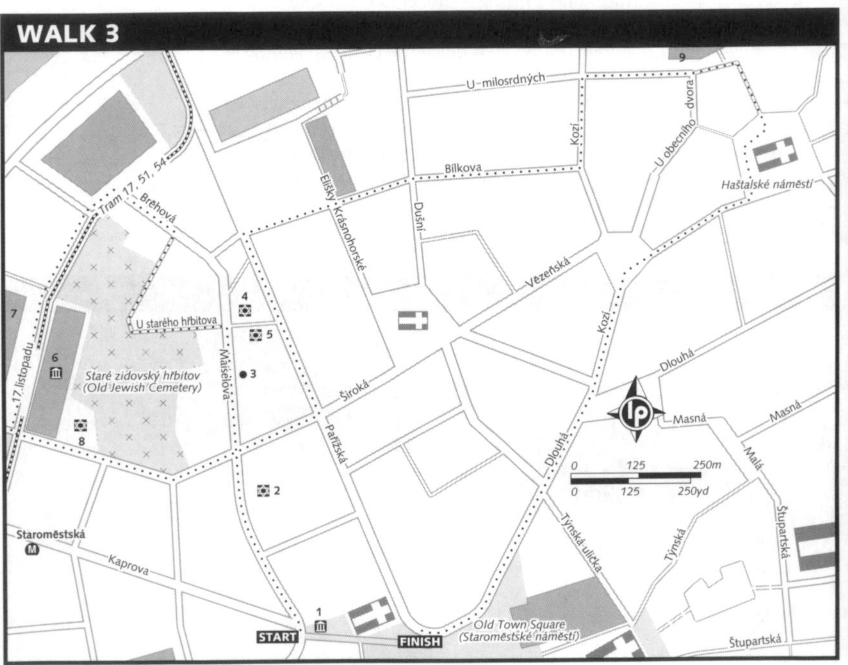

Walk 4: Vltava River & Petřín Hill

Start this walk at Malostranská metro station. At the top of the escalators, turn right and exit through the walled garden. Turn left along Valdštejnská, past Baroque embassies and government ministries.

When it opens onto Valdštejnské náměstí, turn left through the courtyard of the **Valdštejnský palác** (Wallenstein Palace; 1), which houses the Senate of the Czech Republic, and into the beautiful **Valdštejnska zahrada** (Wallenstein Garden). Leave the gardens via the gate on the far side and turn left along Letenská, then right onto U lužického semináře. On the right is leafy **Vojanovy sady** (Vojan Gardens), descendant of Prague's oldest park, established in 1248.

Cross over to Kampa on a small bridge beneath Charles Bridge (Karlův most), with a good view of Prague's most photographed **water wheel**. Pass under Charles Bridge to the little square of **Na Kampě**, once a pottery market. Take one of the little lanes on the right and recross the Čertovka channel to Velkopřevorské náměstí and the **John Lennon Wall** (2).

Return to Kampa island and continue south either through the park or along the river, enjoying the views of Staré Město (Old Town). If the time is right, stop for lunch at the riverside **Rybářský klub** (3) fish restaurant.

Leave the island on Říční and turn right just before the **Church of St John at the Laundry** (4). Continue along Všehrdova to Újezd. Turn left and then right onto U lanové dráhy, then begin the climb up Petřín Hill, either on foot through lush gardens or by funicular railway.

Cross **Strahovská zahrada** (Strahov Gardens) to Strahov Monastery, enjoying fine views of Hradčany, Malá Strana (Little Quarter) and Staré Město. Climb **Petřínská rozhledna** (Petřín Tower; 5) for the best views of all. From **Strahovský klášter** (Strahov Monastery; 6) continue on the final stretch of the Královská cesta (Royal Way) to Prague Castle (Pražský hrad), or catch a tram or bus back to Malostranská metro from Pohořelec.

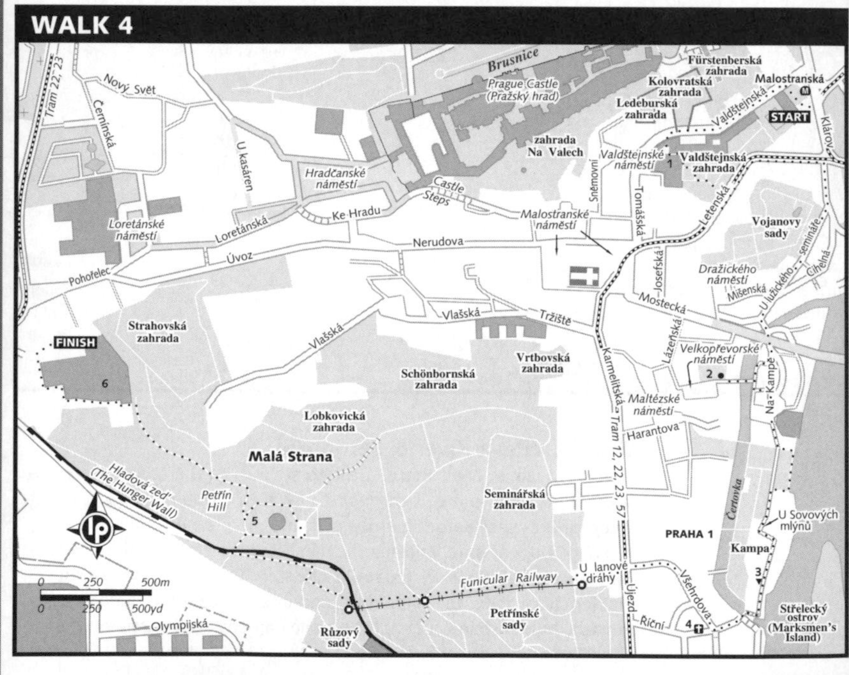

Places to Stay

SEASONS & RATES

Prague is an extremely popular destination; if you're thinking of visiting during Christmas, Easter or from May to September then bookings are strongly recommended, especially if you want to stay in or near the centre.

Other busy periods include public holidays in neighbouring Germany and Austria, when day-trippers and weekenders come in their thousands. At the height of summer, in July and August, the crowding eases off a bit and some hotel rates may drop.

Prices quoted here are for the 'high season', which varies from hotel to hotel. It generally covers April to June, September and October, and the New Year holiday. November to March, July and August are low season, though many places count July and August as 'mid-season', with rates halfway between high and low.

Even high-season rates can be inflated by up to 15% on certain dates, notably at New Year, Easter, and at weekends (Thursday to Sunday) in May, June and September.

Some mid-range and top-end hotels quote rates in euros, and a few quote in US dollars. At these hotels you can pay in Czech koruna, but the price will depend on the exchange rate on the day you settle the bill.

Most hostel, pension and budget hotel rates do not include breakfast; most mid-range and top-end hotel rates do. If only a double-room rate is quoted, then that's what you'll pay for single use too.

TYPES OF ACCOMMODATION

Camping

Most of Prague's camp sites are in the outer suburbs, and are open from March to October. Camping on public land is prohibited.

Prices generally comprise a rate per person (80Kč to 140Kč, with discounts for kids) plus charges per tent (80Kč to 120Kč), caravan (150Kč to 200Kč), car (80Kč to 120Kč) and electrical hook-up (60Kč to 90Kč). Some camp sites have unheated huts or bungalows starting at 130Kč per bed.

All have showers and most have communal kitchens and at least a snack bar. Gas for camping stoves, *technický benzín* (Coleman fuel) and *líh* (methylated spirits) are widely available.

Hostels

Hostel accommodation in Prague can be anything from a dorm full of folding beds in a school gym, to a comfortable double room with private shower. The number of hostel beds explodes from late June to September when the schools are closed and student dorms have empty rooms. Student hostels with *kolej* (college) in the name are usually of a decent standard, and some offer minisuites.

Typical prices range from 300Kč to 500Kč per bed, but they can be as low as 200Kč and as high as 800Kč. Few have places to eat on the premises. Except where noted, most don't have curfews.

Most Czech hostels are not part of the worldwide Hostelling International (HI) system, though many hostels give discounts to HI cardholders. An ISIC, ITIC, IYTC or Euro 26 card may also get you a discount (see Visas & Documents in the Facts for the Visitor chapter for more information).

HI's affiliates in the Czech Republic are **KMC** *(Klub mladých cestovatelů, Young Travellers' Club; Map 6; ☎/fax 222 22 03 47; Ⓦ www.kmc.cz; Karolíny Světlé 30; open 9am-noon & 2pm-5pm Mon-Fri)* and **JSC Travel** *(Map 3; ☎ 220 80 56 84, fax 220 80 69 12; Ⓦ www.iyhf.cz; Strojnicka 999; open 8am-5pm Mon-Fri, 8am-4pm Sat-Sun)*.

Book ahead if you can. Many hostels can be booked from abroad through the computerised IBN booking network, linked to the HI booking service. You can also make bookings at most hostels by email or through their websites.

Pensions

Once upon a time, a *penzión* (pension) meant a boarding house – a home or apartment block fitted out with locking doors,

A Place of Your Own in Prague

More and more travellers are discovering the pleasures of renting their own flat in Prague. This doesn't have to be hideously expensive, but you need to shop around. Before you scoff at the idea, consider that the extra cost of a very basic self-catering flat near the centre means minimal transportation costs, access to cheap local food, and the freedom to come and go as you like.

There are many Prague agencies that will find a flat for you (see Accommodation Agencies later). Typical rates for a modern two-person apartment with living room/bedroom, bathroom, TV and kitchenette range from around 1000/5000/13,000Kč per night/week/month for a place in the outer suburbs, to around 2200/11,000/28,000Kč for a flat near Old Town Square. All short-term rental apartments are fully furnished and serviced, meaning that utilities (gas, water, electricity) and bed linen are included in the price, and a maid will clean up and change the beds at least weekly.

Prague agencies that specialise in short-term rentals include **Happy House Rentals** *(Map 7; ☎ 222 31 24 88, fax 222 31 18 55; W www.happyhouserentals.com; Soukenická 8; open 9am-5pm Mon-Fri)* and **Apartments.CZ** *(Map 6; ☎ 224 99 09 00; W www.apartments.cz; Ostrovní 7; open 9am-5pm Mon-Fri).*

The real estate section of the weekly *Prague Post* newspaper also lists dozens of agencies and private individuals with apartments to rent by the month.

washbasins, extra toilets and sometimes a café – but the term has been hijacked by high-rise hotels that want to sound homely. Real pensions are a nice compromise between hotel comforts and the personal touches of a private home. They're generally no cheaper than a budget hotel, and are often out on the fringes of the city. In the centre they start at about 1500/2000Kč for singles/doubles.

Private Rooms

The renting of rooms in private homes is a booming sector of small-scale capitalism in Prague. Touts swarm on the arrival platforms of Praha hlavní nádraží (Prague's main train station) and Holešovice; most (but not all) are honest amateurs with good deals and pure motives. Check the location and transportation: some are right out in the suburbs. If you fancy a particular neighbourhood, go there and look for *privát* or *Zimmer frei* (rooms for rent) signs.

Away from the city centre, prices per person with bathroom and toilet shared with the family cost about 500Kč to 1000Kč per night. For a private entrance and bathroom, figure about 30% more, and for something near the centre, anywhere from 50% to 100% more. Many people offer discounts for longer stays, but put their prices up for Easter, Christmas and some European holidays.

Hotels

The hotel listings are categorised according to the rate for a double room in high season: budget (under 2500Kč), mid-range (2500Kč to 5000Kč) and top end (over 5000Kč).

If a budget or mid-range hotel claims to be full, ask if there's anything with shared facilities. In addition to being cheaper, these can be quite grand: the 'common bathroom' down the hall is often a private room with a bathtub. Some older hotels have minisuites, with two or three rooms (each with its own lock) sharing toilet and shower. Not many hotels have air-con. We note those hotels that offer wheelchair-friendly, barrier-free rooms.

Nearly all mid-range and top-end hotels have a restaurant, and usually a snack bar, night bar or café as well. A 'Hotel Garni' is equipped only for a simple breakfast – there's no restaurant.

Most mid-range and all top-end hotels accept major credit cards; cheaper hotels and hostels may not do so. Some hotels will offer you a small discount for cash – or a surcharge for using a credit card, depending on how you look at it.

ACCOMMODATION AGENCIES

There are dozens of agencies that will help you find a place to stay – some better than others. Even if you turn up in peak period without a booking, these agencies should be able to find you a bed.

VLADIMIR LIBA

Guardians of the Castle Steps

JULIET COOMBE

Pulling the strings: marionettes abound in Prague.

MARK DAFFEY

A mean fiddler hits his stride on Charles Bridge.

RICHARD NEBESKÝ

Bohemian graffiti: in-your-face street art in Nové Město

RICHARD NEBESKÝ

Sunbathed sculptures on Kostel sv Petra a Pavla (Church of SS Peter & Paul) in Vyšehrad

JULIET COOMBE

A batty sign in Malá Strana

The long-established **AVE** *(☎ 224 22 32 26, fax 224 22 34 63, reservations ☎ 251 55 10 11; W www.avetravel.cz)* has convenient booking offices at Praha hlavní nádraží (Map 6) and Holešovice (Map 4), at Ruzyně airport and in Prague Information Service (PIS) offices (see Tourist Offices in the Facts for the Visitor chapter); the branch at Praha hlavní nádraží opens from 6am to 11pm daily. However, a few readers have reported problems using the online reservation service.

Mary's Travel & Tourist Service *(Map 6; ☎ 222 25 35 10, ☎/fax 222 25 22 15; W www.marys.cz; Italska 31)* offers a wide range of hostels, pensions, hotels and apartments, and it has been recommended by travellers.

Stop City Accommodation *(Map 6; ☎ 222 52 12 33, ☎/fax 222 52 12 52; W www.stopcity.com; Vinohradská 24; open 11am-8pm daily)*, about six blocks from Praha hlavní nádraží, has a large selection of private rooms and apartments, with rates from €20 per person.

Alfa Tourist Service *(Map 6; ☎/fax 224 23 00 37; W www.alfatourist.cz; Opletalova 38; open 9am-5pm Mon-Fri)*, formerly Universitas Tour, can provide accommodation in student hostels (including Hostel and Pension Jednota at the same address), pensions, hotels and private rooms.

Welcome Accommodation Service *(Map 3; ☎ 224 32 02 02, fax 224 32 34 89; W www.bed.cz; Zikova 13)* is based in a student hostel in Dejvice, and offers rooms in student dormitories, hostels and hotels. Go in the main entrance, turn left, and it's the second door on the left; or just say 'Hostel?' to the lady at reception and she'll show you the way.

CKM Travel Centre *(Map 6; ☎ 222 72 15 95; W www.ckm-praha.cz; Mánesova 77)* offers a booking service for hostels to top-end hotels.

Hostels in Prague *(W www.hostel.cz)* is a good online resource for booking hostel accommodation. **TravelGuide** *(W www.travelguide.cz)* is another reliable online booking service with a database of almost 400 hostels, pensions and hotels.

CAMPING

Rates quoted in this section are for a small (two- or three-person) tent; prices for a large frame tent are usually around 50% higher.

Inner Suburbs

Sportovní a Rekreační Areál Pražačka *(Autocamping Žižkov; Map 2; ☎ 267 31 48 62; e info@prazacka.cz; Za Žižkovskou vozovnou 17; camping per person/tent 150/100Kč; open May-Aug)* is a basic camp site in a school sports ground in eastern Žižkov, 3km from the city centre. Take tram No 1, 9 or 16 to the Vápenka stop.

Caravan Camping Císařská louka *(Map 9; ☎ 257 31 75 55, fax 257 31 87 63; e info@caravancamping.cz; Císařska louka 152; camping per person/tent 95/90Kč; open year-round)* is a pleasant riverside site at the tip of the Císařská louka (Imperial Meadow) island, with fine views across to Vyšehrad. Access by public transport is poor – take tram No 12 from Smíchovské nádraží metro station two stops south to Lihovar; it's a five-minute walk past the Shell petrol station.

Troja (Map 2)

There are several quiet camp sites along Trojská ulice in the attractive northern suburb of Troja, less than 10 minutes from Nádraží Holešovice metro station on bus No 112. Tram No 5 from the Hlavní nádraží stop outside Praha hlavní nádraží also passes nearby.

There's a grocery shop about 10 minutes' walk away from the sites, towards the zoo, but the closest restaurants (apart from those on site) are two or three tram stops north.

Autocamp Trojská *(☎/fax 233 54 29 45; e autocamp-trojska@iol.cz; Trojská 157; camping per person/tent 110/90Kč; open year-round)* is the most expensive and generally best equipped of these sites.

Camp Dana Troja *(☎/fax 283 85 04 82; e campdana@volny.cz; Trojská 129; camping per person/tent 115/75Kč; open year-round)* also offers pricey apartments.

Camp Fremunt *(☎/fax 283 85 04 76; e campfremunt@email.cz; Trojská 159; camping per person/tent 80/80Kč; open Apr-Oct)* has only 20 pitches set in a cramped but attractive garden.

Camp-Pension Herzog *(☎ 283 85 04 72; ⓔ info@campherzog.cz; Trojská 161; camping per person/tent 80/80Kč; open Apr-Oct)* is set in an orchard, offers a discount for students (55Kč per person) and has cooking facilities.

Camp Sokol Troja *(☎/fax 233 54 29 08; ⓔ info@camp-sokol-troja.cz; Trojská 171a; camping per person/tent 105/90Kč; open year-round)* is a large, well equipped site with kitchen, laundry, a restaurant and a 24-hour reception.

Northeastern Outskirts

The following sites are north and east, respectively, of Map 2.

Triocamp *(☎/fax 283 85 07 93; ⓔ triocamp.praha@telecom.cz; Ústecká ulice, Dolní Chabry; camping per person/tent 140/80Kč; open year-round)* is a large site with a kids' playground, about 40 minutes from the city centre. From Nádraží Holešovice metro station, take bus No 175 to Kobyliské náměstí, change to bus No 162 and continue for four more stops.

Camping Sokol *(☎/fax 281 93 11 12; ⓔ info@campingsokol.cz; Národních hrdinů 290, Dolní Počernice; camping per person/tent 130/130Kč; open late Mar-Oct)* is a large, well equipped lakeside site, 35 minutes out of town. Take bus No 163 from Skalka metro station to the Škola Dolní Počernice stop.

Southeastern Outskirts (Map 2)

Intercamp Kotva Braník *(☎ 244 46 17 12, fax 244 46 61 10; ⓔ kotva@kotvacamp.cz; U ledáren 1557/55, Braník; camping per person/tent 100/85Kč; open Apr-Oct)* is a peaceful site with a view across the Vltava River, 25 minutes south of the centre. Take tram No 3, 16, 17 or 21 to the Nádraží Braník stop, and walk west for five minutes.

Southwestern Outskirts (Map 2)

USK Caravan Camp *(☎ 257 21 49 91, fax 257 21 50 84; Plzeňská 279, Motol; camping per person/tent 100/85Kč; open year-round)* is Prague's most convenient camp site, just west of Smíchov. Take tram No 7, 9 or 10 from Andel metro to the Hotel Golf stop (10 minutes).

Northwestern Outskirts (Map 2)

Autokemp Džbán *(☎ 235 35 90 06, fax 235 35 13 65; Nad lávkou 5, Vokovice; camping per person/tent 95/90Kč; open May-Oct)* is part of the Aritma sports complex (some 200m on from the sports ground). Facilities include huts and bungalows. Take tram No 20 or 26 from Dejvická metro station to the Nad Džbánem stop; it's a 15-minute walk north from here.

HOSTELS

All the hostels listed here are open year-round unless otherwise indicated.

Malá Strana (Map 5)

Hostel Sokol *(☎ 257 00 73 97; ⓔ hostel@sokol-cos.cz; 3rd floor, Tyršův dům, Nostícova 2; dorm beds/doubles 270/1200Kč)* is fairly central and gets good reports from travellers. Take the metro to Malostranská and then tram No 12, 22 or 23 two stops south.

There are also three summer-only hostels run by Travellers' Hostels (see Staré Město later for other Travellers' Hostels): **Josefska** *(☎ 257 53 07 17; Josefská 5; dorm beds 270Kč; open late June-late Aug)*, a block east of Malostranské náměstí; **Island** *(☎ 224 91 01 88; Strelecký ostrov 36; dorm beds 300Kč; open early June-early Sept)* on the island under Legii most; and **Újezd** *(☎ 257 31 24 03; U lanové dráhy 3; dorm beds 220Kč; open mid-June–mid-Sept)*, at the foot of the Petřín funicular.

Strahov (Map 5)

The Strahov student dormitory complex, just east of the big Strahov Stadium, offers lots of hostel accommodation in dreary, somewhat run-down apartment blocks. The complex also includes several basic cafés, snack shops and bars. But misanthropes and light sleepers take note: in July and August discos pound away into the night in blocks 1, 7 and 11. Take bus No 143, 149 or 217 from Dejvická metro station. The following are all open year-round.

Hostel SPUS *(☎/fax 257 21 07 64; ⓔ reception@spushostels.cz; Chaloupeckého 4; singles/doubles 480/700Kč)* has clean but cramped rooms, and offers breakfast for 60Kč.

Hostel ESTEC *(☎ 257 21 04 10, fax 257 21 52 63; ⓔ estec@jrc.cz; Vaníčkova 5; singles/doubles/triples 400/600/900Kč)* has been recently renovated. It has a 24-hour reception, a lively bar and summer beer garden.

Welcome Hostel Strahov *(☎ 224 32 02 02, fax 224 32 34 89; ⓔ welcome@hostelprague.cz; Vaníčkova 3; dorm beds/singles/doubles 150/350/480Kč)* offers similar accommodation, with a kitchen on each floor.

Staré Město (Map 7)

Travellers' Hostel Dlouhá *(Roxy; ☎ 224 82 66 62, fax 224 82 66 65; ⓔ hostel@travellers.cz; Dlouhá 33; dorm beds/singles/doubles 370/1120/1240Kč)* has basic, clean accommodation and 24-hour service which includes lockers and Internet access. It also has four self-catering apartments that sleep two to six people (2400Kč to 3500Kč).

There are four other Travellers' Hostels in central Prague that are available in summer only. Three are in Malá Strana (see earlier); the other is **Husova** *(☎ 222 22 00 78; Husova 3; bed in 4- or 5-bed room 440Kč; open late July-late Aug)*, near Betlémské náměstí.

Hostel Týn *(☎/fax 224 80 83 33; ⓔ backpacker@razdva.cz; Týnská 19; dorm beds/doubles 400/1100Kč)* is another good central place, only a few minutes' walk from Staroměstské náměstí.

Northern Nové Město (Maps 6 & 7)

These listings include a few places east of Wilsonova in Karlín, near Florenc bus station, but they are most easily reached from northern Nové Město.

Hostel Jednota *(Map 6; ☎/fax 222 24 35 83; ⓔ info@alfatourist.cz; Opletalova 38; dorm beds/singles/doubles/triples 350/550/760/1080Kč; open mid-July–mid-Sept)* is near Praha hlavní nádraží. Booking by fax or email with Alfa Tourist Service (see Accommodation Agencies earlier in this chapter) is recommended.

Alfa Tourist Service can also book beds at **Kolej Petrská** *(Map 7; ☎ 222 31 64 30; Petrská 3)*, north of Na poříčí.

Vesta Hostel *(Map 6; ☎/fax 24 22 57 69; ⓔ info@ckvesta.cz; Wilsonova 2; dorm beds/singles/doubles 350/550/700Kč)* is in the attic of the Art Nouveau Praha hlavní nádraží, and has beds in two- to six-bed rooms. The entrance is at the southern end of the old station building on the Wilsonova street level. Don't be put off by the rough outer appearance; it has been renovated and is quite nice inside.

Hostel TJ Sokol Karlín *(Map 6; ☎ 224 81 74 74, fax 222 31 51 32; ⓔ sokol.karlin@volny.cz; Malého 1; dorm beds 180-200Kč)* is a bit shabby, but it's only a two-minute walk east of Florenc bus station. Reception is only open from 6pm to 10.30pm and 6am to 9am. From 9am to 6pm you have to clear out, though you can leave your gear in a locker.

Juniorhostel *(Map 7; ☎ 224 23 17 54, fax 224 22 15 79; ⓔ euroagentur@euroagentur.cz; Senovážné náměstí 21; dorm beds/singles/doubles 550/700/1100Kč)* is part of the three-star Juniorhotel Praha (see Mid-Range Hotels later), and offers modern accommodation in two- to six-bed rooms.

Southern Nové Město (Maps 6 & 9)

Hostel Advantage *(Map 9; ☎ 224 91 40 62, fax 224 91 40 67; Sokolská 11-13; dorm beds 360-440Kč)* is a cheerful modern place offering two- to seven-bed rooms with shared facilities. It's a five-minute walk south of IP Pavlova metro station.

Hostel Klub Habitat *(Map 6; ☎/fax 224 92 17 06, ⓔ hostel@iol.cz; Na Zderaze 10; dorm beds 350-430Kč)* is clean and bright and has three- to seven-bed rooms. It's a few minutes' walk north from Karlovo náměstí metro station.

Hostel U Melounu *(Map 9; ☎/fax 224 91 83 22; ⓔ info@hostelumelounu.cz; Ke Karlovu 7; dorm beds 380Kč)*, an attractive hostel in a historic building, is on a quiet back street, a 10-minute walk south of metro IP Pavlova.

Hlávkova kolej *(Map 9; ☎ 224 91 65 33; Jenštejnská 1; singles/doubles 600/900Kč)* is a quiet, upmarket hostel in a former college, two blocks west of Karlovo náměstí.

Holešovice (Map 4)

Sir Toby's Hostel *(☎ 283 87 06 35, fax 283 87 06 36; ⓔ info@sirtobys.com; Dělnická 24; dorm beds/singles/doubles 325/750/1150Kč)* is a friendly backpackers' hostel set in a nicely refurbished apartment building – highly recommended. Take tram No 1, 3, 14 or 25 eastbound from Vltavská metro station.

Arena Hostel (*☎ 220 87 02 52; e contact@arenahostel.com; U Výstaviště 1; tram No 5, 12 or 17; dorm beds 290-330Kč*) is a new place that gets rave reviews from the party crowd. With clean sheets, hot showers, 24-hour reception and a late bar it can't be bad.

Hostel Spoas (*☎/fax 220 80 48 91; e spoas@volny.cz; Jankovcova 63a; beds 240-300Kč*) is only recommended for those arriving on a late bus or train – it's in a pale green pre-fab building 100m east of Nádraží Holešovice metro station. Basic accommodation is provided in two- to six-bed rooms.

Žižkov (Map 6)

Hostel Elf (*☎ 222 54 09 63, fax 222 54 09 27; e info@hostelelf.com; Husitská 11; bus No 133 or 207; dorm beds/singles/doubles 280/750/900Kč*) is fast becoming a backpackers' favourite, with good hot showers and a convivial lounge and terrace. It's only five minutes' walk from Florenc bus station.

Clown & Bard Hostel (*☎ 222 71 64 53, fax 222 71 90 26; e reservations@clownandbard.com; Bořivojova 102; tram No 5, 9 or 26; dorm beds/doubles 250/900Kč*) is in the heart of Žižkov's pub district. Under new management and undergoing renovation, it remains one of Prague's most congenial hostels, offering an all-you-can-eat breakfast (99Kč) and a late and lively bar. It also has six-person self-catering flats in the attic for 2400Kč.

Pension 15 (*☎ 222 71 97 68; e pension15@ volny.cz; Vlkova 15; tram No 5, 9 or 26; dorm beds/singles/doubles 300/500/600Kč*) has bright, modern rooms (up to five in a room) with cooking facilities. There are also private apartments that sleep up to five (2500Kč), and private parking (100Kč).

Vinohrady (Maps 2 & 6)

Domov mládeže (*Penzión Jana; Map 2; ☎/fax 222 51 17 77; e jana.dyrsmidova@telecom.cz; Dykova 20; dorm beds/singles/doubles 350/520/800Kč*) is a bargain, and highly recommended. Rates include breakfast. Take tram No 10 or 16 east from náměstí Míru metro station to the Perunova stop; it's a block south.

Švehlova kolej (*Map 6; ☎ 257 09 31 11 ext 145; Slavíkova 22; metro Jiřího z Poděbrad; dorm beds 200Kč; open July & Aug*), a staid student dormitory, is a summer fall-back; the *ubytovaní kancelař* (accommodation desk) is through the third door on the right.

Dejvice (Maps 2 & 3)

Welcome Hostel Dejvice (*Map 2; ☎ 224 32 02 02, fax 224 32 34 89; e welcome@bed.cz; Zikova 13; metro Dejvická; singles/doubles 400/540Kč, with private bathroom 700/1100Kč*) is a newly renovated student residence; it can be booked through the Welcome Accommodation Service (see Accommodation Agencies earlier in this chapter).

Hostel Orlík (*Map 3; ☎ 224 31 12 40; e praguehotel@atlas.cz; Terronská 6; singles/doubles/triples 550/860/1250Kč; open July & Aug*) is a three-minute walk from Dejvická metro station and is run by Hostel ESTEC (see Strahov earlier).

Southeastern Outskirts (Map 2)

Ubytovna Kotva Braník (*☎ 244 46 17 12, fax 244 46 61 10; e kotva@kotvacamp.cz; doubles/triples/quads 520/630/740Kč*) is behind the riverside Intercamp Kotva Braník (see Camping earlier in this chapter).

Hostel Boathouse (*☎ 241 77 00 51, fax 241 77 69 88; e boathouse@volny.cz; Lodnická 1, Braník; dorm beds 300Kč*) is a popular and friendly place that has a peaceful riverbank setting. Extras include bike and boat hire, a minishop and Internet access. It's just off Map 2; take tram No 3 or 17 to the Černý kůň stop, and follow the hostel signs west to the river (it's a five-minute walk).

Hostel Podolí (*☎ 257 21 23 97, fax 257 22 42 28; Na Lysině 12, Podolí; basic singles/doubles/triples 330/450/700Kč, 'hotel' room 405/630/885Kč; open July-late Sept*) is in block A of a student dormitory complex. There are basic rooms with shared bathroom, and 'hotel units' where two rooms share one bathroom. From Pražského Povstání metro station, walk west on Lomnického, then left along Pod Děkankou for 200m; Na Lysině is third on the right.

Southwestern Outskirts (Map 2)

Motorlet Císařka *(☎ 57 21 43 33; Podbělohorská 97, Císařka; singles/doubles/triples 410/800/1140Kč)* has a garden restaurant and free parking for guests, and is in a very quiet neighbourhood. Take bus No 191 from Anděl metro station to the fifth stop (Spiritka).

Northwestern Outskirts (Map 2)

Kolej Kajetánka *(☎ 220 51 34 32; Radimova 12, Střešovice; singles/doubles 420/740Kč)* is another student residence. Take bus No 108 or 174 west from Hradčanská metro station to the Kajetánka stop; the hostel is in building No 1 of two tall, white tower blocks.

SK Aritma Hostel *(☎ 235 35 85 54, fax 235 35 13 65; ⓔ skaritma@mbox.vol.cz; Nad lávkou 5, Vokovice; dorm beds 380Kč)*, at the same address as Autokemp Džbán (see Camping earlier in this chapter), has beds in doubles and four-bed rooms, and a restaurant.

HOTELS – BUDGET

The words 'budget hotel' and 'central Prague' very rarely feature in the same sentence, and when they do they're usually accompanied by 'fully booked'. To find a good, cheap hotel you'll probably have to settle for staying in the suburbs.

Strahov (Map 5)

Hotel Coubertin *(☎ 233 35 31 09, fax 220 51 32 08; ⓔ coubertin@volny.cz; Atletická 4; singles/doubles 1500/2000Kč)*, a modest three-star place in a quiet area beside Strahov Stadium, has a grand view from the roof terrace. Take bus No 176 from náměstí Kinských, or No 143, 149 or 217 from Dejvická metro station.

Staré Město (Map 6)

Unitas Pension *(☎ 224 21 10 20, fax 224 21 08 00; ⓔ unitas@cloisterinn.com; Bartolomějská 9; singles/doubles 1100/1400Kč)* is housed in a convent that was once a prison, and is highly recommended. Václav Havel was held here for a day, and if it's available you can stay in the very same cell (No P6). Rooms are quiet but cramped; rates include breakfast. Booking is advisable.

Nové Město (Maps 6, 7 & 9)

Hotel Imperial *(Map 7; ☎ 222 31 60 12, fax 224 81 63 09; ⓔ reservation@hotelimperial.cz; Na Poříčí 15; singles/doubles/triples/quads 1500/2360/3240/3920Kč)* is a grand old building dating from 1914, with an impressive, ceramic-tiled café. The spartan rooms all have shared toilet facilities.

Pension Museum *(Map 6; ☎ 296 32 51 86, fax 296 32 51 88; ⓔ pension.museum@volny.cz; Mezibranská 15; singles/doubles/4-bed apartments 1990/2520/4450Kč)* just scrapes into the budget category because of its superb central location. All rooms have en-suite bathroom, TV and fridge, and overlook a quiet courtyard.

Pension Březina *(Map 9; ☎ 296 18 88 88, fax 224 26 67 77; ⓔ info@brezina.cz; Legerova 41; economy singles/doubles 900/1100Kč, luxury 1800/2000Kč)* is just south of IP Pavlova metro station. The economy rooms have shared bathrooms; luxury ones have private bathrooms, air-con and Ethernet sockets for your laptop (and free use of the Internet). Rooms facing the street can be pretty noisy.

Vyšehrad (Map 9)

Hotel Amadeus *(☎ 224 93 75 69, ☎/fax 222 51 17 77; Slavojova 8; singles/doubles 2000/2550Kč)* offers 20 en-suite double rooms with cable TV on a quiet street below the fortress.

Holešovice (Map 4)

Hotel Standart *(☎ 220 87 52 58, fax 220 80 67 52; ⓔ standart@jsc.cz; Přístavní 2; tram No 12 or 14; singles/doubles/triples 800/1500/2800Kč)* was completely renovated in 2002, and offers basic, good-value accommodation, plus a pool and sauna in the basement. It's only 10 minutes by tram from the city centre.

Pension Vltava *(☎/fax 222 80 97 95; Dělnická 35; singles/doubles 520/835Kč)*, a block south of Hotel Standart, has a far more welcoming atmosphere than the grim-looking entrance would suggest. Take tram No 1, 3, 14 or 25 east from Vltavská metro station.

Žižkov (Map 8)

Hotel Golden City Garni *(☎ 222 71 10 08, fax 222 71 60 08; ⓔ hotel@goldencity.cz; Táboritská 3; tram No 5, 9 or 26; singles/doubles/*

triples 1650/2450/2700Kč) has been recently modernised, has friendly and helpful staff and is excellent value. Facilities include free Internet access and secure parking close by (250Kč).

Hotel Kafka *(☎ 222 78 13 33, fax 222 78 04 31; Cimburkova 24; tram No 5, 9 or 26; singles/doubles/triples 1700/2200/2600Kč)* has scrupulously clean rooms, some with kitchens (for an extra 150Kč).

Pension Prague City *(☎ 222 78 24 83, fax 222 78 24 81; ⓔ praguecity@cmail.cz; Štítného 13; tram No 5, 9 or 26; singles/doubles/triples 2000/2500/3000Kč)* is a shiny new place round the corner from Hotel Kafka. All 13 en-suite rooms have a TV.

Vinohrady (Map 10)

Hotel/Pension City *(☎ 222 52 16 06, fax 222 52 23 86; ⓔ hotel@hotelcity.cz; Belgická 10; metro Náměstí Míru; singles/doubles 1160/1550Kč, with private bathroom 1670/2320Kč)* has plain, good-value rooms with bathroom, satellite TV and telephone, in a quiet back street. The cheaper rooms share one bathroom between two.

Hotel Hasa *(☎ 271 74 71 28, fax 271 74 71 31; Sámova 1; tram No 6, 7 or 24; singles/doubles/triples 1050/1700/2300Kč)*, south of Havlíčkovy sady, is an ageing but comfortable 1970s-style hotel beside an ice rink; rates include breakfast.

Smíchov (Map 9)

Hotel Balkán *(☎ 257 32 21 50; ⓔ balkan@mbox.dkm.cz; třída Svornosti 28; metro Anděl; singles/doubles/triples 2000/2400/ 2700Kč)* has basic rooms with bath or shower, and a good restaurant.

Pension FD Tour *(☎ 257 31 98 98, fax 257 32 68 08; Svornosti 33; doubles/triples 1500/1800Kč)*, across the road from Hotel Balkán, is a modest, helpful place with just four rooms – bookings need to be made months ahead.

Eastern Outskirts (Map 2)

Hotel Rhea *(☎ 274 77 28 51, fax 274 77 06 23; ⓔ recepce@hotelrhea.cz; V úžlabině 19, Malešice; singles/doubles 2100/2600Kč)* is a renovated, pink high-rise, popular with coach tours. There are few places to eat in the neighbourhood. From Želivského metro station, take bus No 155, 188, 208, 238 or 239 to the Plaňanská stop.

Southeastern Outskirts (Map 2)

Pension Bohemians *(☎/fax 244 46 37 76, Modřanská 51, Podolí; tram No 3 or 21; singles/doubles 990/1290Kč)* is a recommended budget place beside the river, though there are only a few mediocre restaurants nearby. The entrance is around the back and up the stairs.

Hotel Opatov *(☎ 271 19 62 22, fax 271 19 69 66; ⓔ reception-opatov@horst.cz; U chod-ovského hřbitova 2141, Opatov; metro Opatov; singles/doubles/triples 1740/2300/2995Kč)* is a grim-looking, communist-era tower block, but offers bargain three-star accommodation in mini-apartments with TV, phone and fridge. It's just 15 minutes from the city centre. From Opatov metro station head east towards the park then bear right – it's the further away of the two big tower blocks.

Western Outskirts (Map 2)

Hotel Tourist *(☎ 257 21 70 19, fax 257 21 70 22; ⓔ hotel.tourist@quick.cz; Peroutkova 531/81, Košíře; singles/doubles/triples 700/1000/1300Kč)* is a big, 1970s, glass-and-concrete place with bland, functional rooms aimed at big tour groups. Take bus No 137 from Anděl metro station to the end of the line and walk back about 250m.

Hotel Markéta *(☎ 220 51 83 16, fax 220 51 32 83; ⓔ marketa@europehotels.cz; Na Petynce 45, Střešovice; singles/doubles 2000/2500Kč)* is in a quiet residential area within 15 minutes' walk of the castle. Take bus No 108 or 174 from Hradčanská metro station to the Kajetánka stop.

Near the Airport

Until plans to build a hotel at Prague's Ruzyně airport materialise, the nearest accommodation is a few kilometres away in the suburbs of Ruzyně and Liboc. The following are both easily accessible by public transport.

Hotel Radegast *(☎ 235 35 65 17, fax 235 35 90 79; ⓔ cts@ipex.cz; Radčina 11, Liboc;*

singles/doubles/triples 900/1600/1900Kč) is a slightly run-down 1970s throwback, but is the closest budget hotel to the airport – only seven minutes on bus No 119 (get off at the Nová Šárka stop) or No 225 (Vlastina stop).

Pension Větерný Mlyn *(☎/fax 235 30 16 86; ⓔ alex@pensionmlyn.cz; Ruzyňská 3/96, Ruzyně; singles/doubles/triples 1000/1500/1800Kč)* is a more appealing alternative – a friendly, family-run pension where all rooms have TV and en-suite shower. It's only 10 minutes from the airport on bus No 225; the Ruzyňská škola stop is right outside.

HOTELS – MID-RANGE

Malá Strana (Map 5)

Hotel Sax *(☎ 257 53 12 68, fax 257 53 41 01; ⓔ hotelsax@bon.cz; Jánský vršek 328/3; singles/doubles 4100/4400Kč)*, set in a quiet corner of Malá Strana, has sleek, modern interior decor and very reasonable prices considering its location – less than 10 minutes' walk from the castle's main gate.

Staré Město (Maps 6 & 7)

The following hotels are all within five minutes' walk of Old Town Square (Staroměstské náměstí).

Hotel Černý slon *(Map 7; ☎ 222 32 15 21, fax 222 31 03 15; ⓔ slon@hotelcernyslon.cz; Týnská ulička 1; singles/doubles/triples 2730/4890/5820Kč)* has 13 smallish but comfortable four-star rooms, a Gothic-vaulted dining room and a tiny courtyard garden, all barely 30 paces from Old Town Square.

Pension U Lilie *(Map 7; ☎ 222 22 04 32, fax 222 22 06 41; Liliová 15; singles/doubles 1850/2800Kč)* has simply furnished rooms with bathroom and TV that are very reasonably priced considering the central location.

Dům U krále Jiřího *(Map 7; ☎ 222 22 09 25, fax 222 22 17 07; ⓔ rezervace@kinggeorge.cz; Liliová 10; singles/doubles 1800/3100Kč)* is an appealing place; the attic rooms, with exposed wooden beams, are especially attractive.

Hotel U Staré Paní *(Map 7; ☎/fax 224 22 80 90, ☎/fax 224 22 66 59; ⓔ hotel@ustarepani.cz; Michalská 9; singles/doubles 3250/3950Kč)* offers 18 pleasant, modern, en-suite rooms above the jazz club of the same name (see the Entertainment chapter). Be aware that there's no lift. Rates are hiked up 20% over New Year and on certain weekends from April to June.

Pension U zlaté studny *(Map 7; ☎/fax 222 22 02 62; ⓔ info@uzlatestudny.cz; Karlova 3; doubles 4500-4700Kč, suites 5100Kč)*, in a lovely 16th-century house, has two double rooms and four (two-person) suites, some with original painted wooden ceilings and period-style furniture. A third bed in a suite adds 700Kč to the rate.

Hotel U zlatého stromu *(Map 7; ☎/fax 222 22 04 41; ⓔ hotel-zs@zlatystrom.cz; Karlova 6; singles/doubles/suites 3990/4190/5990Kč)* has a historical atmosphere and many timber-ceilinged rooms, but also a basement disco that rages till 6am.

Hotel Central *(Map 7; ☎ 224 81 20 41, fax 222 32 84 04; ⓔ central@orfea.cz; Rybná 8; singles/doubles/triples 3200/3600/4200Kč)*, behind the Kotva department store, has a slightly dated feel, but the rooms are bright and nicely furnished.

The three hotels below are in the southern part of Staré Město.

Hotel U klenotníka *(Map 6; ☎ 224 21 16 99, fax 224 22 10 25; ⓔ info@uklenotnika.cz; Rytířská 3; singles/doubles 2500/3800Kč)* has bland but comfy rooms and a stylish little restaurant – check out the bizarre stained-glass windows.

Cloister Inn *(Map 6; ☎ 224 21 10 20, fax 224 21 08 00; ⓔ cloister@cloister-inn.cz; Konviktská 14; singles/doubles/triples 3400/3800/4750Kč)* has stylish, refurbished convent rooms, private parking and free Internet access.

Pension U medvídků *(Map 6; ☎ 224 21 19 16, fax 224 22 09 30; ⓔ pension@umedvidku.cz; Na Perštýně 7; singles/doubles/triples 2300/3500/4500Kč)* is another historic building with painted Renaissance ceilings, and 32 plain but elegant rooms.

Northern Nové Město (Maps 6 & 7)

Botel Albatros *(Map 7; ☎ 224 81 05 41, fax 224 81 12 14; ⓔ info@botelalbatros.cz; nábřeží Ludvíka Svobody 1; singles/doubles €62/76)* is a converted cruise boat that's a good bargain in the off-season, when rates fall by 30%. Cabins are small and spartan, and come with a tiny private shower and toilet.

Hotel Opera *(Map 6; ☎ 222 31 56 09, fax 222 32 14 77; ⓔ reception@hotel-opera.cz; Těšnov 13; singles/doubles 3550/4200Kč)* is a renovated, neo-Renaissance building (built 1890) near Florenc metro station. It has plush, modern rooms with shower and TV.

Hotel Harmony *(Map 6; ☎ 222 32 00 16, fax 222 31 00 09; Na poříčí 31; singles/doubles 2810/3860Kč)* is aimed mainly at the tour group and conference market. It offers spacious rooms (including six barrier-free doubles) from the 'forgettable modern' school of decor – quieter ones face Biskupská.

Two nearby, group-oriented hotels that occasionally have spare rooms are the **Atlantic Hotel** *(Map 7; ☎ 224 81 10 84, fax 224 81 23 78; ⓔ htlatlantic@mbox.vol.cz; Na poříčí 9; singles/doubles 3500/4400Kč)*, which has three barrier-free rooms; and the plain **Hotel Axa** *(Map 6; ☎ 224 81 25 80, fax 224 21 44 89; ⓔ axapraha@mbox.vol.cz; Na poříčí 40; singles/doubles/triples 2900/3600/4300Kč)*, with fitness centre and indoor 25m pool.

Juniorhotel Praha *(Map 7; ☎ 224 23 17 54, fax 224 22 15 79; ⓔ euroagentur@euroagentur.cz; Senovážné náměstí 21; singles/doubles 2400/3000Kč)* has 14 smartly renovated hotel rooms with en-suite bathroom, minibar and satellite TV – but still offers cheap doubles, triples and dorm beds in a separate part of the building (see Juniorhostel under Hostels earlier in this chapter).

Southern Nové Město (Maps 6 & 9)

Grand Hotel Evropa *(Map 6; ☎ 224 22 81 17, fax 224 22 45 44; ⓔ hotelevropa@iol.cz; Václavské náměstí 25; singles/doubles/triples 1600/2600/3100Kč, with private bathroom 3000/4000/5000Kč)* has a beautiful Art Nouveau facade that conceals a musty warren of run-down 1950s rooms. It still has a certain charm, and considering its location is reasonable value, though some travellers (especially solo women) have found the atmosphere creepy.

Hotel Andante *(Map 6; ☎ 222 21 16 16, fax 222 21 05 91; ⓔ reservations@andante.cz; Ve Smečkách 4; singles/doubles/triples €89/108/140)* has 32 spacious, modern rooms with TV, minibar and a choice of shower or bath.

Novoměstský Hotel *(Map 6; ☎ 224 91 16 74, fax 224 91 19 66; Řeznická 4; singles/doubles 2800/3700Kč)*, on a quiet street near Karlovo náměstí, has plush rooms with shower and TV, and the inexpensive Restaurace U Braunů downstairs.

Hotel Ibis Praha City *(Map 9; ☎ 224 94 12 12, fax 222 94 12 13; ⓔ city@hotelibis.cz; Kateřinská 36; metro IP Pavlova; singles/doubles 2725/3325Kč)* is a soulless but comfortable modern chain hotel, right next door to the metro.

Hotel 16 U sv Kateřiny *(Map 9; ☎ 224 92 06 36, fax 224 92 06 26; ⓔ hotel16@hotel16.cz; Kateřinská 16; singles/doubles 2500/3400Kč)* has 14 smallish, modern rooms with TV, shower and modem socket. It's a five-minute walk southwest from IP Pavlova metro.

Hotel Green Garden *(Map 9; ☎ 224 26 11 81, fax 224 26 21 82; Fügnerovo náměstí 4; singles/doubles 2400/2900Kč)*, a group-oriented place (formerly the Hotel Patty) sandwiched between the raging traffic of Legerova and Sokolská, offers secure parking and wheelchair access. It's a five-minute walk south from IP Pavlova metro.

Vys (Map 9)

Hotel Union *(☎ 261 21 48 12, fax 261 21 48 20; ⓔ hotel.union@telecom.cz; Ostrčilovo náměstí 4; tram No 18 or 24; singles/doubles €94/112)*, just below Vyšehrad, is a grand old family-run hotel that dates from 1906. Nationalised by the communists in 1958, it was returned to the grandson of the former owner in 1991, and thoroughly renovated. The deluxe rooms (€135) are huge.

Holešovice (Map 3)

Hotel Splendid *(☎ 233 37 59 40, fax 233 37 22 32; ⓔ splendid@bon.cz; Ovenecká 33; singles/doubles/triples 2320/2900/3550Kč)* is a tour-group hotel on a quiet side street. From Vltavská metro station, take tram No 1 or 25 three stops west to Letenské náměstí.

Hotel Belvedere *(☎ 220 10 61 11, fax 233 37 23 68; ⓔ prague@belvedere-hotel.com;*

Milady Horákové 19; singles/doubles 2130/2850Kč) has posh three- and four-star rooms at very reasonable rates. Take tram No 1 or 25 two stops west from Vltavská metro station.

Karlín (Maps 2 & 8)

The Karlín district lies east of Florenc bus station, between Vítkov (Žižkov) Hill and the river.

Hotel Brno *(Map 8; ☎ 224 81 18 88, fax 224 81 04 32; Thámova 26; metro Křižíkova; singles/doubles/triples 1920/2810/3340Kč)* is a renovated 1970s hotel in a pedestrianised street, right outside the metro station.

Hotel Ibis Praha Karlín *(Map 8; ☎ 224 81 17 18, fax 224 81 26 81; ⓔ reservation@hotelibis.cz; Šaldova 54; metro Křižíkova; singles/doubles 2425/3025Kč)*, around the block from Hotel Brno, is a comfortable but forgettable chain hotel. Rates are about 35% cheaper from November to March (except for New Year).

Hotel Čechie *(Map 2; ☎ 266 19 41 11, fax 226 83 01 37; ⓔ recepce@hotelcechie.cz; U Sluncové 618; metro Invalidovna; economy singles/doubles 2200/2800Kč, business class 2700/3600Kč)* is owned by a sports centre. There is at least one barrier-free double among the newer and more spacious business-class rooms; all rooms have TV, shower and toilet. Guests can use the swimming pool for free, but all other facilities (tennis and squash courts, bowling alleys and fitness centre) cost extra.

Beside Invalidovna metro station is the four-star, high-rise **Interhotel Olympik** *(Map 2; ☎ 266 18 48 82, fax 266 18 48 46; ⓔ reservation@olympik.cz; Sokolovská 138; singles/doubles €68/97)*, and the neighbouring **Hotel Olympik Tristar** *(Map 2; ☎ 266 18 48 82, fax 266 31 01 06; reservation.tristar@olympik.cz; U Sluncové 14; singles/doubles €60/88)*. Both cater mainly for groups.

Žižkov (Maps 6 & 8)

Western Žižkov has several good-value hotels, mostly aimed at groups but with fair walk-in odds. All are near trams: No 9 from Wenceslas Square (Václavské náměstí), No 5 or 26 from náměstí Republiký, or buses: No 133 or 207 from Florenc bus station.

Hotel Victor *(Map 6; ☎ 222 78 12 91, fax 222 78 31 91; ⓔ hotelvictor@iol.cz; Husitská 72; bus No 133 or 207; singles/doubles 2500/2900Kč)* is a modernised, 19th-century apartment block with comfortable en-suite rooms.

Hotel Ostaš *(Map 6; ☎/fax 226 27 93 86; Orebitská 8; bus No 133 or 207; singles/doubles/triples 1750/2500/2950Kč)* is another late-19th-century apartment block with plain but pleasant rooms.

Hotel U tří korunek *(Map 8; ☎ 222 78 11 12, fax 222 78 01 89; ⓔ hotel@3korunky.cz; Cimburkova 28; bus No 133 or 207; singles/doubles/triples 1900/2900/3900Kč)* has quiet, en-suite rooms (four are barrier-free), with prices that drop about 40% in winter.

If U tří korunek is full, try the **Hotel Bílý Lev** *(Map 8; ☎ 222 78 04 30, fax 222 78 04 65; Cimburkova 20; singles/doubles 1800/2520Kč)* up the hill. It has similar rooms at slightly lower prices.

Hotel Ariston *(Map 6; ☎ 222 78 25 17, fax 222 78 03 47; ⓔ ariston@europehotels.cz; Seifertova 65; tram No 5, 9 or 26; singles/doubles 2800/3700Kč)* is bright and modern and only three tram stops from Wenceslas Square.

Olšanka Hotel *(Map 8; ☎ 267 09 22 02, fax 222 71 33 15; ⓔ rezervace@hotelolsanka.cz; Táboritská 23; tram No 5, 9 or 26; singles/doubles/triples 2100/2700/3500Kč)*, located in an unappealing concrete mall, has unexceptional, modern en-suite rooms with TV; some have balconies. There's an Internet café in the hotel.

Smíchov (Maps 2, 5 & 9)

Hotel Kavalír *(Map 2; ☎ 257 21 65 65, fax 257 21 00 85; ⓔ kavalir@europehotels.cz; Plzeňská 177; singles/doubles 2400/3200Kč)* is yet another ordinary modern hotel, recently refurbished, with five barrier-free double rooms. Take tram No 4, 7, 9 or 10 west from Anděl metro station to the fourth stop, Kavalírka.

Smíchov has two floating hotels: **Admirál Botel** *(Map 9; ☎ 257 32 13 02, fax 257 31 95 16; ⓔ info@admiral-botel.cz; Hořejší nábřeží*

PLACES TO STAY

57; metro Anděl; singles/doubles 2710/2840Kč, triple/quad suites 4520/ 4910Kč) near Palackého most and **Botel Vodník** *(Map 9; ☎ 527 31 56 67, fax 224 81 04 32; Strakonická; singles/doubles/triples 2040/2340/ 2640Kč)*, a five-minute walk from Smíchovské Nádraží metro station.

There are a couple of quiet, unremarkable, modern hotels in the northern part of Smíchov, including the recently renovated **Hotel Mepro** *(Map 9; ☎ 257 31 30 67, fax 257 21 52 63; Viktora Huga 3; singles/doubles from 2500/3200Kč)* and **Hotel Julián** *(Map 5; ☎ 257 31 11 50, fax 257 31 11 49; ⓔ casjul@ vol.cz; Elišky Peškové 11; singles/doubles 3280/3580Kč)*, both hotels have some wheelchair-accessible rooms.

Hotel U Blaženky *(Map 9; ☎/fax 251 56 45 32; ⓔ hotel@ublazenky.cz; U Blaženky 1; singles/doubles 3000/3700Kč)*, in the quiet streets above Bertramka (the elegant 17th-century villa where Mozart stayed), is stylish and comfortable, and hosts a collection of paintings by young Czech artist Markéta Výletalova. From Anděl metro station it's a 15-minute walk uphill through the woods; take the footpath from the top of Ostrovského. You can also take bus No 137 three stops to the Malvazinky stop, then walk five minutes down U Mrázovky.

Near the Airport (Map 2)

The following hotels are accessible by bus from the airport.

Hotel Elegant *(☎ 235 30 05 21, fax 235 30 05 23; Ruzyňská 197, Ruzyně; singles/doubles 3100/3800Kč)* is a stylish, 1930s functionalist building, which has been recently renovated and refurbished. It's only seven minutes from the airport on bus No 225; get off at the Ruzňská škola stop.

Hotel Obora *(☎ 235 35 77 79, fax 235 36 60 93; ⓔ hotel.obora@volny.cz; Libocká 271/1, Liboc; singles/doubles 2200/2850Kč)*, a bland but comfortable 22-room business hotel on the edge of the forest around Letohrádek Hvězda (see the Things to See & Do chapter), is a five-minute walk uphill from the nearest bus stops (Libocká and Petřiny) on the No 179 bus route (12 minutes from the airport).

Southeastern Outskirts (Map 2)

Hotel Braník *(☎ 244 46 28 44, fax 244 46 21 09; Pikovická 199, Braník; singles/doubles/triples 1650/2500/2800Kč)* is close to the river and has a garden restaurant. It's 15 minutes from Wenceslas Square on tram No 3 or from Staroměstská on No 17 (nádraží Braník stop).

Sans Souci Hotel *(☎ 244 46 12 25, fax 244 46 19 50; ⓔ info@hotelsanssouci.cz; V podhájí 12, Podolí; singles/doubles/triples 2200/2600/3000Kč)* is a charming and quiet family hotel in a restored 19th-century villa; en-suite rooms come with TV and breakfast. Rates fall by around 50% in the low season. Take tram No 3 or 17 to the Dvorce stop, walk up Jeremenkova and turn through the underpass just beyond the shops at No 14. At the top of the stairs, walk right on Na Zvoničce for a few minutes until you see the hotel up on the right. By car, follow signs from Jeremenkova.

Botel Racek *(☎ 241 43 16 28, fax 241 43 05 26; ⓔ info@botelracek.cz; Na Dvorecké louce, Podolí; singles/doubles/triples €56/70/104)* is a quiet, floating hotel with dinky little wood-panelled cabins with shower and toilet. It's a five-minute walk from the Dvorce stop on the No 3 or 17 tram line.

Hotel ILF *(☎ 261 09 23 73, fax 261 26 18 46; ⓔ rezervace@ipvz.cz; Budějovická 15/743, Michle; metro Budějovická; singles/doubles 2300/3200Kč)* is a smart business hotel aimed at the medical conference market, but it sells surplus capacity (including seven barrier-free doubles) to all-comers. It's only 10 minutes to the city centre from the neighbouring metro station.

Hotel Globus *(☎ 272 92 77 00, fax 272 93 72 67; ⓔ rezervace@hotel-globus.cz; Gregorova 2115, Horní Roztyly; singles/doubles €71/87)*, a quiet, modern hotel set at the edge of a forest, has eight barrier-free doubles and wheelchair access to the nearby metro. It's easily reached by car via Junction 1 on the D1 from Brno. On foot, it's five minutes from Roztyly metro station – turn right at the top of the stairs and follow the path uphill towards the woods; turn right, then fork left at the first junction – the hotel is 200m further, on the left.

HOTELS – TOP END

Hradčany (Map 5)

Domus Henrici *(☎ 220 51 13 69, fax 220 51 15 02; ⓔ reception@domus-henrici.cz; Loretanska 11; singles US$139-177, doubles US$155-190)*, a historic building in a quiet corner of Hradčany, has eight spacious and elegant rooms, some with private fax, scanner and Internet access, and a sunny terrace with great views.

Romantik Hotel U raka *(☎ 220 51 11 00, fax 233 35 80 41; ⓔ uraka@login.cz; Černínská 10; singles/doubles 5600/6200Kč)*, concealed in a manicured rock garden in a quiet corner of Hradčany, has just six elegant doubles for romantic getaways – kids aged under 10 are not allowed. Book a few months ahead in summer.

Hotel Hoffmeister *(☎ 251 01 71 11, fax 251 01 71 00; ⓔ hotel@hoffmeister.cz; Pod Bruskou 7; singles/doubles €220/310)* is the chosen meeting place for Prague's Rotary Club, which should tell you something about the atmosphere – plush, pink, chintzy and slightly stuffy. It is, however, very comfortable, has excellent service, and is right at the foot of the Old Castle Steps.

Malá Strana (Map 5)

Malá Strana has the highest concentration of top-end hotels in Prague, all within easy walking distance of the castle.

Hotel U tří pštrosů *(☎ 257 53 24 10, fax 257 53 32 17; ⓔ info@utripstrosu.cz; Dražického nám 12; singles/doubles 5900/7900Kč)* is a grand old merchant's house at the foot of the Malá Strana tower on Charles Bridge (Karlův most). It's filled with interesting historical details. The rooms may be expensive, but they have an unbeatable location and some splendid views.

Hotel U Páva *(☎ 57 32 07 43, fax 57 31 58 67; ⓔ hotelupava@tnet.cz; U lužického semináře 32; singles 5400-6400Kč, doubles 5900-6900Kč)*, as its name (At the Peacock) might suggest, proudly shows off its colourfully renovated Gothic and Renaissance interior; some rooms have magical views of Prague Castle (Pražský hrad).

Hotel Neruda *(☎ 257 53 55 57, fax 257 53 14 92; ⓔ info@hotelneruda-praha.cz; Nerudova 44; singles 5500-5800Kč, doubles 5900-6850Kč)*, though set in an old Gothic house, offers a refreshingly modern and stylish alternative to the often tacky, so-called 'historic' hotels in Malá Strana. There's a 10% discount for booking online.

Hotel U krále Karla *(☎ 257 53 28 69, fax 257 53 35 91; ⓔ ukrale@iol.cz; Úvoz 4; singles 6100Kč, doubles 5500-6900Kč)* is set in a lovely, Baroque-style Gothic building. Someone has been a bit heavy-handed with the pastel pink paint, but it vies with Hotel Neruda for the title of closest hotel to the castle – it's just a few minutes' walk from the main gate.

Hotel U Zlaté studně *(☎ 257 01 12 13, fax 257 53 33 20; ⓔ hotel@zlatastudna.cz; singles/doubles US$235/245, apartment US$275-295)* is one of Malá Strana's more tasteful renovations – a 16th-century house (once inhabited by astronomer Tycho de Brahe) perched on the southern slope of the castle hill, and furnished with reproduction antiques. Superb views, too.

Best Western Hotel Kampa *(☎ 257 32 05 08, fax 257 32 02 62; ⓔ euroagentur@euroagentur.cz; Všehrdova 16; singles/doubles 4900/5800Kč)* is set in a quiet location near the southern end of Kampa island. It has slightly cramped modern rooms and a garish, pseudo-Gothic 'Knight's Hall' restaurant.

Kampa Island (Map 5)

Hotel Café Dvořák *(☎ 257 53 21 39, fax 257 53 14 40; ⓔ info@hotel-cafe-dvorak.cz; Na Kampě 3; doubles 4600Kč)*, located on Kampa island's little square, has three luxurious apartments that were renovated in 2001 – ask for the attic apartment, the most atmospheric of the three.

Hotel U červené sklenice *(☎/fax 257 53 29 18; ⓔ recepce@hotel-kampa.cz; Na Kampě 10; doubles/triples 4600/5200Kč)*, on the other side of Na Kampě (Kampa Square), offers five plain but comfortable doubles and three three-bed suites – and a superb view of Charles Bridge from the garden terrace.

Staré Město (Map 7)

The first two hotels listed below are within a few minutes' walk of Old Town Square.

Hotel Ungelt *(☎ 224 82 86 86, fax 224 82 81 81; e hotel@ungelt.cz; Malá Štupartská 1; doubles/quads 6330/9070Kč)*, overlooking the Týnský dvůr, has nine elegant apartments, each with one or two bedrooms, lounge, kitchen and bathroom. Rates include breakfast served in your room, washing and ironing, and free Internet access and fax service.

Hotel Metamorphis *(☎ 221 77 10 11, fax 221 77 10 99; e hotel@metamorphis.cz; Týnský dvůr, Malá Štupartská 5; singles/doubles/suite 4450/5230/5890Kč)*, on historic Týnský dvůr, has luxuriously renovated rooms dating from the 15th and 16th centuries; one of these was used as a family chapel, while another has an original Dutch ceramic stove.

Hotel Clementin *(☎ 222 22 17 98, fax 222 22 17 68; e hotel@clementin.cz; Seminárška 4; singles/doubles 4250/5250Kč)* – a pretty little place that is probably the narrowest hotel in Prague – has nine cosy rooms on a narrow street just off the tourist thoroughfare of Karlova.

Hotel Casa Marcello *(☎ 222 31 02 60, fax 222 31 33 23; e booking@casa-marcello.cz; Řásnovka 783; doubles 7500Kč)* is a former aristocratic residence with stylishly furnished rooms and a pleasant courtyard where you can enjoy a drink or a snack. Prices can fall to almost half the advertised rack rate in July, August and winter.

Hotel Josef *(☎ 221 70 01 11, fax 221 70 09 99; e office@hoteljosef.cz; Rybná 20; singles/doubles €200/400)* opened in July 2002 and is a stunning modern hotel designed by London-based Czech architect Eva Jiřičná. Design highlights include the glass-walled en-suite bathrooms and the suspended spiral staircase in the lobby.

Hotel Paříž *(☎ 222 19 51 95, fax 224 22 54 75; e booking@hotel-pariz.cz; U Obecního domu 1; doubles €320-350)* is a monument to Art Nouveau, with a magnificently marbled and mirrored interior. Its rooms have all mod cons but manage to retain an early-20th-century feel.

Grand Hotel Bohemia *(☎ 224 80 41 11, fax 222 32 95 45; e grand-hotel-bohemia@austria-hotels.icom.cz; Králodvorská 4; standard singles/doubles €218/315)* dates from 1925 but was given a major overhaul in 1993 by an Austrian hotel chain. It has spacious, elegant rooms with desk, fax, voicemail and RJ-11 modem sockets.

Northern Nové Město (Maps 6 & 7)

Hotel Hilton Prague *(Map 6; ☎ 224 84 11 11, fax 224 84 23 78; w www.prague.hilton.com; Pobřežní 3; singles/doubles from €195/205)*, beside the river just north of Florenc metro station, is central Europe's biggest hotel with 788 rooms, a swimming pool, four restaurants, and a vast, glass-roofed atrium. The only thing it hasn't got is atmosphere.

Renaissance Prague Hotel *(Map 7; ☎ 221 82 11 11, fax 221 82 22 00; e renaissance.prague@renaissance.cz; V celnici 1; doubles €195)* is business-traveller friendly, offering rooms with desk, voicemail and modem socket, plus secretarial services and a business centre. There's also an indoor pool, sauna and solarium.

Wenceslas Square & Around (Map 6)

Hotel Esplanade *(☎ 224 50 11 72, fax 224 22 93 06; e esplanade@esplanade.cz; Washingtonova 19; singles/doubles from 3500/4500Kč)*, opposite the Statní opera, is one of the city's older luxury hotels, dating from 1927. The modernised rooms match fussily with the original neobaroque decor.

Palace Hotel *(☎ 224 09 31 11, fax 224 22 12 40; e palhoprg@palacehotel.cz; Panská 12; singles/doubles €295/315)*, a block east of Wenceslas Square, was built in 1906. The Art Nouveau facade is original, but the interior was completely rebuilt in the late 1980s; the luxurious rooms retain plenty of period touches, though.

K+K Hotel Fenix *(☎ 233 09 22 22, fax 222 21 21 41; e hotel.fenix@kkhotels.cz; Ve Smečkách 30; singles/doubles €218/248)*, with design elements by Mies van der Rohe and Philippe Starck among others, has stylish and luxurious rooms just a few paces from Wenceslas Square.

Radisson SAS Alcron Hotel *(☎ 222 82 00 00, fax 222 82 01 00; e mc@prgzh.rdsas.com; Štěpánská 40; doubles €300)* is the modern reincarnation of the 1930s Alcron Hotel.

Much of the original Art Deco marble and glass fittings have been preserved, and the 211 rooms have been far more tastefully renovated than in many other refurbished Prague hotels.

Hotel Adria (☎ *221 08 11 11, fax 221 08 13 00;* ⓔ *info@hoteladria.cz; Václavské náměstí 26; singles/doubles €160/175)* with its yellow Baroque facade is the square's oldest surviving building (late 18th century); the 88 rooms (including two barrier-free doubles), however, are entirely modern. The restaurant (from 1912) is a bizarre blend of Baroque grotto and Art Nouveau decor.

Vyšehrad (Map 10)

Hotel Corinthia Towers (☎ *261 19 11 11, fax 261 22 50 11;* ⓔ *towers@corinthia.cz; Kongresová 1; metro Vyšehrad; doubles €230-360)* is an ultramodern, 26-storey high-rise close to the Congress Centre (and not much else). Recently refurbished, it has first-class service and a spectacular rooftop swimming pool. (Note that American citizens who stay here could, in theory, face criminal charges at home for 'engaging in commercial activity with a Specially Designated National of Libya, as the Corinthia Group is partly Libyan-owned.)

Dejvice (Map 3)

Hotel Crowne Plaza Prague (☎ *224 39 31 11, fax 224 31 06 16;* ⓔ *res@crowneplaza.cz; Koulova 15; tram No 20 or 25; doubles €265-300)*, originally the Hotel International, was built in the 1950s in the style of Moscow University, complete with Soviet star atop the tower. Now modernised, it is comfortable and quiet, tucked away at the end of the tram line.

Smíchov (Map 9)

Anděl's Hotel Prague (☎ *296 88 96 88, fax 296 88 99 99;* ⓔ *info@andelshotel.com; Stroupežnického 21; singles €209-259, doubles €238-294)* is a brand-new boutique hotel in the redeveloped heart of Smíchov, all stark designer chic in beige, black and red. The 200-odd high-tech rooms (half are nonsmoking) all have satellite TV, DVD and Ethernet sockets to connect your laptop to the Internet.

Comfortably Communist

One of Prague's more interesting hotels is hidden away on a hill in Dejvice, surrounded by several hectares of private grounds that were once protected by an electric fence. The **Hotel Praha** *(Map 2;* ☎ *224 34 11 11, fax 224 32 12 18;* ⓔ *reserv@htlpraha.cz; Sušická 20; singles/doubles 5900/6840Kč)* is a luxury complex that was built for the communist party elite in 1981.

The public areas are an intriguing mix of 1970s futuristic-style (sweeping curves and stainless steel) and 1950s Soviet-style splendour (polished marble and cut-glass chandeliers). The bedrooms are very spacious, with all the luxury you'd expect from a five-star establishment, and many are wheelchair-accessible. But the hotel's big draw is the fact that each of its 124 rooms has its own private balcony. The entire southern face of the hotel is a sloping grandstand of stacked balconies, all draped with greenery and commanding a superb view of the castle.

Before 1989, such Soviet-era stalwarts as Nicolae Ceaucescu, Erich Honecker and Eduard Shevardnadze all hung their hats here; in recent years, the clientele has shifted from heads of state to Hollywood, with stars such as Johnny Depp, Alanis Morissette, Kris Kristofferson, Bryan Adams, Suzanne Vega and Paul Simon ringing room service in the small hours. Even Tom Cruise stayed here during the filming of *Mission Impossible* in 1995.

Southeastern Outskirts

Villa Voyta (☎ *261 71 13 07, fax 244 47 12 48;* ⓔ *info@villavoyta.cz; K Novému dvoru 124/54, Lhotka; singles/doubles 4700/5300Kč)* is a beautiful Art Nouveau hotel dating from 1912. Rebuilt in the 1990s when a new 'wing' was added across the road, it's now a small, executive-friendly hotel with elegant rooms, free parking and an excellent, gourmet French restaurant. Rates include breakfast. It's just south of Map 2; take bus No 113, 171, 189 or 215 south from Kačerov metro station to the Zálesí stop, and walk three blocks west on Na Větrově.

Places to Eat

FOOD

Czech cuisine is typically Central European, with German, Austrian, Polish and Hungarian influences. It's very filling, with meat, dumplings, and potato or rice topped with a heavy sauce, and is usually served with a vegetable or sauerkraut.

The standard meal, which is offered in just about every Czech restaurant, is *'knedlo, zelo, vepřo'* (bread dumpling, sauerkraut and roast pork). Caraway seed, salt and bacon are the most common flavourings – most Czech chefs are rather generous with salt. Everything is washed down with alcohol, mainly beer. Diet food it isn't.

Prague's restaurant scene changes fast, with new ethnic and international restaurants opening all the time. There are also plenty of Chinese restaurants (though some visitors report heavy use of monosodium glutamate).

For a full food glossary, see the Language chapter.

Breakfast

A typical Czech *snídaně* (breakfast) consists of *chléb* (bread) or *rohlík* (bread roll) with butter, cheese, eggs, ham or sausage, jam or yogurt, and tea or coffee. Some Czechs eat breakfast at self-service *bufety* that open between 6am and 8am – typically soup or hot dogs washed down with coffee or beer.

A hotel breakfast is typically a cold plate or buffet with cheese, sausage or meat, bread, butter, jam, yogurt, and coffee or tea. Some also offer cereal and milk, pastries, fruit and cakes. Only at top-end hotels and a few restaurants can you get an American or English-style fried breakfast. Some eateries serving Western-style breakfasts are noted in the boxed text 'Best Breakfasts' later in this chapter.

You can also go to a *pekárna* or *pekařství* (bakery), or to one of the French or Viennese bakeries, for *loupáčky*, like croissants but smaller and heavier. Czech bread, especially rye, is excellent and varied.

Lunch & Dinner

Oběd (lunch) is the main meal, but except on Sunday it's a hurried affair. Because Czechs are early risers, they may sit down to lunch as early as 11.30am, though latecomers can still find leftovers in many restaurants at 3pm. Even some of the grungiest spots are nonsmoking until lunch is over. *Večeře* (dinner) might only be a cold platter with bread.

Bufet, jídelna and/or *samoobsluha* are self-service buffets – sit-down or stand-up – for lunch on the run. Common items are *buřt* (mild pork sausages), *chlebíčky* (open sandwiches), *párky* (hot dogs), *klobásy* (spicy sausages), *guláš* (goulash) and good old *knedlo, zelo, vepřo*.

Most *hospoda* and *hostinec* (pubs), *vinárny* (wine bars) and *restaurace* (restaurants) serve sit-down meals with several courses until at least 8pm or 9pm. Some stay open until midnight.

Czechs tend to start their meal with *polévka* (soup). Other common starters are sausage, the famous *Pražská šunka* (Prague ham) and open sandwiches. Salads and condiments may cost extra. The most common main meal is *knedlíky* (dumplings), made from *bramborové knedlíky* (potato) or *houskové knedlíky* (bread), served with pork and sauerkraut. Beef may be served with dumplings and comes with a sauce – usually goulash, *koprová omáčka* (dill cream sauce) or *houbová omáčka* (mushroom sauce). A delicious Czech speciality is *svíčková na smetaně* – roast beef and bread dumplings covered in sour cream sauce, served with lemon and cranberries. Another Czech speciality is *ovocné knedlíky* (fruit dumplings). Unfortunately, the bread and potato dumplings you get in most restaurants are usually factory-produced and pale in comparison to homemade ones.

Fish is common, and is usually *kapr* (carp) or *pstruh* (trout). *Štika* (pike) and *úhoř* (eel) are found on more specialised menus. Seafood – not surprisingly – is found only in a handful of expensive restaurants. Note that the menu price is usually not for the whole fish but per 100g. Ask how much the trout weighs before you order it!

Poultry is also common, either roasted or as *kuře na paprice* (chicken in spicy paprika cream sauce). *Kachna* (duck), *husa* (goose) and *krůta* (turkey) usually come roasted with dumplings and sauerkraut. Turkey is the traditional Christmas Day lunch.

A few restaurants specialise in game. Most common are *jelení* (venison) *bažant* (pheasant), *zajíc* (hare) and *kanec* (boar) – fried or roasted and served in a mushroom sauce or as goulash.

Vegetarian Meals *Bezmasá jídla* ('meatless' dishes) are advertised on most menus, but some may be cooked in animal fat or even with pieces of ham or bacon! If you ask, most chefs can whip up something genuinely vegetarian. Useful phrases include:

Jsem vegetarián/vegetariánka (m/f).
I am a vegetarian.
Nejím maso.
I don't eat meat.
Nejím rybu/kuře/šunku.
I don't eat fish/chicken/ham.

Some common meatless dishes are:

knedlíky s vejci
fried dumplings with egg
omeleta se sýrem a bramborem
cheese and potato omelette
smažené žampiony
fried mushrooms
smažený květák
fried cauliflower with egg and onion
smažený sýr
fried cheese with potatoes and tartar sauce

Fortunately there are several good vegetarian restaurants in Prague.

Dessert

Most Czech restaurants have little in the way of *moučník* (dessert). For cakes and pastries it is better to go to a *kavárna* (café) or *cukrárna* (cake shop). Most desserts consist of *kompot* (canned/preserved fruit), either on its own or *pohár* – in a cup with *zmrzlina* (ice cream) and whipped cream. *Palačinky* or *lívance* (pancakes) are also very common. Other desserts include *jablkový závin* (apple strudel), *makový koláč* (poppy-seed cake) and *ovocné koláče* (fruit slices).

Snacks

The most popular Czech snacks are *buřt* or *vuřt* (thick sausages, usually pork) and *klobása* (spicy pork or beef sausages), fried or boiled, served with mustard on rye bread or a roll. Other snacks are *párky* (hot dogs), *bramborák* (a potato cake made from strips of potato and garlic) and *hranolky* (chips or French fries).

Locally produced *bílý jogurt* (natural white yogurt) is a popular product that is much better than the imported versions. Also good is *Kostka – tvarohový krém*, a

Spanish Birds & Moravian Sparrow

Many Czech dishes have names that don't offer a clue as to what's in them, but certain words will give you a hint: *šavle* (sabre; something on a skewer); *tajemství* (secret; cheese inside rolled meat or chicken); *překvapení* (surprise; meat, capsicum and tomato paste rolled into a potato pancake); *kapsa* (pocket; a filling inside rolled meat); and *bašta* (bastion; meat in spicy sauce with a potato pancake).

Two strangely named dishes that all Czechs know are *Španělský ptáčky* (Spanish birds; veal rolled up with sausage and gherkin, served with rice and sauce) and *Moravský vrabec* (Moravian sparrow; a fist-sized piece of roast pork). But even Czechs may have to ask about *Meč krále Jiřího* (the sword of King George; beef and pork roasted on a skewer), *Tajemství Petra Voka* (Peter Voka's mystery; carp with sauce), *Šíp Malínských lovců* (the Malín hunter's arrow; beef, sausage, fish and vegetables on a skewer) and *Dech kopáče Ondřeje* (Digger Ondřej's breath; fillet of pork filled with extremely smelly Olomouc cheese slices).

frozen yogurt ice cream on a stick and covered in chocolate. In autumn, street vendors offer *kaštany* (roasted chestnuts).

DRINKS

Coffee & Tea

Káva (coffee) and *čaj* (tea) are very popular. Homemade Czech coffee is the strong *turecká* (Turkish) – hot water poured over ground beans that end up as sludge at the bottom of your cup. *Espreso* means 'black coffee', and is sometimes a fair equivalent of the Italian version; *espreso s mlékem* is coffee with milk. *Vídeňská káva* (Viennese coffee) is topped with whipped cream.

Many hotels – even expensive ones – dish up thermos flasks of dismal instant coffee at breakfast. Fortunately, there are lots of cafés which serve excellent coffee, including latte and cappuccino.

Tea tends to be weak and is usually served with a slice of lemon; if you want it with milk, ask for *čaj s mlékem*. *Čajovná* (tea houses) have proliferated in recent years; they serve a wide range of Indian, Sri Lankan, Chinese and herbal teas.

Nonalcoholic Drinks

In Prague it's hard to find *limonády* (soft drinks) other than Western imports. One Czech energy drink – clearly not being marketed just to track and field stars – is Erektus. Another is Semtex, in honour of the infamous plastic explosive made in the former Czechoslovakia. Locally bottled mineral water is widely available, as many Czechs don't like the taste of their tap water. Fruit drinks advertised as 'juices' are widely available, but aren't always 100% juice.

Beer

Czech *pivo* (beer) is among the best in the world, with a pedigree that goes back to the 13th century; see the boxed text 'Pivo' in the Entertainment chapter. The world's first lager was brewed in Plzeň (Pilsen) in West Bohemia. The Czech Republic has for some years been the world's No 1 beer-drinking nation, with an annual per capita consumption of some 158L. Beer is served almost everywhere; even cafeterias and breakfast *bufety* have a tap. Most pubs close at 10pm or 11pm, but some bars and nightclubs are open until 6am.

Most Czech beers are lagers, naturally brewed from malt and flavoured with handpicked hops. Czechs like their beer at cellar temperature with a creamy, tall head. Americans and Australians may find this a bit warm. When ordering draught beer, ask for a *malé pivo* (0.3L) or *pivo* (0.5L).

Most beer is either light or dark, and either *dvanáctka* (12°) or *desítka* (10°). This indicator of specific gravity depends on factors such as texture and malt content, and doesn't directly indicate alcohol content. Most beers are between 3% and 6% alcohol, regardless of their specific gravity.

The best-known Czech beer is Plzeňský Prazdroj (Plzeň's Pilsner Urquell), which is exported worldwide. Many Czechs also like another Plzeň brew, Gambrinus. Sharp marketing (and a tasty brew) has seen Krušovice (from Central Bohemia, west of Prague) rise to national prominence. The most widely exported Czech beer is Budvar (Budweiser in German), the name of which is also used by an unrelated American brew. The Czech Budvar's mild, slightly bitter taste is popular in Austria, Germany and Scandinavia. A newish beer from Prague breweries, with a fine and very smooth taste, is Velvet, in light form, or Kelt, as a dark beer. Other Prague home brands are Smíchovský Staropramen and Braník.

Some pubs brew their own beer; best known are the strong, dark beer served at U Fleků in Nové Město, and a light beer made by its near neighbour, Novoměstský pivovar (see the Entertainment chapter for details of these venues).

Most glass bottles can be returned to the point of purchase for a refund of around 3Kč to 10Kč, a small boost for your beer budget.

Wine

Although not as popular as beer, *víno* (wine) is widely available in *vinárny* (wine bars), restaurants and pubs – but not in many beer halls. *Suché víno* is dry wine and *sladké* is sweet.

Reasonable local wines are available in Prague shops, but the best ones are bought straight from the vineyards. Bohemia's largest wine-producing area, around Mělník (see the Excursions chapter), produces good whites (such as Ludmila bílá or Mělnické zámecké), though its reds don't measure up to Moravia's; Burgundy-like Ludmila is the most popular. The best Moravian label is Vavřinec, a red from the southeast; another good red is Frankovka. A good dry white is Tramín. Rulandské bílé is a semi-dry white, and Rulandské červené a medium red. Czech champagnes are excellent for the price – try Bohemia Sekt Brut or Demi-Sekt.

A popular summer drink is *vinný střik*, white wine and soda water with ice. In winter mulled wine is popular.

Burčak is a wine-based beverage and is only available for about three weeks each year from around the end of September to mid-October. It is a new wine in the passing stage of the fermentation process when it is transforming from grape juice to a full-bodied wine and its taste changes daily. The delicious and sweet taste of Burčak is more

The Rebirth of Absinthe

Absinthe (spelled *absinth* in Czech) is the deadliest spirit in the world. Invented in Switzerland, flavoured with wormwood, and with an alcohol content of 70%, it was first produced commercially by Henry-Louis Pernod in 1797. By the late 19th century it had become a hugely popular drink, especially in France where it was known as *La Feé Verte* (The Green Fairy). The green, slightly soapy-tasting liqueur was linked with creativity and the bohemian lifestyle, and was the favoured tipple of Toulouse-Lautrec, Van Gogh, Oscar Wilde and Ernest Hemingway.

But absinthe had a reputation as a dangerous drink. It was said that wormwood rotted the brain and caused hallucinations, though many put this effect down to the high alcohol content. By the early 20th century it had been banned in many European countries. However, it remained legal in Spain, Portugal, the United Kingdom and Czechoslovakia. It was banned during the communist era but legalised in the Czech Republic in the 1990s when it experienced a renaissance as a trendy, anti-establishment drink.

The following story of the rebirth of absinthe in the Czech Republic comes from a Mr Boháč, one of the founders of an artists' colony in the village of Maříž, just outside of the South Bohemian town of Slavonice. Boháč and his friend (who died in mid-2000) ran the Besídka café in Slavonice. One day in 1990 Radomil Hill of Hill Liquere in the town of Jindřichův Hradec, Southeast Bohemia, visited the café and during their discussion Mr Boháč touched on the subject of absinthe. He suggested that Radomil should start making it again – Hill's family had made absinthe since the 1920s, and though production ceased during the communist era he still possessed the recipe. Not long after their meeting, Radomil Hill returned with a bottle of Czech-made absinthe.

Initially, not many places sold absinthe except for the Besídka café. Apparently, in the late 1990s the band the Sugar Cubes, who were on their way to play a gig, stopped for lunch at Besídka café. But having fallen under the spell of The Green Fairy they stayed until the early hours of the following day.

Absinthe came to Prague via the owner of the Palác Akropolis, who, after discovering it on a visit to Slavonice, began selling it at his nightclub. British and American drinkers rediscovered The Green Fairy in Prague, and Hill's absinthe began to be imported into the UK in 1998.

Arguments still rage about its safety, but one fact is certain – absinthe hangovers are much nastier than normal ones. One traditional way to drink it is to soak a cube of sugar in the absinthe in your glass, set it alight on a spoon, and when the sugar has melted, stir it back into the glass. Add some water, and down the hatch.

Prague's **Kozička** *(Map 7; Kozí, Staré Město)*, makes a 'B-52' shot that includes absinthe (instead of Triple Sec), Baileys and Kahlua. Another popular mix is absinthe and Semtex (the Czech answer to Red Bull) – guaranteed to blow your head off.

reminiscent of cider than wine and contains around 3% to 5% alcohol.

Spirits

Probably the most unique of Czech *lihoviny* (spirits) is Becherovka, with its 'cough-medicine' taste, from the spa town of Karlovy Vary. Another bitter spirit is Fernet. A good brandy-type spirit is Myslivecká.

The fiery and potent *Slivovice* (plum brandy) is said to have originated in Moravia, where the best brands still come from. The best commercially produced *slivovice* is R Jelínek from Vizovice. Other regional spirits include Meruňkovice apricot brandy and juniper-flavoured Borovička. If you have a sweet tooth, try Griotka cherry liqueur.

The deadliest spirit is locally produced Hills Liquere Absinth from Jindřichův Hradec, made from wormwood. While it's illegal in many countries, in part because of its high alcohol content, the liqueur is legal in the Czech Republic. There is still debate about its safety. See the boxed text 'The Rebirth of Absinthe' earlier.

Spirits are drunk neat, and usually cold (an exception is *grog*, a popular year-round hot drink: half rum, half hot water or tea, and lemon). Spirits, including Western brands, are available in all restaurants and most pubs and wine bars.

WHERE TO EAT

There's no shortage of places to eat in Prague. If you like meat and dumplings you'll have no problems, though you may soon begin craving something else. The last few years have seen a boom in good restaurants serving more exotic cuisine, though the selection is constantly changing. Use this book as a guide, but also have a look at the *Prague Post* for current listings and reviews.

Opening hours are variable. Most restaurants seem to stay open on national holidays, except Christmas Eve. Main courses

Best Breakfasts

There are plenty of local *bufety* (buffets) open by 8am, but most visitors probably won't fancy soup and sausage at that time of day. Here are some of the best places to start off the day:

Bohemia Bagel *(Map 5; ☎ 257 31 06 94; Újezd 18, Malá Strana • Map 7; ☎ 224 81 25 60; Masná 2, Staré Město; both open 7am-midnight Mon-Fri, 8am-midnight Sat-Sun)* offers all kinds of bagels and toppings for 40Kč to 100Kč, and 'bottomless' cups of coffee (ie, free refills).

Red, Hot & Blues *(Map 7; ☎ 222 31 46 39; Jakubská 12; dishes 140-240Kč; open 9am-11pm daily)* serves a range of Western breakfasts, including pancakes and maple syrup, and a full British fry-up. Their 'Home Run Special' (bacon, eggs, hash browns, pancakes and toast) will soak up the heaviest hangover, and lay a firm foundation for further debauchery. Breakfast is served until 11.30am on weekdays, brunch till 4pm at weekends.

Café Louvre *(Map 6; ☎ 224 93 09 49; 1st floor, Národní 22; dishes 70-120Kč; open 8am-11pm Mon-Fri, 9am-11pm Sat-Sun)* is an elegant, early-20th-century dining room with smart apron-and-waistcoated waiters serving Czech-, American- and British-style breakfasts.

Káva Káva Káva *(Map 6; Platýz pasáž, Národní 37; dishes 20-80Kč; open 7am-10pm daily)* has some of the best coffee in town – the *grande cappuccino* is big enough to bathe in – and a selection of bagels, croissants, cakes and pastries.

Break Cafe *(Map 6; ☎ 222 23 10 65; Štěpánská 32; dishes 65-90Kč; open 8am-11pm daily)* is an American-style diner that serves breakfasts – croissants, bacon and eggs, fresh fruit and yogurt – until 11am.

Institut Français *(Map 6; ☎ 224 21 66 30; Štěpánská 35; dishes 20-80Kč; open 9am-6pm Mon-Fri)* has a nice little café at the back (go in the main entrance and bear right), frequented by French expats but open to all, where you can read the latest issues of *Le Monde* and *Le Figaro* over *café au lait* and a croissant or *pain au chocolat*.

may stop being served well before the advertised closing time, with only snacks and drinks after that.

Prices soar as you approach Old Town Square (Staroměstské náměstí) and Malostranské náměstí, so if you're on a budget, eat outside the historical centre. We list average price ranges for the main courses, not the total for a full meal.

A few older Prague waiters still suffer from that affliction of the communist-era service industry: surliness. It's nothing personal, and Czechs tend to ignore it. Most younger restaurant staff are pleasant and professional.

Types of Eatery

Restaurace (restaurant) is a catch-all term. A *vinárny* (wine bar) may serve anything from small snacks to a full-blown menu. A *hospoda* or *hostinec* is a pub or beer hall serving basic meals; a *pivnice* is a beer hall serving no meals. A *bufety* is a cafeteria-style place with zero atmosphere but cheap soups and stodge. The occasional *kavárna* (café or coffee shop) has a full menu but most only serve snacks.

Reservations

In high season an advance booking is essential for dinner at most top restaurants; for places near the city centre you may have to plan up to a week ahead. It's not unusual to find restaurants entirely 'reserved' – say, for coach parties – and at dinner time there are always a few anxious tourists marching up and down in search of a meal. That said, in months of Prague research, we mostly did just fine without making any reservations at all. The higher your standards and the larger your group, the more trouble you'll have.

Most places that see tourists have someone who can speak English. If you'd rather dispense with bookings, try eating at odd hours, preferably early – start lunch by 11.30am and dinner by 6pm (many cheaper places run out of food after 3pm and after 10pm). Many pubs will serve you meat and dumplings at any time of day. Don't forget the cheap stand-up *bufety* (buffets), some of which are tucked into the side of *potraviny* (food shops).

HRADČANY (MAP 5)

Sate *(☎ 220 51 45 52; Pohořelec 3; mains 90-110Kč; open 11am-10pm daily)*, which serves tasty Indonesian and Malaysian dishes such as *nasi goreng* and beef *rendang*, is five minutes' walk west of the castle.

Malý Buddha *(☎ 220 51 38 94; Úvoz 46; mains 80-110Kč; open 1pm-10.30pm Tues-Sun)* is a short distance downhill from Sate – just follow the incense fumes. It's an oriental tearoom, complete with Buddhist shrine, offering carefully prepared vegetarian and seafood dishes.

U zlaté hrušky *(☎ 220 51 53 56; Nový svět 3; mains 440-670Kč; open 11.30am-3pm & 6.30pm-midnight daily)* is a cosy, wood-panelled gourmet's corner, serving beautifully prepared Czech fish, fowl and game dishes, frequented as much by locals as by tourists. They also run the cheaper **Zahradní restaurace** *(garden restaurant; Nový svět; mains 88-208Kč; open 11am-11pm daily)* across the street.

Restaurant Peklo *(☎ 220 51 66 52; Strahovské nádvoří 1/132; mains 250-600Kč; open 6pm-midnight Mon, noon-midnight Tues-Sun)* is set in subterranean vaults in the Strahovský klašter (Strahov Monastery) grounds. The name means 'Hell' – because the gardens above are called 'Paradise' – but the only suffering that happens is when you have to pay the bill. The food is Italian and Czech.

See also **Cafe Himalaya** in the Vegetarian section later in this chapter.

MALÁ STRANA (MAP 5)

Cafés & Tearooms

St Nicholas Café *(Tržiště 7; mains 190-235Kč; open noon-1am Mon-Fri, 4pm-1am Sat-Sun)* is a quiet Gothic cellar, a favourite midday refuge in the heart of the tourist zone. Slump into an armchair with your coffee, or enjoy a cocktail before dinner.

U zeleného čaje *(At the Green Tea; ☎ 257 53 00 27; Nerudova 19; tea 30-50Kč; open 11am-10pm daily)*, on the way up to the castle, serves teas from all over the world.

Café Savoy *(☎ 257 32 98 74; Vítězná 5; breakfast 60-115Kč, mains 300-700Kč; open 8am-11pm daily)*, a starkly elegant, renovated 19th-century coffee house, serves breakfasts until 11am, and a range of coffees and cakes, as well as full lunch and dinner.

See also **Bohemia Bagel** in the boxed text 'Best Breakfasts' earlier in this chapter.

Budget Restaurants

Jo's Bar & Garáž *(☎ 257 53 33 42; Malostranské náměstí 7; mains 100-150Kč; open 11am-2am daily)* is a cheerful place serving sandwiches, salads, burgers and Tex-Mex dishes to young expats and tourists. In the club downstairs, drinks keep flowing till 5am.

Cafe Bio Life *(☎ 257 53 28 36; Zámecká 3; mains 88-138Kč; open 11am-10pm daily)* is a cool little place with architecture and antiques magazines scattered around and interesting art on the walls. Settle into a cane chair and order from a menu of organic and macrobiotic grub, both veggie and carnivorous – salads, couscous, pasta and sandwiches made with great home-baked bread.

Restaurace Bar Bar *(☎ 257 31 22 46; Všehrdova 17; mains 75-120Kč; open noon-midnight daily)* is a cellar bar serving giant salads and a zillion kinds of tasty crepes, both savoury and sweet; the food stops at midnight, but drinks go on till 2am.

For inexpensive Bohemian beer snacks and Czech pub grub try **Hostinec U kocoura** *(cnr Nerudova & Zámecká; open 11am-11pm daily)*.

Mid-Range Restaurants

Pasha *(☎ 257 53 24 34; U lužického semináře 23; mains 450-650Kč; open 11am-11pm Tues-Sun)*, decked out in deep blues and reds, has a lush menu of Lebanese *mezzes* (appetisers) with which to carpet your table. Service is polite and attentive, though they keep topping up your wine glass just a little too often…

Vinárna Čertovka *(☎ 257 53 22 05; U lužického semináře 24; mains 210-310Kč; open 11.30am-midnight daily)* serves mediocre, overpriced Czech food – choose a salad instead – but its main attraction is the stunning view of Charles Bridge (Karlův most) and Staré Město (Old Town).

U Maltézských rytířů *(At the Maltese Knights; ☎ 257 53 36 66; Prokopská 10; mains 200-400Kč; open 11am-11pm daily)* is a cosy and romantic little place, with tables tucked in niches in the downstairs Gothic vaults. Book well ahead.

Sushi Bar *(☎ 0603-24 48 82; Zborovská 49; mains 140-360Kč, set menus 360-450Kč; open 11am-10pm daily)* is as compact and neatly ordered as, well, a plate of sushi. It's run by a seafood importer – there's a fresh fish shop next door – so your sushi and sashimi is always superbly fresh.

Meduzzy *(☎ 251 51 05 57; Mělnická 13; mains 100-250Kč; open 11.30am-11pm daily)* seeks to be Greek with its pine and terracotta decor, and windmill and Medusa motifs. Service is friendly, and the food is fairly authentic too – choriatiki salad (feta cheese, olives, tomato and cucumber), freshly made pitta bread, and tsatsiki with enough raw garlic to stun a horse.

See also **Rybářský klub** and **River Club** in the boxed text 'A River Runs Through It…' later in this chapter.

Top-End Restaurants

Circle Line Brasserie *(☎ 257 53 00 23; Malostranské náměstí 12; mains 495-795Kč; open noon-11pm Mon-Fri, 11am-11pm Sat-Sun)* is one of the city's top French restaurants, with dining on separate levels in a plush Gothic and Baroque palace. Frequented by local bon viveurs and business people on expenses.

Restaurace Pálffy Palác Club *(☎ 57 32 05 70, Valdštejnská 14; mains 475-525Kč; open 11am-midnight daily)*, in the neobaroque palace that houses the Prague Conservatoire (music school), is a local institution patronised at lunchtime by workers from the nearby government ministries. The cuisine is high-quality French/International, but the main attraction is a table on the terrace with views of the palace gardens.

U malířů *(At the Painters; ☎ 257 53 00 00; Maltézské náměstí 11; mains 890-960Kč, set menus 1790-2990Kč; open 7pm-10pm daily)* is an opulent enclave of colourful frescoes, starched linen and *haute cuisine*. Opinions vary as to whether the standard is as consistently high as the prices – the lobster in chardonnay sauce (2890Kč per person) is going to be a big letdown if it's the head chef's night off – but when it's good it's very, very good.

U modré kachničky *(☎ 257 32 03 08; Nebovidská 6; open noon-4pm & 6.30pm-11.30pm daily • Map 7; ☎ 224 21 34 18; Michalská 16, Staré Město; open 11.30am-11.30pm daily)* is a chintzy, Baroque hunting lodge on a quiet side street, with quiet nooks perfect for a romantic dinner. Mains cost from 340Kč to 420Kč; it serves good Czech duck and game dishes.

See also **Ostroff** and **Kampa Park** in the boxed text 'A River Runs Through It…', and **U Zlaté studné** and **Restaurant Nebozízek** in the boxed text 'A Table with a View' later in this chapter.

STARÉ MĚSTO

All places in this section are on Map 7, except where indicated.

Cafés & Tearooms

Ebel Coffee House *(Týn 2 • Řetězová 9; both open 9am-10pm daily)* offers superb coffee only a few minutes' walk from Old Town Square, with one branch in Týnský dvůr and another a block south of Karlova. If you can't stand the watery instant served up with your hotel breakfast, head to Ebel for a jolt of full-fat, 98-octane arabica.

Dahab *(☎ 224 82 73 75; cnr Rybná & Haštalská; mains 85-155Kč; open noon-midnight daily)* is a shadowy souk scattered with rugs and cushions, where you can sit at a low table and sip Moroccan mint tea to an oriental-jazz-ragga soundtrack. Food ranges from baklava and other sweet snacks to more substantial hummus and couscous, and there are teas from India, China and Turkey. Or you

A River Runs Through It…

There's no finer way to round off a day's sightseeing than to relax beside the slow-flowing Vltava River with a glass of chilled riesling while you peruse the menu at one of the city's top riverside restaurants. And while you eat, you can watch the setting sun turn the city's spires from gold to rose to ruby.

Here are the four best venues for riverbank dining:

Ostroff *(Map 5; ☎ 224 93 45 76; Střelecký ostrov 336; mains 300-600Kč; open noon-2pm & 7pm-11pm Mon-Fri, 7pm-11pm Sat, 11am-3pm & 7pm-11pm Sun)* has a long bar with picture windows overlooking the river, and in summer there are tables on the rooftop terrace, with a stunning view across the river to Slovanský ostrov and the Narodni divadlo (National Theatre). The food – northern Italian and seafood – is excellent.

Rybářský klub *(Český rybářský svaz; Map 5; ☎ 257 53 31 70; U sovových mlýnů 1; mains 180-270Kč; open 11am-midnight daily)* – the old Fishermen's Guild – is the budget alternative for that riverside dinner. It has a peaceful setting at the southern end of Kampa island, with wooden benches indoors and a handful of outdoor tables beside the river. Try spicy Hungarian fish soup to start, followed by delicious *candát* (pike-perch) cooked with basil.

Kampa Park *(Map 5; ☎ 257 53 26 85; Na Kampě 8b; mains 445-695Kč; open 11.30am-1.30am daily)* is a celebrity magnet at the northern tip of Kampa. Princess Caroline of Monaco, Johnny Depp, Lou Reed, Michael Douglas and Hilary Clinton have all over-tipped the waiters here, and even Salman Rushdie has been seen skulking in a corner. The interior is a designer's wet dream, while the riverside terrace offers a panorama of Charles Bridge (Karlův most) and the Staré Město (Old Town) skyline. The cuisine is as famous as the clientele, from the langoustine tails with tarragon foam to the grilled pompano (it's a fish, darling) with sheep's-milk cheese ravioli and black-truffle-and-orange sauce.

River Club *(Map 7; ☎ 257 31 25 78; U plovárny 8; mains 490-790Kč; open noon-midnight daily)*, housed in a grand, 19th-century swimming clubhouse, has outdoor terrace tables with a view of Mánesův most (Mánes Bridge) and Cechův most (Čech Bridge), and the gilded neo-Renaissance Rudolfinum on the far bank. The inventive international menu ranges through pastas, salads, fish, beef and chicken, while the chef is from the 'Close Encounters of the Third Kind' school. You know: the ones who have a strange compulsion to heap the food into a miniature Devil's Tower…

can kick back with a hookah (hubble-bubble pipe; 155Kč for a chunk of baccy that'll last around 45 minutes).

Café Gaspar Kasper *(Celetná 17; mains 80-150Kč; open 9am-midnight daily)*, upstairs at the divadlo v Celetné (Celetná Theatre; go upstairs from the courtyard), is a pleasant and inexpensive, nonsmoking café-bar, with – not surprisingly – lots of theatrical literature lying around for your perusal.

Kavárna Obecní dům *(☎ 222 00 27 63; náměstí Republiky 5; mains 65-200Kč, breakfast 170Kč; open 7.30am-11pm daily)* offers the opportunity to crunch your cornflakes amid an orgy of Art Nouveau splendour. The café in the **Hotel Paříž** *(U Obecního domu 1)*, just around the block, is another Art Nouveau palace worth the high price of a drink just to have a look around.

Cafe Konvikt *(Map 6; ☎ 224 23 24 27; Bartolomějská 11; mains 50-100Kč; open 9am-1am Mon-Fri, noon-1am Sat-Sun)* is a down-to-earth bar and café serving solid Bohemian fare such as smoked pork, sauerkraut and dumplings – excellent value.

See also **Bohemia Bagel** and **Káva Káva Káva** in the boxed text 'Best Breakfasts' earlier in this chapter.

Budget Restaurants

Restaurace Snack Bar U Černého slunce *(☎ 224 22 47 46; Kamzíkova; mains 65-70Kč; open 10am-10pm)*, in a pedestrian passage off the eastern corner of the square, is good for a beer or a light meal – and excellent value for this area.

U Benedikta *(☎ 222 31 15 27; Benediktská 11; mains 60-180Kč; open 11am-11pm daily)* is a homely little place, with rustic decor and a menu of traditional Czech poultry, fish, steak and game dishes.

Pivnice Radegast *(☎ 222 32 82 37; Templová 2; mains 55-110Kč; open 11am-12.30am daily)*, along an alley off Celetná, has famously no-nonsense service but, considering its location, cheap and tasty traditional Czech food.

Safir Grill *(☎ 224 22 11 43; Havelská 12; mains 65-90Kč; open 10am-8pm Mon-Sat)*, beside the Havelská market stalls, is a stand-up place serving felafel, gyros (doner kebab) and other Middle-Eastern fast food, plus various vegetarian goodies.

Klub architektů *(Map 6; ☎ 224 40 12 14; Betlémské náměstí 5; mains 110-220Kč; open 11.30am-11.30pm daily)* is a popular, subterranean cellar restaurant offering inventive Czech and international dishes, including a wide range of vegetarian ones.

Molly Malone's *(☎ 224 81 88 51; U obecního dvora 4; open midday-1am daily)* is a convivial Irish bar serving not only draught Guinness (80Kč for 0.4L) – of course – but also an excellent menu of high-cholesterol comfort food; this is the place to come for a great bacon sandwich, chip butty, beans on toast, or bacon-and-egg fry-up – even at midnight.

See also **Lotos** and **Country Life** in the Vegetarian section later in this chapter.

Mid-Range Restaurants

Staroměstská restaurace *(☎ 224 21 30 15; Staroměstské náměstí 19; mains 75-245Kč; open 10am-11pm daily)* is easily the best of the tourist restaurants on the square. The meaty Czech and international menu is big, the food good and service pleasant. Try the fruit dumplings. Food and beer prices on the terrace outside are up to 50% higher than those charged inside.

Cafe-Restaurant Metamorphis *(☎ 221 77 10 68; Týnský dvůr, Malá Štupartská 5; mains 85-250Kč; open 9am-1am daily)* is the place to go if you want romantic outdoor dining (April to October) with a view of the Týn Church spires, but without the crowds and inflated prices of places on Old Town Square. The menu is mainly Italian, with excellent service and a good range of wines.

Orange Moon *(☎ 222 32 51 19; Rámová 5; mains 150-220Kč; open 11.30am-11.30pm daily)* is a friendly place set in a cool terracotta cellar and serving excellent Thai, Burmese and Indian dishes.

Ariana *(☎ 222 32 34 38; Rámová 6; mains 180-200Kč; open 11am-11pm daily)*, across the street from Orange Moon, is another welcoming place with a range of unusual Afghani dishes, including *ashak* (a sort of ravioli containing chopped leeks, with a rich sauce of minced lamb and yogurt), various lamb and chicken kebabs, and tasty vegetarian specialities.

Chez Marcel *(☎ 222 31 56 76; Haštalská 12; mains 190-250Kč; open 8am-1am Mon-Thur, 9am-1am Sat-Sun)* is a French café-bar done out in yellow ochre and dark wood. It's a popular hang-out for French expats, a place where you can smoke your Gitanes, sip *café au lait*, and order a *croque monsieur*. The menu also has good bistro dishes such as rabbit with mustard sauce, and tagliatelle with salmon and basil.

Siam-I-San *(☎ 224 81 40 99; Valentínská 11; mains 120-270Kč; open 10am-midnight daily)* is tucked away at the back of the Arzenal designer boutique, in a colourful room designed by a local architect. The cuisine is authentic Thai – probably the best Thai food in Prague – with a good range of dishes, including many vegetarian ones.

Jalapeños *(☎ 222 31 29 25; Valentínská 8; mains 145-245Kč; open 11am-midnight daily)*, across the street from Siam-I-San, is a mock-adobe Tex-Mex place that dishes up decent fajitas, burritos, tacos and nachos.

Red, Hot & Blues *(☎ 222 31 46 39; Jakubská 12; dishes 140-390Kč; open 9am-11pm daily)* is an American-owned, New Orleans-style place with a little courtyard, traditional jazz on the sound system, and live jazz or blues nightly. It serves great nachos, burgers, burritos and shrimp creole, plus some wicked desserts. See also the boxed text 'Best Breakfasts' earlier in this chapter.

Restaurace U medvídků *(Map 6; ☎ 224 21 19 16; Na Perštýně 5-7; mains 80-180Kč; open 11.30am-11pm Mon-Sat, 11.30am-10pm Sun)* is a touristy beer hall and wine bar (bar open until 3am Monday to Saturday, till 1am Sunday) with a nonsmoking restaurant and outdoor garden, all with the same meaty Bohemian menu.

Top-End Restaurants

Le Saint-Jacques *(☎ 222 32 26 85; Jakubská 4; mains 450-950Kč, 3-course menu 650Kč; open noon-3pm & 6pm-midnight Mon-Fri, 6pm-midnight Sat)* is an elegant and intimate, family-run French restaurant with candlelit tables and pleasant service.

Rasoi *(☎ 222 32 84 00; Dlouhá 13; mains 275-500Kč; open 11.30am-3pm & 5pm-11pm Mon-Fri, 11.30am-11pm Sat-Sun)* is an Indian restaurant in a cellar below a busy bar, with a refined, semi-formal atmosphere, and friendly and attentive service. The excellent food draws an appreciative crowd of expat Brits, hankering after authentic chicken tikka *massalam* and *rogan josh*.

Francouzská restaurace *(☎ 222 00 27 70; mains 260-600Kč, 3-course lunch menu 490-590Kč; open noon-4pm & 6pm-11pm daily)*, the 'French Restaurant' in the Obecní dům, is a stunning Art Nouveau dining room. It's hugely popular with visitors, so book a table to avoid disappointment.

V zátiší *(Still Life; Map 6; ☎ 222 22 11 55, Liliová 1; mains 500-900Kč; open noon-3pm & 5.30pm-11pm daily)* is one of Prague's most consistently excellent restaurants, offering traditional Czech cuisine with a gourmet twist; try the roast duck with herb dumplings. There are several vegetarian dishes on the menu too.

Reykjavík *(☎ 222 22 12 18; Karlova 20; mains 250-500Kč; open 11am-midnight daily)* is an Icelandic restaurant – not too many of them around here – serving excellent seafood. As well as chilly northern classics such as pickled herring and salt cod, there's succulent seared tuna, grilled salmon in tarragon cream sauce, and a wicked cheesecake for dessert.

Bellevue *(Map 6; ☎ 224 22 13 87; Smetanovo nábřeží 18; mains 590-790Kč; open noon-3pm & 5.30pm-11pm Mon-Sat, 11am-3pm & 7pm-11pm Sun)* serves up pricey nouvelle cuisine in a formal setting with majestic views of the river, Charles Bridge and Hradčany (and noisy traffic in the foreground if you dine on the balcony). Sunday features a champagne brunch with live jazz from 11am to 3pm.

NOVÉ MĚSTO

Places in this section are on Map 6 unless otherwise noted.

Cafés & Tearooms

Kavárna Imperial *(Map 7; ☎ 222 31 60 12; Na poříčí 15; mains 100-200Kč; open 9am-*

1am daily) has beautiful, early-20th-century decor – oak parquet, walls covered in ornate cream-and-mustard ceramic tiling, and a mosaic ceiling – and is popular with locals and tourists alike, who gather for the live jazz on Friday and Saturday evenings.

Kavárna Arco *(Map 7; Hybernská 16; mains 95-195Kč; open 3pm-9.30pm Mon-Fri, 10am-9.30pm Sat-Sun)* was a regular haunt of writers Franz Kafka and Max Brod in the 1920s. Recently re-opened after a crisp, Art Deco-style renovation in dark wood and teal-green upholstery, it now feels strangely soulless and empty. Worth a coffee for the historical association though.

Grand Hotel Evropa *(☎ 224 22 81 17; Václavské náměstí 25; dishes 100-300Kč; open 9.30am-11pm daily)* has the most stylish café on the square, a fading museum of over-the-top Art Nouveau, but offers only second-rate cakes and coffee, and high tourist prices (including a music cover charge after 3pm on public holidays).

Dobrá Čajovna *(☎ 224 23 14 80; Václavské náměstí 14 • Boršov 2; both open 10am-11pm Mon-Sat, 2pm-11pm Sun)*, along a passage off Wenceslas Square (Václavské náměstí) has snacks for 50Kč to 150Kč and is a little haven of oriental rugs and cushions, away from the heaving crowds on the street. The Bors branch is near the river, just south of Charles Bridge, in Staré Město.

Kavárna Slavia *(☎ 224 22 09 57; Národní 1; mains 100-250Kč; open 8am-midnight Mon-Fri, 9am-midnight Sat-Sun)* is the most famous of Prague's old cafés, a cherrywood and onyx shrine to Art Deco elegance. With the Národní divadlo (National Theatre) across the street, it has been a celebrated literary meeting place since the 1920s, though these days there are more tourists than theatre people.

The Globe *(☎ 224 91 62 64; Pštrossova 6; mains 90-135Kč; open 10am-midnight daily)* is a relaxed and popular expat hang-out, sharing space with a good English-language bookshop. There's a good range of filling veggie sandwiches and healthy snacks including things such as hummus and pitta bread and blackbean burritos, plus burgers, spag bog, nachos etc. See also Internet Cafés in the Facts for the Visitor chapter.

Monica cukrárna *(Národní 32)* is another good place for a caffeine and sugar buzz, down an alley close to Café Louvre. If it's ice cream you're after, to sit in or take away, head for the **Italská cukrárna** *(Vodičkova 4)*.

See also **Café Louvre**, **Break Cafe** and **Institut Français** in the boxed text 'Best Breakfasts' earlier in this chapter.

Budget Restaurants

Pizzeria Václavka *(☎ 222 21 06 97; Václavské náměstí 48; mains 65-120Kč; open 11am-11pm daily)*, in a courtyard through a passage off the southwestern side of Wenceslas Square, serves good, inexpensive pizzas, pastas and salads.

East-West *(☎ 296 23 65 13; Štěpánská 61; mains 85-120Kč; open 11am-11pm daily)* is a unique and exceptionally good-value little place with a cross-cultural menu and decor to match. Dishes include such unusual and wide-ranging offerings as Mohawk Indian corn (sweetcorn kernels with chopped walnuts and herbs) and delicious Tibetan curry.

Branický sklípek *(U Purkmistra; ☎ 224 23 71 03; Vodičkova 26; mains 70-260Kč; open 9am-11pm Mon-Fri, 11am-11pm Sat-Sun)* is an unpretentious restaurant and beer hall, serving meaty but good-value Czech dishes and cheap beer. Menus are in Czech only.

Adoni's bufet *(Anis; ☎ 224 94 84 52; Jungmannova 21; mains 50-100Kč; open 10.30am-7pm Mon-Fri, 11am-5pm Sat)* serves good, cheap Middle Eastern fast food such as kebabs and felafel, to eat in or take away.

Pizzeria Kmotra *(☎ 224 93 41 00; V jirchářích 12; pizzas 70-150Kč; open 11am-midnight daily)* is the place to wash down excellent, wood-fired pizzas with cheap beer. By 8pm crowd control can be a problem, so get there early.

Jihočeská restaurace u Šumavy *(Map 9; ☎ 224 92 11 45; Štěpánská 3; mains 95-155Kč; open 10am-11pm Mon-Fri, 11am-11pm Sat-Sun)* is a smoky, wood-panelled Prague institution, serving tasty, traditional South Bohemian dishes. It has a reputation for overcharging tourists though, so check your bill.

Good inexpensive Czech pub-restaurants in the area include **Restaurace Na poříčí**

(Map 7; ☎ 224 81 13 63; Na poříčí 20; mains 80-150Kč; open 11am-11pm Mon-Sat, noon-11pm Sun) in northern Nové Město; the smoky **Česká hospoda V Krakovské** *(☎ 222 21 02 04; Krakovská 20; mains 90-150Kč; open 11am-11pm daily)* off the top end of Wenceslas Square; and **Hospoda U Nováka** *(☎ 224 93 06 39; V jirchářích 2; mains 70-110Kč; open 11am-midnight Mon-Fri, noon-midnight Sat-Sun)* a block south of the Národní divadlo.

See also **Country Life** and **U Góvindy** in the Vegetarian section later in this chapter.

Mid-Range Restaurants

Restaurace MD Rettigové *(Map 7; ☎ 222 31 44 83; Truhlářská 4; mains 90-290Kč; open 11am-11pm daily)* is named after Magdalena Dobromila Rettigová, the 19th-century exponent of a traditional Czech cuisine – a sort of Czech Mrs Beeton. The rustic dining room dishes up serious traditional dishes such as roast wild boar, baked carp and stuffed quail.

Taj Mahal *(☎ 224 22 55 66; Škrétova 10; mains 250-400Kč; open 11.30am-11.30pm Mon-Sat, 2.30pm-10.30pm Sun)*, tucked behind the Národní divadlo, is one of the city's best Indian restaurants, and offers separate smoking and nonsmoking dining rooms. There's even live sitar-twanging in the evenings.

Titanic Steak House *(☎ 296 22 62 82; Štěpánská 22; mains 90-190Kč; open 11am-11pm Mon-Sat, 3pm-11pm Sun)* is quaintly named – perhaps the food slips down nicely? It's a cool and quiet place with terracotta tiles and cane chairs, offering a range of salads and steaks with various sauces.

Miyabi *(☎ 296 23 31 02; Navrátilova 10; mains 140-270Kč, set lunch 130Kč; open 11am-11pm Mon-Fri, noon-11pm Sat-Sun)* is a relaxed, café-style Japanese restaurant – a refreshing change from more formal Japanese places. The good-value set Japanese lunch is served from 11am to 2pm Monday to Friday.

Restaurant Tbilisi *(Map 9; ☎ 224 91 15 07; Dittrichova 25; mains 190-300Kč; open 11am-midnight daily)* brings a taste of the Caucasus to Prague, with Georgian dishes such as *khinkali* (meat-filled dumplings) and *chakhokhbili* (chicken stew flavoured with mint, basil and coriander); the welcoming waiters speak good English.

Art Diogenes Greek Restaurant *(Map 9; ☎ 224 92 26 45; Gorazdova 22; metro Karlovo náměstí; mains 195-295Kč; open 11.30am-11.30pm daily)*, west of Karlovo náměstí, is an authentic Greek restaurant with a Mediterranean blue-and-white courtyard at the back, and a menu rich in seafood, feta cheese, vine leaves and garlic.

Top-End Restaurants

El Gaucho *(☎ 221 62 94 10; Václavské náměstí 11; mains 390-590 Kč; open 11.30am-midnight daily)* is carnivore heaven – a rustic, rug-draped basement serving charcoal-grilled steaks, and also beef heart, liver, pickled tongue and all the other bits of a cow you just never knew what to do with. For the offally adventurous only.

Restaurant Pod Křídlem *(☎ 224 95 17 41; cnr Voršilska & Národní; mains 185-365Kč; open 10am-midnight Mon-Fri, 11.30am-midnight Sat-Sun)* is a stylish place with Art Deco-style decor and bottle-juggling cocktail waiters, excellent modern Czech food and wine, and live jazz at weekends.

HOLEŠOVICE

Restaurant Corso *(Map 4; ☎ 220 80 65 41; Dukelských hrdinů 7; tram No 5, 12 or 17; mains 95-270Kč; open 9am-11pm daily)* has 'interesting' decor – a cross between Aztec and Art Nouveau on acid. The food is good though – top-notch traditional Czech dishes, steaks, pasta and half a dozen decent veggie options.

Caffé Dante *(Map 4; ☎ 220 87 01 93; Dukelských hrdinů 16; tram No 5, 12 or 17; mains 60-100Kč; open 8am-11pm Mon-Fri, 11am-11pm Sat-Sun)*, along the road from Restaurant Corso, dishes up decent pizzas, pastas and salads under a huge, mystical painting of Heaven and Hell.

La Bodega Flamenca *(Map 3; ☎ 233 37 40 75; Šmerlova 5; tram No 1, 8, 25 or 26; mains 100-200Kč; open 5pm-1am Sun-Thur, 5pm-3am Fri-Sat)* is a candlelit, red-brick cellar bar serving a range of delicious Spanish tapas.

A Table with a View

Prague abounds in good viewpoints, and the best way to enjoy them is over wine and a good meal. Many well placed restaurants have let the view go to their heads, and overpriced, mediocre food is the norm, but there are some exceptions. It's best to make a reservation for these places.

U Zlaté studně *(Map 5; ☎ 257 53 33 22; U Zlaté studně 4, Malá Strana; metro Malostranská; mains 400-650Kč; open noon-4pm & 6pm-11pm daily)* enjoys one of the best situations in Prague, perched beneath the castle gardens and commanding a view across the rooftops of Malá Strana (Little Quarter) to the river. The food, which has a Mediterranean motif, and wine are superb too.

Restaurant Nebozízek *(Map 5; ☎ 257 31 53 29; Petřínské sady 411, Malá Strana; mains 200-450Kč; open 11am-11pm daily)*, on Petřín Hill, serves Czech standards, fish dishes and good salads in a terrace-conservatory with wide views across the Vltava River to Staré Město (Old Town). From Újezd, take the funicular railway to the halfway station.

Hanavský pavilón *(Map 7; ☎ 233 32 36 41; Letenské sady, Letná; mains 550-650Kč; open 11.30am-1am daily)* is an ornate, neobaroque pavilion dating from 1891, housing a smart restaurant with a Czech/International menu. From April to September you can dine on the terrace (open 11am to 10pm daily) and enjoy a postcard-perfect view of the Vltava bridges. Take tram No 18 from Malostranská metro station to Chotkovy sady.

La Perle de Prague *(Map 9; ☎ 221 98 41 60; Rašínovo nábřeží 80, Nové Město; metro Karlovo náměstí; mains 470-670Kč, 4-course menu 900Kč; open noon-2pm & 7pm-10.30pm Tues-Sat)*, on the 7th floor of the spectacular Tančiči dům (Dancing Building), offers stunning views across the rivers to Malá Strana and Prague Castle (Pražský hrad). The cuisine is French, with the accent on seafood and meat dishes – nothing for veggies here – and the atmosphere is crisply formal.

Zvonařká *(Map 10; ☎ 224 25 19 90; Šafaříkova 1; dishes 70-150Kč; open 11am-11pm daily)* sits at the far end of a quiet residential street, where Vinohrady spills over into the Nusle valley. The outdoor terrace commands a wide view across the valley towards Vyšehrad. The menu offers 'Plzeň-style' Czech dishes. The restaurant is 10 minutes' walk south of Náměstí Míru metro station.

Restaurace Televizní Věž *(Map 8; ☎ 267 00 57 78; Mahlerovy sady 1, Žižkov; metro Jiřího z Poděbrad; mains 150-350Kč; open 11am-11pm daily)* sits 63m above ground level, halfway up the TV Tower in Žižkov. It serves so-so Czech dishes at modest prices, but the main attraction is the view. You have to pay the normal admission fee (adult/child 120/60Kč) for the tower's sightseeing deck, but this gets you 10% off the menu prices.

Take the tram to Letenské náměstí and walk north for a few minutes.

For good, cheap Chinese eats close to Hotel Standart and Sir Toby's Hostel, try the **Čínské bistro** *(Map 4; Komunardů 13; mains 50-70Kč; 11am-11pm daily)*.

See also **Hanavský pavilón** in the boxed text 'A Table with a View' above.

ŽIŽKOV

U radnice *(Map 8; ☎ 222 78 27 13; Havlíčkovo náměstí 7; tram No 5, 9 or 26; mains 50-85Kč; open 11am-11pm Mon-Fri, 11am-10pm Sat-Sun)* is a cheerful neighbourhood *pivnice* (pub; with its own six- to 10-person sauna, no less!). Wash down generous helpings of Czech standards with Budvar beer. The sauna needs to be booked ahead.

Restaurace Panda Palace *(Map 6; ☎ 269 76 610; Seifertova 18; mains 120-180Kč; open 10.30am-11pm daily)*, at the corner with Přibyslavská, is a quiet place with attentive service and a vast menu of mainly northern Chinese food, including vegetarian dishes.

Mailsi *(Map 8; ☎ 290 05 97 06; Lipanská 1; tram No 5, 9 or 26; mains 150-300Kč; open noon-11pm daily)* is Prague's first Pakistani restaurant. The outside is inconspicuous, and it's only the *qawwali* music that gives it away. Service is courteous, the food good and prices modest for a speciality restaurant – though helpings are small.

Hanil *(Map 6; ☎ 222 71 58 67; Slavíkova 24; metro Jiří z Poděbrad; mains 280-450Kč; open 11am-2.30pm & 5pm-11pm Mon-Sat, 5.30pm-11pm Sun)* is a relaxed and intimate place serving Japanese and Korean cuisine without the fuss and formality of more expensive Japanese places. It's four blocks north of the metro station.

VINOHRADY

Cafés

Caffé Kaaba *(Map 6; ☎ 222 25 40 21; Mánesova 20; tram No 11; snacks 40-100Kč; open 8am-10pm Mon-Sat)* is a colourful little café-bar with furniture and decor straight out of the 1959 Ideal Homes Exhibition – you half expect to see a Kenwood Chef sitting on the counter. It serves good coffee, and has an extensive list of Czech and imported wines.

Kavárna Medúza *(Map 10; ☎ 222 51 51 07; Belgická 17; snacks 50-120Kč; open 11am-1am Mon-Fri, noon-1am Sat-Sun)*, a quiet spot in a quiet street off náměstí Míru, offers snacks, juices and a long list of coffees, in a room covered in old photos and an atmospheric mix-and-match of furniture and decor.

Restaurants

Modrá řeka *(Map 6; ☎ 222 25 16 01; Mánesova 13; tram No 11; mains 100-200Kč; open 3pm-11pm Mon-Fri, 5pm-11pm Sat-Sun)* is a homely Yugoslav restaurant run by a couple who fled to Prague from Serbia in 1992. The deliciously spicy menu includes Yugoslav classics such as *čevapčiči* (minced meat kebabs) with *adžvar* (roast red pepper puree) and *gibanica* (a rich cake filled with fruit, nuts and poppy seeds).

Tai Wan *(Map 10; ☎ 224 24 75 49; Vinohradská 48; tram No 11; mains 100-150Kč, lunch menus 49-79Kč; open 11am-11pm daily)* is a great little Chinese restaurant, with authentic Taiwanese cuisine and good-value set menus from 11am to 3pm on weekdays.

Restaurace Pravěk *(Map 10; ☎ 224 25 22 87; Budečská 6; mains 100-200Kč; open 11am-11pm daily)*, southeast of náměstí Míru, is a popular Czech place offering duck, venison and wild boar, plus a few veggie dishes.

See also **FX Café** in the Vegetarian section later in this chaper, and **Zvonařka** in the boxed text 'A Table with a View' earlier.

SMÍCHOV

Il Giardino *(Map 9; ☎ 257 15 42 62; Mozartová 1; mains 300-500Kč; open 5.30pm-11pm daily)* is a smart, modern Mediterranean restaurant – think tortellini and seared tuna – in the smart, modern Mövenpick Hotel. Perched on top of a rise, it commands a great view across Smíchov towards Vyšehrad.

Smíchov has a couple of decent Czech restaurants, including the **Vinárna U Mikuláše Dačického** *(☎ 257 32 23 34; Viktora Huga 2; mains 95-230Kč; open 4pm-1am Mon-Fri, 6pm-1am Sat-Sun)*, and the noisy, smoky down-to-earth **Hospoda U Starého lva** *(☎ 257 32 99 46; Lidická 13; mains 60-75Kč; open 11am-11pm daily)*.

DEJVICE

Pizzeria Grosseto *(Map 3; ☎ 233 34 26 94; Jugoslávských partyzánů 8; metro Dejvická; mains 70-125Kč; open 11.30am-11pm daily)* is a lively and friendly place that pulls in crowds of students from the nearby university campus with its genuine, wood-fired pizza oven and Moravian Radegast beer.

Haveli *(Map 3; ☎ 233 34 48 00; Dejvická 6; metro Hradčanská; mains 170-230Kč, lunch buffet 149Kč; open 11am-11pm daily)* is a new and authentic Indian restaurant in a cosy red-brick and whitewash cellar. It offers a good-value lunch buffet on weekdays.

Restaurant U cedru *(Map 3; ☎ 233 34 29 74; Národní obrany 27; metro Dejvická; mains 200-300Kč; open 11am-11pm daily)* is a welcoming Lebanese restaurant offering tasty *mezzes* such as *baba ganoush* (aubergine puree), taboulleh salad and stuffed vine leaves; a spread of 10 *mezzes* costs 775Kč.

Two good Czech restaurants in this area are **Restaurace Sokolovna** *(Map 3; ☎ 224 31 78 34; Dejvická 2; mains 50-70Kč; open 10.30am-11.30pm Mon-Fri, 11.30am-11.30pm Sat-Sun)*, near Hradčanská metro, and **Pivnice U Švejka** *(Map 3; ☎ 233 33 07 62; Nikoly Tesly 1; mains 60-800Kč; open 11am-11pm daily)*, one tram stop north from Dejvická metro.

VEGETARIAN

An increasing number of mainstream Prague restaurants cater to vegetarians, many offering up to half a dozen veggie dishes on their otherwise meat-ridden menus. The following places, however, are wholly vegetarian.

Cafe Himalaya *(Map 5; ☎ 233 35 35 94; Chaloupeckého 7; mains 30-60Kč; open 3pm-5am Mon-Thur, 3pm-3am Fri-Sun)*, next to block 7 in the Strahov student dormitory complex, serves very cheap Indian and Nepalese vegetarian food.

Lotos *(Map 7; ☎ 222 32 23 90; Platnéřská 13; mains 70-150Kč; open noon-10pm daily)*, just north of the Klementinum, does gourmet veggie, vegan and macrobiotic food with many dishes modelled on Bohemian cuisine. It's wholly nonsmoking.

Country Life *(Map 7; ☎ 224 21 33 66; Melantrichova 15; open 9am-8.30pm Mon-Fri • Map 6; Jungmannova 1; open 9.30am-6.30pm Mon-Thur, 10am-6pm Fri)*, with mains for 75Kč to 150Kč, is Prague's best health-food shop and vegetarian salad-and-sandwich bar (there is pizza and goulash too). The Melantrichova branch has sit-down service at the back, Jungmannova is cafeteria-style. Both get crowded at lunchtime, so go early or get a takeaway.

U Góvindy *(Map 7; ☎ 224 81 66 31; Soukenická 27; open 11am-5.30pm Mon-Sat)* takes a 'donation' of around 50Kč, which gets you a generous, imaginatively seasoned set meal of vegetable soup, salad, rice, cake and herbal tea. It's run by Hare Krishnas, but nobody's preaching.

FX Café *(Map 10; ☎ 224 25 47 76; Bělehradská 120; metro IP Pavlova; mains 100-200Kč; open 11.30am-2am daily)* offers some of the best food in Prague in its price range – and it's all veggie. This hippy-chic café at the entrance to the Radost FX nightclub (see the Entertainment chapter) – all draped chiffon, tasselled lampshades and distressed walls, like a faded bordello – dishes up imaginative dishes ranging from Indian-spiced aubergine with mint yogurt to Thai veggies in coconut sauce.

SELF-CATERING

There are *potraviny* (food shops) and supermarkets everywhere, the best stocked and priciest being in flash department stores near the centre.

Note that some perishable supermarket food items bear a date of manufacture *(datum výroby)* plus a 'consume-within...' *(spotřebujte do...)* period, whereas others (such as long-life milk) have a stated minimum shelf-life *(minimální trvanlivost)* date, after which the freshness of the product is not guaranteed.

The city has several open-air produce markets; see Open-Air Markets in the Shopping chapter for a list of some near the centre.

Malá Strana

J+J Mašek & Zemanová *(Map 5; Karmelitská 30; open 8am-6pm Mon-Fri, 8am-noon Sat)* is a fine Czech deli near Malostranské náměstí; this is the place to buy the best *šunka od kosti* (ham off the bone), smoked cheese and sausage.

Around the block at the corner of Mostecká and Lázeňská is **Vacek Bio-Market** *(Map 5; Mostecká 3; open 7am-10pm Mon-Sat, 10am-10pm Sun)*, a well stocked mini supermarket open until late in the evening.

Staré Město

Fresh produce is sold at the daily **market** *(Map 7; open 8am-6pm daily)* on Havelská, south of Old Town Square.

Bakeshop Praha *(Map 7; Kozí 1; open 7am-7pm daily)* is a fantastic bakery that sells some of the best bread in the city, along with pastries, cakes and takeaway sandwiches, salads and quiche.

Two other bakeries near Old Town Square are **Michelské pekařství** *(Map 7; Dlouhá 1; open 6.30am-6pm Mon-Fri, 11am-6pm Sun)* and **Chléb pečivo** *(Map 7; Kaprova 13; open 6.30am-6pm Mon-Fri, noon-6pm Sat)*.

For supermarket supplies, try **Julius Meinl** *(Map 6; entrances at Rytířská 10 & 28.října 5; open 7am-8pm Mon-Fri, 7am-4pm Sat, 10am-6pm Sun)* or **Kotva** *(Map 7; náměstí Republiky; open 9am-8pm Mon-Fri, 9am-6pm Sat, 10am-6pm Sun)*. For picnic supplies there's a good **supermarket-deli** on Masná near Old Town Square.

Nové Město

The concentration of supermarkets in Nové Město (Map 6) – **Julius Meinl** *(Václavské náměstí 21; open 9am-8pm Mon-Fri, 9am-7pm Sat, 10am-6pm Sun)* in the basement of the Krone department store, **Tesco** *(Národní 26; open 8am-9pm Mon-Fri, 9am-8pm Sat, 10am-7pm Sun)* and **Bílá Labuť** *(Na poříčí 23; open 9am-8pm Mon-Fri, 9am-6pm Sat, 10am-6pm Sun)* – should satisfy any shopping list. Krone's supermarket tends to be the most expensive, Bílá Labuť's the cheapest.

Fruits de France *(Map 6; Jindřišská 9; 9.30am-6.30pm Mon-Fri, 9.30am-1pm Sat)* sells French wine, cheese, pastries and more, but not cheaply. Next door is the similar **Paris-Praha** *(Map 6; Jindřišská 7; open 7am-6.30pm Mon-Fri)*.

Cellarius *(Map 6; Hvězda pasáž, Václavské náměstí 36; open 9.30am-9pm Mon-Sat, 3pm-9pm Sun • Map 10; Budečská 29, Vinohrady; open 9am-9pm Mon-Sat, 3pm-8pm Sun)*, at the intersection of the Lucerna and Hvězda passages, is the place to try for imported wines. The Vinohrady branch is in the Pavilón shopping centre.

Entertainment

Across the spectrum, from ballet to blues, jazz to rock, theatre to tennis, there's a bewildering range of entertainment on offer in this eclectic city. Prague is now as much a European centre for jazz, rock and hip-hop as it is for classical music. The big draw, however, is still the Prague Spring (Pražské jaro) festival of classical music and opera.

For reviews, day-by-day listings, and an up-to-the-minute directory of venues, consult the 'Night & Day' section of the weekly *Prague Post*, or the fortnightly free newspaper *The Prague Pill*. Monthly listings booklets include *Culture in Prague* and the Czech-language *Přehled*, available from PIS offices (see Tourist Offices in the Facts for the Visitor chapter). The fortnightly pamphlet *Do města – Downtown*, free at bars and restaurants, lists clubs, galleries, cinemas and theatre events. For online listings and reviews, check out **W** www.prague.tv.

If you can find it, the alternative, Czech-language monthly magazine *14* lists the entertainment that other publications miss. It's also worth keeping an eye on the posters and bulletin boards around town.

Buying Tickets

For classical music, opera, ballet, theatre and some rock concerts – even the most thoroughly 'sold-out' events – you can often find a ticket or two on sale at the box office a half-hour or so before show time.

If you want to be sure of a seat, Prague is awash with ticket agencies. Their advantage is convenience: most are computerised, quick, and accept credit cards. Their drawback is a probable 10% to 15% mark-up. Touts will sell tickets at the door, but avoid them unless all other avenues have been exhausted.

At the box office, non-Czechs normally pay the same price as Czechs. Many venues have discounts for students, and sometimes for the disabled. Most performances have a certain number of tickets set aside for foreigners – for a premium price, of course.

'Wholesalers' with the largest agency networks are Bohemia Ticket International (BTI), FOK and Ticketpro; the others probably get their tickets from them.

Ticketpro *(Map 7; ☎ 296 32 99 99, fax 296 32 88 88; **W** www.ticketpro.cz; Salvátorská 10; open 9am-12.30pm & 1pm-5.15pm Mon-Fri)* is the biggest agency, with branches in PIS offices (see Tourist Offices in the Facts for the Visitor chapter) and many other places around Prague, including **Ticketcentrum** *(Map 7; Rytířská 31; open 8.30am-8.30pm daily)*.

Bohemia Ticket International *(BTI; Map 7; ☎ 224 22 78 32; **W** www.ticketsbti.cz; Malé náměstí 13; open 9am-5pm Mon-Fri, 9am-2pm Sat • Map 7; ☎/fax 224 21 50 31; Na příkopě 16; open 10am-7pm Mon-Fri, 10am-5pm Sat, 10am-3pm Sun)* and **Ticketstream** *(Map 10; ☎ 224 26 30 49; Koubkova 8, Vinohrady; open 9am-6pm Mon-Sat)* are the other big agencies in town.

FOK Box Office *(Map 7; ☎ 222 00 23 36, fax 222 32 25 01; U Obecního domu 2; open 10am-6pm Mon-Fri)* mainly sells tickets for Prague Symphony Orchestra concerts.

For rock and jazz clubs you can turn up at the door, but advance bookings are recommended for big names. A good agency for rock-concert tickets is **Ticketpro Melantrich** *(Map 6; ☎ 224 22 84 55; Pasáž Rokoko, Václavské náměstí 36; open 9.30am-1pm & 2pm-6pm Mon-Fri)* in Nové Město.

Pub Etiquette

Always ask if a chair is free before sitting down: *Je tu volno?* (Is it free?). Service is usually quick – in better places you may find a beer in front of you almost before your bum touches the seat – but if it's slow, chasing the waiter is a sure way to be ignored. Your bill is run up on a slip of paper left at your table, and at the end it's usually rounded up to the nearest koruna. Tipping is similar to restaurants, that is 5% to 10% of the total.

PUBS & BARS

Most pubs serve beer snacks; some of the most popular are *utopenci* (sliced sausage pickled in vinegar with onion), *topinky* (fried toast) and, of course, the famous *Pražská šunka* (Prague ham) with gherkin. Many of the following places also serve inexpensive Czech food or pricier non-Czech food.

Bars come and bars go with alarming speed in Prague, and trendspotters are forever flocking to the latest 'in' place only to desert it as soon as it becomes mainstream. There's only space here to list the best of the long-term survivors, along with a few of the newer places; pick up a listings magazine to check what the latest 'in' places are (see the start of this chapter for details).

Hradčany & Malá Strana (Map 5)

Pivnice U černého vola *(☎ 220 51 34 81; Loretánské náměstí 1; open 10am-10pm daily)* is an authentic and surprisingly cheap Czech beer hall barely a bottle's throw from the tourist-thronged Loreta.

Hostinec U kocoura *(☎ 257 53 01 07; Nerudova 2; open 11am-11pm daily)* is an old, but now very touristy, pub, still enjoying its reputation as a former favourite of President Havel. See also the Places to Eat chapter.

U krále Brabantského *(☎ 257 31 09 29; Thunovská 15; open noon-11pm daily)*, around the corner from Hostinec U kocoura, is a similarly Gothic place but with cheaper beer (26Kč) and much less crowded.

Jo's Bar (see the Places to Eat chapter), a popular backpackers' hang-out, and **Malostranská Beseda** (see Rock & Other Music later in this chapter) are good places for a drink on Malostranské náměsti.

U Malého Glena *(Little Glen's; ☎ 290 00 39 67; Karmelitská 23; open 10am-2am daily)* is a bar (with Guinness on tap), café, restaurant and jazz club (see also Jazz later in this chapter). You can chill out over a late breakfast of bagels and coffee, or relax with a beer in the afternoon, but in the evenings the place really starts to rock.

Zanzi bar *(cnr Lázeňská & Saská; open 5pm-3am daily)* is a little haven of cool jazz and superb cocktails tucked away in the medieval lanes beside Charles Bridge (Karlův most). The drinks list is the size of a Jeffrey Archer novel, but far more interesting.

U Zlatého hada *(☎ 257 53 14 72; Maltézské náměstí 3; open 3pm-9pm Mon-Fri, 2pm-9pm Sat-Sun)* is a cosy *vinný sklep* (wine cellar) where you can work your way through a list of top Bohemian and Moravian wines.

Klub Újezd *(☎ 257 31 65 37; Újezd 18; open 11am-4am daily)*, a former live-rock venue tamed by noise complaints, remains an agreeable bar, with a wide range of music (harder sounds downstairs, mellower upstairs), a retro underground setting and a grungy crowd. No food though.

Staré Město

All places in this section are on Map 7, unless otherwise noted, and are listed from north to south.

Žíznivý pes *(The Thirsty Dog; ☎ 224 81 98 30; Elišky Krásnohorské 5; open 11am-2am daily)* is a bustling bar with cheapish beer (20Kč for 0.4L), good cheap pub food, and televised sports events.

Blatouch *(☎ 222 32 86 43; Vězeňská 4; open 11am-midnight Mon-Thur, 11am-2am Fri, 1pm-2am Sat, 1pm-midnight Sun)* is a pleasantly relaxed literary hang-out, with a long, narrow bar lined with antique bookcases and Edward Hopper prints, and a tiny garden courtyard at the back.

Kozička *(The Little Goat; ☎ 224 81 83 08; Kozí 1; open noon-4am Mon-Fri, 6pm-4am Sat-Sun)* is a permanently buzzing basement bar with taped mainstream music, a young clientele and standing-room only after midnight.

Chateau *(☎ 222 32 62 42; cnr Malá Štupartská & Jakubská; open noon-5am daily)* is a busy bar that draws a mixed crowd of expat regulars, Czechs and tourists; by mid-evening it's standing-room only.

Bambus *(☎ 224 82 81 10; Benediktská 12; open 9am-1am Mon-Fri, 11am-2am Sat, 11am-11pm Sun)* is a laid-back café-bar whose bamboo chairs are filled by a mixed crowd of young locals and backpackers who have found their way from the Travellers' Hostel Dlouhá (see the Places to Stay chapter) nearby.

The following places are all south of Old Town Square (Staroměstské náměstí):

U zlatého tygra *(The Golden Tiger; ☎ 222 22 11 11; Husova 17; open 3pm-11pm daily)* is one of the few old-town drinking holes that has hung on to its soul – and its low prices. It was novelist Bohumil Hrabal's favourite hostelry – there are photos of him on the walls – and the place that President Havel took Bill Clinton to show him a real Czech pub.

James Joyce *(☎ 224 24 87 93; Liliová 10; open 11am-12.30am daily)* is a small but often raucous Irish pub in the dům U krále Jiřího (see the Places to Stay chapter), full of good-timers knocking back expensive Guinness (90Kč for 0.4L). It serves a tasty and filling Irish stew or beef-and-Guinness hotpot.

O'Che's Cuban-Irish Bar *(☎ 222 22 11 78; Liliová 14; open 10am-1am daily)* – yes, you read that correctly – is an expat bar that juxtaposes images of Che Guevara with Guinness taps, dartboards and sports-channel TV.

Keltic Bar *(Map 6; ☎ 602 87 45 82; Betlémské náměstí 8; open 11am-1am daily)*, as the name suggests, is a popular bar which takes Bohemia's Celtic history as its theme, and has live music and dancing on Thursday to Saturday nights.

Nové Město (Map 6)

U Fleků *(☎ 224 91 51 18; Křemencová 11; open 9am-11pm daily)*, a festive warren of drinking and dining rooms, is a Prague institution, increasingly clogged with tour groups high on oompah music and the tavern's home-brewed, 13° black beer (49Kč for 0.4L). Purists grumble but go along anyway because everybody has a good time, though tourist prices have nudged out many locals. You might still find an empty seat at 7pm on a weekday.

Novoměstský pivovar *(☎ 224 23 35 33; Vodičkova 20; 8am-11.30pm Mon-Fri, 11.30am-11.30pm Sat, noon-10pm Sun)*, like U Fleků, brews its own beer on the premises and suffers from coach-party invasions. But it's considerably cheaper (30Kč for 0.5L), and the food is not only edible but actually rather good, including a delicious *svíčková* (beef and dumplings with cream sauce).

Jáma *(The Hollow; ☎ 224 22 23 83; V jámě 7; open 11am-1am daily)*, south off Vodičkova, is a popular expat bar, with restaurant and beer garden, whose clientele includes tourists and young Praguers; beer is medium priced at 28Kč for 0.5L of Gambrinus.

Velryba *(The Whale; ☎ 224 91 24 84; Opatovická 24; open 11am-midnight Sat-Thur, 11am-2am Fri)* is an arty café-bar – quiet enough to have a real conversation – with vegie-friendly snacks, a smoky back room and a basement art gallery.

Žižkov (Maps 6 & 8)

U Vystřeleného oka *(The Shot-Out Eye; Map 6; ☎ 226 27 87 14; U Božích bojovníků 3; bus No 133 or 207; open 4.30pm-1am Mon-Sat)* – the name pays homage to the one-eyed Hussite hero atop the hill behind it – is a bohemian (with a small 'b') hostelry with a beer garden whose cheap food and beer pulls in a typically heterogeneous Žižkov crowd, ranging from art students to tattooed bikers.

Hapu *(Map 8; ☎ 222 72 01 58; Orlická; metro Jiřího z Poděbrad; open 6pm-2am daily)* is almost in Vinohrady – geographically and socially on the opposite side of Žižkov from U Vystřeleného oka (see above). It's a tiny, smoky, and immensely cool cocktail bar – and all the fruit juice in those mixed drinks is freshly squeezed.

DISCOS & CLUBS

With few exceptions, Prague's dance clubs cater to teenagers weaned on MTV Europe and techno/tribal beats. Most venues open late (after 9pm) and keep the music going until 4am or 5am. Clubs have notoriously short life spans; check the *Prague Post* and *Prague Pill* for current listings.

Klub 007 Strahov *(Map 5; ☎ 257 21 14 39; W www.klub007strahov.cz; Block 7, Chaloupeckého, Strahov; open 7.30pm-1am Tues-Sat)* is one of several grungy student clubs in the basements of the big dormitory blocks in Strahov; 007 offers a menu of hip-hop, ragga, punk, ska and reggae served very, very loud. Take bus No 143, 149 or 217 from Dejvická metro station.

Garáž *(Map 5; ☎ 257 53 33 42; Malostranské náměstí 7; metro Malostranská; open*

CHRIS MELLOR

The Staroměstská Radnice's astronomical clock

RICHARD NEBESKÝ

The vibrant Jubilejní synagóga dates from 1906.

JONATHAN SMITH

Images of Kafka crop up all over Prague.

RICK GERHARTER

Prague's Starý židovský hřbitov (Old Jewish Cemetery) is the oldest in Europe.

RICHARD NEBESKÝ

The Televizní vysílač (TV Tower) in Žižkov

RICHARD NEBESKÝ

The baroque Dvořák museum in Nové Město

JONATHAN SMITH

The latest incarnation of the John Lennon Wall

MARTIN MOOS

An evening stroll over the Charles Bridge

6pm-5am daily) is a dark and decadent dance venue in the basement of Jo's Bar (see Pubs & Bars earlier in this chapter), popular with backpackers who flock here for the four-hour happy hour (6pm to 10pm). There's no cover charge.

Karlovy Lázně *(Map 7; ☎ 222 22 05 02; Novotného lávka 1, Staré Město; metro Staroměstská; admission 50-100Kč; open 9pm-5am daily)*, down by the river near Charles Bridge, is Central Europe's biggest music club. A single cover charge admits you to four venues – MCM Café (various live bands); Discotheque (classic disco music); Kaleidoskop ('60s, '70s and '80s revival); and Paradogs (house, techno, drum 'n' bass etc).

Mecca *(Map 4; ☎ 283 87 05 22; W www.mecca.cz; U Průhonu 3, Holešovice; metro Nádraží Holešovice; admission 150-250Kč; open 10pm-6am Fri-Sat)* is a deeply hip dance venue with DJs spinning house, drum 'n' bass and techno.

Pivo

Pivo is Czech for beer, and the Czech Lands, including Prague, have been famous for centuries as one of the finest producers of the amber liquid. The first-ever historical documentation of beer-making and hop-growing goes back to the Opatovice monastery's founding charter in 1088. Apparently the taste of beer was quite different in those days and by today's standards it would be considered undrinkable. It was not until 1842 that a smart group of Plzeň brewers pooled their experience, installed 'modern' technology and founded a single municipal brewery, with spectacular results. Their golden lager beer, labelled Plzeňský Prazdroj (*prazdroj* is old Czech for 'the original source') – Pilsner Urquell in German – is now one of the world's best, and most imitated, beers.

The Czech Republic has the largest per capita beer consumption (158L per head of population) of any country in the world, easily beating both Germany and Australia. This means, of course, that the 'average' adult drinks about 330L per year.

The world famous Pilsner Urquell and Budvar (Budweiser) beers are brewed in the smaller, provincial towns of the Czech Republic, but Prague has its own brews. The largest concern is Prague Breweries, which operates the Staropramen and Braník breweries in Prague, and the Ostravar brewery in Ostrava (in Northern Moravia). Its brands include the traditional Staropramen lager, and the newer Kelt stout and Velvet bitter, and account for around 13% of the domestic beer market. Prague Breweries is owned by the Belgian company Interbrew, the second-largest brewery in the world after Anheuser Busch.

There are several microbreweries in Prague – beer halls that brew their own beer on the premises. The most famous, and probably the oldest, is **U Fleků** (see Pubs & Bars earlier in this chapter), a Prague institution. Though very touristy, its 13° black beer is still excellent. The newer **Novoměstský pivovar** (see Pubs & Bars earlier) is another place that brews its own beer but is cheaper all round. Newly opened in 1998, the **Pivovarský pivovar** *(Map 9; ☎ 296 21 66 66; Lípová 15, Nové Město)* offers some very unusual beers such as coffee beer, beer champagne, wheat beer and other interesting flavours.

Czech beers are predominantly bottom-fermented lagers. As in neighbouring Germany, there are no chemicals in the beer. The whole fermentation process uses only natural ingredients – water, hops and barley.

The strong beer culture here is centuries old and is one of the few traditions to survive the communist era relatively intact. Today the art of beer drinking is celebrated at numerous Czech festivals. Beer-inspired competitions include speed drinking (the record for 1L of beer is 3.44 seconds) and the largest beer gut, to name but a few.

Czechs have many sayings that celebrate beer drinking, but the claims are often dubious. One of the favourites is *'Pivo dělá pěkná těla'* (Beer makes beautiful bodies). And home-brew fans might adopt *'Kde se pivo vaí tam se dobe daí'* (Life flourishes where beer is brewed).

Sedm Vlků *(Seven Wolves; Map 6; ☎ 222 71 17 25; Vlkova 7, Žižkov; open 6pm-3am Mon-Sat)* is a cool, two-level, art-studenty kind of café-bar and club. Upstairs, the music's low enough to have a conversation without shouting; downstairs, the DJs pump out drum 'n' bass and ragga.

Radost FX *(Map 10; ☎ 224 25 47 76; W www.radostfx.cz; Bělehradská 120, Vinohrady; metro IP Pavlova; admission 100-250Kč; open 10pm-5am)* has stainless-steel walls, leopard-skin sofas and lava lamps, and is the best place to catch top DJs spinning hip-hop, house and funk. See also **FX Café** in the Places to Eat chapter.

Futurum *(Map 9; ☎ 257 32 85 71; W www.musicbar.cz; Zborovská 7, Smíchov; metro Anděl; cover 80-130Kč; open 9pm-3am daily)* is a former heavy-metal venue where DJs now play techno, garage and tribal. There are regular '80s and '90s parties, and live bands a couple of times a week.

See also **Roxy** and **Palác Akropolis** under Alternative Venues later in this chapter.

GAY & LESBIAN VENUES

The gay scene in Prague changes fast – check out the listings in *Amigo* magazine (see Gay & Lesbian Travellers in the Facts for the Visitor chapter). There's no 'gay district' in Prague – places are spread across the inner city.

Friends *(Map 7; ☎ 221 63 54 08; Náprstkova 1, Staré Město; metro Národní třídá; open 4pm-3am daily)* is a welcoming music and video bar with excellent coffee and wine; there are DJs from 10pm, and Thursday night is '60s music.

Sauna Babylonia *(Map 6; ☎ 224 23 23 04; Martinská 6, Staré Město; admission 200Kč, massage 500Kč; open 2pm-3am daily)* offers a bar, sauna, fitness room, Jacuzzi and whirlpool.

A-Club *(Map 8; ☎ 222 78 16 23; Miličova 25, Žižkov; tram No 5, 9 or 26; cover Fri 25Kč, Sat 50Kč; open 7pm-6am daily)* is Prague's only lesbian club – Friday nights are women-only.

Piano Bar *(Map 8; ☎ 222 72 74 96; Milešovská 10, Žižkov; metro Jiřího z Poděbrad; open 5pm-midnight or later daily)* is another highly recommended spot, a homely little cellar bar cluttered with junk and bric-a-brac.

Club Stella *(Map 10; ☎ 224 25 78 69; Lužická 10, Vinohrady; tram No 4, 22 or 23; open 8pm-5am daily)* is an intimate, candlelit café-bar that seems to be the first place everyone recommends when you ask about gay bars in Prague. Ring the doorbell to get in.

Gejzee..r *(Map 6; ☎ 222 51 60 36; Vinohradská 40, Vinohrady; metro Náměstí Míru; cover 50-70Kč, Thur & before 10.30pm Fri & Sat free; open 8pm-4am Thur, 9pm-5am Fri, 9pm-6am Sat)* is Prague's biggest G&L club, with two bars, a huge dance floor and a video-projection system.

Restaurant Arco *(Map 10; ☎ 271 74 29 08; Voroněžská 24, Vinohrady; tram No 4, 22 or 23; open 8am-1am Mon-Fri, 9am-1am Sat-Sun)* is a friendly and popular restaurant and café-bar, with Internet access and pension accommodation.

Angel Club *(Map 9; ☎ 257 31 61 27; Kmochova 8, Smíchov; bus No 176; open 7pm-5am daily)* is a gay disco club, with a Green Room full of chill-out sofas, a black-lit Dark Room out back, and a romantic, candlelit Red Room.

ROCK & OTHER MUSIC

Prague has a high-energy live-music scene, with rock, metal, punk, rap and newer sounds at a score of legitimate DJ and live-music venues.

During the last five years or so, noise regulations and increasing rents have forced the closure of several big venues in historical city-owned properties, but new ones have since opened in the suburbs. For current listings and reviews, see the entertainment periodicals noted at the start of this chapter – and watch the posters.

Except as noted, clubs have a bar, usually a dance floor, and cover charges from around 80Kč.

Klub 007 Strahov (see Discos & Clubs earlier) offers cheap beer and raw music from up-and-coming heavy rock, punk or alternative bands (or DJs), and attracts a mainly student crowd, from 7.30pm to 1am daily except Sunday (music from 8pm).

Malostranská Beseda *(Map 5; ☎ 257 53 20 92; Malostranské náměstí 21, Malá Strana; bar open 5pm-1am daily, music from 8pm)* is a large café-bar that hosts anything from hard rock to bluegrass via jazz and folk, for a young and mostly Czech crowd.

Batalion *(Map 6; ☎ 220 10 81 48; 28.října 3, Staré Město; bar open 24 hrs, music from 9pm)* is a grungy bar that offers anything from rock 'n' roll to punk performed by up-and-coming Czech bands (DJs on most Saturdays), and attracts a young, mainly local crowd.

Lucerna Music Bar *(Map 6; ☎ 224 21 71 08; Vodičkova 36, Nové Město; open 8pm-3am daily)* is a quality venue, now looking a little dog-eared, with mainly Czech artists playing jazz, blues, pop, rock and more. It's becoming increasingly touristy but still has a local feel.

Rock Café *(Map 6; ☎ 224 91 44 16; Národní 20, Nové Město; open 10am-3am Mon-Fri, 7pm-3am Sat-Sun, music from 8pm)* is a stripped-down venue for DJs and live rock, with a café downstairs, popular with locals but increasingly touristy.

Futurum (see Discos & Clubs earlier in this chapter) has live rock or alternative bands playing several nights a week from 9pm to 3am.

Klub Delta *(Map 2; ☎ 233 31 13 98; Vlastina 887, Na Dědině; open from 7pm, music from 8pm)* is a theatre venue hosting mainly alternative and underground Czech bands. It's almost at the airport – take bus No 218 from Dejvická metro station to the Sídliště Na Dědině stop.

JAZZ & BLUES

The following clubs have cover charges of between 50Kč and 100Kč except as noted, and some double as restaurants; most of these jazz clubs usually have live bands playing blues rather than jazz.

Malostranská Beseda (see Rock earlier in this chapter) has jazz on some nights at 8.30pm.

U Malého Glena *(Map 5; ☎ 290 00 39 67; Karmelitská 23, Malá Strana; open 10am-2am daily, music from 9pm)* is a good bar where hard-swinging local jazz or blues bands play in the stone cellar most nights. It's a small venue so get there early. See also Pubs & Bars earlier in this chapter.

Red, Hot & Blues *(Map 7; ☎ 222 31 46 39; Jakubská 12, Staré Město; open 9am-11pm daily, music 7pm-10pm)* is a New Orleans-style restaurant (see the Places to Eat chapter) with live blues or jazz most nights (check the board outside).

U Staré paní Jazz Club *(Map 7; ☎ 222 24 80 90; Michalská 9, Staré Město; open 7pm-1am daily, music from 9pm Tues-Sat)* is in the basement of the hotel with the same name (see the Places to Stay chapter) – ISIC and IYTC cardholders get 50% off the cover charge.

Metropolitan Jazz Club *(Map 6; ☎ 224 94 77 77; Jungmannova 14, Nové Město; open 6pm-1am Mon-Fri, 7pm-1am Sat, music from 9pm)* is a smallish basement venue with a restaurant.

Reduta Jazz Club *(Map 6; ☎ 224 91 22 46; Národní 20, Nové Město; open 9pm-3am daily)* is Prague's oldest jazz club, founded in the communist era, with live jazz daily. Book a few hours ahead at the ticket office, open from 3pm Monday to Friday and from 7pm Saturday and Sunday.

AghaRTA Jazz Centrum *(Map 6; ☎ 222 21 12 75; Krakovská 5, Nové Město; music from 9pm)* is a venerable basement venue with '70s decor, a café (open 7pm to midnight daily) and a music shop (open 5pm to midnight weekdays and 7pm to midnight Saturday and Sunday).

ALTERNATIVE VENUES

These are combined theatres and clubs with an underground look and feel. Mainly experimental venues, they combine bands, DJs, drama, dance, art and films; check their websites to see what's on.

Roxy *(Map 7; ☎ 224 82 62 96; W www.roxy.cz; Dlouhá 33, Staré Město; open 1pm-1am daily)* is a decrepit old theatre complex with surprising longevity as an 'experimental space', staging avant-garde drama and dance, experimental cinema, live music and some of Prague's most popular club nights.

Palác Akropolis *(Map 6; ☎ 222 71 22 87; W www.palacakropolis.cz; Kubelíkova 27,*

Žižkov) is another sticky-floored shrine to alternative music and drama. At the time of writing there were rumours that it might close or be redeveloped, much to the horror of its loyal fans.

FOLK & TRADITIONAL MUSIC

Dlabačov Hall *(Map 2; ☎ 233 37 34 75; Bělohorská 24, Střešovice; tram No 8 or 22; admission 450Kč; shows 8.30pm Mon-Sat Apr-Nov)*, in the Hotel Pyramida, is the home venue of the Český soubor písní a tanců (Czech Song & Dance Ensemble), the only professional troupe of its kind in the Czech Republic. Performances, a stylised amalgam of traditions from around Bohemia, are undeniable crowd-pleasers.

CLASSICAL MUSIC, OPERA & BALLET

Don't believe anyone who says it's impossible to get concert tickets. There are half a dozen concerts of one kind or another almost every day during the summer, making a fine soundtrack to the city's visual delights. Many of these are chamber concerts by aspiring musicians in the city's churches – gorgeous but chilly (take an extra layer, even on a summer day) and not always with the finest of acoustics. An increasing number of church concerts have been second-rate, despite the premium prices foreigners pay.

Concert Venues

The city's top venues for classical concerts are:

Dvořák Hall *(Map 7; ☎ 227 05 93 52; W www.rudolfinum.cz; náměstí Jana Palacha 1, Staré Město; tickets 150-900Kč; box office open 10am-12.30pm & 1.30pm-6pm Mon-Fri)*, in the neo-Renaissance Rudolfinum, is home to the Český národní symfonický orchestr (Czech National Symphony Orchestra); it has wheelchair access.

Smetana Hall *(Map 7; ☎ 22 00 21 01; náměstí Republiky 5, Staré Město; tickets 150-900Kč; box office open 10am-6pm daily)*, in the Obecní dům (Municipal House), houses the Symfonický orchestr hlavního města Prahy (Prague Symphony Orchestra).

The Original Music Theatre of Prague can be seen performing Dvořák's vocal and instrumental works in period costume in the salon of the **Vila Amerika** *(Dvořák Museum; Map 9; ☎ 224 91 80 13; Ke Karlovu 20, Nové Město; tickets 495Kč; concerts 8pm Tues & Fri Apr-Oct)*; tickets are available through BTI (see Buying Tickets earlier in this chapter).

There are also regular concerts held in the salon and garden of the **Vila Bertramka** *(Map 9; ☎ 257 31 74 65; Mozartova 169, Smíchov; tickets 230-450Kč; salon 5pm, garden 7pm Tues-Sat Apr-Oct & New Year)*, home of the Mozart Museum (see Smíchov in the Things to See & Do chapter).

Opera & Ballet

The two main venues for opera and ballet are the **Státní opera Praha** *(Prague State Opera; Map 6; ☎ 0800 135 784; W www.opera.cz; Wilsonova 4, Nové Město; tickets 200-950Kč; box office open 10am-5pm Mon-Fri, 10am-noon & 1pm-5pm Sat-Sun)*, which has a gilded, neo-Rococo auditorium; and the **Národní divadlo** *(National Theatre; Map 6; ☎ 224 91 34 37; Národní 2, Nové Město; tickets 200-1000Kč; box office open 10am-6pm Mon-Fri, 10am-12.30pm Sat-Sun)*, which has wheelchair access.

The **Stavovské divadlo** *(Estates Theatre; Map 7; ☎ 224 21 50 01; Ovocný trh 1, Staré Město)* also stages opera and drama. It is equipped for the hearing-impaired and has wheelchair access (wheelchair bookings can be made up to five days in advance); the **box office** *(☎ 224 90 16 38; Ovocný trh 6; open 10am-6pm Mon-Fri, 10am-12.30pm Sat-Sun)* is around the corner in the Kolowrat Palace.

Box offices are also open from 30 minutes to one hour before the start of a performance.

Other Venues

Prague's many churches and Baroque palaces also serve as concert venues, staging anything from choral performances and organ recitals to string quartets, brass ensembles and occasionally full orchestras. You can get details of these concerts from PIS offices (see Tourist Offices in the Facts for the Visitor chapter). Following is a selection of the more popular venues.

Hradčany & Malá Strana (Map 5)

Bazilika sv Jiří (Basilica of St George) St George Square, Prague Castle (Pražský hrad)
Kostel sv Vavčince (Church of St Lawrence) Hellichova 18
Liechtensteinský palác (Liechtenstein Palace) Malostranské náměstí
Lobkovický palác (Lobkowicz Palace) Jiřská 3, Prague Castle
Kostel sv Mikuláše (St Nicholas Church) Malostranské náměstí
Chrám sv Víta (St Vitus Cathedral) 2nd Courtyard, Prague Castle
Strahovský klášter (Strahov Monastery) Strahovské nádvoří 1
Vojanovy sady (Vrtbov Garden) Karmelitská 25
Valdstejnsky palac (Wallenstein Palace) Valdštejnské náměstí

Staré Město

Betlémská kaple (Bethlehem Chapel; Map 6) Betlémské náměstí 1, Staré Město
Zrcadlová kaple (Chapel of Mirrors; Map 7) Klem- entinum, Mariánské náměstí
Klašter sv Anězsky (Convent of St Agnes; Map 7) U milosrdných 17
Kostel sv Františka (Church of St Francis; Map 7) Křížovnické náměstí
Chrám sv Mikuláše (St Nicholas' Church; Map 7) Old Town Square

Take care when buying tickets through people handing out flyers in the street – some of these concerts are OK, but some may turn out to be a disappointment. Make sure you know exactly where the concert will be held – if you are told just 'the Municipal House', don't expect the magnificent Smetana Hall, as it may be in one of the smaller concert halls.

Prague Spring

Prague Spring (Pražské jaro) is the Czech Republic's best-known annual cultural event, and is now a major tourist event too. It begins on 12 May, the anniversary of Smetana's death, with a procession from his grave at Vyšehrad to the Obecní dům, and a performance there of his *Má vlast* song cycle. The festival runs until 2 June. The beautiful venues are as big a draw as the music.

The cheapest tickets are from the official **Prague Spring Box Office** *(Map 5; ☎ 257 31 25 47, fax 257 31 37 25; ⓔ info@festival.cz; ⓦ www.festival.cz; Hellichova 18, Malá Strana, 118 00 Praha 1)*, off Karmelitská; it's open from 10am to 6pm Monday to Friday during the run-up to the festival (from April), but only until 5pm during the festival. Bookings can also be made through **Ticketpro** (see Buying Tickets at the start of this chapter).

If you want a guaranteed seat at a Prague Spring concert, book it by mid-March. A few seats may be available as late as the end of May: watch the papers.

THEATRE

Prague's most famous stage show is probably **Laterna Magika** (Magic Lantern; *Map 6; ☎ 224 93 14 82; ⓦ www.laterna.cz; Národní 4, Nové Město; tickets 600-690Kč; box office open 10am-8pm Mon-Sat)*), a multimedia show interweaving dance, opera, music and film, which caused a stir when it premiered in 1958 at the Brussels World Fair. It has been going strong ever since, and today it still offers clever, expensive, mainstream entertainment, now enjoyed mainly by tourists.

Laterna Magika is the futuristic glass-block building next to the Národní divadlo. It has been home to the Laterna Magika show since it moved here from its birthplace in the basement of the Adria Palace in the mid-1970s. Some agencies may tell you it's booked out, but you can often bag a leftover seat at the box office on the day before a performance, or a no-show half-hour beforehand.

Drama

Most Czech drama is, not surprisingly, performed in Czech, which rather diminishes its appeal to non Czech-speakers. Nevertheless, here are Prague's main drama venues; most theatres close during the summer months, from July to mid-September:

Stavovské divadlo (Estates Theatre; Map 7; ☎ 224 21 50 01) Ovocný trh 1, Staré Město. Box office (☎ 224 90 16 38; Ovocný trh 6) open 10am to 6pm Monday to Friday and 10am to 12.30pm Saturday and Sunday. See Classical

Music, Opera & Ballet earlier in this chapter for details; some plays include simultaneous translation on headphones.

Divadlo v Celetné (Celetná Theatre; Map 7; ☎ 222 32 68 43) Celetná 17, Staré Město. Box office open 1pm to 7.30pm daily. Stages old and new Czech drama, and some foreign plays (in Czech).

Divadlo Na Zábradlí (Theatre on the Balustrade; Map 7; ☎ 222 22 20 26) Anenské náměstí 5, Staré Město. Box office open 2pm to 7pm Monday to Friday plus two hours before the show on Saturday and Sunday. Main venue for serious Czech-language drama, including the occasional play by Václav Havel; tickets cost from 90Kč to 250Kč.

Činoherní Klub (Dramatic Club; Map 6; ☎ 296 22 21 23; W www.cinoherni.cz) Ve Smečkách 26, Nové Město. Box office open from 3pm Monday to Friday, from 6pm Saturday and Sunday. Stages Czech-language modern drama; tickets cost from 130Kč to 160Kč.

Divadlo Na Vinohradech (Vinohrady Theatre; Map 10; ☎ 224 25 76 01) náměstí Míru 7, Vinohrady. Box office open 11am to 7pm Monday to Friday, plus 1pm to 4pm and 4.30pm to 7pm Saturday. Stages Czech-language drama and ballet; tickets cost from 40Kč to 190Kč.

Black-Light Theatre

Black-light theatre – occasionally called just 'black theatre' – is a hybrid of mime, drama and puppetry. Live or animated actors wearing fluorescent costumes do their thing on a stage or in front of a black backdrop lit only by ultraviolet light, thus eliminating the usual distractions of stage management and scenery. It's a growth industry in Prague, with at least half a dozen venues. The main ones are:

Image Theatre (Map 7; ☎ 222 32 91 91) Classic Club, Pařížská 4, Staré Město. Box office open 9am to 8pm daily. Black-light theatre, pantomime and modern dance; tickets 400Kč.

Ta Fantastika (Map 7; ☎ 222 22 13 66) Karlova 8, Staré Město. Box office open 11am to 9.30pm daily. Black-light theatre based on classic literature such as *Gulliver's Travels* and *Alice in Wonderland*; tickets 490Kč.

Reduta Theatre (Map 6; ☎ 224 93 34 87) Národní 20, Nové Město. Box office open from 3pm Monday to Friday, from 7pm Saturday and Sunday. Home to the Black Theatre of Jiří Srnec, who was a founding member of Prague's original black-light theatre; tickets cost 490Kč.

Children's Theatre

Divadlo Minor *(Minor Theatre; Map 6; ☎ 222 23 13 51; Vodičkova 5, Nové Město; tickets 150Kč; box office open 9am-noon & 12.30pm-8pm Mon-Fri)* is a wheelchair-accessible children's theatre that puts on puppet shows, clown shows and performances that celebrate 'humour, verse and fantasy'.

Národní divadlo marionet *(National Marionette Theatre; Map 7; ☎ 224 81 93 23; Žatecká 1, Staré Město; tickets 490Kč; box office open 10am-8pm daily)* has been staging puppet performances of Mozart's *Don Giovanni* almost continuously since 1991.

CINEMAS

Prague has over 30 *kino* (cinemas), some showing first-run Western films, some showing Czech films. Admission costs from around 90Kč to 160Kč. For listings check the 'Night & Day' section of the *Prague Post*, or the free bi-monthly pamphlet *Do města – Downtown*. Except for Hollywood blockbusters, which may be dubbed into Czech, films are usually shown in their original language; *anglický verze* means 'English version' and *České titulky* means 'Czech subtitles'.

Ster Century *(Map 7; ☎ 221 45 12 14; Na příkopě 22, Nové Město; admission 159Kč)*, in the posh Slovanský dům shopping centre, is central Prague's Western-style, 10-screen multiplex, showing big-name Hollywood films.

Kino MAT *(Map 6; ☎ 224 91 57 65; Karlovo náměstí 19, Nové Město; metro Karlovo náměstí; admission 60-100Kč)* is a former film studio turned hip, arthouse cinema. This is the place to see Czech films with English subtitles, or *Casablanca* with Czech ones.

Kino Aero *(Map 2; ☎ 271 77 13 49; Biskupcova 31, Žižkov; bus No 133; admission 50-90Kč)*, in eastern Žižkov, is another excellent arthouse cinema, showing re-runs of classics from *Smrt v Benátkách* (Death in Venice) to *Dobrodružství Priscilly, Královny Pouště* (The Adventures of Priscilla, Queen of the Desert).

There are several older cinemas around Wenceslas Square (Václavské náměstí; Map 6) that screen first-run films, including the

Kino Lucerna *(☎ 224 21 69 72; Vodičkova 36)*, **Kino Hvězda** *(☎ 224 21 68 22; Václavské náměstí 38)* and **Kino Jalta** *(☎ 224 22 88 14; Václavské náměstí 43)*. **Kino 64 U hradeb** *(Map 5; ☎ 257 53 11 58; Mostecká 21)* is a similar place in Malá Strana.

SPECTATOR SPORTS

Prague International Marathon

The Prague International Marathon (Pražský Mezinárodní maraton), started in 1989, is now an annual event (normally mid- to late May), attracting more foreign runners than Czechs. There is also a half-marathon, held in late March.

If you'd like to compete, contact **Prague International Marathon** *(☎ 224 91 92 09; W www.pim.cz; Záhořanského 3, 120 00 Praha 2)*. The entry fee in 2002 was US$50 for foreigners and 400Kč for Czechs. Entries must be received at least 10 days before the race. For dates and details, check the official website.

Ice Hockey

The Czech national *lední hokej* (ice hockey) team has won the European championship 17 times, the world title 10 times (most recently in 2001), and one Olympic gold medal. HC Sparta Praha and HC Slavia Praha are Prague's two big teams. The season runs from September to early April.

You can see Sparta play at the **T-Mobile Aréna** *(Map 4; ☎ 266 72 74 43; Za Elektrárnou 419, Holešovice; metro Nádraží Holešovice)* by the Exhibition Grounds in Holešovice (take tram 12 one stop west from the metro station); tickets cost from 40Kč to 100Kč. Slavia's games are played at **Zimní stadión Eden** *(Map 2; ☎ 267 31 14 17; Vladivostocká 10, Vršovice)*; tickets cost from 50Kč to 100Kč.

Football

Slavia Praha and Sparta Praha are leading teams in the national *fotbal* (football) league; two other Prague teams are the Bohemians and Viktoria Žižkov. Each has its own stadium where you can watch matches, mostly on Sunday afternoons. The season runs from August to December and February to June.

AC Sparta Praha stadium (Map 3; ☎ 20 57 16 67) Milady Horákové 98, Bubeneč. Tickets cost 50Kč to 150Kč; take tram No 1, 8, 25 or 26 east from Hradčanská metro station.

FC Bohemians stadium (Map 2; ☎ 71 72 14 59) Vršovická 31, Vinohrady. Tickets cost 75Kč to 100Kč; take tram No 4 or 22 from Karlovo náměstí.

FK Viktoria Žižkov stadium (Map 6; ☎ 222 72 20 45) Seifertova, Žižkov. Tickets cost 40Kč to 60Kč; take eastbound tram No 9 from Wenceslas Square or tram No 5 or 26 from náměstí Republiky.

SK Slavia Praha stadium (Map 5; ☎ 257 21 32 90) Diskařská 100, Strahov. Tickets cost 40Kč to 120Kč; take bus No 176 from Karlovo náměstí.

Horse Racing

Check out the *dostihy* (racing) scene at **Velká Chuchle závodiště Praha** *(Prague Racecourse; Map 2; ☎ 257 94 14 31; Radotínská 69, Velká Chuchle)*; take bus No 129, 172, 243, 244 or 255 from Smíchovské Nádraží metro station. There are races every Sunday from April to October. Contact PIS offices (see Tourist Offices in the Facts for the Visitor chapter) about other venues and events, as these constantly change. Tickets are cheap and usually available at the grounds.

Shopping

In recent years Prague has succumbed to a wave of rampant consumerism, with glitzy new shopping malls crammed with designer outlets, smart cafés and big Western brand names springing up all over the place. Opened in 2001, **Slovanský dům** *(Map 7; Na příkopě)* is the newest, and still more are planned.

Imports carry Western European prices, but Czech products are affordable for Czechs and cheap for Westerners. While tourist-zone gift shops outside Prague (such as in Karlštejn or Mělník, see the Excursions chapter) have smaller selections, prices are significantly lower.

WHAT TO BUY

Antiques & Bric-a-Brac

There are dozens of *starožitnictví* (antique shops) in Prague. In Staré Město, there are several along Celetná and Týnská.

Bric á Brac *(Map 7; Týnská 7, Staré Město)* is a wonderfully cluttered Aladdin's Cave of odds and ends and old household junk, along with glassware, toys, apothecary jars and 1940s leather jackets.

Starožitnosti Alma *(Map 7; Valentinská 7, Staré Město)* and **Art Deco Galerie** *(Map 7; Michalská 21, Staré Město)* specialise in early-20th-century stuff, including clothes, handbags, jewellery, glassware and ceramics. **Starožitnosti V Andrie** *(Map 7; cnr Platneřská and Křížovnická)* is also worth a look.

Eduard Čapek *(Map 7; Dlouhá 32, Staré Město)* was founded in 1911 and has been doing a roaring trade ever since. You may not need an old door knob, a rusty typewriter or a cracked teapot, but you might find something of interest among the household junk.

Starožitností Z Križek *(Map 6; Žitna 3, Nové Město)* is a dusty treasure-trove of old furniture, porcelain toilet bowls and old postcards and photographs.

There's also an **Antiques Fair** *(Map 3; cnr Bechyňova & Kolejní, Dejvice; open 8am-noon every 2nd Sun)*, organised by a commercial dealer, offering everything from old books, coins and postcards to cameras and militaria.

Books & Maps

Prague is full of interesting *knihupectví* (bookshops). Those that stock English-language titles also tend to have books on Czech history and culture, and translations of well-known Czech writers. Paperback classics in English abound. Bookshops listed in this section are the best options for English-speaking book junkies.

Big Ben *(Map 7; ☎ 224 82 65 65; Malá Štupartská 5, Staré Město; open 9am-6.30pm Mon-Fri, 10am-5pm Sat-Sun)* is a small but well-stocked, English-language-only bookshop, with a selection of Czech history, essays and fiction. Nearby **Anagram** *(Map 7; Týn 4; open 10am-8pm Mon-Sat, 10am-6pm Sun)* is also good, and has a broad range of second-hand books as well.

Kanzelsberger *(Map 6; ☎ 224 21 92 14; Václavské náměstí 4, Nové Město; open 9am-7pm daily)*, in the tall, glass Lindt building at the foot of Wenceslas Square (Václavské náměstí), has five floors of bookshelves – you'll want the top floor, where there's an extensive selection of books in English, German and French, plus hiking and city maps covering the whole of the Czech Republic and Slovakia.

Famous expat hang-out **The Globe** *(Map 6; Pštrossova 6, Nové Město; open 10am-midnight daily)* is a cosy English-language bookshop with a good selection of second-hand material, and a bar and Internet café (see Cafés & Tearooms in the Nové Město section of the Places to Eat chapter and Internet Cafés in the Facts for the Visitor chapter).

Maps **Mapis** *(Map 5; ☎ 257 31 54 59; Štefánikova 63, Smíchov; open 9am-6.30pm Mon-Fri)* is a specialist map shop with a wide selection of local, national and international maps.

Kiwi *(Map 6; Jungmannova 23, Nové Město; open 9am-6.30pm Mon-Fri, 9am-2pm*

Sat) has an excellent range of maps and Lonely Planet guidebooks.

Antiquarian Books The many *antikvariát* (second-hand bookshops) dotted around Staré Město (Old Town) and Malá Strana (Little Quarter) have few English titles – most are in Czech and German – but make for interesting browsing.

Antikvariát Karel Křenek *(Map 7; Celetná 31, Staré Město)* has old maps, photographs and watercolours, and books in Czech, German and French dating from the 16th to the 19th centuries.

Galerie-Antikvariát U bílého zajíce *(Map 7; Michalská 15, Staré Město)* stocks early-20th-century books, prints, drawings and illustrations from both Czechoslovakia and the rest of Europe.

Ceramics

Keramika v Ungeltu *(Map 7; Týn 7, Staré Město)* is a good place to look for traditional Bohemian pottery and blue-and-white ware, with prices up to 25% lower than many other outlets in Staré Město.

Tupesy lidová keramika *(Map 7; Havelská 21, Staré Město)* has a good selection of work from the Slovácko region of Moravia and the Chodsko region of Bohemia.

Dům Slovenské kultury *(House of Slovak Culture; Map 6; Purkyňova 4, Nové Město)* is the place to go to for Slovak folk handicrafts.

Gemstones & Jewellery

Amber and gemstones mined in the Czech Republic are good value, and popular as souvenirs or gifts. *Jantar* (amber) is better value here than over the border in Germany. This fossilised tree resin is usually honey yellow in colour, although it can be white, orange, red or brown. *Český granát* (Czech garnets) – sometimes called 'Czech rubies' – are usually red but can be many other colours, or even colourless.

Wenceslas Square, Na příkopě, Národní and Karlova abound in jewellers.

Granát Turnov *(Map 4; Dlouhá 28–30, Staré Město)* is part of the country's biggest jewellery chain, with a huge range of gold and silver jewellery set with garnets.

Jewellery Ametyst *(Map 7; Maiselova 3, Staré Město)* is another good place to try; as well as garnets it offers chunky amber necklaces and bracelets.

Gifts & Souvenirs

Česká hračká *(Map 5; Maltézské náměstí, Malá Strana)* offers a good selection of traditional Bohemian toys and other crafts.

Česká lidová řemesla *(Czech Traditional Handicrafts; Map 7; Melantrichova 17, Staré Město)* is the biggest of at least nine shops of the same name between Prague Castle (Pražský hrad) and Old Town Square (Staroměstské náměstí), all with quality items of wood, ceramic, straw, textiles and other materials, handmade in traditional styles and/or with traditional materials. Things to look for include painted Easter eggs, wooden utensils, ceramics with traditional designs, linen with traditional stitching, and Bohemian lacework.

Wooden marionettes (and more delicate and lifelike ones made of plaster) are available in many Staré Město shops; worth a look are **Bonum** *(Map 7; Husova 8)* and **Obchod U Sv Jiljí** *(Map 7; Jilská 7)*.

Beruška *(Map 6; Václavské náměstí 15, Nové Město)*, in a passage off the square, sells animated wooden toys.

Ivana Follová Art & Fashion Gallery *(Map 7; Týn 1, Staré Město)* has some excellent, if pricey, locally produced paintings, jewellery and sculpture.

Nearby **Botanicus** *(Map 7; Týn 3, Staré Město)* sells cosmetic, culinary and medical products made from herbs and plants grown on an organic farm at Ostrá, east of Prague.

There are souvenir stalls everywhere in Wenceslas Square, Na můstku and Old Town Square, on Charles Bridge (Karlův most) and along the steps to Prague Castle. Though many of these stalls have now descended into kitsch, a few still offer good drawings, paintings and photographs of the city.

Glass & Crystal

One of Prague's best buys is Bohemian crystal – anything from simple glassware to stupendous works of art, sold at some three dozen upmarket places in the shopping zone. Prices aren't radically different from shop to shop, though they are highest in the city centre. The following shops are all in Staré Město (Map 7).

Moser *(Na příkopě 12)*, the most exclusive (and expensive) crystal shop, is worth a browse as much for the decor as the goods: it's in an originally Gothic building called the dům U černé růže (House of the Black Rose).

Rott Crystal *(Malé náměstí 3)* is housed in a beautifully restored neo-Renaissance building – originally an ironmongers' – with 1890s wall paintings on the facade. It has four floors of crystal, jewellery and ceramics

Other worthwhile crystal shops include **Výtvarná Řemesla** *(Karlova 23)* and **Sklo Bohemia** *(Na příkopě 17)*.

Many accept credit cards, and most will ship goods abroad. If you want to ship them out yourself you must take your parcel, unsealed, to the customs post office (see Customs in the Facts for the Visitor chapter). Note that parcels containing glass and crystal are not accepted by the US, Australian and New Zealand postal systems.

Music

Good buys include CDs of the works of the famous Czech composers (such as Smetana, Dvořák, Janáček and Martinů), as well as folk music – even *dechovka* (brass-band 'polka' music) if you like it. There are almost as many music shops in Prague as bookshops.

Supraphon *(Map 6; Jungmannova 20, Nové Město)* is a good option for classical music buffs, while **Bontonland** *(Map 7; Václavské náměstí 1-3, Nové Město)* is a mainstream music megastore in the basement of the Koruna Palace.

If vinyl is your thing, head for **Diskoduck** *(Map 7; Karlova 12, Staré Město)*, which has racks of techno, trance and house singles and remixes tucked away in a dark alley.

The AghaRTA Jazz Centrum club (see Jazz in the Entertainment chapter) has a music shop selling jazz recordings.

Sporting Goods

YMCA Sportcentrum *(Map 7; Na poříčí 12, Nové Město)* has a good sports shop with modest prices (and a range of serious backpacks). It's through the separate entrance to the left.

Gigasport *(Map 7; Na příkopě 19–21, Nové Město)*, in the Myslbek Shopping Centre, has three floors of brand-name sportswear and equipment.

Other good shops include **Hudy Sport** *(Map 6; Na Perštýně; Staré Město • Map 7; Havlíčkova 11, Nové Město)* and **Sport Slivka** *(Map 5; Újezd 42, Malá Strana)*, which both sell climbing and camping gear and other inexpensive outdoor equipment.

The big department stores (see below) also have sizable sports departments. Locally made equipment is of good quality and moderately priced.

WHERE TO SHOP

Prague's principal shopping area is around Wenceslas Square and the streets at its northwestern end – Na příkopě, 28.října and Národní třída – but there are also lots of interesting shops in the maze of streets and alleys around Old Town Square. There are new shopping centres on náměstí Republiky, and in Smíchov and Vinohrady, and more will no doubt be open by the time you read this.

Department Stores

The major department stores in the city centre are:

Bílá Labuť (Map 6) Na poříčí 23, Nové Město • cnr Václavské náměstí & Wilsonova, Nové Město. Both open 9am to 8pm Monday to Friday, 9am to 6pm Saturday and 10am to 6pm Sunday.

Kotva (Map 7) náměstí Republiky 8, Staré Město. Open 9am to 8pm Monday to Friday, 9am to 6pm Saturday and 10am to 6pm Sunday.

Krone (Map 6) cnr Václavské náměstí & Jindřišská, Nové Město. Open 9am to 8pm Monday to Friday, 9am to 7pm Saturday and 10am to 6pm Sunday.

Tesco (Map 6) Národní 26, Nové Město. Open 8am to 9pm Monday to Friday, 9am to 8pm Saturday and 10am to 7pm Sunday.

Open-Air Markets

The city has a number of open-air markets where you can buy not only fresh produce but also souvenirs, clothing and the odd antique. The biggest one in the city centre is the rather pricey daily **produce and souvenir market** *(Map 7; Havelská)*, south of Old Town Square. Less expensive ones – mainly open in the morning and closed Sunday – include:

Dejvice (Map 3); take the Praha Dejvice exit from metro Hradčanská and turn left onto Dejvická
Dejvice (Map 3); just off Vítězné náměstí
Holešovice (Map 4); Bubenské nábřeží
Smíchov (Map 9); Arbesovo náměstí and nearby náměstí 14.října

Excursions

The Central Bohemian countryside, within an hour's train or bus ride from Prague, is rich in landscapes, good walks, interesting architecture and historical sights. Following are a few day or overnight trips you can do on your own.

Top of the list are photogenic Karlštejn Castle, harrowing Terezín, the silver-mining town of Kutná Hora and – barely outside the city limits – Průhonice Park. Be ready for summer crowds at Karlštejn and Konopiště castles; staying the night, after the tour buses return to Prague, lets you see these places in a kinder light.

Of the castles and chateaux described here, Křivoklát and Karlštejn are open year-round, Mělník from March to December, and the others from April to October, except Konopiště which is open until November. All the sights in this chapter are closed on Monday except the Terezín Memorial, the Lidice Museum, Mělník zámek (Mělník Chateau) and – in July and August – Křivoklát Castle.

Guided Tours

The risk of theft has prompted most castles and chateaux to only admit visitors in guided groups, though most will let you pay the Czech price (typically around 30Kč to 80Kč) and lend you a written English text (ask for the *anglický text*). If you want to catch every detail, be prepared to fork out around 70Kč to 260Kč for an English-language tour, easily available only at the major tourist sights.

If you don't want to arrange a trip on your own, a range of operators offer a variety of daylong excursions in the high season, with lunch included. See Organised Tours in the Getting Around chapter.

Walks

Only a few walks are noted in this chapter, but there are many routes mapped and described on SHOCart's excellent map, *Praha a okolí* (Prague and Around) and in the excellent series of 1:50,000 hiking maps produced by Klub českých turistů/VKÚ (in Czech). Trails are well marked and colour-coded.

North

MĚLNÍK

On a prominent hill above the confluence of rivers Vltava and Labe, Mělník began as a 9th-century Slavonic settlement. Its castle was the second home of Bohemia's queens from the 13th century until the time of George of Poděbrady. A solidly Hussite town, it was demolished by Swedish troops in the Thirty Years' War, and the original castle gave way to the present chateau.

The town, about 30km north of Prague, is the centre of Bohemia's wine-growing region. The best vineyards are descended from Burgundy vines imported by Charles IV.

This is an easy day trip, good for lazy strolling and wine tasting.

Orientation & Information

Across the road from the bus station, take any street that angles about 45° to the right (west). It's a 10- to 15-minute uphill slog to the town's old gate tower, **Pražská brana**. Inside, bear right into náměstí Míru, an arcaded square lined with pastel-tinted Renaissance and Baroque facades. Take the first left along Svatováclavská to the chateau and church.

The municipal **Tourist Information Centre** *(TIC; ☎/fax 315 62 75 03; e infocentrum@melnik.cz; náměstí Míru 30/16; open 9am-5pm daily May-Sept, 9am-5pm Sat-Sun Oct-Apr)* offers town maps and help with accommodation. **Česká spořitelna banka** *(náměstí Míru)* and **Komerční banka** *(Svatováclavská)* have currency exchanges and ATMs.

Mělník Zámek

Marriage brought this Renaissance chateau *(☎ 315 62 21 21; Mělník; adult/child 60/40Kč; open 10am-5pm daily Mar-late Dec)* into the Lobkowicz family in 1753. Since getting it back from the state in 1990, they've opened it to the public.

The 40-minute self-guided tour looks at the **former apartments**, crowded with the family's rich collection of Baroque furniture and 17th- and 18th-century paintings. Additional rooms are given over to changing exhibits of modern works.

You can also visit the 14th-century **wine cellars** *(admission 25Kč; open 10am-6pm daily)* where you can taste the chateau's wines (70Kč to 350Kč, depending on how tipsy you want to get). A shop in the courtyard sells the chateau's own label.

The **Okresní muzeum** *(District Museum; ☎ 315 62 19 17; náměstí Míru 54; adult/child 30/15Kč; open 9am-noon & 1pm-5pm Tues-Sun)*, next to the town hall, has exhibits on Bohemian wine-making and the history of prams.

Kostel sv Petra a Pavla

The town's 15th-century kostel sv Petra a Pavla (Church of SS Peter & Paul), with Baroque furnishings and bell tower, is worth a look. Remnants of its Romanesque predecessor have been incorporated into the rear of the building, south of the bell tower.

The old **crypt** *(adult/child 30/15Kč; open 9.30am-12.30pm & 1pm-5pm Tues-Sun)* is now an ossuary, packed with the bones of some 15,000 people dug up to make room for 16th-century plague victims, and arranged in macabre patterns. It has an unintentionally hilarious show every half-hour. The ticket also lets you have a look inside the church; children aged under five get in free.

Lookout & Walks

The view from behind the chateau takes in the confluence of the rivers Vltava and Labe, and a once-busy 10km canal from the Vltava. The big bump on the horizon to the northwest is a hill called Říp where, legend says, the brothers Čech and Lech stopped on a journey from the east. The former stayed and founded the Czech nation, while the latter went on to sire the Poles.

Lobkowicz vineyards carpet the wedge of land between the Vltava River and the canal. To the right of the canal is the thickly wooded Hořínský Park, which offers some pleasant walking. A 2km marked trail passes Hořín village, Hořín Chateau (the old Lobkowicz family home) and the canal lock, which is still in use.

Places to Stay

Autocamp Mělník *(☎ 315 62 38 56, fax 315 62 65 68; ⓔ autocamp.melnik@seznam.cz; Klášterní 717; camping per person/tent 45/80Kč)* is a few kilometres northeast of the centre.

Two modest and fairly central places offer rooms with shower and toilet: **Penzion V podzámčí** *(☎ 315 62 28 89; Seiferta 167; beds per person 750Kč)* and the **Hotel Jaro** *(☎ 315 62 68 52, fax 315 62 68 51; 17. listopadu 174; singles/doubles 1150/1890Kč)*. Both are two to three blocks from náměstí Míru, to the left as you face the chateau. The TIC can direct you to others.

Places to Eat

The best local wines, both white and red, are called Ludmila, after the saint and grandmother of St Wenceslas. One of the best places to taste them is in the chateau. On the ground floor are the **Restaurant Zámecká** *(mains 150-200Kč; open 10am-11pm daily)*, with good food and a smashing view, and a pricier **vinárna** (wine bar). The **Stará škola** vinárna behind the church has similar views and prices.

For cheaper eats, **U sv Václava** *(Svatováclavská 22; mains 90-110Kč)* is a modern and trendy place with very good Czech and international main courses, served with good local wines.

Getting There & Away

There are daily buses from Prague to Mělník, departing every 30 to 60 minutes from Nádraží Holešovice metro station (32Kč, 45 minutes).

TEREZÍN

Even were it not for their barbaric use by the Nazis, the massive strongholds at Terezín (Theresienstadt in German) would still be a chilling sight. Though founded in 1780 by Emperor Joseph II as a state-of-the-art

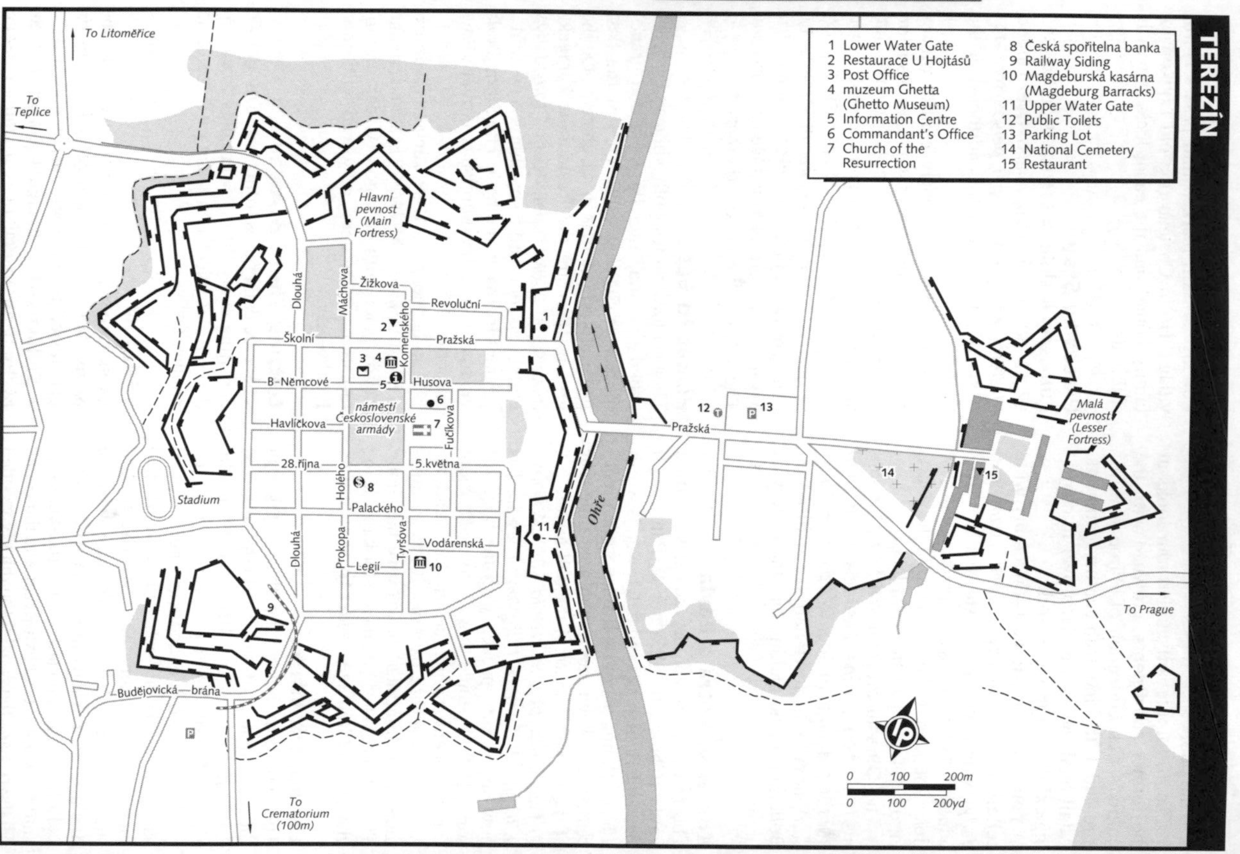
TEREZÍN
1 Lower Water Gate
2 Restaurace U Hojtášů
3 Post Office
4 muzeum Ghetta (Ghetto Museum)
5 Information Centre
6 Commandant's Office
7 Church of the Resurrection
8 Česká spořitelna banka
9 Railway Siding
10 Magdeburská kasárna (Magdeburg Barracks)
11 Upper Water Gate
12 Public Toilets
13 Parking Lot
14 National Cemetery
15 Restaurant
To Litoměřice
To Teplice
Hlavní pevnost (Main Fortress)
Dlouhá
Máchova
Žižkova
Revoluční
Komenského
Školní
Pražská
B-Němcové
Husova
náměstí Československé armády
Havlíčkova
Fučíkova
28.října
5.května
Holého
Stadium
Palackého
Prokopa
Tyršova
Vodárenská
Legií
Ohře
Malá pevnost (Lesser Fortress)
To Prague
Budějovická brána
To Crematorium (100m)
0 100 200m
0 100 200yd

bulwark against the Prussians, they never saw military action. In the 19th century the town within the Hlavní pevnost (Main Fortress) became a garrison, while the so-called Malá pevnost (Lesser Fortress) served as a jail and a WWI prisoner-of-war camp.

In 1940 the Gestapo established a prison in the Malá pevnost. At the end of 1941 they evicted the townspeople from the Hlavní pevnost and turned it into a transit camp and ghetto, through which some 150,000 European Jews eventually passed en route to extermination camps.

Terezín became the centrepiece of an extraordinary public-relations hoax. Official visitors to the fortress, which was billed as a kind of Jewish 'refuge', saw a clean town with a Jewish administration, banks, shops, cafés, schools and a thriving cultural life – plays, recitals, concerts, even a jazz band – a charade that completely fooled the International Red Cross, among others.

The reality was a relentlessly increasing concentration of prisoners (some 60,000 eventually, in a town built for a garrison of 5000), regular trains departing for Auschwitz, and the death by starvation, disease or suicide of some 35,000 Jews in the camp.

Though lacking the immediate horror of places such as Auschwitz, Terezín still has a powerful impact. This is a highly recommended, and fairly straightforward, day trip from Prague.

Orientation & Information

Public buses stop at náměstí Československé armády, the central square of the town within the Hlavní pevnost. The Malá pevnost is a 10-minute walk east across the Ohře River, beside furious traffic on the Prague–Ústí nad Labem highway (which cuts through the middle of the village). In between is a huge tour-bus and car parking lot.

The town's **Information Centre** *(☎ 416 78 26 16; náměstí Československé armády; open 9am-12.30pm & 1pm-4pm Tues-Sun)* is in the town hall.

There's an ATM at the **Česká spořitelna banka** on the southern side of the main square, and a **post office** *(open 8am-4pm Mon-Fri, 8am-9am Sat)* on the northern side.

Památník Terezín

The Památník Terezín *(Terezín Memorial; ☎ 416 78 22 25; W www.pamatnik-terezin.cz; both parts adult/child 160/120Kč, one part 140/110Kč)* consists of the Malá pevnost and the muzeum Ghetta (Ghetto Museum), including the Magdeburská kasárna (Magdeburg Barracks) and the Crematorium in the Hlavní pevnost. The museum has good multilingual self-guide pamphlets, a large selection of books for sale, and guides for hire (a few of them ghetto survivors).

If you are pushed for time, just visit the Malá pevnost and the main branch of the muzeum Ghetta. Smoking, and still and video photography are not allowed inside the monuments. All venues are usually closed Christmas Eve to Boxing Day, and New Year's Day. However, during the 2002 floods, buildings were badly damaged and much of the original furniture was destroyed, meaning that parts of the memorial may remain closed until 2006.

Malá Pevnost The self-guided tour of the Malá pevnost *(Lesser Fortress; open 8am-6pm daily Apr-Sept, 8am-4.30pm daily Oct-Mar)* takes you through the prison barracks, isolation cells, workshops and morgues, past execution grounds and former mass graves. It'd be hard to invent a more menacing, ghost-ridden place than these cell blocks, with wooden bunks worn smooth by the passage of bodies. An eternity of tunnels leads beneath the walls to the execution place, which exudes an atmosphere of evil. The Nazis' mocking concentration-camp slogan, *Arbeit Macht Frei* (work makes you free), hangs above a gate. In front of the fortress is the **National Cemetery**, founded in 1945 for those exhumed from mass graves here. Many have no name, just a concentration camp number.

Hlavní Pevnost From the ground, the scale of the massive fortifications of the Hlavní pevnost (Main Fortress) is impossible to grasp – take a look at the aerial photograph in the muzeum Ghetta. Within the walls sits the colourless town of Terezín.

The absorbing **muzeum Ghetta** *(Ghetto Museum; Komenského • corner of Tyršova &*

Vodárenska; open 9am-6pm daily Apr-Sept, 9am-5.30pm daily Oct-Mar), which has two branches, is the main attraction here. The main museum (Komenského) explores the rise of Nazism and life in the Terezín ghetto, with moving displays of artefacts, paintings, letters, photos and video documentaries.

The other branch (corner of Tyršova and Vodárenska) is in the former **Magdeburská kasárna** (Magdeburg Barracks), which served as the seat of the Jewish 'administration'. Here you can visit a reconstructed dormitory for prisoners, and look at exhibits on the extraordinarily rich cultural life – music, theatre, fine arts and literature – that somehow flourished among these condemned souls.

Apart from the museum, there's little to look at in town except the chunky, 19th-century **Church of the Resurrection**, the arcaded **commandant's office**, the neoclassical **administrative buildings** on the square, and the surrounding grid of houses with their awful secrets.

In the southwestern corner are the remains of a **railway siding**, built by prisoners, on which loads of further prisoners arrived. Close by, in vaults beneath the fortifications, are the **Columbarium**, where the ashes of cremated bodies were stored, and **exhibits** on death and burial in the ghetto.

Another 10 minutes' walk south of here is the gruesome **Crematorium** *(open 10am-5pm Sun-Fri Apr-Nov)* in the Jewish Cemetery, where candles burn in memory of those who died.

Places to Stay

There's very little in the way of accommodation in Terezín – the thought of staying the night in a former concentration camp makes most people's skin crawl – and what there is isn't recommendable. It's far nicer to stay in the attractive town of Litoměrice, just 3km north and easily reached by bus. The following three places are in Litoměrice.

The best bargain is **Penzion U pavouka** *(☎ 416 73 44 09; Pekařská 7; doubles 550Kč)*, where the price includes breakfast. The new **Pension U svatého Václava** *(☎ 416 73 75 00; Svatováclavská 12; singles/doubles 600/1000Kč)* is a bit more posh.

The top place in town, **Hotel Salva Guarda** *(☎ 416 73 25 06, fax 416 73 27 98; Mírové nám 12; singles/doubles 920/1400Kč)*, is in the historic House at the Black Eagle, where cosy rooms come with bathroom and TV.

Places to Eat

There's a restaurant in the former officers' mess in the Malá pevnost, and fast-food stands in the parking lot outside.

Restaurace U Hojtásů *(☎ 416 78 22 03; Komenského 152; mains 60-100Kč; open 10am-9pm Sun-Thur, 10am-10pm Fri-Sat)*, near the main branch of the museum, is the most popular place in Terezín – should you have any appetite after your tour.

Getting There & Away

There are hourly buses from Prague to Terezín (61Kč, one hour), departing from Florenc bus station.

East

KUTNÁ HORA

It's hard to imagine today, but in its time Kutná Hora, 70km southeast of Prague, was Bohemia's second-most important town. In 1996 it was added to Unesco's World Heritage List.

In the late 13th century, silver ore was found in these hills, and a town sprouted. In 1308 Wenceslas II imported a team of Italian minters and established his central Royal Mint here. The town's power grew, splendid churches and palaces arose, and in 1400 Wenceslas IV moved the royal residence here. In less than 150 years Kutná Hora had become one of Europe's biggest, richest towns, and Bohemia's economic mainstay.

But in the 16th century the silver began to run out and decline set in, hastened by the Thirty Years' War. A Baroque building boom came to an end with a devastating fire in 1770.

Today Kutná Hora is a shadow of its old self, but still sports a fine collection of architectural monuments. With its pastel-hued town square dotted with cafés, medieval alleys with facades ranging from

Gothic to neoclassical, and a cathedral to rival sv Víta (St Vitus), comparisons with Prague are hard to resist.

Orientation

The main train station, Kutná Hora hlavní nádraží, is 3km northeast of the centre along Masarykova. The bus station is more conveniently located just on the northeastern edge of the old town.

To walk into town from the train station (40 minutes), turn right out of the station building, then first left. When you reach the main road (Vítězná), turn left. After five minutes you'll see a huge church on the left; Sedlec (see Around Kutná Hora later in this chapter) is along the street (Zámecká) to the right here. Keep straight ahead along the main road, which becomes Masarykova after the big intersection, to reach the town centre.

The historical centre is compact enough to cover on foot. Most attractions lie between the central square, Palackého náměstí, and the kostel sv Barbora (Cathedral of St Barbara) in the southwestern corner of town.

The user-friendly town centre has almost too many signs. Chronological (red) house numbers are in more common use than sequential (blue) ones. Quite a few places accommodate disabled visitors.

Information

The helpful **Culture and Information Centre** *(Kulturní a informační centrum; ☎ 327 51 23 78; ⓔ infocentrum@kutnohorsko.cz; Palackého námesti 377; open 9am-6.30pm Mon-Fri, 9am-5pm Sat-Sun Apr-Oct; 9am-5pm Mon-Fri Nov-Mar)* can arrange accommodation, tours and guides. The information centre also offers public Internet access *(1Kč per minute, 15Kč minimum)*, and sells a good 30-page booklet about the town.

Komerční banka *(Tylova 9/390; open 9am-5pm Mon-Fri)* and **Česká spořitelna banka** *(Lierova 148/2; open 9am-4.30pm Mon-Fri)* both have ATMs. The **post office** *(Husova; open 9am-7pm Mon-Fri, 9am-1pm Sat)* is west of the town square.

Vlašský Dvůr

The Vlašský dvůr *(Italian Court; ☎ 327 51 28 73; Havlíčkovo náměstí; adult/child 70/50Kč; open 9am-6pm daily Apr-Sept, 10am-5pm daily Mar & Oct, 10am-4pm daily Nov-Feb)* was built by Wenceslas II as a royal seat and later became the Royal Mint. The old Czech name refers to its original Italian architects. A palace, chapel and tower were added a century later by Wenceslas IV, who made it his home.

When the mint closed in the early 18th century it became the town hall. The guided tour in Czech (with English/French/German text – or pay 50/30Kč per adult/child extra for a foreign-language tour) is worth it for a look at the few historical rooms open to the public. The oldest remaining part, the (now bricked-up) niches in the courtyard, were **minters' workshops**. The original **treasury rooms** now hold an exhibit on coins and minting.

In Wenceslas IV's **Audience Hall** are 19th-century murals of two important events that took place here: the 1471 election of Vladislav II Jagiello as king (the angry man in white is Matthias Corvinus, the loser), and an agreement between Wenceslas IV and Jan Hus (then rector of Charles University) to increase the number of Czech students.

About all that remains of Wenceslas IV's **kaple sv Václava a Vladislava** (Chapel of SS Wenceslas & Vladislav) is the oriel, which is best seen from the courtyard – although the 1904 Art Nouveau interior renovation is very striking.

The **Galérie Félixe Jeneweina**, just inside the courtyard, has changing art exhibits with the same opening hours as the mint.

From Vlašský Dvůr to Kostel sv Barbora

Around the corner from Vlašský dvůr is the huge **kostel sv Jakuba** (St James Church), begun in 1330 but only completed a century later. Passing south of the church, you come to Ruthardská, a very old and photogenic lane running up beside the old town walls. It's named after Rozina Ruthard who, according to local legend, was sealed alive in a closet by her father, a medieval burgher.

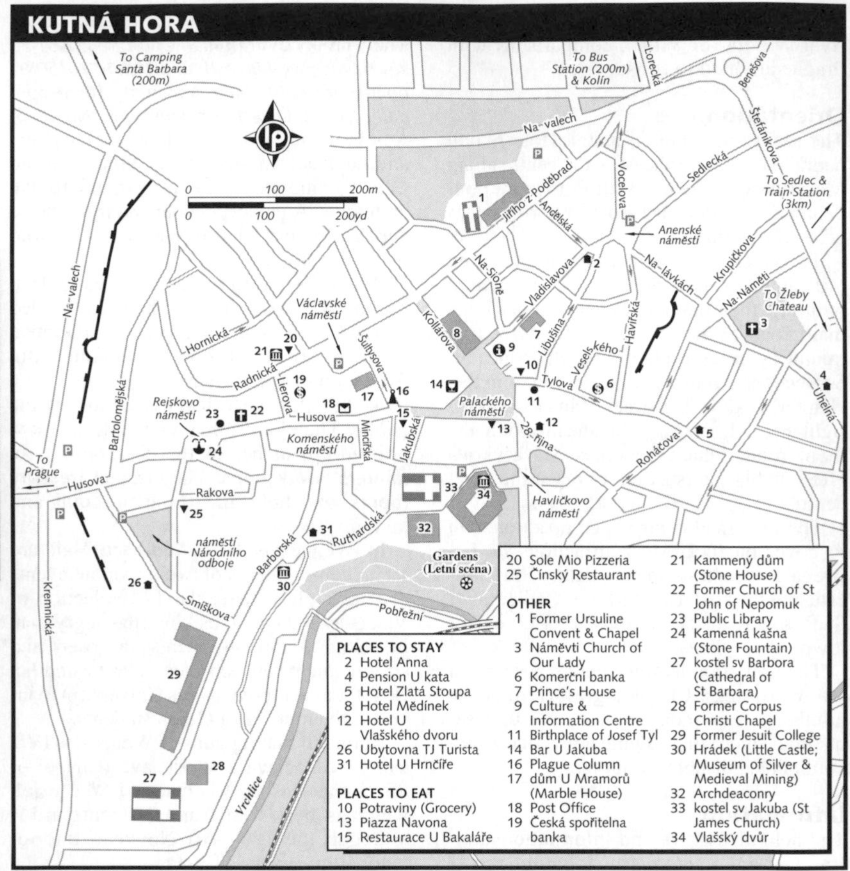

At the top of the lane is the **Hrádek** (Little Castle), originally part of the town's fortifications. It was rebuilt in the 15th century as the residence of Jan Smíšek, administrator of the royal mines, who grew rich from the silver that he mined illegally right under the building. It's now the **Museum of Silver and Medieval Mining** *(☎ 327 51 21 59; Barborská 28; admission with/without tour of mine 110/60Kč; open 10am-6pm Tues-Sun July & Aug; 9am-6pm Tues-Sun May, June & Sept; 9am-5pm Tues-Sun Apr & Oct)*. Note the huge wooden device used in the Middle Ages to lift up to 1000kg of rock from 200m-deep shafts. The museum's main attraction, however, is the 45-minute guided tour through 500m of claustrophobia-inducing **medieval mine shafts** beneath the town.

The final approach to the cathedral along Barborská ulice passes between 13 crumbling **Gothic statues** on one side and the **former Jesuit College** (1700), the biggest in the Czech Republic after Prague's Klementinum, on the other.

Kostel sv Barbora

The miners' guilds of Kutná Hora pipped Prague in the cathedral league: their kostel sv

Barbora *(Cathedral of St Barbara; ☎ 327 51 21 15; admission 30Kč; open 9am-5.30pm Tues-Sun May-Sept, 10am-11.30am & 1pm-4pm Tues-Sun Apr & Oct, 10am-11.30am & 2pm-3.30pm Nov-Mar)* is a masterpiece dedicated to the patron saint of miners, and is one of the finest Gothic churches in Europe.

Work was started in 1380, interrupted during the Hussite Wars and abandoned in 1558 when the silver began to run out. As with Prague's sv Víta (St Vitus), the western end was completed in neogothic style only at the end of the 19th century.

Inside, eight **ambulatory chapels** surround the main altar, some with vivid frescoes – including mining scenes – dating from the 15th century. The lofty **ceiling vault** is covered in a tangle of ribs, stars and floral patterns, and the coats of arms of the miners' guilds and local nobility. In the southwestern chapel are **murals** of 15th-century minters at work. The northwestern chapel has an eye-popping mural of the *Vision of St Ignatius*.

On the hillside below the cathedral is the former **kaple Božího těla** (Corpus Christi Chapel), built in the 14th century.

Other Attractions

From the Jesuit College, walk through náměstí Národního odboje and turn left on Husova to see bits of the **old city walls**. Return along Husova to Rejskovo náměstí, with its 1495 Gothic **Kamenná kašna** (Stone Fountain).

Cross via Lierova to Radnická. The Gothic confection is the **Kamenný dům** *(Stone House; ☎ 327 51 28 21; Václavské náměstí 24; adult/child 40/20Kč; open 10am-6pm Tues-Sun July-Aug; 9am-6pm Tues-Sun May-June & Sept; 9am-5pm Tues-Sun Apr & Oct)*, a burgher's house dating from 1490, now a local museum. Some of the more interesting exhibits include guild emblems, a fully equipped 'black' kitchen, folk furniture and the interior of the building itself. An English-language tour is available for 100Kč.

East and then south is Šultysova, once part of the town's medieval marketplace, and lined with handsome town houses, in particular the **dům U Mramorů** *(Marble House; Šultysova 173)*. At the bottom of the street is a 1715 **plague column**.

Cross Palackého náměstí and walk down Tylova to the **birthplace of Josef Tyl** *(☎ 327 51 15 04; Tylova 507; adult/child 20/10Kč; open 10am-4pm Tues-Sun Apr-Oct)*, the 19th-century playwright who wrote *Kde domov můj?* (Where Is My Home?), which later became part of the Czech national anthem. On the Baroque facade is a statue of three miners.

Places to Stay

Camping Santa Barbara *(☎ 327 51 20 51; Česká ulice; camping per person/tent 80/40Kč; open Apr-Oct)* is 600m northwest of the town square off Česká, near the cemetery *(hřbitov)*.

Ubytovna TJ Turista *(☎ 327 51 49 61; náměstí Národního odboje 56; dorm beds with/without youth card 140/160Kč; reception open 5pm-6pm)* offers the best budget accommodation. Rooms have six beds, communal shower and toilet, and a little kitchen.

Pension U kata *(☎ 327 51 50 96; Uhelná 569; singles/doubles 300/400Kč)*, on the eastern edge of the old town, is another good, low-priced option.

Hotel U Hrnčíře *(☎ 327 51 21 13; Barborská 24; doubles 1000Kč)*, a romantic place set in a listed 14th-century building, has only five plain doubles with shower and toilet; rates include breakfast.

Hotel Anna *(☎/fax 327 51 63 15; Vladislavova 372; singles/doubles/triples from 690/990/1465Kč)* offers comfortable, modern rooms with shower, TV and breakfast.

Hotel U Vlašského dvoru *(☎ 327 51 46 18, fax 327 51 46 27; e kh_hotels@iol.cz; 28. října 511; doubles/triples 1290/1890Kč)* is a modern place with 10 bright and spacious rooms – highly recommended. Its restaurant is popular with locals and is often packed out.

Hotel Mědínek *(☎ 327 51 27 41, fax 327 51 27 43; e hotel.medinek@worldonline.cz; Palackého náměstí 316; singles/doubles 1050/1540Kč)* is the modern monstrosity looming over the northern side of the square. It may be ugly, but it's also quiet and friendly.

Hotel Zlatá Stoupa *(☎ 327 51 15 40, fax 327 51 38 08; e zlatastoupa@iol.cz; Tylova 426; singles/doubles from 1070/1800Kč)*, the most luxurious place in town, has 25 rooms with period-style furniture, en-suite bathroom, TV and mini-bar. Its restaurant is also recommended.

Places to Eat

Restaurace U Bakaláře *(☎ 327 51 25 47; Husova 103; mains 85-110Kč; open 10am-midnight Mon-Thur, 10am-6pm Fri-Sat)* serves tasty and filling Czech grub, plus a few veggie dishes.

Čínský Restaurant *(☎ 327 51 41 51; náměstí Národního odboje 48; mains 90-150Kč; open 11am-2.30pm & 5.30pm-10pm Tues-Sat, 11am-2.30pm Sun)* is a little heavy on the MSG but still manages a tasty Chicken Gung-Pao – makes a change from dumplings.

Piazza Navona *(☎ 327 51 25 88; Palackého náměstí 90; pizzas 80-100Kč; open 11am-10pm Mon-Fri, 11am-11pm Sat, noon-10pm Sun)*, on the main square, does decent pizzas.

Sole Mio Pizzeria *(cnr Václavské náměstí & Česká)* serves reasonable pizzas and good salads, while **Bar U Jakuba** *(Palackého náměstí)* has Guinness on tap.

There's a convenient **potraviny** *(grocery; open 6am-6pm Mon-Fri, 7am-noon Sat)* on the eastern side of the main square.

Getting There & Around

Kutná Hora is about an hour's drive away from Prague. The fastest route is Highway 12 via Kolín and Sedlec; the prettiest is road 333 via Kostelec.

There are direct trains from Praha hlavní nádraží (Prague's main train station) to Kutná Hora hlavní nádraží (62Kč, 55 minutes, seven daily), which is about 3km northeast of the town centre. From here there are local trains to Kutná Hora město station (8Kč, seven minutes, 15 daily) on the edge of the town centre.

There are half a dozen buses to/from Prague (60Kč, 1¼ hours) on weekdays but far fewer at weekends. If your timing doesn't coincide with a bus direct to Prague, take one to Kolín (12km), where there are better connections. At Kutná Hora bus station, buses to Prague leave from stand No 6, those to Kolín from stand Nos 2 and 10.

Local *(městská doprava)* buses on Masarykova ulice go to/from Sedlec and the train station around once an hour on weekdays, less often at weekends. Buy a ticket from the driver (6Kč).

AROUND KUTNÁ HORA

Sedlec

Today Sedlec is a suburb of Kutná Hora, but it's been around much longer, since the founding of Bohemia's first Cistercian monastery here in 1142. It's famous for one of Bohemia's most gruesome tourist attractions – the **Kostnice** *(Ossuary; ☎ 327 76 11 43; adult/child 30/20Kč; open 8am-6pm daily Apr-Sept, 8am-noon & 1pm-5pm daily Oct, 9am-noon & 1pm-4pm daily Nov-Mar)*.

After a 13th-century abbot brought back some earth from Jerusalem and sprinkled it on the monastery's graveyard, its popularity grew. Demand for grave plots was augmented by plague epidemics; within a century there were tens of thousands of graves, and bones began to pile up. The small 14th-century kaple Všech svatých (All Saints' Chapel) was pressed into service as an ossuary.

When Joseph II abolished the monasteries, the Schwarzenberg family bought this one, and in 1870 a Czech woodcarver named František Rint turned the bones into the ghoulish artistic attraction you can see in the chapel cellar today. There are bone chalices and bone crosses; the Schwarzenberg coat of arms in bones; and an extraordinary chandelier made from at least one of every bone in the human body. Rint even signed his name in bones, at the foot of the stairs.

You have to pay an extra 30Kč if you want to take photos, or 60Kč to video.

Down on the main road is the monastery's **kostel Nanebevzetí Panny Marie** (Church of the Ascension of the Virgin), renovated at the beginning of the 18th century by Giovanni Santini in his 'Baroque-Gothic' style, unique to Bohemia; at the time of writing, it was scheduled for a major reconstruction that could last several years.

Getting There & Away The Kostnice is 2km northeast of Kutná Hora town centre.

See Getting There & Around under Kutná Hora earlier in this chapter for details of local transport.

PŘEROV NAD LABEM

This village east of Prague is home to the **Polabské národopisné muzeum** *(Labe River Region Ethnographic Museum; ☎ 325 56 52 72; adult/child 40/20Kč; open 9am-5pm Tues-Sun Apr-Oct, 10am-4pm Fri-Sun Dec)*, the Czech Republic's oldest open-air museum of traditional architecture. It was begun in 1895, soon after the first such museum opened in Stockholm (the Swedish word for these museums, *skansen*, has stuck). Contrived as skansens are, they are a great help in visualising life in an earlier time.

This one was started around an existing Přerov house: the 'Old Bohemian Cottage', dressed in herringbone clapboard and carved ornaments. Other exhibits have been brought in piecemeal from around the region: over a dozen houses have been reconstructed, as well as bell towers, pigsties, decorated beehives and a pigeon house. Staff tend gardens and raise bees using traditional methods.

Getting There & Away

There are around eight buses a day Monday to Friday (three at weekends) from the bus stand outside Černý Most metro station to Přerov (23Kč, 30 minutes).

There are also frequent trains from Prague's Holešovice train station to Čelakovice (28Kč, 40 minutes), from where you can catch a bus to Přerov (9Kč, 12 minutes).

South

PRŮHONICE

The little village of Průhonice, just south of Prague, has a photogenic 13th-century chateau, restored at the end of the 19th century in a mix of neo-Renaissance and neogothic styles, fronting onto a 250-hectare landscaped park, one of the finest of its kind in Europe.

Průhonický zámek (Průhonice Chateau) is now occupied by the Botanical Institute of the Czech Academy of Sciences and is closed to the public. The little **kostel narození Panny Marie** (Church of the Birth of Our Lady) beside the chateau, consecrated in 1187, still has some 14th-century frescoes visible. It too is closed to the public, unless you attend Sunday Mass at 5pm.

Průhonický Park *(adult/child 20/10Kč; open 7am-7pm daily Apr-Oct, 8am-5pm daily Nov-Mar)* – now a state botanical garden – is the main attraction. At weekends it's packed with Czech families, but on a drizzly weekday morning you could have the exotic gardens, sweet-smelling woods and three artificial lakes literally to yourself. In May, rhododendrons come out in rainbows.

A map of the park, with some English text, is available at the entrance.

Getting There & Away

On weekdays, buses to Průhonice leave every 15 minutes (20 minutes at weekends) from the ČSAD stand (not the city bus stop) at Prague's Opatov metro station (17Kč, 15 minutes).

KONOPIŠTĚ

The French-style chateau at Konopiště dates from 1300. It had a neogothic face-lift in the 1890s from its best-known owner, Archduke Franz Ferdinand, heir to the Austro-Hungarian throne, whose assassination in 1914 set off WWI.

The archduke was an obsessive hunter, as you will see from a tour through the wood-panelled chateau, packed with a grossly over-the-top collection of dead animals and an armoury of hunting weapons. In 25 years, he dispatched several hundred thousand creatures on his 225 hectare estate – and kept a detailed tally of them all.

Nowadays the wooded grounds, dotted with lakes, gardens and statuary, are really the best reason to visit – and a relaxing antidote to the heavy tourist scene around the chateau.

Orientation & Information

The nearest town is Benešov. Its train and bus stations are opposite one another and less than five minutes on foot from the town square, Masarykovo náměstí (turn left out of the train station, then right at Tyršova). The **IPB** bank on the square has a currency exchange and an ATM.

The chateau is 2km from town, a pleasant half-hour walk through the estate. Cross the bridge over the railway, take the first left into Ke stadiónu and the third right down Spartakládní. Drivers can go straight down Konopištská from the bridge.

Konopiště Zámek

The chateau *(☎ 317 72 13 66; open 9am-12.30pm & 1pm-5pm daily May-Aug, 9am-12.30pm & 1pm-4pm daily Sept; 9am-12.30pm & 1pm-3pm Mon-Fri, 9am-12.30pm & 1pm-4pm Sat-Sun Apr & Oct; 9am-12.30pm & 1pm-3pm Sat-Sun Nov)* offers a choice of three tours, which tend to become little more than tedious inventories. For tours I and II (50 minutes each) you can join a Czech group for 80Kč with English text, or pay 120Kč for a tour in English, French, German, Italian or Spanish. Tour III lasts one hour 10 minutes and costs 140Kč in Czech and 260Kč in a foreign language. Tours in French, Spanish and Italian are only available in July and August.

All three tours take in the archduke's trophies, a forest of mounted heads, antlers, claws and teeth. **Tour I** also looks at the stately rooms with their Italian cabinets, Dürer graphics and Meissen porcelain. **Tour II** takes in hunting weapons, the chapel and a plush men's party room. **Tour III**, limited to groups of eight, is the most interesting and intimate, taking in the archduke's living quarters and the music salon of Princess Sophie.

If that's not enough, go round the back of the chateau to see the archduke's St George fetish: scores of paintings, statues and other renderings of the mythical dragon-slayer (and what you see here is only some 10% of the hoard).

The chateau is closed the day after a public holiday. The last tour starts one hour before closing time.

Places to Stay

Hotel Nová Myslivna *(☎ 317 72 24 96; singles/doubles 300/600Kč)*, a big chalet-style place at the chateau's car park, has basic rooms and a touristy restaurant.

Hotel Pošta *(☎ 317 72 10 71; Tyršova 162; singles/doubles 310/620Kč)*, off Masarykovo náměstí in Benešov, has plain rooms with toilet and shower (the price can more than triple whenever the hotel is heavily booked).

Getting There & Away

From Praha hlavní nádraží, Benešov is a pleasant train ride through broadly rolling farmland and forests (42Kč, one hour). There are 12 fast trains a day. Alternatively, buses depart hourly from Roztyly metro station (35Kč, 35 minutes). There's also one bus daily from Florenc bus station direct to Konopiště zámek, departing at 8am (50Kč, 40 minutes).

ČESKÝ ŠTERNBERK

This hulking castle, on a sheer ridge above the Sázava River, dates from the 13th century. It probably owes its survival not only to its impregnable position, but to being owned by the same family, the Sternbergs (Šternberk to the Czechs), for almost its entire life. It suffered heavy Baroque remodelling in the 17th and 18th centuries, and the only remaining traces of its Gothic personality are in the fortifications.

Nowadays its most impressive features are the views – up from the river, and out from the castle windows. The scenery on the train journey up the Sázava River valley is itself worth the ride. Don't get off at Český Šternberk station, but one stop on at Český Šternberk zastávka, across the river from the castle. A road and then a footpath climb around behind the castle.

The tedious 45-minute tour of the castle *(☎ 317 85 51 01; open 9am-6pm Tues-Sun June-Aug, 9am-5pm Tues-Sun May & Sept, 9am-4pm Sat-Sun Apr & Oct)* reveals an Italian Baroque renovation, very heavy on stucco ornamentation. Highlights include the rococo **kaple sv Šebestiána** (St Sebastian Chapel) and the **'Yellow Room'**, with fine views over the countryside. From here you can see trees marking out a 17th-century French-style park across the river, the only part of a planned Sternberg chateau that was completed before the money ran out.

Tours in Czech/English cost 50/120Kč; the last tour begins an hour before closing time.

Places to Stay & Eat

Parkhotel Český Šternberk *(☎ 317 85 51 68, fax 317 85 51 08; singles/doubles 750/800Kč)*, just above the train stop (zastávka), has smallish rooms with shower, and a restaurant. It's best to book in summer.

The castle has a pricey **vinárna**; the **Restaurace Pod hradem u Marků** in the hamlet below is cheaper.

Getting There & Away

There are trains from Praha hlavní nádraží to Český Šternberk (62Kč, 2½ hours) every two hours or so; change at Čerčany, from where trains lumber up the Sázava valley to the castle.

On weekdays there is one direct bus from Prague's Roztyly metro station to Český Šternberk (56Kč, two hours), departing at 11.25am. Returning buses depart at 6.08pm.

West

LIDICE

When Czechoslovak paratroopers assassinated Reichsprotektor Reinhard Heydrich in June 1942 (see the boxed text 'The Assassination of Heydrich' in the Facts about Prague chapter), the Nazis took savage revenge. Picking – apparently at random – the mining and foundry village of Lidice, northwest of Prague, on 10 June they proceeded to obliterate it from the face of the earth. All the men were shot, all the women and most of the children were shipped to Ravensbrück concentration camp, and the remaining children farmed out to German foster homes. The village was systematically burned and bulldozed so that no trace remained. Of its 500 inhabitants, 340 were killed.

News of the atrocity swiftly spread, and despite the fact that war was raging, the entire globe responded. A Chicago suburb was named Lidice, Illinois, and a city square in Montevideo, capital of Uruguay, became Plaza Lidice. In the UK, in 1944, a Mass was said for Lidice in the ruins of Coventry Cathedral, and a week-long demonstration of solidarity filled the streets of Nottingham.

The outrage triggered a campaign to preserve the village's memory and create a kind of symbolic Lidice. The site is now a park and rose garden, eloquent in its silence, dotted with a few memorials and the reconstructed foundations of the farm where most of the men were shot and buried.

A small **museum** *(☎ 312 25 30 63; adult/child 50/20Kč; open 8am-6pm daily Apr-Oct, 9am-4pm daily Nov-Mar)* tells the harrowing story in photographs and artefacts, along with chilling SS film footage of its destruction. A path leads downhill from the museum through green fields that were once a village, the site of the school marked by a sad huddle of small bronze figures, a moving memorial to the 82 former pupils who died in the gas chambers.

Getting There & Away

Buses from Prague to Kladno via Lidice (18Kč, 20 minutes) depart every 30 minutes or so from the Dejvická bus stop on Evropská, outside Dejvická metro station. Direct *(přímý spoj)* buses to Kladno don't stop at Lidice, but anything serving Buštěhrad does.

KŘIVOKLÁT

Křivoklát Castle was built in the late 13th century as a royal hunting lodge. In the 15th century Vladislav II gave it its present Gothic face. There's no hunting any more: much of the upper Berounka basin, one of Bohemia's most pristine forests, is now the Křivoklát Protected Landscape Region and a Unesco 'biosphere preservation' area.

Half the pleasure of a trip to Křivoklát is getting there by train up the wooded valley hemmed in by limestone bluffs. On weekdays you'll find none of the crowds associated with Karlštejn Castle.

Orientation & Information

Křivoklát is a drowsy village, across the Rakovnický creek (a tributary of the Berounka River) from the train station. From Hotel Sýkora (see Places to Stay & Eat later in this section), climb up the road for about 10 minutes to the castle turn-off.

Křivoklát Castle

The castle's **chapel** is one of the Czech Republic's finest unaltered late-Gothic interiors, full of intricate polychrome carvings. The altar is decorated with angels carrying instruments of torture – not entirely surprising in view of the castle's 16th-century use as a political prison.

The **prison** and the **torture chambers** are under the chapel. The **Knights' Hall** features a permanent collection of late-Gothic religious sculpture and painted panels. On the 1st floor is the 25m-long **King's Hall**, the second-biggest non-church Gothic hall in the republic, after Vladislavský sál (Vladislav Hall) in Prague Castle (Pražský hrad).

Guided tours of the castle *(☎ 313 55 81 20; open 9am-noon & 1pm-5pm daily July & Aug, 9am-noon & 1pm-5pm Tues-Sun June, 9am-noon & 1pm-4pm Tues-Sun May & Sept, 9am-noon & 1pm-3pm Sat-Sun Oct-Apr)* in English or German cost 140/70Kč per adult/child; a tour of the Great Tower costs an extra 70/35Kč. If you're content to join a Czech-language tour (with an English text) you'll pay about half this.

Walking from Křivoklát to Skryje

If you've got the necessary gear and an extra day or two, consider walking the fine 18km trail (marked red; if the markings disappear, follow the river) southwest up the Berounka valley to Skryje. It starts on the western side of Rakovnický creek near the train station. Beyond the bridge to Roztoky are the **Nezabudické skály** (Nezabudice cliffs), part of a state nature reserve, and the village of Nezabudice. Across the river from Týřovice village is **Týřov**, a 13th-century French-style castle used for a time as a prison and abandoned in the 16th century. Surrounding this is another nature reserve.

The summer resort of **Skryje** has some old thatched houses. You can also walk back down the other side of the river for a closer look at Týřov. From Skryje, local buses travel down the valley to the train at Roztoky, or on to Beroun.

Placards around Křivoklát village (labelled *Okolí Křivoklátska*) describe some shorter walks through the woods.

Places to Stay & Eat

There are **camp sites** about 3km up the Berounka River from Křivoklát at Višňová, across the river at Branov (cross at Roztoky), and at Skryje.

Hotel Sýkora *(☎/fax 313 55 81 14; náměstí sv Čecha 85; doubles 1100Kč)* in Křivoklát village has basic doubles with shared toilet and shower (breakfast included), and a restaurant and beer hall with modest prices. Both restaurant and hotel are closed on Monday.

Pension restaurace U Jelena *(☎ 313 55 85 29; Hradební 53; doubles 1500Kč)* is on the other side of the road from Hotel Sýkora. It has modern doubles; rates include breakfast.

Getting There & Away

You can get from Prague to Křivoklát and back in a long day. There is just one departure from Praha hlavní nádraží at 8.11am with a reasonable connection at Beroun (62Kč, 1¾ hours), and just one similarly convenient return departure from Křivoklát at 4.39pm (terminating at Prague's Smíchov station).

Staying the night at Beroun allows you to do more than just visit the castle. Rakovník-bound trains leave Beroun every two hours or so, and Křivoklát is 50 minutes up the line.

BEROUN

Though of little interest itself, Beroun acts as a jumping-off point for Křivoklát and Karlštejn, the Koněprusy Jeskyně (Koněprusy Caves) and hikes in the beautiful Berounka river basin.

The main square, Husovo náměstí, is a 10-minute walk straight out (north) from the train station. The GE Capital bank on the square has a currency exchange and an ATM. The bus station is east of the square, across the river.

Places to Stay & Eat

Hotel U Blažků *(☎/fax 311 62 13 76; ⓔ blazek@terminus.cz; Česká 176; doubles/triples 1150/1350Kč)*, off the square to the northeast, offers good-value accommodation with ensuite bathroom and TV. Its restaurant serves up big helpings of Czech/international standards until 9pm.

Cheaper options include basic rooms with toilet and shower at **Hotel Český dvůr** *(☎ 311 62 14 11; Husovo náměstí 86; beds 450Kč)*; and spic-and-span doubles with shower but shared toilet (breakfast included) at **Hotel Barbora Garni** *(☎ 311 62 54 42; Na Podole 741; doubles 600Kč)*. From the train station, turn first right beyond the motorway.

Getting There & Away

It's a pleasant train ride from Prague to Beroun along the Berounka River (42Kč, 40 minutes). Express trains leave about every two hours from Praha hlavní nádraží, while local trains leave more frequently from the Smíchov station. See Getting There & Away under Křivoklát earlier in this chapter for more on times.

KONĚPRUSY JESKYNĚ

The 600m-long tour through these impressive limestone caves *(adult/child 60/30Kč; open 8am-5pm daily June-Aug; 8am-4pm Mon-Fri, 8am-5pm Sat-Sun May; 8am-4pm daily Apr & Sept; 8am-3pm Mon-Fri, 8am-3.30pm Sat-Sun Oct)*, 6km south of Beroun, reveals colourful formations, the bones of humans and a woolly rhinoceros, and a 15th-century underground forge used to make counterfeit coins. Take a pullover: it's a constant, chilly 10ºC, and you'll be down there for 45 to 60 minutes.

There's a snack bar at the caves.

Getting There & Away

Buses from Beroun to Koněprusy village below the caves (12Kč, 20 minutes) run at least every two hours on weekdays; useful departures include 9.25am and 2.20pm (for Zadní Třebáň) from Boroun bus station, and 11.30am (for Liteň) from the train station. They depart from Koněprusy at 1.07pm and 3.33pm for Beroun bus station, and at 3.32pm for the train station. There are less frequent services on Saturday and Sunday.

It's worth checking at the train or bus station (and the caves office when you arrive) about changes to these times, or look up the latest times on **w** www.vlak.cz at an Internet café in Prague before you go.

KARLŠTEJN

Karlštejn Castle was founded by Charles IV in 1348 as a royal hideaway and a treasury for the crown jewels and his holy relics. Perched on a crag above the Berounka River, looking taller than it is wide, it's unquestionably the most photogenic castle in the Prague region – and the most visited in the Czech Republic, with coachloads of tourists trooping through all day. Get there early to beat the crowds.

Heavily remodelled in the 19th century, it's now in amazingly good shape. The best views are from the outside, so if the tours are sold out, relax and enjoy a good tramp in the woods (see Walks later in this section).

Orientation

It's a 10-minute walk from the train station to the village, and another 10 minutes up to the castle past a strip of overpriced restaurants and souvenir shops.

Karlštejn Castle

There are two 45-minute guided tours of the castle *(☎ 311 68 16 95; **w** www.hradkarlstejn.cz; open 9am-noon & 12.30pm-6pm Tues-Sun July-Aug; 9am-noon & 12.30pm-5pm Tues-Sun May, June & Sept; 9am-noon & 1pm-4pm Tues-Sun Apr & Oct; 9am-noon & 1pm-3pm Tues-Sun Nov-Mar)*. Route I includes the Imperial Palace and the Marianská věž (Marian Tower), and costs 200/100Kč per adult/child. Route II, which takes in the kaple sv Kříže (Chapel of the Holy Cross), runs from July to November only, and must be prebooked *(☎ 274 00 81 54; **e** rezervace@spusc.cz)*, for a maximum of 10 people, at 300/100Kč per adult/child plus a 20Kč booking fee.

The south-facing **Císařského palác** (Imperial Palace) is where most of the open rooms are, including a handsome audience hall and the imperial bedroom. You must use your imagination since they have been largely stripped of their furnishings. Several scale models indicate just how drastic the 19th-century renovation was.

North of the palace is the **Marianská věž**, with Charles' private quarters and the **kostel Panny Marie** (Church of Our Lady), with fragments of its beautiful original frescoes.

Charles' private **kaple sv Kateřiny** (Chapel of St Catherine) is in a corner of the church.

The centre of the complex is the **Velká věž** (Great Tower), where the royal regalia, jewels and relics were kept. At its heart is the lavish **kaple sv Kříže** (Chapel of the Holy Cross), its walls covered in gilt panels set with thousands of semiprecious stones, and 127 priceless panels by Master Theodoric, Bohemia's best-known painter of the time.

Muzeum Betlémů

Below the castle on the road to the car park, in the 14th-century parsonage, is the curious muzeum Betlémů *(Museum of Nativity Scenes; adult/child 40Kč/free; open 9am-5pm Tues-Sun)* with over two dozen nativity scenes, from a few centimetres to several metres across, made of everything from sugar to sheet metal. Some are even animated.

Walks

On a red-marked path east from Karlštejn village, it's 7km via Mořinka (not Mořina) village into the **Karlícké údolí** (Karlík valley), a nature reserve where you can find the remains of Charles IV's Karlík Castle, abandoned in the 15th century. Karlík village, 1km down the valley, has a 12th-century rotunda. From Karlík, a road and a green-marked trail run 1.5km southeast to Dobřichovice, on the Prague–Beroun railway line.

From Srbsko, one train stop west of Karlštejn, a red trail climbs 8km up the wooded valley of Buboviský creek to the ridge-top **klášter sv Jan pod Skálou** (Monastery of St John under the Rock), allegedly once a StB (secret police) training camp. About 1.5km farther, on a blue-marked trail and just beyond the highway, is Vráž, with buses back to Beroun or to Prague.

Either walk takes less than three hours.

Places to Stay

There's a **camp site** on the northern side of the river, 500m west of the bridge.

The village has a few overpriced pensions.

Penzión U královny Dagmar *(☎ 311 68 12 50, fax 311 68 13 83; doubles 990Kč)*, one of the cheapest options, is a bright-yellow, well kept mini-hotel with a good restaurant, and is located where the road turns up towards the castle. Rates include breakfast.

Pension & restaurace Pod Dračí skalou *(☎/fax 311 68 11 77; ⓔ pod.draci@seznam.cz; rooms per person 450Kč)*, just north of the village, offers a good deal; rates include breakfast. You'll need to book ahead.

Pension Slon *(☎ 311 68 15 50; rooms per person 500Kč)* is a tranquil, family-run place; rooms have shared facilities, and rates include breakfast. From the train station, turn right and right again over the tracks, then follow the elephant-shaped signs for 300m.

You'll find other riverside pensions on the road to Prague.

Places to Eat

An alternative to the overpriced touristy restaurants on the path to the castle is the simple **Restaurant Česká hospoda** *(☎ 311 68 11 79; mains 60-160Kč; open 10am-9pm daily)* about halfway up on the left.

The friendly **Restaurant Blanky z Valois** *(mains 100-150Kč)* is another good choice, with fresh specials daily.

Getting There & Away

Local trains depart at least hourly for Karlštejn from Praha hlavní nádraží (32Kč, 45 minutes) and Smíchov station (28Kč, 35 minutes). There are return departures from Karlštejn until at least 10.30pm.

Drivers must pay 60Kč to use the village parking lot. If you don't fancy walking up to the castle, you can take a minibus (100Kč) or horse-drawn carriage (150Kč) from the car park.

Language

Czech *(čeština)* is the main language spoken in the Czech Republic. It belongs to the West Slavonic group of Indo-European languages, along with Slovak, Polish and Lusatian.

For a more comprehensive guide to the language, get a copy of Lonely Planet's *Czech phrasebook*.

Pronunciation

It's not easy to learn Czech pronunciation, and you may have to learn a few new linguistic tricks to do so (see the boxed text below). It is, however, spelt the way it's spoken, and once you become familiar with the sounds, it's easy to read. Stress is usually on the first syllable.

Vowels

Vowels have long and short variants; they have the same pronunciation, but long vowels are simply held for longer. Long vowels are indicated by an acute accent. The following approximations reflect British pronunciation:

a as the 'u' in 'cut'
á as the 'a' in 'father'
e as in 'bet'
é as the word 'air'
ě as the 'ye' in 'yet'
i/y as the 'i' in 'bit'
í/ý as the 'i' in 'marine'
o as in 'pot'
ó as the 'aw' in 'saw'
u as in 'pull'
ú/ů as the 'oo' in 'zoo'

Diphthongs (Vowel Combinations)

aj as the 'i' in 'ice'
áj as the word 'eye'
au as the 'ow' in 'how'
ej as the 'ay' in 'day'
ij/yj short; as 'iy'
íj/ýj longer version of **ij/yj**
oj as the 'oi' in 'void'
ou as the 'o' in 'note', though each vowel is more strongly pronounced than in English
uj as the 'u' in 'pull', followed by the 'y' in 'year'
ůj longer version of **uj**

Consonants

c as the 'ts' in 'lets'
č as the 'ch' in 'chew'
ch like 'ch' in Scottish *loch*
f as in 'fever', never as in 'of'
g as in 'get', never as in 'age'
h as in 'hand'
j as the 'y' in 'year'
r a rolled 'r' (at the tip of the tongue)
ř no English equivalent; a rolled 'rzh' sound, as in the composer, Dvořák
s as in 'sit', never as in 'rose'
š as the 'sh' in 'ship'
ž a 'zh' sound, as the 's' in 'treasure'
ď, ň, ť very soft palatal sounds – ie, consonants followed by a momentary contact between the tongue and the hard palate, as if followed by 'y' (like the 'ny' in canyon). The same applies to **d**, **n** and **t** when followed by **i**, **í** or **ě**.

All other consonants are similar to their English counterparts, although **k**, **p** and **t** are unaspirated, ie, pronounced with no puff of breath after them.

Greetings & Civilities

Hello/Good day.	*Dobrý den.*
	Ahoj. (informal)
Goodbye.	*Na shledanou.*
	Ahoj/Čau. (informal)
Yes.	*Ano/Jo.* (informal)

Bg Prdn?

The frustrating thing about Czech is its aversion to vowels. Many words contain nothing identifiable as a vowel. A famous tongue twister goes, *strč prst skrz krk*, which means 'stick your finger through your neck'. It's pronounced just as it's spelt!

No.	*Ne.*
May I? (asking permission)	*Dovolte mi?*
Sorry/Excuse me. (apologising or seeking assistance)	*Promiňte.*
Could you help me, please?	*Prosím, můžete mi pomoci?*
Please.	*Prosím.*
Thank you (very much).	*(Mockrát) děkuji.*
You're welcome.	*Není zač.*
Good morning.	*Dobré jitro/ráno.*
Good afternoon.	*Dobré odpoledne.*
Good evening.	*Dobrý večer.*
Good night.	*Dobrou noc.*
How are you?	*Jak se máte?*
Well, thanks.	*Děkuji, dobře.*

Language Difficulties

Do you speak English?	*Mluvíte anglicky?*
Does anyone here speak English?	*Mluví někdo anglicky?*
I speak a little ...	*Mluvím trochu ...*
I don't speak ...	*Nemluvím ...*
I understand.	*Rozumím.*
I don't understand.	*Nerozumím.*
Could you write it down, please?	*Můžete mi to napsat, prosím?*

Getting Around

What time does the train/bus leave?
V kolik hodin odjíždí vlak/autobus?
What time does the train/bus arrive?
V kolik hodin přijíždí vlak/autobus?
Excuse me, where is the ticket office?
Prosím, kde je pokladna?
I want to go to ...
Chci jet do ...

I'd like ...	*Rád bych* ... (m) *Ráda bych* ... (f)
a one-way ticket	*jednosměrnou jízdenku*
a return ticket	*zpáteční jízdenku*
two tickets	*dvě jízdenky*
a student's fare	*studentskou jízdenku*

Directions

Where is ...?	*Kde je ...?*
Go straight ahead.	*Jděte přímo.*
Turn left.	*Zatočte vlevo.*
Turn right.	*Zatočte vpravo.*
behind	*za*
in front of	*před*
far	*daleko*
near	*blízko*
opposite	*naproti*

Signs

Otevřeno	**Open**
Zavřeno	**Closed**
Vchod	**Entrance**
Východ	**Exit**
Nouzový Východ	**Emergency Exit**
Informace	**Information**
Vstup Zakázán	**No Entry**
Zákaz Parkováni	**No Parking**
Zákaz Kouření	**No Smoking**
Pěší Zóna	**Pedestrian Zone**
Policie	**Police**
Tam	**Push**
Sem	**Pull**
Zadáno	**Reserved**
WC/Záchody/ Toalety	**Toilets**
Páni/Muži	**Men**
Dámy/Ženy	**Women**

Accommodation

Do you have any rooms available?
Máte volné pokoje?
How much is it per night?
Kolik stojí jedna noc?

I'd like ...	*Přál bych si* ... (m) *Přála bych si* ... (f)
a single room	*jednolůžkový pokoj*
a double room	*dvoulůžkový pokoj*
a room with a bathroom	*pokoj s koupelnou*

cheap hotel	*laciný hotel*
good hotel	*dobrý hotel*
nearby hotel	*blízký hotel*
room number	*číslo pokoje*
key	*klíč*
shower	*sprcha*
toilet	*záchod/WC*
toilet paper	*toaletní papír*
hot/cold water	*horká/studená voda*
clean/dirty	*čistý/špinavý*

light/dark	*světlý/tmavý*
quiet/noisy	*tichý/hlučný*
cheap/expensive	*levný/drahý*

Around Town

I'm looking for (a/the) ...	*Hledám ...*
art gallery	*uměleckou galérii*
bank	*banku*
city centre	*centrum*
embassy	*velvyslanectví*
exchange office	*směnárna*
my hotel	*muj hotel*
laundry	*prádelna*
main square	*hlavní náměstí*
market	*tržiště*
museum	*muzeum*
police	*policii*
post office	*poštu*
public toilet	*veřejné záchody*
telephone centre	*telefonní ústřednu*
tourist office	*turistické informační středisko*

What's the exchange rate?	*Jaký je výměnný kurs?*
What's the commission?	*Jaký je poplatek?*
Can I have my change, please?	*Můžete mě vrátit drobné, prosím?*
What time does it open/close?	*V kolik hodin otevírají/ zavírají?*

Time & Dates

What time is it?	*Kolik je hodin?*
When?	*Kdy?*

in the morning	*ráno*
in the afternoon	*odpoledne*
in the evening	*večer*
today	*dnes*
now	*teď*
yesterday	*včera*
tomorrow	*zítra*
next week	*příští týden*

Monday	*pondělí*
Tuesday	*úterý*
Wednesday	*steda*
Thursday	*čtvrtek*
Friday	*pátek*
Saturday	*sobota*
Sunday	*neděle*

Map Jargon

Terms you'll encounter on maps and throughout this book include:

dům	house
galérie	gallery, arcade
hora	mountain
hrad	castle
hřbitov	cemetery
kaple	chapel
kopec	hill
kostel	church
most	bridge
nábřezí	embankment (abbreviated *nábř*)
náměstí	square (abbreviated *nám*)
ostrov	island
palác	palace
potok	stream
řeka	river
sad(y)	garden(s), park(s), orchard(s)
silnice	road
třída	avenue
ulice	street (abbreviated *ul*)
ulička	lane
zahrada	gardens, park
zámek	chateau (live-in castle, manor)

January	*leden*
February	*únor*
March	*březen*
April	*duben*
May	*květen*
June	*červen*
July	*červenec*
August	*srpen*
September	*září*
October	*říjen*
November	*listopad*
December	*prosinec*

Dates in Museums

year	*rok*
century	*století*
millennia	*milénium/tisíciletí*
beginning of ...	*začátek ...*
first half of ...	*první polovina ...*
middle of ...	*polovina ...*
second half of ...	*druhá polovina ...*
end of ...	*konec ...*
around ...	*kolem ...*

Emergencies

Help!	*Pomoc!*
Please, call ...	*Prosím, zavolejte ...!*
a doctor	*doktora*
an ambulance	*sanitku*
the police	*policii*
Where is the nearest ...?	*Kde je nejbližší ...?*
police station	*policejní stanice*
dentist	*zubař*
hospital	*nemocnice*
I'm ill.	*Jsem nemocný.* (m) *Jsem nemocná.* (f)
I'm lost.	*Zabloudil jsem.* (m) *Zabloudila jsem.* (f)
Go away!	*Běžte pryč!*
Where are the toilets?	*Kde jsou záchody?*
I wish to contact my embassy/consulate.	*Přeji si mluvit s mým velvyslanectvím/konzulátem.*

Numbers

It's quite common for Czechs to say the numbers 21 to 99 in reverse; for example, *dvacet jedna* (21) becomes *jedna dvacet*.

0	*nula*
1	*jedna*
2	*dva*
3	*tři*
4	*čtyři*
5	*pět*
6	*šest*
7	*sedm*
8	*osm*
9	*devět*
10	*deset*
11	*jedenáct*
12	*dvanáct*
13	*třináct*
14	*čtrnáct*
15	*patnáct*
16	*šestnáct*
17	*sedmnáct*
18	*osmnáct*
19	*devatenáct*
20	*dvacet*
21	*dvacet jedna*
22	*dvacet dva*
23	*dvacet tři*
30	*třicet*
40	*čtyřicet*
50	*padesát*
60	*šedesát*
70	*sedmdesát*
80	*osmdesát*
90	*devadesát*
100	*sto*
1000	*tisíc*
1 million	*jeden milión*

FOOD

breakfast	*snídaně*
lunch	*oběd*
dinner	*večeře*
Table for ..., please.	*Stůl pro ... osob, prosím.*
The menu, please.	*Jídelní lístek, prosím.*
What's today's special?	*Jaká je specialita dne?*
children's menu	*dětský jídelníček*
Bon appétit!	*Dobrou chuť!*
Cheers!	*Nazdraví!*
I'd like to pay, please.	*Zaplatím, prosím.*
I'm a vegetarian.	*Jsem vegetarián.* (m) *Jsem vegetariánka.* (f)
I don't eat ...	*Nejím ...*
meat	*maso*
fish	*rybu*
chicken	*kuře*
ham	*šunku*
ashtray	*popelník*
drink	*pití*
fork	*vidlička*
glass	*sklenice*
knife	*nůž*
plate	*talíř*
spoon	*lžíce*
toothpick	*párátko*

Food Glossary

biftek	beefsteak
bílý jogurt	natural white yogurt
brambory	potato
chléb	bread
chlebíčky	open sandwiches

cibule	onion
citrón	lemon
cukr	sugar
česnek	garlic
džem	jam
fazolky	beans
guláš	goulash
houby	mushrooms
hovězí (maso)	beef
hranolky	chips/French fries
hrášek	peas
husa	goose
játra	liver
kachna	duck
kapr	carp
karbanátek	hamburger
kaštany	roasted chestnuts
klobása	sausage
kmín	caraway
knedlíky	dumplings
koláč	cake
kompot	stewed fruit
kotleta	cutlet/chop
křen	horseradish
krůta	turkey
kuře	chicken
květák	cauliflower
máslo	butter
maso	meat
med	honey
moučník	dessert
mrkev	carrot
okurka	cucumber/pickle
omáčka	sauce
ovoce	fruit
palačinky	pancakes
paprika	capsicum
párky	hot dogs
pepř	pepper
polévka	soup
pstruh	trout
rajče	tomato
řízek	cutlet
rohlík	bread roll
ryba	fish
rýže	rice
smetana	cream
špenát	spinach
sterelizované zelí/ sterelizovaná kapusta	pickled cabbage
sůl	salt
šunka	ham
sýr	cheese
telecí (maso)	veal
těstoviny	pasta
tvaroh	cottage cheese
úhoř	eel
vejce	egg
míchaná vejce	scrambled egg
omeleta	omelette
smažená vejce	fried egg
vejce na měkko	soft-boiled egg
vejce na tvrdo	hard-boiled egg
vejce se slaninou	egg with bacon
vepřové (maso)	pork
zelenina	vegetables
zelí	sauerkraut
zmrzlina	ice cream

spotřebujte do ...	consume within ...
datum výroby	date of manufacture
minimální trvanlivost	minimum shelf-life date

Cooking Terms

čerstvý	fresh
domácí	home-made
dušený	steamed
grilovaný	grilled/on the spit
pečený	roasted/baked
roštěná/na roštu	broiled
sladký	sweet
smažený	fried
uzený	smoked
vařený	boiled

DRINKS

voda	water
káva	coffee
espreso	black coffee
espreso s mlékem	coffee with milk
čaj	tea
čaj s mlékem	tea with milk
limonády	soft drinks
grog	a popular year-round hot drink: half rum, half hot water or tea, and lemon
lihoviny	spirits
pivo	beer
víno	wine
vinný střik	white wine and soda water with ice
suché víno	dry wine
sladké víno	sweet wine

Glossary

You may encounter the following terms and abbreviations while in Prague. For other terms, see the Language chapter.

Autobus – bus
autoplyn – LPG

bankomat – ATM
benzín – petrol (gasoline)
bez poplatku – free of charge

celnice – customs
chrám – cathedral
cizinec, cizinci (pl) – foreigner
cukrárna – cake shop

čajovna – tearoom
ČD – Czech Railways, the state railway company
Čedok – the former state tour operator and travel agency, now privatised
čeština – the Czech language
čistřína – drycleaners
ČSA – Czech Airlines, the national carrier
ČSAD – Czech Automobile Transport, the state bus company
ČSSD – Social Democratic Party

dámy – sign on women's toilet
divadlo – theatre
dům – house or building

fin-de-siècle – relating to the last part of the 19th century, as in *fin-de-siècle* architecture

galérie – gallery, arcade

h. or **hod** – hour; designates the hour in a timetable
hlavní nádraží or **hl. nád.** – main train station
hora – mountain
hospoda – pub
hostinec – pub
hrad – castle
hřbitov – cemetery

impuls, impulsů (pl) – 'beep' or time increment used for determining telephone charges

jídelní lístek – menu
jízdenka – ticket
jízdní řád – timetable

kaple – chapel
kavárna – café or coffee shop
Kč (Koruna česká) – Czech crown
kino – cinema
knihkupectví – bookshop
kolej – college
kolky – duty stamps, for payment at certain government offices, such as for a visa extension; sold at post offices and elsewhere
kostel – church
kreditní karta – credit card

lékárna – pharmacy
lístek – ticket

maso uzeniny – meat, smoked meat and sausages (sign on a butcher's shop)
město – town
místenka – reservation (such as on a train)
mlékárna – dairy
most – bridge
muži – sign on men's toilet

nábřeží or **nábř.** – embankment
nádraží – station
nafta – diesel fuel
náměstí or **nám.** – square
natural – unleaded petrol (gasoline)
nemocnice – hospital

ODS – Civic Democratic Party
ostrov – island
otevŷeno – open (such as a shop)
ovoce – fruit

palác – palace
páni – sign on men's toilet
paragon – receipt or docket
pekárna – bakery

RICHARD NEBESKÝ

A beer in the sun in Hostinec U kocoura on Kampa

VLADIMIR LIBA

A plethora of tipples

RICHARD NEBESKÝ

A formidable array of beverages in Nové Město

RICHARD NEBESKÝ

Elegant dining in Staré Město

RICHARD NEBESKÝ

Follow the clown to get to Ta Fantastika theatre.

RICHARD NEBESKÝ

The hugely popular Konopiště is over 700 years old and still going strong.

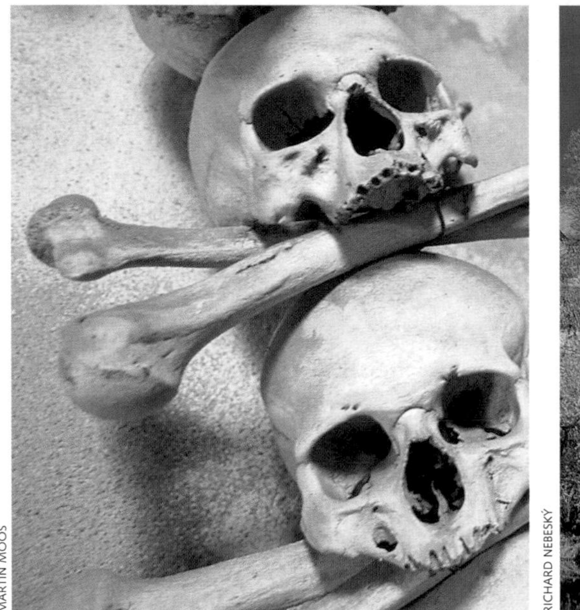

MARTIN MOOS

Skeletal tourism in Sedlec, Kutná Hora

RICHARD NEBESKÝ

Photogenic Karlštejn Castle

penzíon – pension
pěší zóna – pedestrian zone
pivnice – small beer hall
pivo – beer
pivovar – brewery
platební karta – cash/ATM card
počítač – computer
potraviny – grocery or food shop
prádelna – laundry
Praha – Prague's Czech name
provozní doba – business hours, opening times
přestup – transfer or connection

sad(y) – garden(s), park(s), orchard(s)
samizdat – underground press during the communist years
samoobsluha – self-service; mini-market
samoobslužná prádelna – self-service laundry
sem – pull (sign on door)
sgraffito – mural technique in which the top layer of plaster is scraped away or incised to reveal the layer underneath
skansen – open-air museum of traditional architecture
stanice – train stop or station
sv. or **svatý** – Saint

tam – push (sign on door)
tel. č. or **telefonní číslo** – telephone number
telecard or **telefonní karta** – telephone card
toalet – toilet
toaletní papír – toilet paper
tramvaj – tram
třída or **tř.** – avenue

ubytovna – accommodation, usually of the dormitory-style
účet volaného – a reverse-charge (collect) call
ulice or **ul.** – street
uložené zásilky – poste restante
úschovna – left-luggage office

'Velvet Divorce' – separation of Czechoslovakia into fully independent Czech and Slovak republics in 1993
'Velvet Revolution' – bloodless overthrow of Czechoslovakia's communist regime in 1989
věž – tower
vchod – entrance
vinárna – wine bar
vlak – train
vstup – entrance
vstup zakázán – no entry
východ – exit
výstup – exit

WC (vé cé) – toilet

zadáno – reserved
zahrada – gardens, park
záchod – toilet
zakázán – prohibited
zámek – chateau
zastávka – bus, tram or train stop
zavřeno – closed (such as a shop)
zelenina – vegetables
Zimmer frei – German for 'room(s) free' – ie, room(s) for rent

žel. st. – small local train station
ženy – sign on women's toilet

Acknowledgments

Thanks

Many thanks to the following travellers who used the last edition and wrote to us with helpful hints, useful advice and interesting anecdotes:

Naomi Adam, Janice Albert, Carole Amaio, Bashar Amso, Brian & Mary Ashmore, Jorg Ausfelt, Ivan Babiuk, Kate Bamberg, Matt Beks, Tony Bellette, Tony Benfield, Brenda Bierman, Gerry Bierman, Maurizio Bilotta, Melissa Bogursky, Stephen Boswell, Joel Brazy, Graeme Bridges, Bernie Brown, Nancy Bruno, Sarah Carmichael, Fred Carreon, Steven Carrick, Matt Chaffe, C W Chen, Gina Clark, Martha W Connor, Peter Dedman, Philippe Dennler, Johanna Derry, Floris Dirks, Annick Donkers, Ravit & Sagi Dror, Christine Durrant, Michael Durrant, Helen Frakes, Trudy Fraser, Paul Gallagher, Paul W Gioffi, Irene Gomez, Meahan Grande, Catherine Holland, Aryeh Houminer, Jeff & Karri & Erika Howlett, Petr Hruska, Jan Hruza, Martyn Hughes, Lisa Israel, Greta Janzow, Angela Johnston, Margaret Jones, Kerry King, David Klur, Timo Knaebe, Donna Krupa, David & Caroline Lee, M S Lewis, Zhixin Li, Alicia López-Miedes, Don Lowman, Nick Lux, Deirdre MacBean, Andrea MacLeod, Dee Mahan, John Malcolm, Paul Mastaglio, Sinead McCambridge, Pat McFeely, Ian McLoughlin, Kate Meredith, Joan Midgely-Wood, Lee Gerard Molloy, David Morris, Jason Mote, Elke Mueller, Grainne Murphy, Petra Naavalinna, Jamie Norris, Jacqui O'Connell, Robin O'Donoghue, Michelle Orme, Manuel Padilla, Thomas Paetzold, P A Path, Miguel A Pérez-Torres, Michel Pinton, Kevin Presto, Kathy Prunty, Maria Ralph, Kelly Rattray, Val Renegar, Wayne Roelke, Vicki Roubicek, Graddon Rowlands, Julie Sadigursky, Leo H Sano, C Schupp, Robin Seager, Tal Shany, Paul Shema, Tara Sims, Raewyn Somerville, Agnes Stassen, Lyn Steele, Julie Stenberg, Samo Stritof, Gary Thomas, Roger & Chris Thornback, Sinead Thornton, Chester A Troy, Boaz Ur, Carolyn Urquhart-Barham, Sergio Valdes, Caroliena van den Bos, Marian van der Maat, Benedict Wabunoha, Aled Williams, Fiona Wilson, Caroline Worthington, Niki and Shlomo Yom Tov, Will Zucker.

LONELY PLANET

You already know that Lonely Planet produces more than this one guidebook, but you might not be aware of the other products we have on this region. Here is a selection of titles that you may want to check out as well:

Eastern Europe
ISBN 1 74059 289 1
US$27.99 • £15.99

Central Europe
ISBN 1 74059 285 9
US$27.99 • £15.99

Czech & Slovak Republics
ISBN 1 86450 212 6
US$19.99 • £12.99

Europe on a Shoestring
ISBN 1 74059 314 6
US$24.99 • £14.99

Read This First: Europe
ISBN 1 86450 136 7
US$14.99 • £8.99

Czech Phrasebook
ISBN 1 86450 184 7
US$7.99 • £4.50

Central Europe Phrasebook
ISBN 1 86450 226 6
US$7.99 • £4.50

Eastern Europe Phrasebook
ISBN 1 86450 227 4
US$8.99 • £4.99

Prague City Map
ISBN 1 86450 012 3
US$5.95 • £3.99

Prague Condensed
ISBN 1 74059 349 9
US$11.99 • £5.99

Available wherever books are sold

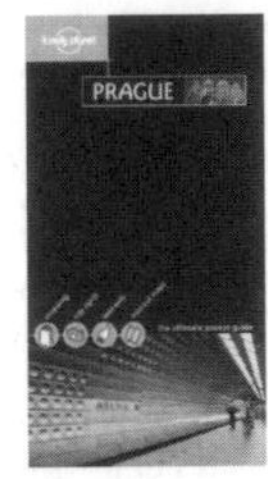

Lonely Planet Guides by Region

Lonely Planet is known worldwide for publishing practical, reliable and no-nonsense travel information in our guides and on our Web site. The Lonely Planet list covers just about every accessible part of the world. Currently there are 16 series: Travel guides, Shoestring guides, Condensed guides, Phrasebooks, Read This First, Healthy Travel, Walking guides, Cycling guides, Watching Wildlife guides, Pisces Diving & Snorkeling guides, City Maps, Road Atlases, Out to Eat, World Food, Journeys travel literature and Pictorials.

AFRICA Africa on a shoestring • Botswana • Cairo • Cairo City Map • Cape Town • Cape Town City Map • East Africa • Egypt • Egyptian Arabic phrasebook • Ethiopia, Eritrea & Djibouti • Ethiopian Amharic phrasebook • The Gambia & Senegal • Healthy Travel Africa • Kenya • Malawi • Morocco • Moroccan Arabic phrasebook • Mozambique • Namibia • Read This First: Africa • South Africa, Lesotho & Swaziland • Southern Africa • Southern Africa Road Atlas • Swahili phrasebook • Tanzania, Zanzibar & Pemba • Trekking in East Africa • Tunisia • Watching Wildlife East Africa • Watching Wildlife Southern Africa • West Africa • World Food Morocco • Zambia • Zimbabwe, Botswana & Namibia

Travel Literature: Mali Blues: Traveling to an African Beat • The Rainbird: A Central African Journey • Songs to an African Sunset: A Zimbabwean Story

AUSTRALIA & THE PACIFIC Aboriginal Australia & the Torres Strait Islands •Auckland • Australia • Australian phrasebook • Australia Road Atlas • Cycling Australia • Cycling New Zealand • Fiji • Fijian phrasebook • Healthy Travel Australia, NZ & the Pacific • Islands of Australia's Great Barrier Reef • Melbourne • Melbourne City Map • Micronesia • New Caledonia • New South Wales • New Zealand • Northern Territory • Outback Australia • Out to Eat – Melbourne • Out to Eat – Sydney • Papua New Guinea • Pidgin phrasebook • Queensland • Rarotonga & the Cook Islands • Samoa • Solomon Islands • South Australia • South Pacific • South Pacific phrasebook • Sydney • Sydney City Map • Sydney Condensed • Tahiti & French Polynesia • Tasmania • Tonga • Tramping in New Zealand • Vanuatu • Victoria • Walking in Australia • Watching Wildlife Australia • Western Australia

Travel Literature: Islands in the Clouds: Travels in the Highlands of New Guinea • Kiwi Tracks: A New Zealand Journey • Sean & David's Long Drive

CENTRAL AMERICA & THE CARIBBEAN Bahamas, Turks & Caicos • Baja California • Belize, Guatemala & Yucatán • Bermuda • Central America on a shoestring • Costa Rica • Costa Rica Spanish phrasebook • Cuba • Cycling Cuba • Dominican Republic & Haiti • Eastern Caribbean • Guatemala • Havana • Healthy Travel Central & South America • Jamaica • Mexico • Mexico City • Panama • Puerto Rico • Read This First: Central & South America • Virgin Islands • World Food Caribbean • World Food Mexico • Yucatán

Travel Literature: Green Dreams: Travels in Central America

EUROPE Amsterdam • Amsterdam City Map • Amsterdam Condensed • Andalucía • Athens • Austria • Baltic States phrasebook • Barcelona • Barcelona City Map • Belgium & Luxembourg • Berlin • Berlin City Map • Britain • British phrasebook • Brussels, Bruges & Antwerp • Brussels City Map • Budapest • Budapest City Map • Canary Islands • Catalunya & the Costa Brava • Central Europe • Central Europe phrasebook • Copenhagen • Corfu & the Ionians • Corsica • Crete • Crete Condensed • Croatia • Cycling Britain • Cycling France • Cyprus • Czech & Slovak Republics • Czech phrasebook • Denmark • Dublin • Dublin City Map • Dublin Condensed • Eastern Europe • Eastern Europe phrasebook • Edinburgh • Edinburgh City Map • England • Estonia, Latvia & Lithuania • Europe on a shoestring • Europe phrasebook • Finland • Florence • Florence City Map • France • Frankfurt City Map • Frankfurt Condensed • French phrasebook • Georgia, Armenia & Azerbaijan • Germany • German phrasebook • Greece • Greek Islands • Greek phrasebook • Hungary • Iceland, Greenland & the Faroe Islands • Ireland • Italian phrasebook • Italy • Kraków • Lisbon • The Loire • London • London City Map • London Condensed • Madrid • Madrid City Map • Malta • Mediterranean Europe • Milan, Turin & Genoa • Moscow • Munich • Netherlands • Normandy • Norway • Out to Eat – London • Out to Eat – Paris • Paris • Paris City Map • Paris Condensed • Poland • Polish phrasebook • Portugal • Portuguese phrasebook • Prague • Prague City Map • Provence & the Côte d'Azur • Read This First: Europe • Rhodes & the Dodecanese • Romania & Moldova • Rome • Rome City Map • Rome Condensed • Russia, Ukraine & Belarus • Russian phrasebook • Scandinavian & Baltic Europe • Scandinavian phrasebook • Scotland • Sicily • Slovenia • South-West France • Spain • Spanish phrasebook • Stockholm • St Petersburg • St Petersburg City Map • Sweden • Switzerland • Tuscany • Ukrainian phrasebook • Venice • Vienna • Wales • Walking in Britain • Walking in France • Walking in Ireland • Walking in Italy • Walking in Scotland • Walking in Spain • Walking in Switzerland • Western Europe • World Food France • World Food Greece • World Food Ireland • World Food Italy • World Food Spain **Travel Literature:** After Yugoslavia • Love and War in the Apennines • The Olive Grove: Travels in Greece • On the Shores of the Mediterranean • Round Ireland in Low Gear • A Small Place in Italy

Lonely Planet Mail Order

Lonely Planet products are distributed worldwide. They are also available by mail order from Lonely Planet, so if you have difficulty finding a title please write to us. North and South American residents should write to 150 Linden St, Oakland, CA 94607, USA; European and African residents should write to 10a Spring Place, London NW5 3BH, UK; and residents of other countries to Locked Bag 1, Footscray, Victoria 3011, Australia.

INDIAN SUBCONTINENT & THE INDIAN OCEAN Bangladesh • Bengali phrasebook • Bhutan • Delhi • Goa • Healthy Travel Asia & India • Hindi & Urdu phrasebook • India • India & Bangladesh City Map • Indian Himalaya • Karakoram Highway • Kathmandu City Map • Kerala • Madagascar • Maldives • Mauritius, Réunion & Seychelles • Mumbai (Bombay) • Nepal • Nepali phrasebook • North India • Pakistan • Rajasthan • Read This First: Asia & India • South India • Sri Lanka • Sri Lanka phrasebook • Tibet • Tibetan phrasebook • Trekking in the Indian Himalaya • Trekking in the Karakoram & Hindukush • Trekking in the Nepal Himalaya • World Food India **Travel Literature:** The Age of Kali: Indian Travels and Encounters • Hello Goodnight: A Life of Goa • In Rajasthan • Maverick in Madagascar • A Season in Heaven: True Tales from the Road to Kathmandu • Shopping for Buddhas • A Short Walk in the Hindu Kush • Slowly Down the Ganges

MIDDLE EAST & CENTRAL ASIA Bahrain, Kuwait & Qatar • Central Asia • Central Asia phrasebook • Dubai • Farsi (Persian) phrasebook • Hebrew phrasebook • Iran • Israel & the Palestinian Territories • Istanbul • Istanbul City Map • Istanbul to Cairo • Istanbul to Kathmandu • Jerusalem • Jerusalem City Map • Jordan • Lebanon • Middle East • Oman & the United Arab Emirates • Syria • Turkey • Turkish phrasebook • World Food Turkey • Yemen **Travel Literature:** Black on Black: Iran Revisited • Breaking Ranks: Turbulent Travels in the Promised Land • The Gates of Damascus • Kingdom of the Film Stars: Journey into Jordan

NORTH AMERICA Alaska • Boston • Boston City Map • Boston Condensed • British Columbia • California & Nevada • California Condensed • Canada • Chicago • Chicago City Map • Chicago Condensed • Florida • Georgia & the Carolinas • Great Lakes • Hawaii • Hiking in Alaska • Hiking in the USA • Honolulu & Oahu City Map • Las Vegas • Los Angeles • Los Angeles City Map • Louisiana & the Deep South • Miami • Miami City Map • Montreal • New England • New Orleans • New Orleans City Map • New York City • New York City City Map • New York City Condensed • New York, New Jersey & Pennsylvania • Oahu • Out to Eat – San Francisco • Pacific Northwest • Rocky Mountains • San Diego & Tijuana • San Francisco • San Francisco City Map • Seattle • Seattle City Map • Southwest • Texas • Toronto • USA • USA phrasebook • Vancouver • Vancouver City Map • Virginia & the Capital Region • Washington, DC • Washington, DC City Map • World Food New Orleans **Travel Literature**: Caught Inside: A Surfer's Year on the California Coast • Drive Thru America

NORTH-EAST ASIA Beijing • Beijing City Map • Cantonese phrasebook • China • Hiking in Japan • Hong Kong & Macau • Hong Kong City Map • Hong Kong Condensed • Japan • Japanese phrasebook • Korea • Korean phrasebook • Kyoto • Mandarin phrasebook • Mongolia • Mongolian phrasebook • Seoul • Shanghai • South-West China • Taiwan • Tokyo • Tokyo Condensed • World Food Hong Kong • World Food Japan **Travel Literature:** In Xanadu: A Quest • Lost Japan

SOUTH AMERICA Argentina, Uruguay & Paraguay • Bolivia • Brazil • Brazilian phrasebook • Buenos Aires • Buenos Aires City Map • Chile & Easter Island • Colombia • Ecuador & the Galapagos Islands • Healthy Travel Central & South America • Latin American Spanish phrasebook • Peru • Quechua phrasebook • Read This First: Central & South America • Rio de Janeiro • Rio de Janeiro City Map • Santiago de Chile • South America on a shoestring • Trekking in the Patagonian Andes • Venezuela **Travel Literature**: Full Circle: A South American Journey

SOUTH-EAST ASIA Bali & Lombok • Bangkok • Bangkok City Map • Burmese phrasebook • Cambodia • Cycling Vietnam, Laos & Cambodia • East Timor phrasebook • Hanoi • Healthy Travel Asia & India • Hill Tribes phrasebook • Ho Chi Minh City (Saigon) • Indonesia • Indonesian phrasebook • Indonesia's Eastern Islands • Java • Lao phrasebook • Laos • Malay phrasebook • Malaysia, Singapore & Brunei • Myanmar (Burma) • Philippines • Pilipino (Tagalog) phrasebook • Read This First: Asia & India • Singapore • Singapore City Map • South-East Asia on a shoestring • South-East Asia phrasebook • Thailand • Thailand's Islands & Beaches • Thailand, Vietnam, Laos & Cambodia Road Atlas • Thai phrasebook • Vietnam • Vietnamese phrasebook • World Food Indonesia • World Food Thailand • World Food Vietnam

ALSO AVAILABLE: Antarctica • The Arctic • The Blue Man: Tales of Travel, Love and Coffee • Brief Encounters: Stories of Love, Sex & Travel • Buddhist Stupas in Asia: The Shape of Perfection • Chasing Rickshaws • The Last Grain Race • Lonely Planet ... On the Edge: Adventurous Escapades from Around the World • Lonely Planet Unpacked • Lonely Planet Unpacked Again • Not the Only Planet: Science Fiction Travel Stories • Ports of Call: A Journey by Sea • Sacred India • Travel Photography: A Guide to Taking Better Pictures • Travel with Children • Tuvalu: Portrait of an Island Nation

Index

Text

Bold indicates maps.

Bold indicates maps.

Places to Stay

Places to Eat

Boxed Text

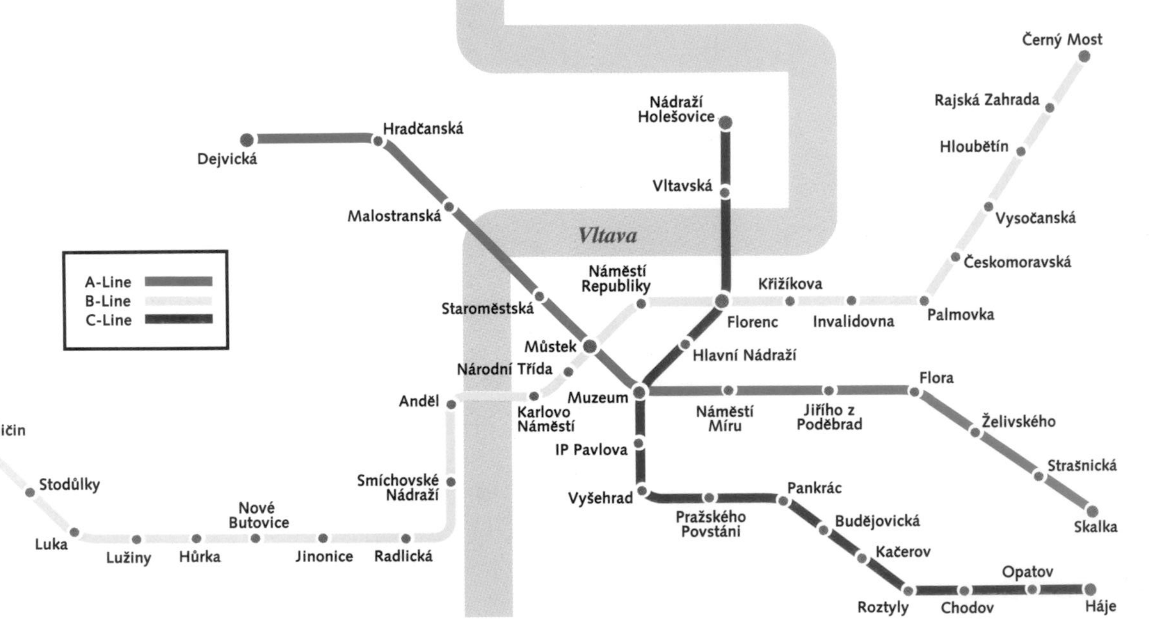
Černý Most
Rajská Zahrada
Hloubětín
Vysočanská
Českomoravská
Palmovka
Invalidovna
Křižíkova
Florenc
Hlavní Nádraží
Nádraží Holešovice
Vltavská
Vltava
Náměstí Republiky
Můstek
Národní Třída
Karlovo Náměstí
Muzeum
IP Pavlova
Vyšehrad
Flora
Želivského
Strašnická
Skalka
Jiřího z Poděbrad
Náměstí Míru
Pražského Povstáni
Pankrác
Budějovická
Kačerov
Roztyly
Chodov
Opatov
Háje
Dejvická
Hradčanská
Malostranská
Staroměstská
Anděl
Smíchovské Nádraží
Radlická
Jinonice
Nové Butovice
Hůrka
Lužiny
Luka
Stodůlky
Zličin
A-Line
B-Line
C-Line

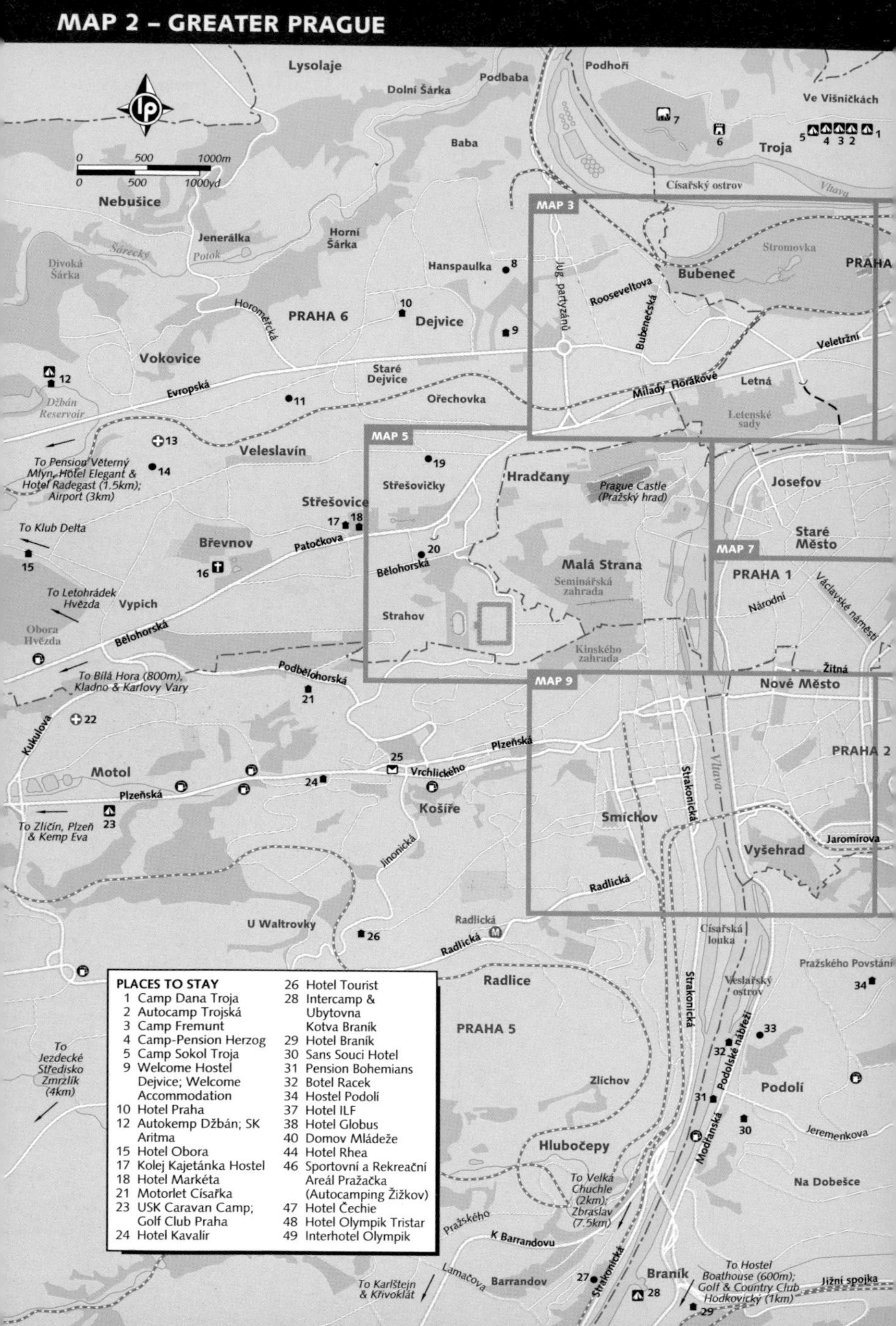

MAP 2 – GREATER PRAGUE
0 500 1000m
0 500 1000yd
Lysolaje
Dolní Šárka
Podbaba
Podhoří
Ve Višničkách
Baba
Troja
5 4 3 2 1
7
6
Císařský ostrov
Vltava
Nebušice
Jenerálka
Šárecký
Potok
Horní Šárka
Divoká Šárka
Hanspaulka
8
MAP 3
Jug. partyzánů
Roosveltova
Bubenečská
Bubeneč
Stromovka
PRAHA
Horoměřická
PRAHA 6
10
Dejvice
9
Veletržní
Vokovice
12
Staré Dejvice
Evropská
Milady Horákové
Letná
Džbán Reservoir
11
Ořechovka
Letenské sady
MAP 5
13
Veleslavín
19
Hradčany
Prague Castle (Pražský hrad)
Josefov
To Pension Větrný Mlýn, Hotel Elegant & Hotel Radegast (1.5km); Airport (3km)
14
Střešovičky
Střešovice
17
18
Staré Město
To Klub Delta
Břevnov
Patočkova
20
MAP 7
15
16
Bělohorská
Malá Strana
PRAHA 1
Seminářská zahrada
Národní
Václavské náměstí
To Letohrádek Hvězda
Vypich
Obora Hvězda
Strahov
Bělohorská
Kinského zahrada
Žitná
To Bílá Hora (800m), Kladno & Karlovy Vary
Podbělohorská
MAP 9
Nové Město
21
22
Kukulova
Plzeňská
PRAHA 2
25
Motol
Vrchlického
24
Plzeňská
Košíře
Strakonická
Vltava
To Zličín, Plzeň & Kemp Eva
23
Smíchov
Jaromírova
Vyšehrad
Jinonická
Radlická
U Waltrovky
Radlická
26
Radlická
Císařská louka
Radlice
Pražského Povstání
Veslařský ostrov
34
PLACES TO STAY
1 Camp Dana Troja
2 Autocamp Trojská
3 Camp Fremunt
4 Camp-Pension Herzog
5 Camp Sokol Troja
9 Welcome Hostel Dejvice; Welcome Accommodation
10 Hotel Praha
12 Autokemp Džbán; SK Aritma
15 Hotel Obora
17 Kolej Kajetánka Hostel
18 Hotel Markéta
21 Motorlet Císařka
23 USK Caravan Camp; Golf Club Praha
24 Hotel Kavalír
26 Hotel Tourist
28 Intercamp & Ubytovna Kotva Braník
29 Hotel Braník
30 Sans Souci Hotel
31 Pension Bohemians
32 Botel Racek
34 Hostel Podolí
37 Hotel ILF
38 Hotel Globus
40 Domov Mládeže
44 Hotel Rhea
46 Sportovní a Rekreační Areál Pražačka (Autocamping Žižkov)
47 Hotel Čechie
48 Hotel Olympik Tristar
49 Interhotel Olympik
PRAHA 5
Strakonická
33
32
Podolské nábřeží
To Jezdecké Středisko Zmrzlík (4km)
Zlíchov
Podolí
31
Modřanská
30
Jeremenkova
Hlubočepy
To Velká Chuchle (2km); Zbraslav (7.5km)
Na Dobešce
Pražského
K Barrandovu
Strakonická
Lamačova
Barrandov
27
Braník
28
To Hostel Boathouse (600m); Golf & Country Club Hodkovický (1km)
Jižní spojka
To Karlštejn & Křivoklát
29

MAP 2 – GREATER PRAGUE

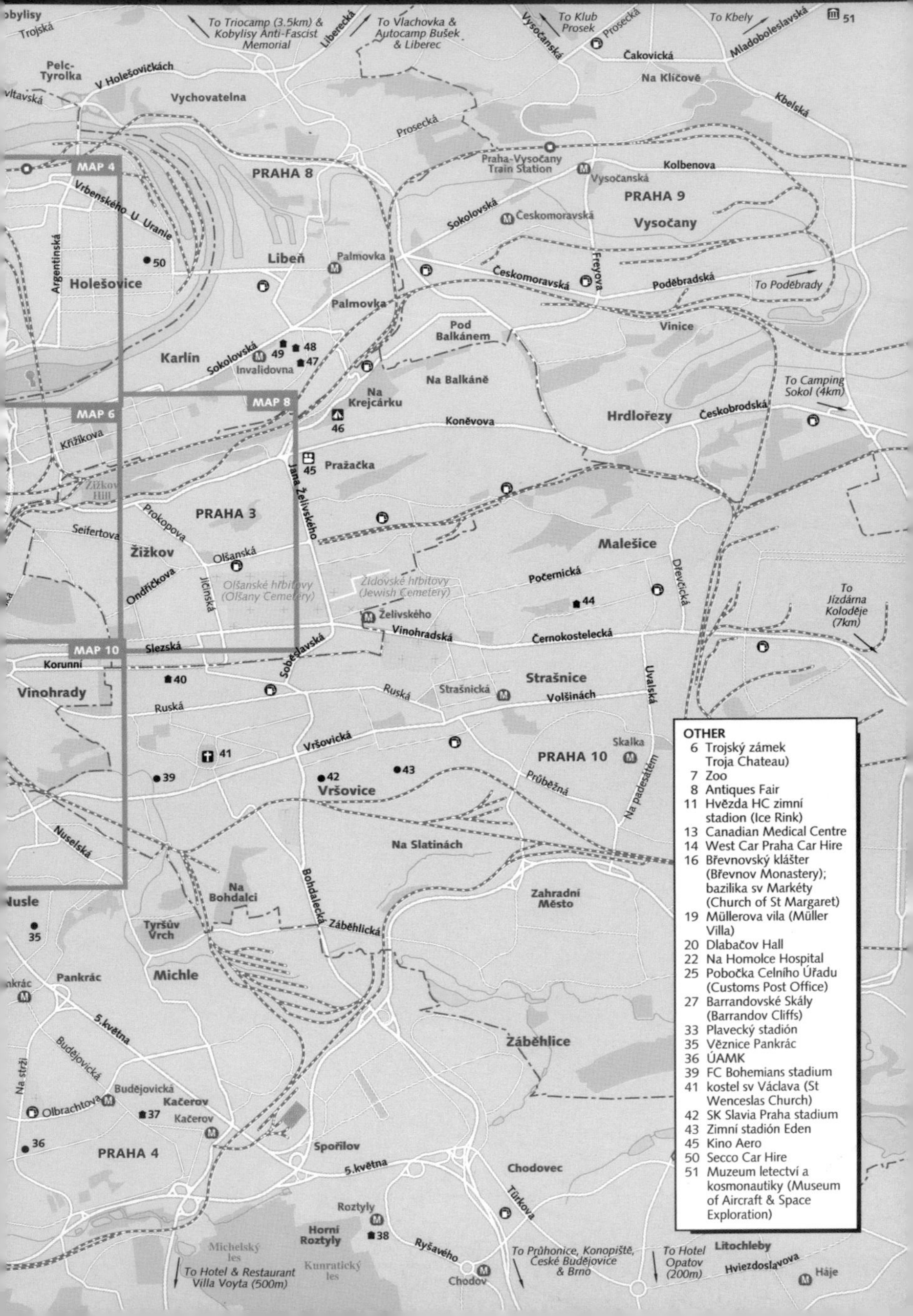

OTHER

6 Trojský zámek Troja Chateau)
7 Zoo
8 Antiques Fair
11 Hvězda HC zimní stadion (Ice Rink)
13 Canadian Medical Centre
14 West Car Praha Car Hire
16 Břevnovský klášter (Břevnov Monastery); bazilika sv Markéty (Church of St Margaret)
19 Müllerova vila (Müller Villa)
20 Dlabačov Hall
22 Na Homolce Hospital
25 Pobočka Celního Úřadu (Customs Post Office)
27 Barrandovské Skály (Barrandov Cliffs)
33 Plavecký stadión
35 Věznice Pankrác
36 ÚAMK
39 FC Bohemians stadium
41 kostel sv Václava (St Wenceslas Church)
42 SK Slavia Praha stadium
43 Zimní stadión Eden
45 Kino Aero
50 Secco Car Hire
51 Muzeum letectví a kosmonautiky (Museum of Aircraft & Space Exploration)

MAP 3

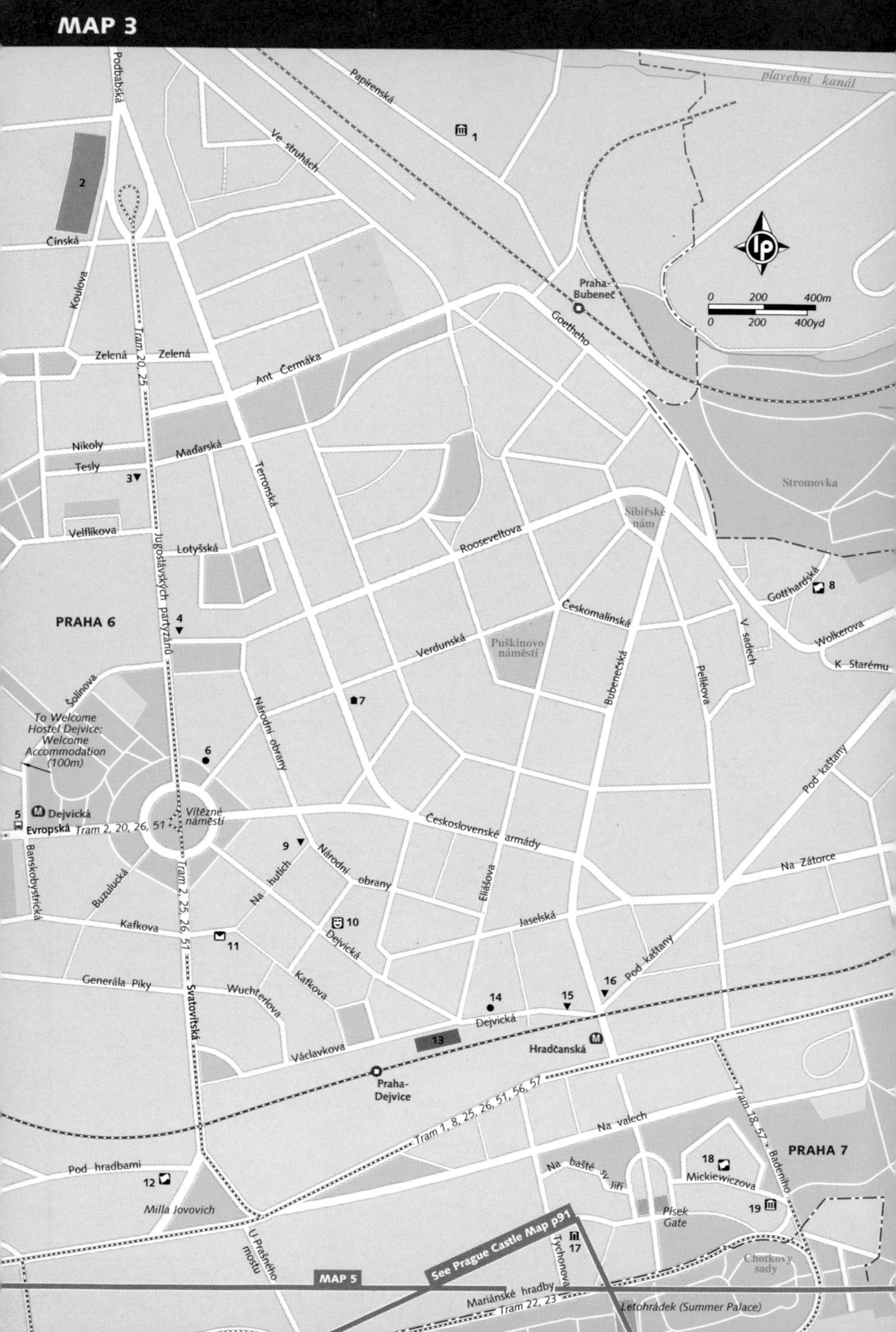

Podbabská
Papírenská
plavební kanál
Ve struhách
Čínská
Koulova
Zelená
Zelená
Ant Čermáka
Tram 20, 25
Nikoly Tesly
Maďarská
Terronská
Velflíkova
Lotyšská
Jugoslávských partyzánů
Rooseveltova
Praha-Bubeneč
Goetheho
Stromovka
Sibiřské nám
Gotthardská
Českomalínská
Verdunská
Puškinovo náměstí
Wolkerova
K Starému
V sadech
Pelléova
Bubenečská
PRAHA 6
Šolínova
To Welcome Hostel Dejvice; Welcome Accommodation (100m)
Národní obrany
Pod kaštany
Dejvická
Evropská
Tram 2, 20, 26, 51
Vítězné náměstí
Československé armády
Banskobystrická
Buzulucká
Na hutích
Národní obrany
Tram 2, 25, 26, 51
Ellášova
Na Zátorce
Kafkova
Jaselská
Dejvická
Generála Piky
Svatovítská
Wuchterlova
Kafkova
Pod kaštany
Dejvická
Hradčanská
Václavkova
Praha-Dejvice
Tram 1, 8, 25, 26, 51, 56, 57
Na valech
Tram 18, 57
PRAHA 7
Badeniho
Pod hradbami
Na baště sv Jiří
Mickiewiczova
Milla Jovovich
Písek Gate
U Prašného mostu
See Prague Castle Map p91
Tychonova
Chotkovy sady
MAP 5
Mariánské hradby
Tram 22, 23
Letohrádek (Summer Palace)
0 200 400m
0 200 400yd
1 2 3 4 5 6 7 8 9 10 11 12 13 14 15 16 17 18 19

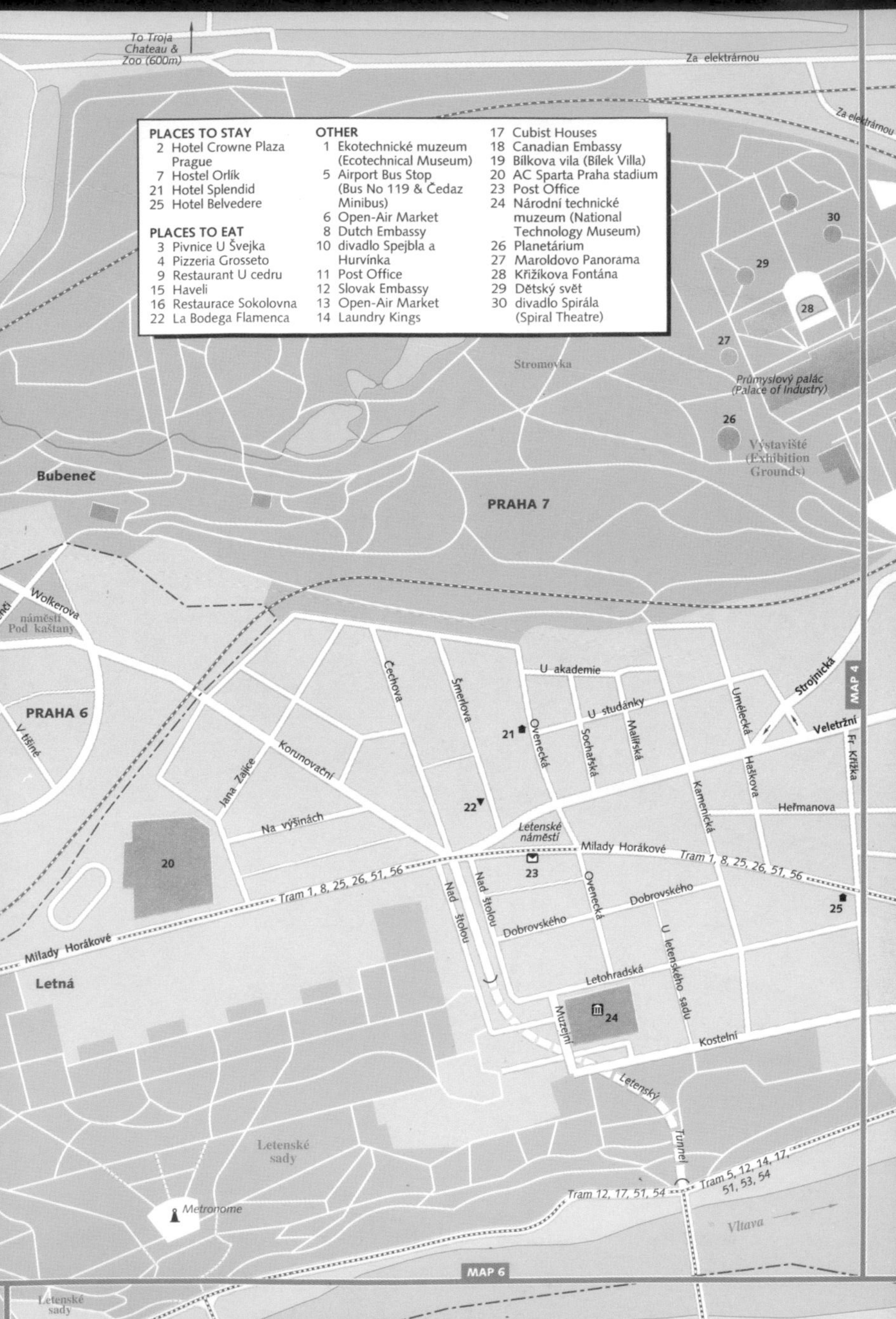

PLACES TO STAY
2 Hotel Crowne Plaza Prague
7 Hostel Orlík
21 Hotel Splendid
25 Hotel Belvedere
PLACES TO EAT
3 Pivnice U Švejka
4 Pizzeria Grosseto
9 Restaurant U cedru
15 Haveli
16 Restaurace Sokolovna
22 La Bodega Flamenca
OTHER
1 Ekotechnické muzeum (Ecotechnical Museum)
5 Airport Bus Stop (Bus No 119 & Čedaz Minibus)
6 Open-Air Market
8 Dutch Embassy
10 divadlo Spejbla a Hurvínka
11 Post Office
12 Slovak Embassy
13 Open-Air Market
14 Laundry Kings
17 Cubist Houses
18 Canadian Embassy
19 Bílkova vila (Bílek Villa)
20 AC Sparta Praha stadium
23 Post Office
24 Národní technické muzeum (National Technology Museum)
26 Planetárium
27 Maroldovo Panorama
28 Křižíkova Fontána
29 Dětský svět
30 divadlo Spirála (Spiral Theatre)
To Troja Chateau & Zoo (600m)
Za elektrárnou
Stromovka
Průmyslový palác (Palace of Industry)
Výstaviště (Exhibition Grounds)
Bubeneč
PRAHA 7
PRAHA 6
Wolkerova
náměstí Pod kaštany
V tišině
U akademie
Strojnická
U studánky
Čechova
Šmeralova
Ovenecká
Sochařská
Malířská
Umělecká
Haškova
Veletržní
Fr Křížka
Korunovační
Jana Zajíce
Na výšinách
Kamenická
Heřmanova
Letenské náměstí
Milady Horákové
Tram 1, 8, 25, 26, 51, 56
Nad štolou
Dobrovského
U letenského sadu
Letohradská
Muzejní
Kostelní
Letenský Tunnel
Letná
Letenské sady
Metronome
Tram 12, 17, 51, 54
Tram 5, 12, 14, 17, 51, 53, 54
Vltava
MAP 4
MAP 6

RICHARD NEBESKÝ
Snow-sprinkled rooftops in Malá Strana

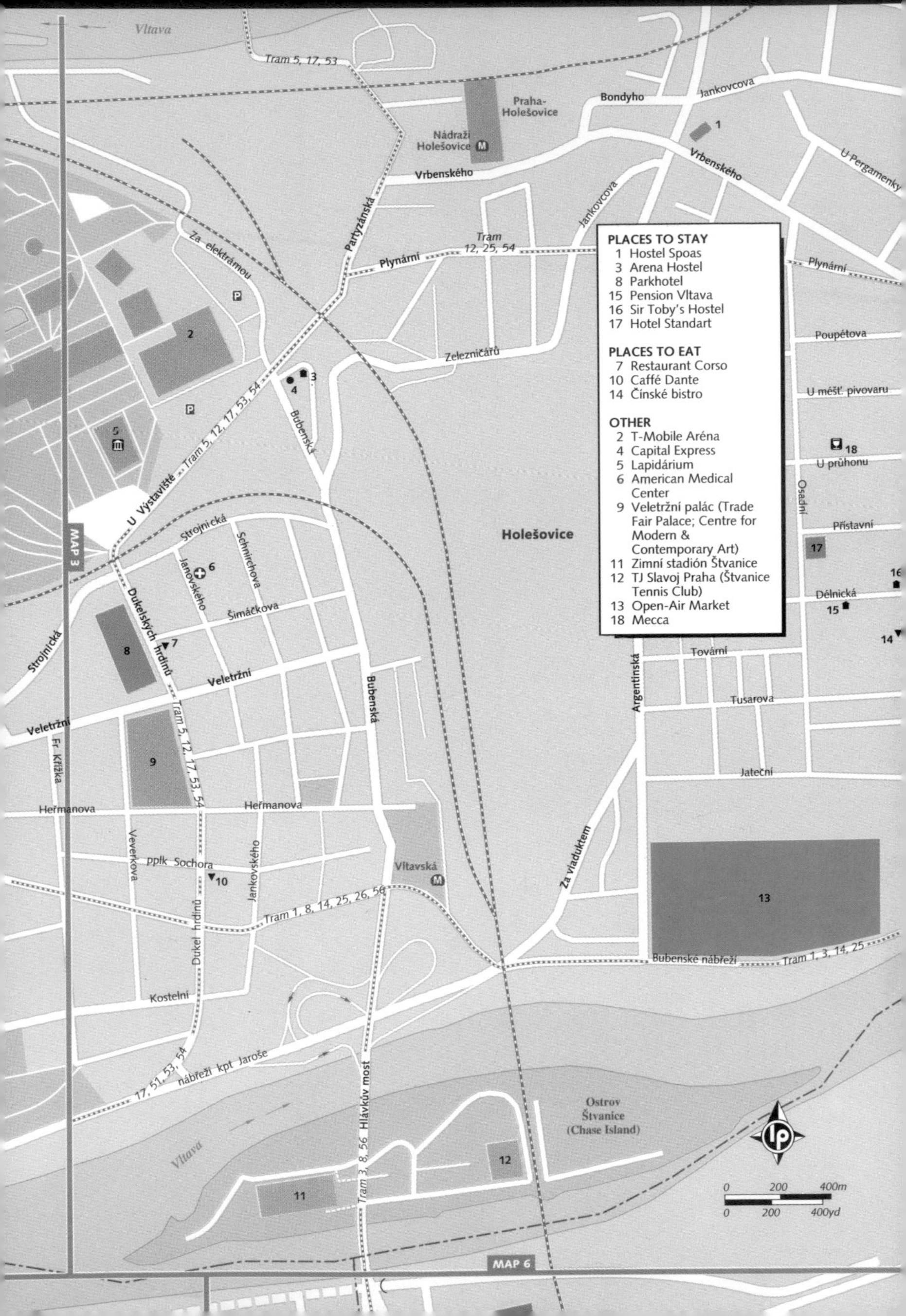

PLACES TO STAY
1 Hostel Spoas
3 Arena Hostel
8 Parkhotel
15 Pension Vltava
16 Sir Toby's Hostel
17 Hotel Standart
PLACES TO EAT
7 Restaurant Corso
10 Caffé Dante
14 Čínské bistro
OTHER
2 T-Mobile Aréna
4 Capital Express
5 Lapidárium
6 American Medical Center
9 Veletržní palác (Trade Fair Palace; Centre for Modern & Contemporary Art)
11 Zimní stadión Štvanice
12 TJ Slavoj Praha (Štvanice Tennis Club)
13 Open-Air Market
18 Mecca
Vltava
Tram 5, 17, 53
Praha-Holešovice
Nádraží Holešovice
Bondyho
Jankovcova
Vrbenského
U Pergamenky
Partyzánská
Za elektrárnou
Plynární
Tram 12, 25, 54
Poupětova
Železničářů
U měšť. pivovaru
Bubenská
U průhonu
Osadní
U Výstaviště
Tram 5, 12, 17, 53, 54
Holešovice
Přístavní
Strojnická
Schnirchova
Janovského
Délnická
Šimáčkova
Dukelských hrdinů
Továrni
Veletržní
Argentinská
Tusarova
Fr. Křížka
Jateční
Heřmanova
Veverkova
pplk Sochora
Jankovského
Vltavská
Za viaduktem
Tram 1, 8, 14, 25, 26, 56
Dukel. hrdinů
Bubenské nábřeží
Tram 1, 3, 14, 25
Kostelní
nábřeží kpt Jaroše
17, 51, 53, 54
Hlávkův most
Tram 3, 8, 56
Ostrov Štvanice (Chase Island)
MAP 3
MAP 6
0 200 400m
0 200 400yd

MAP 5

PLACES TO STAY

2 Romantik Hotel U raka
7 Domus Henrici
9 Hotel U krále Karla
12 Hotel Neruda
25 Hotel & Restaurant U Zlaté studně
31 Hotel Hoffmeister
34 Hotel U Páva
41 Hotel U červené sklenice
42 Hotel Café Dvořák
45 Hotel U tří pštrosů
56 Travellers' Hostel Josefská
67 Hotel Sax
90 Travellers' Hostel Újezd
95 Hostel Sokol
98 Best Western Hotel Kampa
107 Travellers' Hostel Island
109 Hotel Julián
114 Hostel SPUS
115 Welcome Hostel Strahov
117 Hostel ESTEC
122 Hotel Coubertin

PLACES TO EAT

3 U zlaté hrušky
8 U Stoletýho Café
15 U zeleného čaje
21 Hostinec U kocoura
22 Café Bio Life
27 Restaurace Pálffy Palác Club
33 Pasha
35 Vinárna Čertovka
36 Kampa Park
47 Vacek Bio-Market
52 U malířů
53 U Maltézských rytířů
59 Jo's Bar & Garaž
60 J+J Mašek & Zemanová
61 St Nicholas Café
64 Circle Line Brasserie
75 Malý Buddha
76 Sate
79 Restaurant Peklo
88 Restaurant Nebozízek
94 U modré kachničky
97 Restaurace Bar Bar
99 Rybářský klub
103 Bohemia Bagel
104 Sushi Bar
105 Café Savoy
106 Ostroff
108 Meduzzy
113 Café Himalaya

OTHER

1 muzeum MHD (Public Transport Museum)
4 Šternberský palác (Sternberg Palace)
5 Arcibiskupský palác (Archbishop's Palace)
6 Švarcenberský palác (Schwarzenberg Palace); Vojenské historické muzeum (Museum of Military History)
10 U dvou slunců (House of Two Suns)
11 Bretfeld Palace
13 dům U zlaté podkovy (House of the Golden Horseshoe)
14 Expozica Historických lékáren (Museum of Historical Pharmacies)
16 kostel Panny Marie ustavičné pomoci (Church of Our Lady of Unceasing Succour)
17 U krále Brabantského
18 House of St John of Nepomuk
19 dům U tří housliček (House of the Three Fiddles)
20 Liechtenstein Palace
23 British Embassy
24 Sněmovna (Parliament House)
26 Pedagogické muzeum JA Komenského (Pedagogical Museum of JA Comenius)
28 Valdštejnský palác (Wallenstein Palace)
29 Main Entrance to Palácový zahrady pod Pražským hradem (Palace Gardens Beneath Prague Castle)
30 Polish Embassy
32 Valdštejnská jízdárna (Wallenstein Riding School)
37 Water Wheel
38 Prague Venice (Boat Trips)
39 Children's Playground
40 PPS Boat Landing
43 French Embassy
44 John Lennon Wall
46 Malostranská mostecká věž (Malá Strana Bridge Tower); Prague Information Service (PIS)
48 Zanzi bar
49 kostel Panny Marie pod řetězem (Church of Our Lady Below the Chain)
50 U Zlatého hada
51 Česká hračká
54 Kino 64 U hradeb
55 Post Office
57 Malostranská beseda (Former Town Hall)
58 kostel sv Mikuláše (St Nicholas Church)
62 U Malého Glena
63 Irish Embassy
65 US Embassy
66 Police Station
68 German Embassy
69 Children's Playground
70 Loreta
71 klášter Kapucínů (Capuchin Monastery)
72 Černínský palác (Černín Palace)
73 Tram Stop (Nos 22 & 23)
74 Pivnice U Černého vola
77 Hradčany Tennis Courts
78 Esquo Squashcentrum
80 Strahovská knihovna (Strahov Library); Museum of Czech Literature
81 Strahovská obrazárna (Strahov Picture Gallery)
82 Strahovský klášter (Strahov Monastery of Our Lady)
83 kostel Nanebevzetí Panny Marie (Church of the Assumption of Our Lady)
84 Petřínská rozhledna (Petřín Tower)
85 Bludiště (The Maze)
86 kostel sv Vavřince (Church of St Lawrence)
87 Štefánikova hvězdárna (Štefánik Observatory)
89 Statue of Karel Hynek Mácha
91 Prague Spring Box Office
92 kostel Panny Marie Vítězné (Church of Our Lady Victorious); muzeum Pražského Jezulátka (Museum of the Infant Jesus of Prague)
93 Prague Center for Further Education
96 Sport Slivka
100 kostel sv Jana Na prádle (Church of St John at the Laundry)
101 Pop Museum
102 Klub Újezd
110 Mapis Map Shop
111 Children's Playground
112 kostel sv Michala (Church of St Michael)
116 Klub 007 Strahov
118 Esquo Relax Club
119 Bus Stop (Nos 143, 149 & 217)
120 Strahov stadium
121 Bus Stop (No 176)
123 SK Slavia Praha stadium

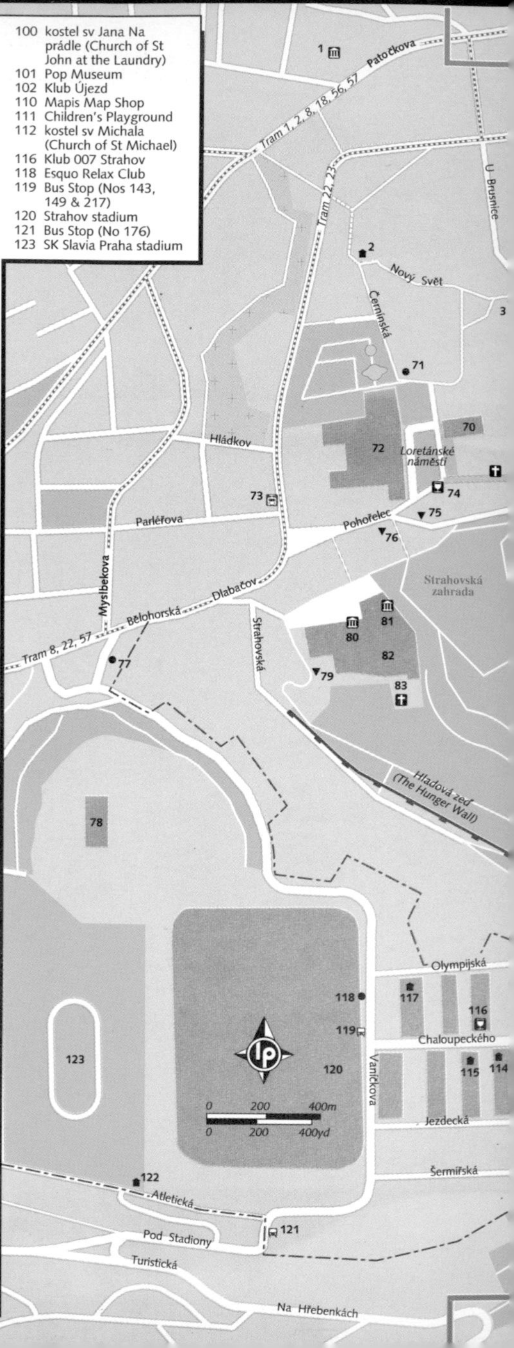

Patočkova
Tram 1, 2, 8, 18, 56, 57
Tram 22, 23
U Brusnice
Nový Svět
Černínská
Hládkov
Loretánské náměstí
Parléřova
Pohořelec
Strahovská zahrada
Myslbekova
Bělohorská
Dlabačov
Tram 8, 22, 57
Strahovská
Hladová zeď (The Hunger Wall)
Olympijská
Chaloupeckého
Vaníčkova
Jezdecká
Šermířská
Atletická
Pod Stadiony
Turistická
Na Hřebenkách
0 200 400m
0 200 400yd

MAP 3
MAP 7
MAP 6
MAP 9
See Prague Castle Map p91
Hradčany
Malá Strana
Petřín Hill
Klárov
PRAHA 1
Královská zahrada
Ball-Game House
Stag Moat (Jelení příkop)
Brusnice
Pražský hrad (Prague Castle)
Zahrada Na Valech
Summer Palace
Chotkovy Sady
Letenské sady
Old Castle Steps
Palácový zahrady pod Pražským hradem (Palace Gardens Beneath Prague Castle)
Valdštejnské náměstí
Valdštejnská zahrada
Vojanovy sady
Hradčanské náměstí
Malostranské náměstí
Dražického náměstí
Velkopřerovské náměstí
Maltézské náměstí
Vrtbovská zahrada
Schönbornská zahrada
Lobkovická zahrada
Seminářská zahrada
Petřínské sady
Růžový sad
Kinského zahrada
Kampa
Na Kampě
Čertovka
Vltava
U Sovových mlýnů
Střelecký ostrov (Marksmen's Island)
Dětský ostrov (Children's Island)
Charles Bridge (Karlův most)
Mánesův most
most Legií
Funicular Railway
U lanové dráhy
náměstí Kinských
Mariánské hradby
Tram 22, 23
Tram 18, 22, 23, 57
Tram 12 nábřeží Edvarda Beneše
Tram 18
Tram 12, 22, 23, 57
Tram 6, 9, 22, 23, 57, 58
Jelení
U Prašného mostu
Pod Bruskou
Chotkova
Malostranská
Valdštejnská
Klárov
Kosárkovo nábřeží
Letenská
Tomášská
Sněmovní
Thunovská
Zámecké schody
Ke Hradu
Loretánská
Úvoz
Nerudova
U kasáren
Šporkova
Vlašská
Tržiště
Mostecká
Josefská
Míšeňská
U lužického semináře
Cihelná
Lázeňská
Saská
Prokopská
Karmelitská
Harantova
Nebovidská
Nosticova
Hellichova
Újezd
Všehrdova
Říční
Besední
Vítězná
Plaská
Mělnická
Petřínská
Zborovská
Janáčkovo nábřeží
Holečkova
Vodní
Malátova
Elišky Peškové
Štefánikova
Kroftova
Drtinova
Zubatého
1 2 3 4 5 6 7 8 9 10 11 12 13 14 15 16 17 18 19 20 21 22 23 24 25 26 27 28 29 30 31 32 33 34 35 36 37 38 39 40 41 42 43 44 45 46 47 48 49 50 51 52 53 54 55 56 57 58 59 60 61 62 63 64 65 66 67 68 69
84 85 86 87 88 89 90 91 92 93 94 95 96 97 98 99 100 101 102 103 104 105 106 107 108 109 110 111 112 113

MAP 3
MAP 5
MAP 7
MAP 9
Letenské sady
nábřeží Edvarda Beneše
Tram 12
Čechův most
Tram 17, 51, 54
Na Františku
nábřeží Ludvíka Svobody
Klášterská
Řásnovka
Tram 5, 8, 14, 53
Nové mlýny
Klimentská
U milosrdných
Josefov
Dušní
Kozí
U obecního dvora
Haštalské náměstí
Haštalská
Hradební
Bílkova
Soukenická
Dlouhá
Eližky Krásnohorské
Revoluční
Truhlářská
Klárov
Dvořákovo nábřeží
Kosárkovo nábřeží
Vltava
Starý židovský hřbitov (Old Jewish Cemetery)
Maiselova
Široká
Rybná
Benediktská
Mánesův most
Tram 18
17.listopadu
náměstí Jana Palacha
Dlouhá
Masná
Pařížská
Malá Štupartská
náměstí Republiky
Alšovo nábřeží
Staroměstská
Kaprova
Valentinská
Žatecká
Týnská
Jakubská
Králodvorská
U Obecního domu
V celnici
Náměstí Republiky
Křižovnická
Old Town Square (Staroměstské náměstí)
Štupartská
Platnéřská
Mariánské náměstí
Linhartská
Celetná
Hybernská
Charles Bridge (Karlův most)
Staré Město
Železná
Ovocný trh (Former Fruit Market)
Na příkopě
Senovážná
Karlova
Melantrichova
Havířská
Liliová
Jilská
Michalská
Nekázanka
Panská
Betlémské náměstí
Husova
Havelská
Provaznická
Na můstku
Můstek
Náprstkova
Rytířská
Uhelný trh
Skořepka
Betlémská
Karoliny Světlé
Konviktská
Perlová
28.října
Jungmannovo náměstí
Wenceslas Sq
V cípu
Jindřišská
Politických vězňů
Růžová
U půjčovny
Martinská
Na Perštýně
Bartolomějská
PRAHA 1
Můstek
Divadelní
Smetanovo nábřeží
Frantíškánská zahrada
(Václavské náměstí)
Národní třída
Tram 6, 9, 18, 21, 22, 23, 51, 54, 57
Mikulandská
Národní Třída
Voršilská
Purkyňova
Palackého
Nové Město
Tram 3, 9, 14, 24, 52, 53, 55, 56
Lucerna Palace
Ostrovní
Jungmannova
Vladislavova
Vodičkova
V jámě
Školská
Štěpánská
Muzeum
Tram 17, 21
Na struze
V jirchářích
Opatovická
Křemencova
Spálená
M Rettigové
Lazarská
Ve Smečkách
Krakovská
Mezibranská
Šítkova
Slovanský ostrov (Žofín)
Masarykovo nábřeží
Vojtěšská
Pštrossova
Černá
Ordinace dinářů
Navrátilova
Řeznická
Příčná
Myslíkova
Odborů
Na zbořenci
Karlovo náměstí
Žitná
Legerova
Anglická
0 200 400m
0 200 400yd

MAP 4
MAP 7
MAP 8
MAP 10
Karlín
Nové Město
Žižkov
Pobřežní
Sokolovská
Tram 8, 24, 52
Klimentská
Barvířská
Samcova
Mlynářská
Těšnov
Tram 3, 26, 56
Petrské náměstí
Biskupská
Zlatnická
Na poříčí
Tram 3, 8, 24, 26, 52, 56
Florenc
Ke Štvanici
Za Poříčskou bránou
Křižíkova
Prvního pluku
Vítkova
Karlínské náměstí
Peckova
Kollárova
Pernerova
Mařího
Havlíčkova
Na Florenci
Náměstí Republiky
Masarykovo nádraží
Wilsonova
Trocnovská
U památníku
Žižkov Hill (Vítkov)
Husitská
Řehořova
Orebitská
Husinecká
Seifertova
Tram 5, 9, 26, 55
Cimburkova
Štítného
Dlážděná
Senovážné náměstí
Opletalova
Jeruzalémská
Italská
U Rajské zahrady
Havelkova
Hlavní Nádraží
Praha hlavní nádraží (Main Train Station)
Vrchlického sady
Washingtonova
U divadla
Rajská zahrada
Vlkova
Krásova
Víta Nejedlého
Bořivojova
Kubelíkova
Ježkova
Křížkovského
Fibichova
Slavíkova
Chopinova
Riegrovy sady
Mahlerovy sady
Španělská
Helénská
Krkonošská
Čerchovská
Vinohradská
Mánesova
Polská
Budečská
Třebízského
U Kanálky
Tram 11
Blanická
Římská
náměstí Jiřího z Poděbrad
Jiřího z Poděbrad
154 153 152 151 150 149 155 156 157 158 159 148 147 146 145 144 143 142 141 160 161 162 163 164 165 166 167 168 169 170 171 172 173 140 139 138 137 136 135 134

MAP 6

PLACES TO STAY

6 Cloister Inn
7 Unitas Pension
16 Hotel U Klenotníka
31 Palace Hotel
34 Grand Hotel Evropa
46 Hotel Adria
91 Hostel Klub Habitat
94 Novomêstský Hotel
106 Radisson SAS Alcron Hotel
126 K+K Hotel Fenix
129 Hotel Andante
132 Pension Museum
143 Vesta Hostel
144 Hotel Esplanade
147 Hostel Jednota; Alfa Tourist Service
149 Hotel Axa
151 Hotel Harmony
153 Hotel Opera
154 Hotel Hilton Prague; Cybex Health Club & Spa
158 Hostel TJ Sokol Karlín
160 Hostel Elf
161 Hotel Ostaš
163 Hotel Victor
164 Hotel Ariston
168 Pension 15
169 Clown & Bard Hostel
172 Švehlova kolej

PLACES TO EAT

1 Bellevue
3 Dobrá čajovna
9 Cafe Konvikt
11 V zátiší
13 Klub architektů
17 Julius Meinl Supermarket
22 Dobrá čajovna
23 El Gaucho
28 Paris-Praha Food Shop
29 Fruits de France
38 East-West
54 Adoni's bufet
57 Tesco
58 Monica cukrárna
60 Káva Káva Káva
63 Restaurace & Pension U Medvídků
65 Café Louvre
71 Restaurant pod Křídlem
77 Kavárna Slavia
83 Hospoda U Nováka
84 Pizzeria Kmotra
96 Italská cukrárna (Ice Cream Shop)
98 Country Life
101 Miyabi
104 Titanic Steak House
105 Break Cafe
108 Branický sklípek
111 Pizzeria Václavka
131 Česká hospoda V Krakovské
134 Taj Mahal
137 Caffé Kaaba
139 Modrá řeka
165 Restaurace Panda Palace
171 Hanil

OTHER

2 KMC (Klub mladých cestovatelû)
4 Drop In Foundation
5 kaple sv Kâí¢e (Chapel of the Holy Cross)
8 kostel sv Barolomêje (St Bartholomew Church)
10 Ňáprstkovo muzeum (Náprstek Museum)
12 Betlémská kaple (Bethlehem Chapel)
14 Keltic Bar
15 Hudy Sport
18 Batalion
19 Police Station
20 Bat'a Shoe Store; Lindt Building; Kanzelsberger Bookshop
21 Peterkûv dûm
24 Western Union
25 Assicurazioni Generali (Kafka's Workplace 1907-08)
26 Beruška Toy Shop
27 Astera Laundrette
30 Muchovo muzeum (Mucha Museum)
32 Main Post Office
33 Krone Department Store; Julius Meinl Supermarket
35 Best Tour
36 Alimex ÀR Car Hire
37 Kanzelsberger Bookshop
39 Cellarius Wine Shop; Ticketpro Melantrich
40 Lucerna Music Bar; Kino Lucerna
41 Milan Škoda Fototechnika PhotoShop
42 Melantrich Building
43 Wiehl House
44 Àeskoslovenská obchodní banka
45 Kino Hvêzda
47 kostel Panny Marie Sněžné (Church of Our Lady of the Snows)
48 Austrian Cultural Institute
49 Adria Palace
50 Supraphon Music Shop
51 Bohemiatour
52 District Clinic; 24-hour Pharmacy
53 Metropolitan Jazz Club
55 Kiwi Map Shop
56 dûm Slovenské kultury
59 Thomas Cook/TravelEx
61 Sauna Babylonia
62 kostel sv Martina ve zdi (Church of St Martin in the Wall)
64 Internet Cafe Prague
66 Reduta Jazz Club; Reduta Theatre; Rock Café
67 Student Memorial
68 Confederation of Czech Industries
69 Fischer Travel Agency
70 British Council
72 klášter sv Voršila (Church & Convent of St Ursula)
73 Poliklinika na Národní
74 Lost & Found Office
75 Viola Building
76 Nová scéna (Laterna Magika)
78 Národní divadlo (National Theatre)
79 Boat Hire
80 Boat Hire
81 Boat Hire
82 Goethe Institut
85 Velryba
86 Holy Trinity Church
87 U Fleků
88 Šitovská věž; Mánes Building & Gallery
89 Artlingua
90 The Globe (Bookshop, Bar & Café)
92 Kino MAT
93 Starožitností Z Križek
95 Novoměstská radnice (New Town Hall & Tower)
97 divadlo Minor
99 Novoměstský pivovar
100 Charles University Information & Advisory Centre (IPC)
102 Institut Français de Prague; Café
103 Cybeteria
107 Jáma
109 CK Srdce Evropy
110 Foto Jan Pazdera
112 GTS International
113 Fotolab
114 DHL
115 Centrum Krásy (Beauty Centre)
116 Kino Jalta
117 ČTK Foto Shop
118 Pečkův palác
119 A-Rent Car/Thrifty Car Hire
120 Bílá Labut' Department Store
121 St Wenceslas Statue
122 Čedok
123 Polish Cultural Centre
124 Memorial to Victims of Communism

MAP 6

125 American Express (AmEx)
127 Union of the Blind and Weak Sighted
128 Činoherní klub (Dramatic Club)
130 AghaRTA Jazz Centrum
133 Národní muzeum (National Museum)
135 Stop City Accommodation
136 Gejzee..r
138 Mary's Travel & Tourist Service
140 Wittmann Tours
141 Radio Free Europe
142 Státní opera Praha (Prague State Opera)
145 Prague Information Service (PIS)
146 Autoklub Bohemia Assistance
148 Non-Stop Post Office
150 Bílá Labut' Department Store
152 Petrská Tower
155 Kingscourt Express Coach Stand
156 Muzeum hlavního města Prahy (Museum of the City of Prague)
157 Florenc Bus Station; Bohemia Euroexpress International; Tourbus
159 Armádní muzeum (Army Museum)
162 U Vystřeleného oka
166 FK Viktoria Žižkov stadium
167 Sedm Vlků
170 Palác Akropolis
173 CKM Travel Centre

RICHARD NEBESKÝ

A selection of elegant ways to cross the Vltava

VLADIMIR LIBA

A tram trundles through the city streets.

MAP 7

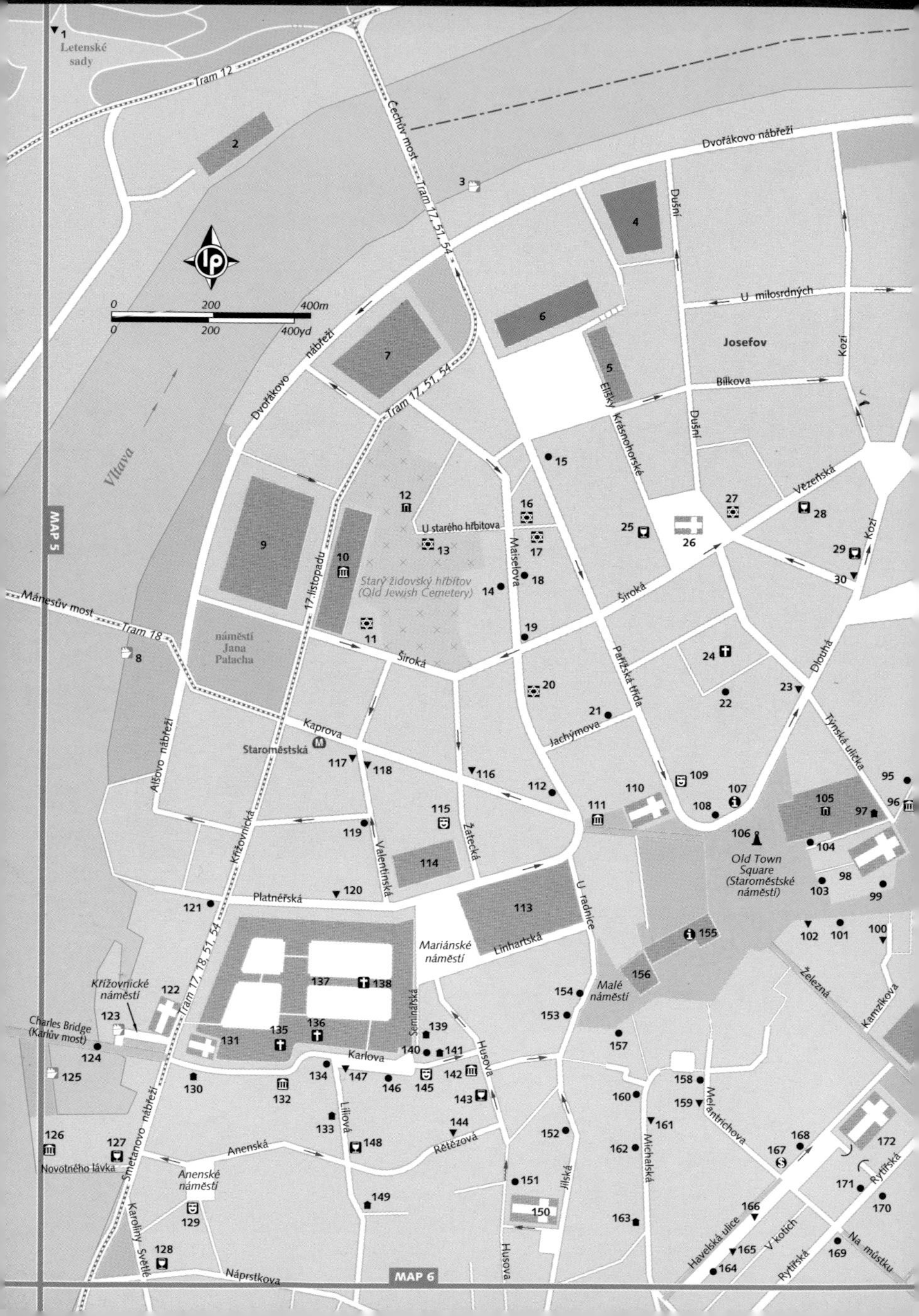

Letenské sady

Tram 12

Čechův most

Tram 17, 51, 54

Dvořákovo nábřeží

Dušní

U milosrdných

Josefov

Kozí

Bílkova

Elišky Krásnohorské

Vltava

Vězeňská

U starého hřbitova

Maiselova

Starý židovský hřbitov (Old Jewish Cemetery)

17.listopadu

Mánesův most

Tram 18

náměstí Jana Palacha

Široká

Pařížská třída

Dlouhá

Týnská ulička

Jachymova

Kaprova

Staroměstská

Alšovo nábřeží

Křižovnická

Valentinská

Žatecká

Platnéřská

U radnice

Old Town Square (Staroměstské náměstí)

Mariánské náměstí

Linhartská

Malé náměstí

Železná

Kamzíkova

Křižovnické náměstí

Tram 17, 18, 51, 54

Charles Bridge (Karlův most)

Seminářská

Karlova

Husova

Liliová

Řetězová

Anenská

Anenské náměstí

Novotného lávka

Smetanovo nábřeží

Karoliny Světlé

Náprstkova

Jilská

Michalská

Melantrichova

Havelská ulice

V kotcích

Rytířská

Na můstku

MAP 5

MAP 6

nábřeží Ludvíka Svobody
Na Františku
Klášterská
Řásnovka
Tram 5, 8, 14, 53
Novomlýnská
Nové mlýny
Klimentská
Barvířská
Samcova
Lodecká
Petrské náměstí
Petrská
Soukenická
Hradební
Haštalská
Haštalské náměstí
Dlouhá
Rámová
Benediktská
Revoluční
Truhlářská
Zlatnická
Rybná
Masná
Malá
Štupartská
Na Poříčí
Tram 3, 8, 24, 26, 52, 56
Havlíčkova
Týnská
Týnský dvůr
Jakubská
Králodvorská
U Obecního domu
náměstí Republiky
Na Florenci
V celnici
Náměstí Republiky
Tram 3, 5, 14, 24, 26, 52, 53, 56
Masarykovo nádraží
Celetná ulice
Hybernská
Staré Město
Ovocný trh (Former Fruit Market)
Rathova pasáž
Na příkopě
Senovážná
Dlážděná
Nové Město
Tram 5, 9, 26, 55, 58
Havířská
Provaznická
Nekázanka ulice
Panská
Jindřišská ulice
Tram 3, 9, 14, 24, 52, 53, 55, 56, 58
Jeruzalémská
Opletalova
Můstek
MAP 6

MAP 7

PLACES TO STAY

4 President Hotel
39 Travellers' Hostel Dlouhá
45 Hotel Casa Marcello
46 Botel Albatros
53 Kolej Petrská
54 Hotel & Kavárna Imperial
58 Renaissance Prague Hotel
59 Atlantic Hotel
70 Hotel Josef
72 Hotel Paříž & Café
74 Hotel Central
77 Grand Hotel Bohemia
81 Hotel Ungelt
85 Hotel Metamorphis
88 Hostel Týn
97 Hotel Černý Slon
130 Hotel U zlatého stromu
133 Pension U Lilie
139 Hotel Clementin
141 Pension U zlaté studny
149 Dům U krále Jiřího; James Joyce Pub
163 Hotel U Staré paní & Jazz Club
207 Juniorhotel Praha; Juniorhostel

PLACES TO EAT

1 Hanavský pavilón
2 River Club
23 Michelské pekářství
30 Bakeshop Praha
31 Supermarket-Deli
32 Bohemia Bagel
33 Rasoi
34 Orange Moon
35 Ariana
41 Dahab
42 Chez Marcel
50 U Góvindy
56 Restaurace Na poříčí
64 Restaurace MD Rettigové
67 U Benedikta
75 Red, Hot & Blues
78 Pivnice Radegast
83 Le Saint-Jacques
89 Cafe-Restaurant Metamorphis
94 Ebel Coffee House
100 Restaurace Snack Bar U Černého slunce
102 Staroměstská restaurace
116 Chléb pečivo
117 Siam-I-San
118 Jalapeňos
120 Lotos
144 Ebel Coffee House
147 Reykjavík
159 Country Life
161 U modré kachničky
165 Safir Grill
166 Open-Air Market
200 Kavárna Obecní dům; Francouzská restaurace
202 Kavárna Arco

OTHER

3 Evropská vodní doprava (EVD) Pier
5 Cubist Apartment Building
6 Hotel Inter-Continental
7 Charles University Law Faculty
8 Boat Hire
9 Rudolfinum; Dvořák Hall
10 Umělecko-průmyslové (Museum of Decorative Arts)
11 Pinkasova synagóga (Pinkas Synagogue)
12 Obřadní síň (Ceremonial Hall)
13 Klauzová synagóga (Klaus Synagogue); Jewish Museum Ticket Office
14 Matana Travel Agency
15 Europcar Car Hire
16 Staronová synagóga (Old-New Synagogue)
17 Vysoká synagóga (High Synagogue)
18 Židovská radnice (Jewish Town Hall)
19 Precious Legacy Tours
20 Maiselova synagóga (Maisel Synagogue)
21 Central European Adventures
22 Ticketpro
24 Church of the Holy Saviour
25 Žíznivý pes
26 Church of the Holy Spirit
27 Španělská synagóga (Spanish Synagogue); Jewish Museum Ticket Office
28 Blatouch
29 Kozička
36 Granát Turnov
37 Eduard Čapek
38 Roxy
40 Kussova Prádelna
43 Molly Malone's
44 klášter sv Anežky (Convent of St Agnes)
47 Petrská vodárenská věž (Petrská Waterworks Tower)
48 Poštovní muzeum (Postal Museum)
49 Australian Consulate
51 GTS International
52 Avis Car Hire
55 Bank of Czechoslovak Legions
57 Hudy Sport
60 Former Headquarters of Workers' Accident Insurance Company (Kafka's Workplace 1908-22)
61 YMCA Sportcentrum
62 ČSA Service Centre
63 Čedaz Airport Minibus Stop
65 Happy House Rentals
66 Bambus
68 Prague Wheelchair Users Organisation
69 Police Station
71 Kotva Department Store
73 FOK Box Office
76 City Bike (Bike Hire)
79 dům U Černé Matky Boží (House of the Black Madonna); České muzeum výtvarných umění (Czech Museum of Fine Arts)
80 divadlo V Celetné (Celetná Theatre); Café Gaspar Kasper
82 Chateau
84 kostel sv Jakuba (St James Church)
86 Big Ben Bookshop
87 American Chamber of Commerce
90 Botanicus
91 Ivana Follová Art & Fashion Gallery
92 Keramika v Ungeltu
93 Anagram Bookshop
95 Bríc á Brac
96 dům U zlatého prstenu (House at the Golden Ring); Prague Municipal Gallery
98 kostel Panny Marie Před Týnem (Church of Our Lady Before Týn)
99 The Three Kings, Kafka's Home 1896-1907
101 Kafka's Home 1888-89
103 Týn School
104 dům U Kamenného Zvonu (House of the Stone Bell)
105 palác Kinských (Kinský Palace)
106 Jan Hus Statue
107 Czech Tourist Authority (ČCCR)
108 American Express
109 Image Theatre
110 kostel sv Mikuláše (St Nicholas Church)
111 Expozice Franze Kafky (Kafka's Birthplace)
112 Jewellery Ametyst
113 City Hall
114 City Library
115 Národní divadlo Marionet (National Marionette Theatre)
119 Starožitnosti Alma
121 Starožitností V Andrie
122 kostel sv Františka Serafinského (Church of St Francis Seraphinus); galerie Křižovníků (Knights of the Cross Gallery)

RICHARD NEBESKÝ

Walking on thin ice: ice hockey on the Vltava under the shadow of Vyšehrad

MAP 8

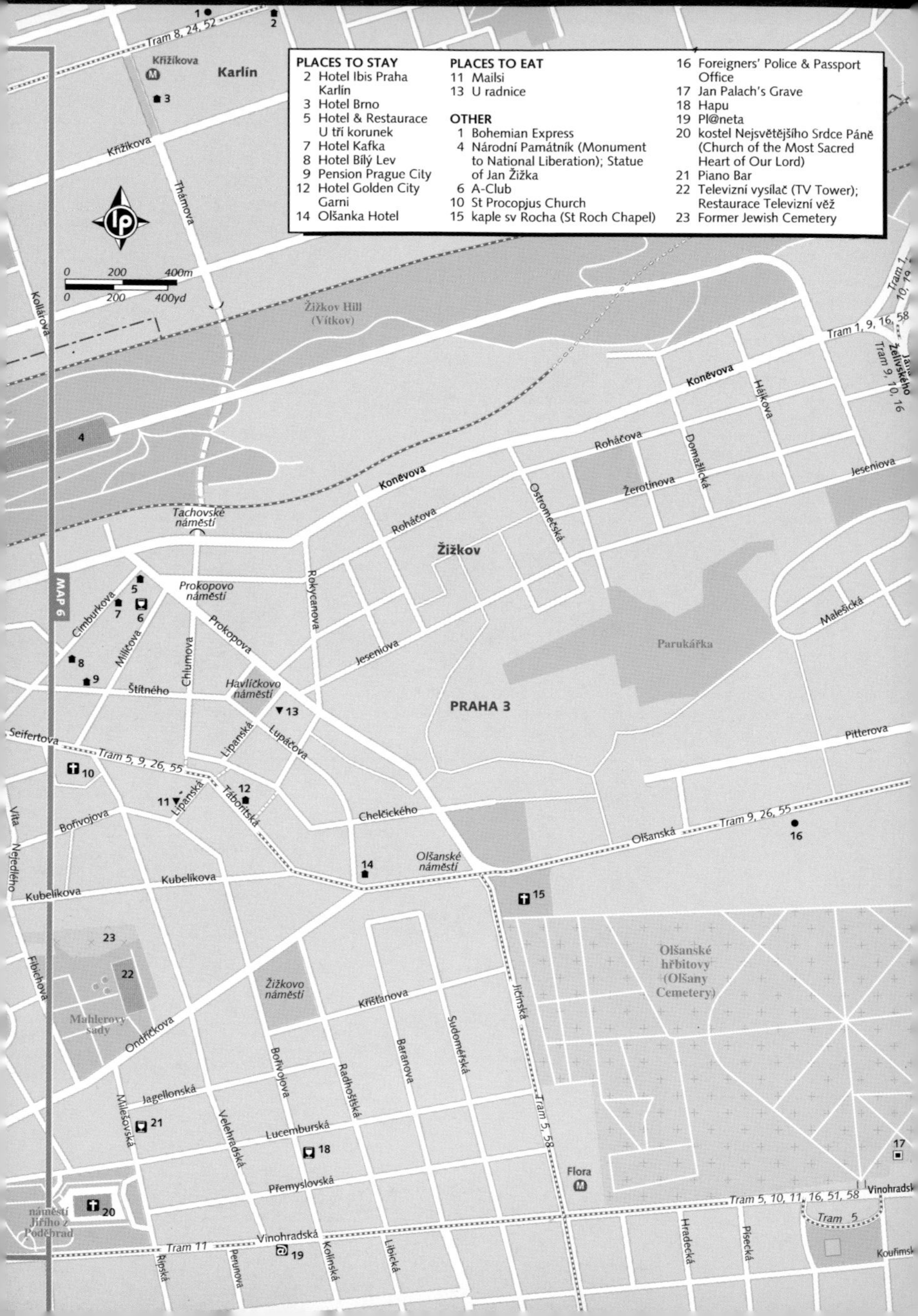

PLACES TO STAY
2 Hotel Ibis Praha Karlín
3 Hotel Brno
5 Hotel & Restaurace U tří korunek
7 Hotel Kafka
8 Hotel Bílý Lev
9 Pension Prague City
12 Hotel Golden City Garni
14 Olšanka Hotel
PLACES TO EAT
11 Mailsi
13 U radnice
OTHER
1 Bohemian Express
4 Národní Památník (Monument to National Liberation); Statue of Jan Žižka
6 A-Club
10 St Procopjus Church
15 kaple sv Rocha (St Roch Chapel)
16 Foreigners' Police & Passport Office
17 Jan Palach's Grave
18 Hapu
19 Pl@neta
20 kostel Nejsvětějšího Srdce Páně (Church of the Most Sacred Heart of Our Lord)
21 Piano Bar
22 Televizní vysílač (TV Tower); Restaurace Televizní věž
23 Former Jewish Cemetery
0 200 400m
0 200 400yd
Karlín
Křižíkova
Thámova
Kollárova
Žižkov Hill (Vítkov)
Tram 8, 24, 52
Tram 1, 9, 16, 58
Tram 9, 10, 16
Želivského
Koněvova
Roháčova
Hájkova
Domažlická
Jeseniova
Žerotínova
Ostromečská
Tachovské náměstí
Žižkov
Rokycanova
Prokopovo náměstí
Prokopova
Cimburkova
Milíčova
Chlumova
Štítného
Havlíčkovo náměstí
Lupáčova
Lipanská
Táboritská
Seifertova
Tram 5, 9, 26, 55
Malešická
Parukářka
PRAHA 3
Pitterova
Chelčického
Olšanská
Tram 9, 26, 55
Olšanské náměstí
Bořivojova
Víta Nejedlého
Kubelíkova
Fibichova
Mahlerovy sady
Ondříčkova
Žižkovo náměstí
Křišťanova
Baranova
Sudoměřská
Radhošťská
Jičínská
Olšanské hřbitovy (Olšany Cemetery)
Tram 5, 58
Jagellonská
Milešovská
Velehradská
Lucemburská
Přemyslovská
Flora
Tram 5, 10, 11, 16, 51, 58
Vinohradská
Tram 5
náměstí Jiřího z Poděbrad
Tram 11
Řipská
Perunova
Kolínská
Libická
Hradecká
Písecká
Kouřimská
MAP 6

HAVELSKÁ
STARÉ MĚSTO-PRAHA 1

NEIL WILSON

An ornate street sign in the heart of the Old Town

RICHARD NEBESKÝ

The night lights of Prague Castle and Charles Bridge from across the Vltava

MAP 9

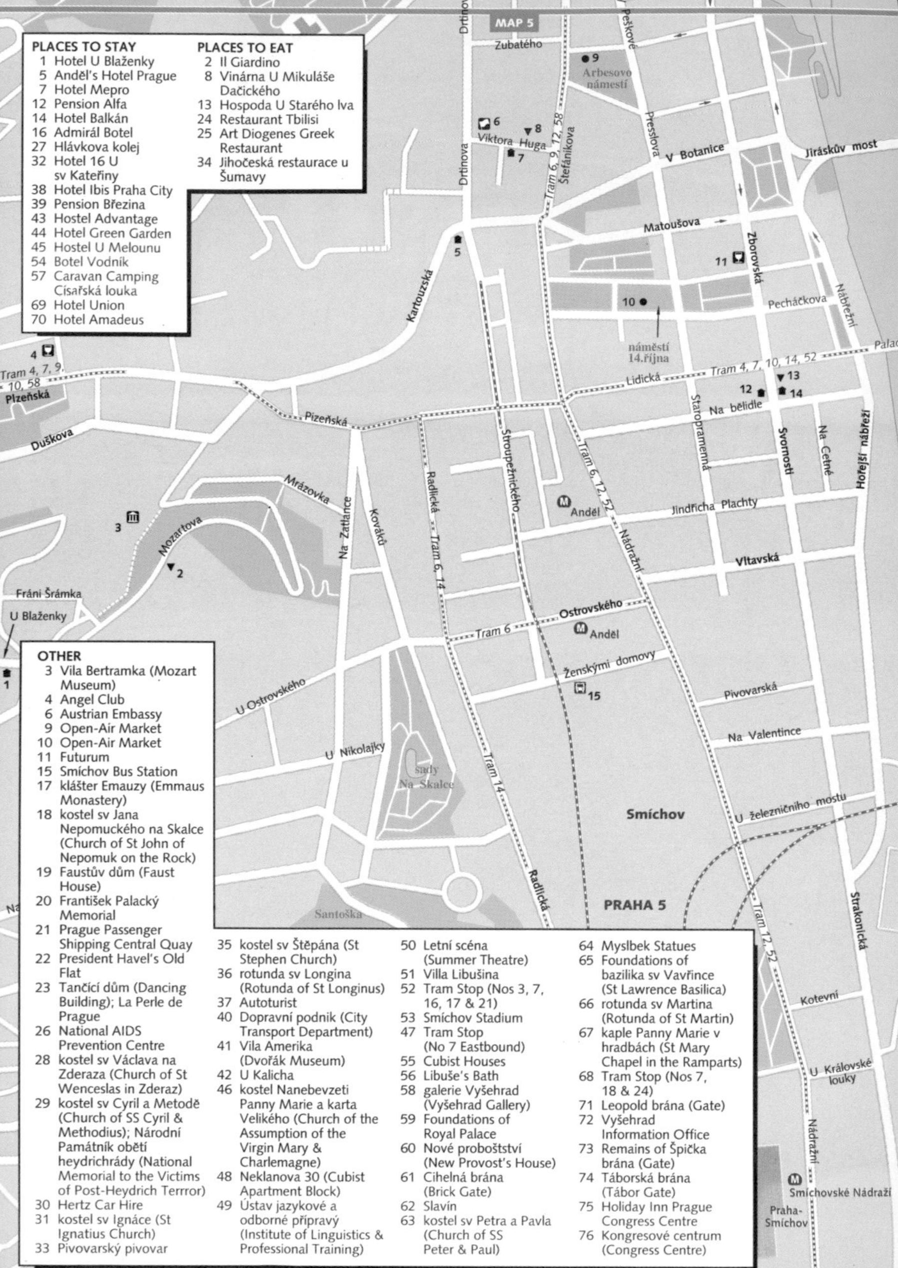

MAP 5
PLACES TO STAY
1 Hotel U Blaženky
5 Anděl's Hotel Prague
7 Hotel Mepro
12 Pension Alfa
14 Hotel Balkán
16 Admirál Botel
27 Hlávkova kolej
32 Hotel 16 U sv Kateřiny
38 Hotel Ibis Praha City
39 Pension Březina
43 Hostel Advantage
44 Hotel Green Garden
45 Hostel U Melounu
54 Botel Vodník
57 Caravan Camping Císařská louka
69 Hotel Union
70 Hotel Amadeus
PLACES TO EAT
2 Il Giardino
8 Vinárna U Mikuláše Dačického
13 Hospoda U Starého lva
24 Restaurant Tbilisi
25 Art Diogenes Greek Restaurant
34 Jihočeská restaurace u Šumavy
OTHER
3 Vila Bertramka (Mozart Museum)
4 Angel Club
6 Austrian Embassy
9 Open-Air Market
10 Open-Air Market
11 Futurum
15 Smíchov Bus Station
17 klášter Emauzy (Emmaus Monastery)
18 kostel sv Jana Nepomuckého na Skalce (Church of St John of Nepomuk on the Rock)
19 Faustův dům (Faust House)
20 František Palacký Memorial
21 Prague Passenger Shipping Central Quay
22 President Havel's Old Flat
23 Tančící dům (Dancing Building); La Perle de Prague
26 National AIDS Prevention Centre
28 kostel sv Václava na Zderaza (Church of St Wenceslas in Zderaz)
29 kostel sv Cyril a Metodě (Church of SS Cyril & Methodius); Národní Památník obětí heydrichrády (National Memorial to the Victims of Post-Heydrich Terrror)
30 Hertz Car Hire
31 kostel sv Ignáce (St Ignatius Church)
33 Pivovarský pivovar
35 kostel sv Štěpána (St Stephen Church)
36 rotunda sv Longina (Rotunda of St Longinus)
37 Autoturist
40 Dopravní podnik (City Transport Department)
41 Vila Amerika (Dvořák Museum)
42 U Kalicha
46 kostel Nanebevzetí Panny Marie a karta Velikého (Church of the Assumption of the Virgin Mary & Charlemagne)
48 Neklanova 30 (Cubist Apartment Block)
49 Ústav jazykové a odborné přípravý (Institute of Linguistics & Professional Training)
50 Letní scéna (Summer Theatre)
51 Villa Libušina
52 Tram Stop (Nos 3, 7, 16, 17 & 21)
53 Smíchov Stadium
47 Tram Stop (No 7 Eastbound)
55 Cubist Houses
56 Libuše's Bath
58 galerie Vyšehrad (Vyšehrad Gallery)
59 Foundations of Royal Palace
60 Nové proboštství (New Provost's House)
61 Cihelná brána (Brick Gate)
62 Slavín
63 kostel sv Petra a Pavla (Church of SS Peter & Paul)
64 Myslbek Statues
65 Foundations of bazilika sv Vavřince (St Lawrence Basilica)
66 rotunda sv Martina (Rotunda of St Martin)
67 kaple Panny Marie v hradbách (St Mary Chapel in the Ramparts)
68 Tram Stop (Nos 7, 18 & 24)
71 Leopold brána (Gate)
72 Vyšehrad Information Office
73 Remains of Špička brána (Gate)
74 Táborská brána (Tábor Gate)
75 Holiday Inn Prague Congress Centre
76 Kongresové centrum (Congress Centre)
Malátova
Elišky Peškové
Drtinova
Zubatého
Arbesovo náměstí
Viktora Huga
Tram 6, 9, 12, 58
Štefánikova
Presslova
V Botanice
Jiráskův most
Matoušova
Zborovská
Kartouzská
Pecháčkova
Nábřežní
náměstí 14.října
Palackého
Tram 4, 7, 9, 10, 58
Plzeňská
Lidická
Tram 4, 7, 10, 14, 52
Na bělidle
Duškova
Stroupežnického
Tram 6, 12, 52
Staropramenná
Svornosti
Na Četné
Hořejší nábřeží
Mrázovka
Anděl
Jindřicha Plachty
Mozartova
Radlická
Tram 6, 14
Na Zatlance
Kováků
Nádražní
Vltavská
Fráni Šrámka
U Blaženky
Ostrovského
Tram 6
Ženskými domovy
U Ostrovského
Pivovarská
Na Valentince
U Nikolajky
sady Na Skalce
Tram 14
Smíchov
U železničního mostu
Radlická
PRAHA 5
Santoška
Strakonická
Tram 12, 52
Kotevní
U Královské louky
Nádražní
Smíchovské Nádraží
Praha-Smíchov
Kesnerkou

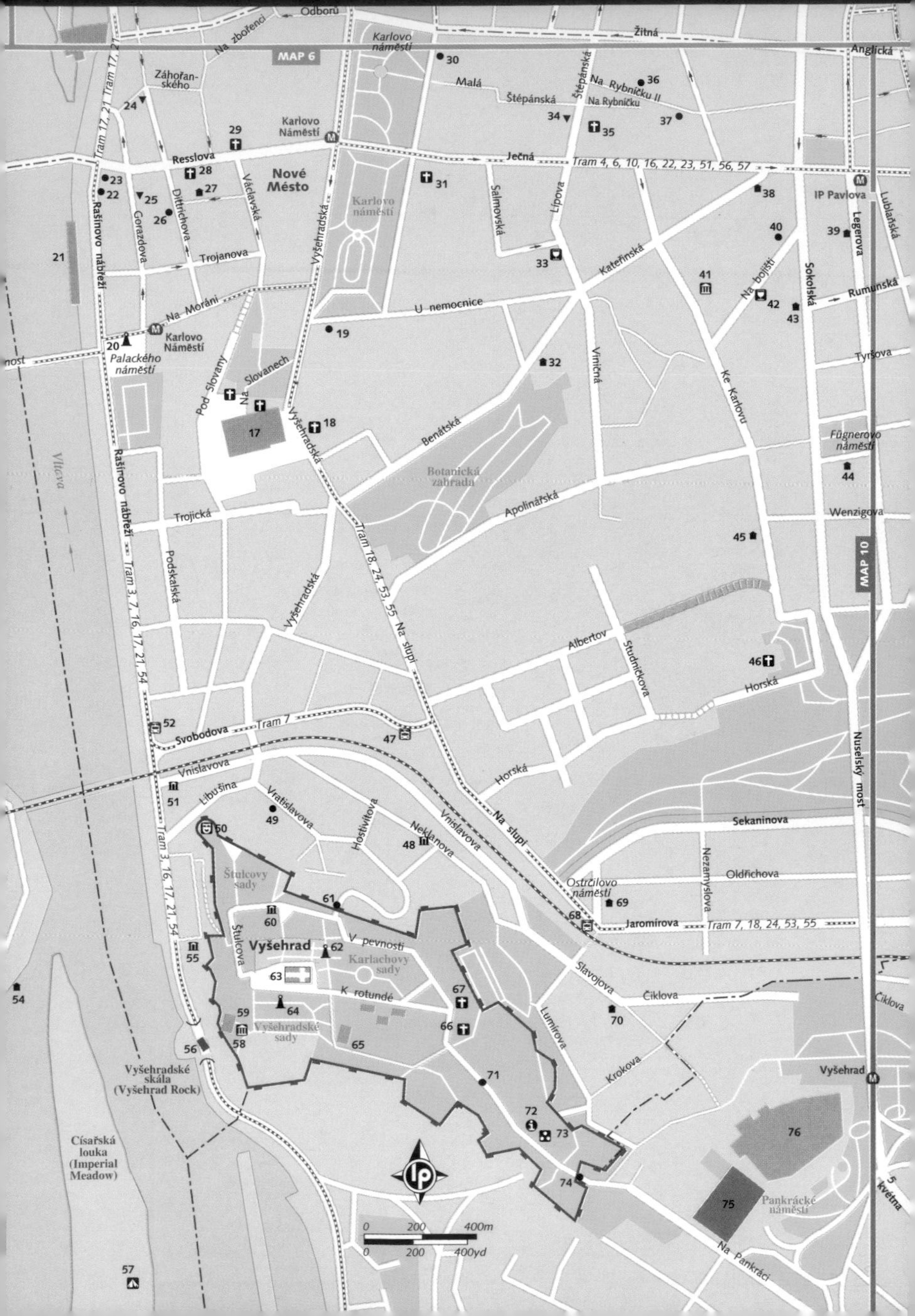
MAP 6
MAP 10
Odborů
Žitná
Anglická
Na zbořenci
Karlovo náměstí
30
Záhořanského
Malá
Štěpánská
Na Rybníčku II
Na Rybníčku
36
37
34
35
24
29
Karlovo Náměstí
Resslova
Ječná
Tram 4, 6, 10, 16, 22, 23, 51, 56, 57
Tram 17, 21
Tram 17, 21
28
23
22
27
25
26
Nové Město
31
Karlovo náměstí
38
IP Pavlova
Lublaňská
Legerova
39
40
Gorazdova
Dittrichova
Václavská
Vyšehradská
Salmovská
Lípova
Rašínovo nábřeží
21
Trojanova
33
Kateřinská
41
Na bojišti
42
43
Sokolská
Rumunská
Na Moráni
U nemocnice
19
Karlovo Náměstí
20
Palackého náměstí
most
Tyršova
Pod Slovany
Na Slovanech
32
Viničná
Ke Karlovu
18
17
Vyšehradská
Benátská
Fügnerovo náměstí
44
Vltava
Rašínovo nábřeží
Botanická zahrada
Trojická
Apolinářská
Wenzigova
Podskalská
Tram 3, 7, 16, 17, 21, 54
Tram 18, 24, 53, 55 Na slupi
45
Vyšehradská
Albertov
Studničkova
46
Horská
52
Svobodova
Tram 7
47
Nuselský most
Vnislavova
Libušina
51
Vratislavova
49
Horská
Hostivítova
Neklanova
48
Vnislavova
Na slupi
Sekaninova
50
Tram 3, 16, 17, 21, 54
Štulcovy sady
61
Nezamyslova
Oldřichova
Ostrčilovo náměstí
69
60
68
Jaromírova
Tram 7, 18, 24, 53, 55
Štulcova
Vyšehrad
62
V pevnosti
55
Karlachovy sady
Slavojova
63
54
67
Čiklova
Čiklova
K rotundě
64
70
59
Vyšehradské sady
66
Lumírova
58
65
56
Krokova
Vyšehradské skála (Vyšehrad Rock)
71
Vyšehrad
72
73
76
Císařská louka (Imperial Meadow)
74
5 května
75
Pankrácké náměstí
0
200
400m
0
200
400yd
Na Pankráci
57

MAP 10

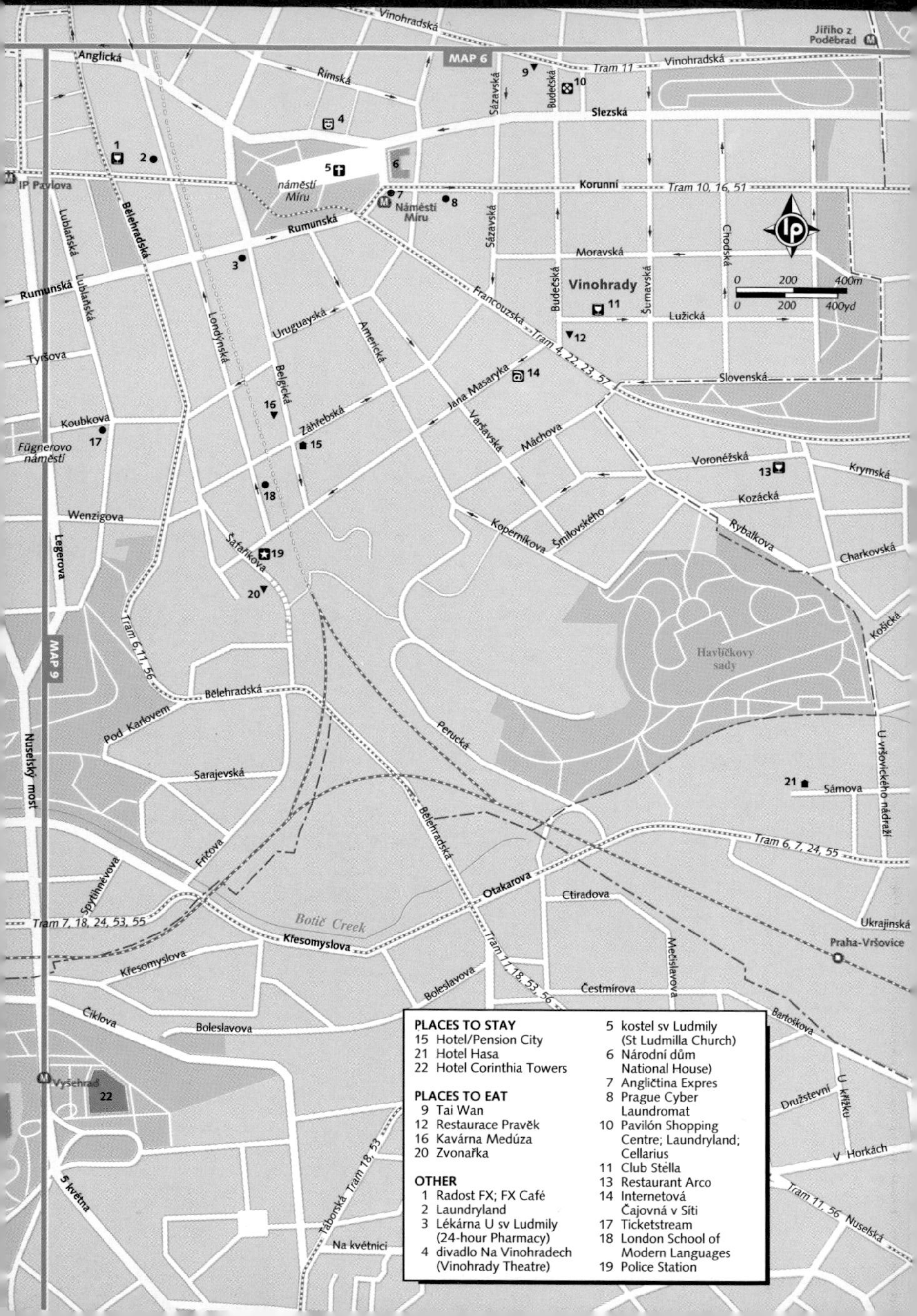

PLACES TO STAY
- 15 Hotel/Pension City
- 21 Hotel Hasa
- 22 Hotel Corinthia Towers

PLACES TO EAT
- 9 Tai Wan
- 12 Restaurace Pravěk
- 16 Kavárna Medúza
- 20 Zvonařka

OTHER
- 1 Radost FX; FX Café
- 2 Laundryland
- 3 Lékárna U sv Ludmily (24-hour Pharmacy)
- 4 divadlo Na Vinohradech (Vinohrady Theatre)
- 5 kostel sv Ludmily (St Ludmilla Church)
- 6 Národní dům National House)
- 7 Angličtina Expres
- 8 Prague Cyber Laundromat
- 10 Pavilón Shopping Centre; Laundryland; Cellarius
- 11 Club Stella
- 13 Restaurant Arco
- 14 Internetová Čajovná v Síti
- 17 Ticketstream
- 18 London School of Modern Languages
- 19 Police Station

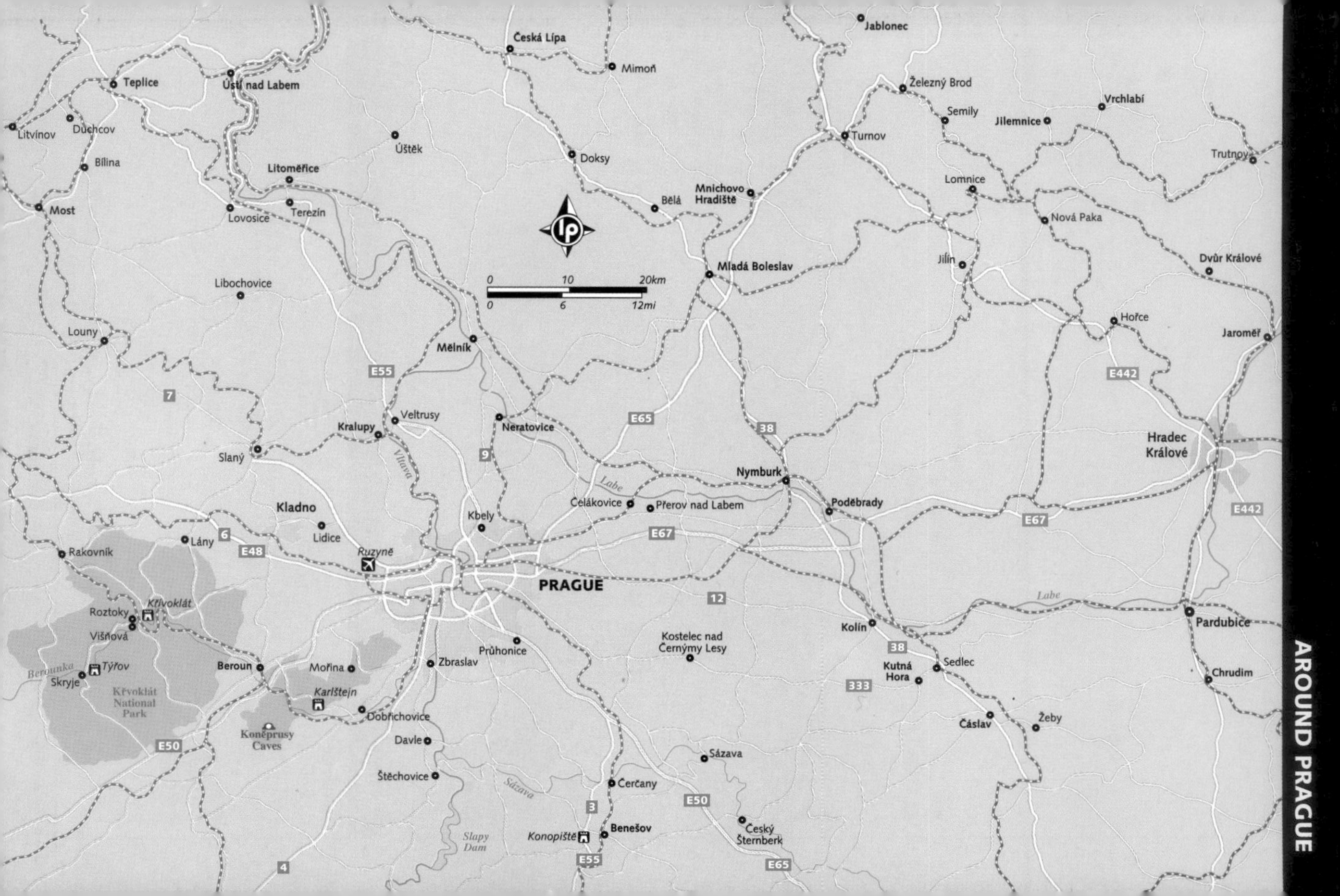

Jablonec
Česká Lípa
Mimoň
Teplice
Ústí nad Labem
Železný Brod
Vrchlabí
Semily
Jilemnice
Litvínov
Duchcov
Turnov
Úštěk
Trutnov
Bílina
Doksy
Litoměřice
Lomnice
Mnichovo Hradiště
Most
Bělá
Lovosice
Terezín
Nová Paka
Mladá Boleslav
Jičín
Dvůr Králové
Libochovice
0
10
20km
0
6
12mi
Hořice
Louny
Jaroměř
Mělník
E55
E442
7
Veltrusy
E65
Kralupy
Neratovice
38
Vltava
9
Hradec Králové
Slaný
Nymburk
Labe
Kladno
Čelákovice
Přerov nad Labem
Poděbrady
E442
Kbely
E67
6
Lány
Lidice
E67
Rakovník
E48
Ruzyně
PRAGUE
12
Labe
Křivoklát
Roztoky
Pardubice
Višňová
Kolín
Průhonice
Kostelec nad Černými Lesy
38
Berounka
Týřov
Beroun
Mořina
Zbraslav
Kutná Hora
Sedlec
Chrudim
Skryje
Křivoklát National Park
Karlštejn
333
Dobřichovice
Čáslav
Žeby
E50
Koněprusy Caves
Davle
Sázava
Štěchovice
Čerčany
Sázava
3
E50
Benešov
Český Šternberk
Slapy Dam
Konopiště
4
E55
E65

MAP LEGEND

BOUNDARIES

International
Departmental
Suburb

HYDROGRAPHY

Coastline
River, Creek
Lake
Canal

ROUTES & TRANSPORT

Freeway
Highway
Major Road
Minor Road
Unsealed Road
City Freeway
City Highway
City Road
City Street, Lane
Pedestrian Mall
Tunnel
Train Route & Station
Metro & Station
Tramway & Tram Stop
Cable Car or Chairlift
Path
Walking Tour
Ferry Route & Terminal

AREA FEATURES

Building
Hotel
Park, Gardens
Cemetery
Market
Pedestrian

MAP SYMBOLS

Prague Capital
Pardubice Town
Churdim Village
Point of Interest
Place to Stay
Camp Site
Place to Eat
Pub or Bar
Airport
Ancient or City Wall
Archaeological Site
Bank
Bus Stop, Station
Castle or Fort
Church or Cathedral
Cinema
Embassy or Consulate
Fountain
Golf Course
Hospital
Internet Cafe
Lookout
Monument
Mosque
Museum
One Way Street
Palace or Stately Home
Parking
Petrol Station
Police Station
Post Office
Shopping Centre
Swimming Pool
Synagogue
Taxi
Telephone
Theatre
Toilet
Tourist Information
Transport
Zoo

Note: not all symbols displayed above appear in this book

LONELY PLANET OFFICES

Australia
Locked Bag 1, Footscray, Victoria 3011
☎ 03-8379 8000 fax 03-8379 8111
email: talk2us@lonelyplanet.com.au

USA
150 Linden St, Oakland, CA 94607
☎ 510-893 8555 TOLL FREE: 800-275 8555
fax 510-893 8572
email: info@lonelyplanet.com

UK
10a Spring Place, London NW5 3BH
☎ 020-7428 4800 fax 020-7428 4828
email: go@lonelyplanet.co.uk

France
1 rue du Dahomey, 75011 Paris
☎ 01 55 25 33 00 fax 01 55 25 33 01
email: bip@lonelyplanet.fr
www.lonelyplanet.fr

World Wide Web: www.lonelyplanet.com *or* AOL keyword: lp
Lonely Planet Images: lpi@lonelyplanet.com.au